D0214401

LANGUAGE FOR HUMANS AND ROBOTS

LANGUAGE FOR

HUMANS AND ROBOTS

PATRICK SUPPES

BLACKWELL
Oxford UK & Cambridge USA

First published 1991
First published in USA 1992

Blackwell Publishers
Three Cambridge Center
Cambridge, Massachusetts 02142
USA

108 Cowley Road
Oxford OX4 1JF   UK

Library of Congress Cataloging in Publication Data
Suppes, Patrick 1922–
Language for humans and robots/Patrick Suppes.
p.   cm.
Includes bibliographical references and index.
ISBN 0–631–18262–4
1. Language and languages.   I. Title.
P106.S837   1992   91–27584
401—dc20   CIP

A CIP catalogue record for this book is available from the British Library

Printed and bound in Great Britain by
Biddles Ltd, Guildford and King's Lynn

This book is printed on acid-free paper

PREFACE

The 21 papers collected in this volume represent the bulk of the articles
that I have published on language over the past 20 years. The articles are
arranged under four main headings. Part I contains four articles on the
concept of congruence of meaning I have been developing for a number
of years. Part II contains five articles on the psychology of children's
language. These articles report a variety of empirical studies. Part III is
on the topic of variable-free semantics and is more formal in character.
The six articles of this part develop an alternative to first-order logic as
a framework for analyzing the semantics of natural-language utterances.
Part IV contains six articles on language interaction with robots. Within
each part the articles are arranged chronologically. I turn now to a more
detailed overview of the content of each part.

Part I is concerned with congruence of meaning as a generalization
of the standard concept of synonymy. I like to call this approach to
meaning a geometric theory of meaning because it draws on the analogy
of the role of congruence in geometry. There is no single concept of
congruence in geometry; for example, affine congruence is not the same
thing as Euclidean congruence. So I maintain there should be no single
concept of synonymy in the theory of meaning, but weaker and stronger
notions of congruence. As is familiar from algebra and geometry, a notion
of congruence can then be used to define, by abstraction, i.e., by a creative
definition of identity, propositions. Thus if u and u' are two utterances
that are congruent, which we write in the usual form, $u \simeq u'$, then the
condition of identity for propositions is:

$$[u] = [u'] \text{ if and only if } u \simeq u' .$$

Here u and u' are concrete utterances and $[u]$ is the proposition expressed
by u or u' — explicitly, the proposition expressed by u relative to the con-

gruence relation $\simeq$. The philosophical habit of believing in propositions simpliciter is not an easy one to break, just as it was not easy as late as the 18th century when Kant was writing *The Critique of Pure Reason* to break away from the idea of Euclidean geometry as the one true geometry. Fundamental to all of the articles in this section is the view that there is no one true concept of proposition, but only one relative to a congruence relation for concrete utterances. Many different kinds of congruence relations, weak and strong, are spelled out in the various articles. In the final article of this section, relations are made between the theory of congruence and Grice's theory of utterer's meaning.

Part II represents a shift in focus, even though the concern with semantics continues. The five articles reproduced here represent in all cases specific empirical studies of children's language use. The first article in this part is an experimental study of children's comprehension of logical connectives. It is a strictly experimental study and in that sense is different from the other articles which are based on the collection of the actual speech of children in noncontrolled, nonexperimental settings. Use is made in these articles of data collected from children speaking English, Chinese, and French, except for Article 9, which is wholly concerned with English. Running through this work is the conviction, expressed in different ways, that semantics is more important than grammar from the standpoint of the child's acquisition of language and from the standpoint of understanding what the child is trying to do in his or her early speech. Another conviction that is evident from the viewpoint expressed in these articles is that linguists have as yet had little of real interest to say about semantics, but the conceptually rich tradition of semantical analysis and logic in philosophy can be used successfully in detailed empirical studies. On the other hand, I am under no illusion that the empirical and theoretical results presented in these articles represent anything like a definitive analysis. The data are far too complex and rich for that to be possible at the present stage of scientific development.

Part III contains six articles devoted to the use of variable-free semantics for the analysis of natural language. The general objective is to provide formal apparatus that will impose a logically explicit semantics on natural language utterances, but do so in a notation that is close to the structure of the natural language itself. The aim here is simplicity, not maximum generality. The apparatus builds on Tarski's relation algebras but extends them in obvious ways needed for natural language, for instance, by inclusion of the image operation. It is easy enough to give elementary sentences of geometry, for example, that cannot be expressed in such extended relation algebras, but the subtle use of quantifiers, characteristic of such examples, is not a feature of most ordinary-language

sentences. Since the introduction of quantifiers as explicit logical notation by Frege, the separation of semantics from the syntax of natural
language seems to have widened. An objective of the use of variable-free
semantics is to reverse such matters and to narrow the gap for large fragments of natural language. In the last article of this part (Article 15) the
apparatus is applied to inference in English. The aim is to show how in
many familiar uses it is much easier and simpler to generalize the familiar
apparatus of syllogistic inference to the semantical structure fixed by relation algebras rather than to make an awkward translation into first-order
logic.

Part IV contains six articles that explore various aspects of using language with robots. The first three articles in this part develop the concept of instructable robot. By this is meant a robot having the ability
to understand verbal instruction on what to do. The use of rapid verbal
interaction is in strong contrast to much of the current interest in robotics
on autonomous planning. In using the concept of instructability, there is
no emphasis on language learning, for the robot's ability to understand
language can just as well as not, from the standpoint of the concept of
instructability, be preprogrammed. On the other hand, the complexity
of the semantics of the language of action as it needs to be implemented
in robots is stressed, especially the difficult problem of context, which is
close to what has been called the frame problem in artificial intelligence.
Article 18 formulates a more general philosophical view of robots being
instructed to perform given actions.

The last three articles turn to the still more fundamental problem
of language learning for robots. Article 19 gives a simple application
of learning models to speech recognition, a problem that is fundamental for the development of robotic language capacities. This is the only
article in the volume concerned with speech recognition. Article 20 outlines a general view of robotic learning and argues that learning, rather
than intentionality, is a better test of intelligence for robots. Article 21,
the final article in the book, is concerned with robotic machine learning of
natural language. Here the attempt is to build a theory of language learning on semantics rather than grammar. No knowledge of the grammar
of any natural language is assumed, but concepts and their semantical
categories are given a priori in order to concentrate solely on language
learning. Psychological processes of association are central to the theory
of learning developed, but not in a version that would necessarily be acceptable to old-fashioned associationists. The other key ingredient of the
theory is generalization from concrete utterances to grammatical forms,
the process which is central to learning the grammar of a natural language in the theory proposed. The research described in this last article

has just begun. What is reproduced here is the first published report of a larger program on machine learning of natural language. Consequently many of the details of the theory as outlined in Article 21 will be subject to change, but I have confidence that the general approach will serve as a robust framework for some time to come.

As is evident from this brief summary, the articles in this book exemplify different approaches to the study of language. It is not my intention or hope to have one overarching view of how language should be studied, either from a theoretical or empirical standpoint. To have some single theoretical position seems to me as foolish as holding to a single theory of all physical phenomena, for in its own way language is as complicated as any phenomenon to be found in nature. It is hopeless now, and probably will remain hopeless for the foreseeable future, to believe that any single theory that consists of more than platitudes will be useful in studying most of the important features of language. In the study of language, as in other areas of philosophy and science, I remain a dedicated pluralist.

The reader will find some technical preliminaries briefly repeated at the beginning of several articles, e.g., the formal characterization of context-free grammars. Because the articles vary greatly both in content and in the depth of details that are spelled out, it seemed best to leave these preliminaries untouched, so that the articles can be read more or less independently of each other.

For a quick and accessible overview of each part, I recommend Article 3 in Part I, Article 6 in Part II, Article 14 in Part III and Chapter 20 in Part IV.

Two of the empirical articles in Part II are co-authored, Article 5 with Shirley Feldman and Article 9 with Elizabeth Macken. But the other articles in Part II summarize research involving a number of collaborators. All of the articles in Part IV on robots are co-authored: Article 16 with Robert Maas; Article 17 with Colleen Crangle and Stefan Michalowski; Articles 18 and 20 with Colleen Crangle; Article 19 with Douglas Danforth and David Rogosa; and Article 21 with Michael Böttner and Lin Liang. The publication here of these articles has been generously agreed to by my co-authors.

Acknowledgments for permission to reproduce the various articles are given at the bottom of the first page of each article, but thanks are extended here to the many editors and publishers who generously granted this permission. No substantive or real stylistic changes have been made in any of the articles; only the manner of referring to published articles and books has been standardized, as has the format of section headings. The references to the literature given in the various articles are all collected together at the end in a single list. Footnotes in the original articles are numbered, beginning anew with each article. An index of authors referred to is given. In place of a subject index there is a detailed table of contents at the beginning of the volume.

Finally, I want to acknowledge the able assistance of Laura Tickle and Emma Pease in preparing this volume for publication, which in the spirit that has come to dominate academic publications, means actual preparation of the camera-ready copy in TeX. I also want to express my appreciation to Michael Böttner for his careful reading of the proofs.

PATRICK SUPPES

Stanford, California, June 1991

CONTENTS

xi

PART I

CONGRUENCE OF MEANING

1

CONGRUENCE OF MEANING

GEOMETRIC CONGRUENCE

A large literature in philosophy attempts to give criteria for the identity of two propositions. Those who do not like talk about propositions have been much involved in the closely related problem of stating when two sentences or expressions are synonymous. A good review of the earlier work may be found in Quine's *Word and Object* (1960). The contributions of Church, Mates, Sheffler, and others show how difficult it is to get an appropriate concept of synonymy of expressions or criterion of identity for propositions. The efforts of Carnap, for example, to develop a concept of intensional isomorphism in *Meaning and Necessity* (1947) was not brought to a finished state. To a large extent, the same difficulties arise in giving a criterion of identity for proofs, with about as little progress in the case of proofs as in the case of propositions. (Recently, almost the same difficulties have been faced again in trying to say when two computer programs are identical.)

The theme I shall develop today is that by looking at the history of geometry and the concept of congruence in geometry we can get a new perspective on how to think about the closeness in meaning of two sentences. (Hereafter, to avoid any commitment to propositions, I shall

---

*Reprinted from *Proceedings and Addresses of the American Philosophical Association*, 1973, **46**, 21-38. Presidential address delivered at the Forty-seventh Annual Meeting of the Pacific Division of the American Philosophical Association in Seattle, Washington, March 30, 1973.

3

talk about sentences and not about propositions.) I shall not try to say
when two sentences express the same proposition or when two sentences
have the same meaning, but rather shall talk about the congruence of
meaning of two sentences or expressions. I say *expressions*, because the
concepts I introduce need not be restricted to sentences but can deal with
noun phrases, verb phrases, and so forth.

In the long history of the concept of equality or congruence in geometry, there is almost no discussion of the criterion of identity for two
figures. Of course, for many formal treatments of geometry, the concept
of identity follows directly from the logic of identity in first-order logic,
together with the definitions of concepts like those of triangle, quadrilat-
eral, etc. The important point is that the criterion of identity is not an
issue in geometry and is not the important or significant concept.

What does have a long and interesting history in geometry is the
concept of congruence. Because the axiomatic treatment of the concept
is obscure and unsatisfactory in Greek geometry, I shall not review the
role of superposition of figures in Euclid. The Euclidean notion of superposition expressed cryptically in Greek geometry is given an admirable
intuitive formulation in Kiselyov's well-known Russian textbook on plane
geometry: "Two geometric figures are said to be congruent if one figure,
by being moved in space, can be made to coincide with the second figure
so that the two figures coincide in all their parts."

The theory of congruence for Euclidean geometry was put on a rigorous
and explicit basis at the end of the nineteenth century by Hilbert and
others. Intuitively, Hilbert's concept of congruence is such that any two
figures with the same shape and size are congruent. The important fact
for purposes of later discussion is that any two figures of the same shape
and size can be related by what is called in geometry a rigid motion. This
means that we can transform the spatial origin and orientation as well as
the handedness of the axes of reference, without changing the size or shape
of a figure. From the standpoint of ordinary experience, one can certainly
see demanding a stronger sense of congruence than that characterized by
Hilbert. We could, for instance, require that congruent figures also have
the same orientation. So, for example, if a triangle has a horizontal base,
then any triangle congruent to it must also have its base oriented along
the horizontal. To do this, of course, is to strengthen Euclidean geometry,
which has no preferred direction and therefore no nonarbitrary definition
of *horizontal*. It is straightforward, however, to introduce such directions
in geometry, and we all recognize that the absence of a sense of preferred
direction in Euclidean geometry is an abstraction from our ordinary ways
of thinking about space.

On the other hand, we can move in the opposite direction and develop weaker concepts of congruence. The next, most natural weaker concept is that of two figures being congruent if they have the same shape, but not necessarily the same size. This concept of congruence is ordinarily termed *similarity of figures*.

From this definition we can move on to the concept of congruence in affine spaces. Roughly speaking, in affine spaces lines are carried into lines and, consequently, triangles into triangles, but the shape and size of the triangles are not preserved, and in a general affine space any two triangles are congruent. This weakening of the concept of geometrical congruence can proceed much further. A significant example is topological congruence. Two figures are topologically congruent when one is a homeomorphic image of the other, that is, one can be obtained from the other by a one-one bicontinuous transformation. In this case, for example, a square and a triangle are topologically congruent. On the other hand, dimensionality is preserved under topological congruence, and therefore a sphere is not homeomorphic to a circle or a pyramid to a triangle. Beyond topological congruence we can go on to the broadest concept of congruence, namely, that which is preserved under one-one transformations. In this case, cardinality is preserved but not much else. Thus, for example, a line segment is in this one-one sense congruent to a square, etc.

Each of these concepts of congruence in geometry, some weak and some strong, has a useful and important role, both in geometrical theory and in widespread applications of geometry to physics and other sciences. It is not my purpose here to make a case for the significance of the concept of congruence in geometry, for it will be generally accepted without much argument. Rather, my purpose is to work on an analogy and to develop corresponding strong and weak definitions of congruence of meaning for sentences or even expressions that are not sentences.

Before looking at some examples that will motivate the definitions I want to give, let me interject that I intend to keep the treatment of these matters reasonably informal and reserve the technical and formal presentation of the concepts for another occasion.

Consider the first pair of sentences:

(1) *The book is red.*
    Le livre est rouge.

In spite of general problems about translating from one language to another, we all recognize the closeness in meaning of these two sentences, and my purpose is to give definitions that catch this closeness. As a second pair, consider the following:

(2) *John and Mary are here.*
    Mary and John are here.

In the case of this pair, we recognize that commuting the order of the proper names in the noun phrase *John and Mary* makes little difference in the literal meaning of the sentence. The closeness in meaning in this case, however, is different from the closeness of the first pair of sentences.

Consider next the pair of sentences:

(3) *John has three apples.*
John has more than two, but less than four apples.

In this case the content of the two sentences is very similar, but the second is more pedantic and elaborate in formulation than the first. We can probably agree that the second sentence is an approximate *paraphrase* of the first.

THEORETICAL FRAMEWORK

As in the analysis of congruence in geometry, a definite and concrete set of proposals about congruence of meaning depends essentially on the kind of theoretical framework assumed. For the analysis in this paper, I shall assume a fixed, context-free grammar. Such a grammar consists of a finite vocabulary of which a given subset is the nonterminal vocabulary, a set of production rules that have the restricted form required for a context-free grammar, and a start symbol usually labelled S (for *sentence*). These ideas are familiar and have been around for more than a decade (Chomsky, 1956, 1959). What is less familiar is the semantical apparatus that I shall assume. The details of the semantical setup are given in an earlier paper (Suppes, 1973b); therefore, I shall not repeat all the detailed definitions, but rather shall give an intuitive sense of the main ideas. (The main predecessors of my approach to semantics of context-free languages are to be found in the literature on computer programming languages, in particular, Irons (1961) and Knuth (1968). I have also been influenced by the work of Montague (1970, 1973) on English as a formal language.)

The context-free semantics that is added to the context-free grammar, and that is closely wedded to the grammar, consists of two main parts. One part consists of giving a model structure in the sense of classical model theory in order to assign a reference (relative to a model) to various terminal words, although not necessarily to all terminal words. (By *terminal word* I mean the ordinary words of the language and not the nonterminal grammatical vocabulary like *noun phrase, verb phrase, intransitive verb*.) The important point is that a model structure consists of a nonempty domain D of individuals and an evaluation function that assigns a denotation to each terminal word. The denotation of a word is a set-theoretical object that is part of the natural Zermelo hierarchy built up from the domain by taking sets of objects, sets of sets of objects, and so forth. I shall not have more to say about the model structure, because I do not want to enter into the technical definitions relevant to the construction. The intuitive idea is straightforward and a natural extension of Tarskian semantics for first-order theories.

A more important and interesting point in the application of model-theoretic semantics to natural languages is that set-theoretical functions must enter in telling us how denotations of the various parts of the sentences are related. The analysis of how the various parts of a sentence are related in terms of meaning, that is, what set-theoretical functions relate the denotations of the words occurring in the sentences, constitutes one important part of our intuitive idea of meaning. Like the denotations of individual words, the set-theoretical functions that relate the denotations of individual words are ordinarily relatively simple in character. If, for example, I use the phrase *red flowers*, then the natural set-theoretical function for this phrase is the intersection of the set of red things and the set of flowers.

The problem is how to bring order into the method for introducing the set-theoretical functions relating the parts. Fortunately, a completely straightforward answer is available for context-free languages. With each production rule of the grammar we associate a semantic function, and thus we may convert each derivation tree of the grammar into a *semantic tree* by attaching not only labels to the nodes of the tree, but also denotations generated by the semantic functions. (The idea of identifying the meaning of a sentence with an appropriate tree is developed rather thoroughly in terms of categorical grammars, but in a different direction from the consideration of congruence of meaning by Lewis, 1970.)

In previous writings I have termed the grammar and model structure *simple* if the following conditions are met: Each terminal word has a denotation, and each production rule of the grammar has exactly one semantic function associated with it. There is no reason to insist that simple grammars have a position of widespread applicability; I mention them only because they give a feeling for the natural place to begin the analysis. It is easy to move on to more complicated characterizations.

All this is by way of preliminary analysis; let me quickly summarize what I have said. First, I introduce model structures that are fairly natural extensions of Tarskian relational structures for first-order theories to serve as the model structures for context-free languages. Second, a semantic function is assigned to each production rule of the grammar. By this means, any derivation tree of the grammar is converted to a semantic tree. In the simple case, a semantic tree is merely a derivation tree with the addition of a denotation for each node.

A brief remark about grammatical and semantical ambiguity is needed. It is often the case that more than one derivation tree in a given grammar is possible for a sentence. When there are at least two such trees we say that the sentence is grammatically ambiguous. If in addition the denotations of the roots of the trees differ for a fixed model structure, then the sentence is also semantically ambiguous (relative to the given model structure).

A second remark about the class of model structures is also needed. In classical model theory of first-order logic, it is natural ordinarily to consider the set of all possible models of a sentence or of a theory or of a language, but in the context of natural language, it is more appropriate to hold certain aspects of the models constant and to vary only some restricted part. For example, we may in our analysis of paraphrase want to assume that arithmetic is constant across all the models considered and, consequently, restrict the set of models to those in which arithmetic has its standard interpretation. In my view it is a mistake always to test the meaning of a sentence of natural language by asking for its logical consequences. It is often more appropriate and informative to narrow the class of models to those in which variously broadly accepted nonlogical theories like arithmetic are satisfied.

Thus, the definitions of congruence are for a fixed set $\mathcal{M}$ of model structures, not in general for the set of all possible model structures of a language. I also allow for the possibility that a sentence may have more than one semantic tree (up to isomorphism) with respect to the given grammar and a fixed model structure.

FOUR DEFINITIONS OF CONGRUENCE

I begin with a strong notion of congruence.

Definition 1. Let S_1 and S_2 be sentences of the given language, that is, derivable by means of the given grammar of the language. Then S_1 is strongly $\mathcal{M}$-congruent to S_2 if and only if the set of semantic trees of S_1 and S_2 can be made identical with respect to each model structure of $\mathcal{M}$, except perhaps for labelling, by identifying isomorphic trees.

The force of this definition is that the denotations of each node must be identical, and the tree structures themselves must be isomorphic, but both terminal and nonterminal labels of corresponding nodes can differ. Examples of congruent sentences under this definition are the following:

All men are mortal.
Every man is mortal.

This pair exemplifies the fact that shifting from the plural to the singular should not really affect the meaning of universal affirmative sentences, and thus they should be congruent in a strong sense.

On the other hand, if we use a noun phrase rather than an adjective for predication, we cannot satisfy strong congruence in going from the plural to the singular:

All men are animals.
Every man is an animal.

The second sentence has an additional word, the indefinite article, with no corresponding terminal node in the first sentence, and thus the tree structures are not isomorphic.

If we think of our language as containing both elementary parts of French and Russian, as well as of English, then of the following three sentences that essentially express the same idea in the three languages, the English and French sentences are strongly congruent but the Russian is not, because of the absence of a definite article and the copula:

The book is red.
Le livre est rouge.
Kniga krasnaya.

I give now a second definition incomparable to the first. By *incomparable* I mean there exist pairs of sentences that are congruent in the sense of the first definition, but not in the sense of the second, and conversely. I call this second sense permutational congruence in meaning and form.

Definition 2. Let S_1 and S_2 be sentences of a given language as before. Then S_1 is permutationally $\mathcal{M}$-congruent to S_2 in meaning and form if and only if each semantic tree of S_1 can be obtained from a semantic tree of S_2 by a sequence of permutations of branches of subtrees for every model structure of $\mathcal{M}$.

Thus in the sense of this definition the following sentences, mentioned earlier, are permutationally congruent in meaning and form, but are not congruent in the sense of strong congruence.

John and Mary are here.
Mary and John are here.

In this pair we have a natural permutation of the order of proper names in the subject, something we would ordinarily consider fairly unimportant in conveying the sense of the sentence. We would also ordinarily treat as permutationally congruent in meaning and form a sentential conjunction that results from another conjunction by interchanging the components, and similarly for a disjunction, but not when an implicit temporal order of events is implied by the order of the components. Consider *They got married and had a baby* versus *They had a baby and got married.*

Looking at the first two definitions, we are naturally led to a third definition that is weaker than either of the other two, namely, that of being permutationally congruent in meaning, but not necessarily in form.

Definition 3. Let S_1 and S_2 be sentences of a given language. Then S_1 is permutationally $\mathcal{M}$-congruent in meaning to S_2 if and only if each semantic tree of S_1 can be obtained from a semantic tree of S_2, except possibly for labelling, by a sequence of permutations of branches of subtrees for every model structure in $\mathcal{M}$.

Given this definition, we then have permutational congruence of sentences in different languages, because we are again no longer looking at the labelling itself. For example, the following three sentences in French, English, and German would be permutationally congruent.

> *John and Mary are here.*
> *Marie et Jean sont ici.*
> *Marie und Johann sind hier.*

Under the natural grammar for arithmetical expressions, the following pair would also be permutationally congruent:

$$2 + 2 = 4$$
$$4 = 2 + 2$$

Let me guard against one kind of misinterpretation of permutational congruence. It might be thought that simply by permuting the branches of the tree we could show mistakenly that there was permutational congruence of the sentences *John loves Mary* and *Mary loves John.* This is of course not the case, because the semantic function that is the root of the two trees is different for these two sentences.

I turn now to the fourth definition. It is easy to show that each of the three definitions of congruence already given implies $\mathcal{M}$-paraphrase, which is the most general and therefore the weakest concept of congruence I shall introduce.

Definition 4. Two sentences are $\mathcal{M}$-paraphrases of each other if and only if the roots of their trees denote the same object with respect to every model structure in $\mathcal{M}$.

If $\mathcal{M}$-paraphrase is replaced by logical paraphrase, we get the definition that Montague, for example, liked: Two sentences are L-paraphrases of each other if and only if they denote the same function from possible worlds to truth values. Closely connected with this latter definition is

Frege's characterization of sentences being paraphrases of each other if and only if they have the same logical consequences. It seems to me that the condition of logical consequence or logical paraphrase is too strong. In ordinary language we regard the following two sentences as paraphrases of each other, but of course they are not logical paraphrases:

Mary has three apples and John has four.
Mary has three apples and John has one more.

Unless arithmetic is assumed as a part of logic, these two sentences are not paraphrases of each other in the logical sense, although under the intended treatment of $\mathcal{M}$-paraphrase they would be because arithmetic would be held constant across the set $\mathcal{M}$ of model structures, i.e., the elementary laws of arithmetic would be satisfied in every model structure of $\mathcal{M}$.

Another example on the assumption that arithmetic is not part of logic is the following pair of even simpler sentences:

$$2 < 4$$
$$4 > 2$$

(at least under the treatment I prefer of definitions as noncreative axioms in the object language).

The four definitions given do not in any sense exhaust the possible definitions of congruence of sentences. They are meant to exhibit the possibilities and to show how we may deal in a natural and simple way with sentences that all of us accept as being close to each other in meaning.

PROPERTIES OF CONGRUENCE

Turning once again to the classical geometrical tradition, we should be able to ask many questions about congruence of meaning if our concepts of congruence are remotely similar to those that have been so useful in geometry. I have divided this topic into three parts. First, I look at the natural analogues of classical geometric theorems about congruence of figures. Second, I examine the relation between congruences and groups of transformations. A new way of talking about transformational grammars arises from this discussion. Finally, I consider some conjectures about the expressiveness of languages when the congruence relation is that of paraphrase.

A familiar concept in Euclidean geometry is that of congruence of polygons. Two polygons are said to be congruent if there is a one-to-one correspondence between their vertices, so that the corresponding segments and the corresponding angles of the two polygons are in every case congruent to each other. We assume of course in this definition that we already have a characterization of the congruence of segments and the congruence of angles. What is interesting about polygons is that the only rigid polygon is a triangle. The meaning of this is that the only polygon whose shape is determined by its sides alone is the triangle. We may ask a similar question of congruence about sentences, with terminal words corresponding to segments. If two sentences are such that their terminal words are congruent, that is, have the same denotations, under the natural left-to-right ordering, then are the sentences strongly congruent? In other words, is the meaning of sentences within strong congruence rigid with respect to terminal words? It is easy to see that in general the answer is negative for sentences that have two or more words. It is trivial to construct examples of context-free languages to show that this is so.

On the other hand, for a wide variety of formal languages, rigidity of congruence with respect to the terminal symbols of expressions is a fundamental property. Essentially, such rigidity is characteristic of the language of all theories with standard formalization, that is, of all theories formulated in first-order logic with identity, which includes such standard examples as the algebraic theory of fields, elementary number theory, and axiomatic set theory.

By looking at languages for theories with standard formalization, it is easy enough to find languages rigid with respect to strong congruence. Also evident for such languages as ordinarily formulated is that the concept of strong congruence reduces to this. The only sentences strongly congruent to a given sentence are the alphabetic variants of the sentence itself.

Further, in first approximation most sentences of ordinary language used in a literal or scientific sense are rigid. The interesting comparisons are probably between languages that have been subsumed under a single grammar as in the case of machine translation. Although simple examples of rigidity have already been given, the fragments of grammars of English, French, and German can be put together to form a rigid grammar in the sense of strong congruence, the very absence of rigidity in the sense of strong congruence is a major contributing factor to the difficulty of machine translation.

In the case of permutational congruence of meaning for both formal languages and natural languages, we have many congruent sentences. Examples have already been given, but here is another: The first-order theory of commutative groups contains numerous expressions that are permutationally congruent, and of course many of these expressions are congruent just because of the symmetry of the logical predicate of identity.

Something that we all recognize as fundamentally conventional is properly reflected in the definition of permutational congruence. For example, the axioms for commutive groups, all of which have as a single predicate identity, can be written with the left-hand and right-hand terms reversed; there are only more or less standard conventions as to what to put on the left side and what on the right side.

Examples of permutational congruence of sentences of ordinary language have already been given, and others may be constructed in terms of sentential connectives or in terms of noun phrases or verb phrases. On the other hand, there seems to be no straightforward generalization of the concept of a language being rigid with respect to strong congruence to its being rigid with respect to permutational congruence. The reason is transparent. If the terminal words of two languages are congruent under a permutation, it does not follow at all that the sentences are permutationally congruent. Perhaps the simplest examples may be constructed from any transitive verb. For instance, as already remarked, *John loves Mary* is not permutationally congruent with *Mary loves John*, even though the terminal words can be put into one-to-one correspondence under a permutation.

I reserve for the moment discussion of the concept of congruence corresponding to paraphrase and turn to the relation between transformations and congruence.

TRANSFORMATIONS

The geometrical analogy developed at the beginning of this paper can be pushed further to suggest a relation between congruence of meaning and transformational grammars that does not yet seem to have been explored in the literature on linguistics and the philosophy of language. Let me briefly review the situation in geometry. Given the idea of motion to obtain superposition of figures, it was gradually realized that a motion may be conceived as a geometric transformation of the plane (or space) and that such a geometric transformation is in its most general form any one-one function mapping the plane (or space) onto itself. The particular transformations that correspond to motions admissible in Euclidean geometry are just the transformations that form what has to come to be called the group of rigid motions or Euclidean motions.

Originally, transformations were looked upon as a rigorous way of talking about superpositions. At an early date the connection between transformations and symmetries of figures was also recognized. For example, in late Hellenistic times, Pappus discussed earlier work by Apollonius showing that a transformation by central symmetry, or by circular inversion, would carry a line or a circle into a line or circle. Probably the first person to have a definite idea of using a transformation to determine the properties of a general figure from the simpler properties of a special one was Poncelet (1822) who, at the beginning of the nineteenth century, used projective transformations for purposes of simplification.

The connection, however, between transformations and congruence was set forth in the latter part of the nineteenth century by Felix Klein in his famous inaugural dissertation that formulated his Erlanger Program. To each group of transformations there corresponds a congruence relation, and to each congruence relation there corresponds a group of transformations. Klein's program was to study the significant groups of transformations to identify the congruence relation or, put another way, the geometric properties preserved under the group, and correspondingly, given a congruence relation, to determine the group of transformations under which it remains invariant (see Klein, 1893).

It is sometimes said that Klein's lucid and explicit characterization of the relation between groups of transformations and invariant properties of congruence relations is the most important conceptual contribution to geometry since ancient Greeks. In any case, the subsequent history of geometry has certainly been deeply affected by his viewpoint, and today it is probably more common to think of a given group of transformations and the properties that are held invariant under this group than it is to think about a particular concept of congruence.

In principle, the same program should be feasible for congruence relations of meaning. Although we can ask for the transformations that preserve the congruence relation, there are several conceptual problems that we must first deal with. In fact the way in which we shall deal with these problems that are in a sense preliminary is not yet accepted or fully agreed upon. The problem is this. In the case of geometry it is easy to say what a transformation is. It is a one-one function mapping the entire space onto itself. We thereby have a simple and straightforward mathematical characterization of transformations as objects. The situation would have been quite different if the attempt had been made to define transformations not on points, but on figures, so that transformations take as their arguments not points, but figures. It is probably intuitively easier to use the latter definition. In talking, for example, about one figure being superimposed or moved to coincide with another, it is not natural to think about transforming the entire space. Physically and empirically we certainly do not think in such terms, but rather in terms of local effects only on the two figures in question. Mathematically, however, it is much simpler to talk about transforming the entire space rather than individual figures.

Geometrically speaking, transformational grammars are more or less currently defined as transformations on figures rather than on points, for in the standard approach, it is customary to define transformations in the linguistic sense as mappings of trees into trees. Thus we can start with a context-free grammar and consider the trees generated by this grammar; the transformations then map these trees into other trees. The attempts to give an exact definition of the concept of transformation, as for example that given by Ginsburg and Partee (1969), is awkward from a mathematical standpoint and certainly encourages the search for a definition closer in spirit to that used in geometry.

Unfortunately, we do not have anything like the natural distance function between points to use in defining transformations on tree nodes, terminal words, or sentences of a language. Certainly, a one-one transformation on the finite set of terminal words is not satisfactory and will not permit the deletions and insertions as required, for instance, in the transformation from the active to the passive voice. There is the possibility of defining the transformations on the sentences, but this is in effect almost the same as defining the transformations on the trees, and the technical reason for choosing the trees rather than the sentences is that the sentences themselves are syntactically ambiguous. Thus the move from trees to sentences is not one that will improve the conceptual situation. If the nodes of the trees are not put in the context of the tree itself, they are too unconnected from other objects and therefore do not seem suitable as objects to be transformed.

One natural suggestion is that transformations should operate on the production rules of the grammar. The reason for doing this is that we can require that the transformation of a production rule use the same semantic function as the original production rule. Thus, when I transform the rule that carries a sentence in the active voice into one with a passive voice, I do not actually change the semantic function that establishes a relation between the denotation of the noun phrase that is the subject, the denotation of the transitive verb, and the denotation of the noun phrase that is the object. The idea of defining transformations on the production rules is closely connected to the concept of a syntax-directed translation scheme in computer science, but it would lead too far afield to develop the relevant formal machinery in this paper.

Establishing a close connection between transformations and congruence relations of meaning does not depend upon the particular definition of transformations just mentioned. One can work with the definition already familiar in the literature, that is, having transformations map trees into trees, and still look for the group of transformations that preserve a given congruence relation.

Without entering into technical details, it is easy to state in an informal way what transformations correspond to strong congruence or permutational congruence. In the case of strong congruence, the group of transformations can be characterized in terms of transformations of individual vocabulary words into other words. In the case of terminal words, the mapping must be into terminal words having the same denotation, and in the case of nonterminal words the mapping must be into nonterminal words that yield isomorphic semantic trees. My point is that strong congruence can be characterized in terms of such point transformations, so to speak, once we apply them to the production rules of the grammar, including the lexical rules.

For permutational congruence, the group of transformations can be characterized in terms of appropriate subgroups of the full permutation group, but different permutations may be applied to different production rules of the grammar. Of course, as in the case of strong congruence, a mapping of terminal words into terminal words with the same denotation is also required.

There is a natural question to ask about the language generated by the group of transformations corresponding to a given concept of congruence. It is especially appropriate to ask this question, because the standard results in the literature indicate that the general concept of transformations mapping trees into trees is far too powerful, in the sense that in applying the transformations to a context-free language we may generate any recursively enumerable set over the given finite vocabulary. Salomaa (1971) has shown that any recursively enumerable language may be generated by a transformational grammar over a regular language, which is much more restricted than a context-free base. In view of the simplicity of the register machines or Turing machines that may be used to generate any partially recursive function over a finite alphabet, it is not surprising that results of the simplicity of Salomaa's are obtainable.

On the other hand, the situation is quite different for highly restricted senses of transformation. For example, the group of transformations corresponding to a strong congruence relation over a regular language leads only to a regular language, and the group of transformations corresponding to strong congruence over a context-free language leads only to a context-free language. The transformations corresponding to permutational congruence can lead from a regular language to a context-free language, but not to something more powerful.

It is not my purpose here to present results of this kind in formal detail and to prove appropriate theorems. Thus I have only sketched some of the ways in which the concept of transformation assumes a more restricted character when it is tied to semantical notions, particularly to a semantical congruence relation.

The results of Salomaa suggest an interesting conjecture regarding paraphrase. Given the extent to which a regular language can be transformed to generate any recursively enumerable set, and therefore any language over a finite alphabet, it might seem that the expressive power of any language can be paraphrased in the simple structure of a regular language. The syntactic results suggest this as a serious possibility. But the well-known results about the limited power of finite-state machines that correspond to regular languages suggest that once we tie the semantics explicitly to the power of the language as well, no such reduction by paraphrase to a regular language will be possible. We know, for example, that a finite-state machine cannot multiply any two arbitrary integers. Already, this suggests that once we include the semantics of the simple recursive language of arithmetic, we shall not be able to reduce by paraphrase to a regular language. The intuitive argument seems clear, but the formal analysis is not yet completely explicit. Almost certainly the group of transformations corresponding to the very general sense of congruence expressed by the concept of paraphrase will require considerably more effort to characterize than do the groups corresponding to the stronger senses of congruence I have discussed.

CONCLUDING REMARKS

I have tried to outline the beginnings of what I think might properly be called a geometric theory of meaning. It has been remarked by many people that semantical theory as applied to natural language has not yet led to a series of results comparable in depth to those obtained in the theory of models for formal languages. One possible feeling is that this can hardly be expected, because natural languages are fundamentally empirical phenomena in contrast to formal languages, which may be studied as a part of pure mathematics. However, this seems to me a mistake. My hope is that semantical theory or, more generally, the tools of logic, may play the role in the study of natural languages that classical mathematical analysis has played in physics.

My final point is that the emphasis in the philosophy of language should be on analysis and not on reduction. The reduction of much systematic discourse to first-order logic has been important and represents a long tradition that begins with Aristotle. What is more important for the philosophy of language of the future is to concentrate on the analysis of natural language as it is used in practice and not to be concerned with the reduction of that practice to an artificial regime. One direction to move in obtaining greater empirical fidelity is to widen the concept of sentence or sentence utterance to that of speech act. Unfortunately, the theory of speech acts is still in a nascent state. Unlike the theory of language I have been able to draw on in characterizing congruence of meaning, correspondingly clear and definite concepts have not yet been developed for speech acts. Intuitively, significant concepts of congruence are used continually in abstracting sentences from speech acts, but the theory of that abstraction is left wholly informal. Development of an explicit theory of congruence for speech acts is a task for the future, but one that seems far from hopeless. The tools of analysis I have described should be useful in that enterprise as well.

2

A PUZZLE ABOUT RESPONSES
AND CONGRUENCE OF
MEANING

This paper has been stimulated by reading Almog (1984) and even more by conversations with Joseph Almog, as well as with Howard Wettstein. I discuss Almog's own paper in the last section but first I begin with a stronger puzzle than Mates', a puzzle about responses, and then in the next section I relate the puzzle to my idea about congruence of meaning.

By bringing in other psychological variables it is easy to formulate a test for sameness of meaning that is stronger than that required by Mates' puzzle. The kind of context I have in mind depends upon statements about the responses of an individual to individual propositions. As would be expected, the examples use indirect discourse.

(1) Jones responds more quickly in judging the truth of the proposition that Cicero was bald than he does in responding to the proposition that Tully was bald.

---

*Reprinted from *Synthese*, **58**, 1984, 39-50.

Ordinarily permutation of the words 'Cicero' and 'Tully' will change the truth value of this sentence and only one of the permutations will make it true. The truth of (1) depends upon the detailed, highly idiosyncratic behavior of an individual. There is a great deal of data showing that fine distinctions will exist between any two words, no matter how frequent they both are in the individual's vocabulary or how frequently they serve as approximate synonyms. The point of this kind of example is that there is no fixed relation of synonymy that will patch it up—my proposed solution in terms of a hierarchy of congruences is set forth in the next section.

I label the puzzle generated by (1) *a puzzle about responses* to match Kripke's phrase concerning a puzzle about beliefs.

We can ignore the complicated comparative structure of (1) and consider sentences like the following.

(2) Jones responds affirmatively in less than 200 milliseconds to the assertion that Cicero was bald, and in more than 200 milliseconds to the assertion that Tully was bald.

A possible objection is that indirect discourse is inappropriate, but this objection as far as I can see would apply equally well to the belief cases. The inability to go directly from indirect discourse to direct quotation in the belief cases has been well accepted since Church's discussion (1950). The same thing can be said about (1) and (2) above. These are propositions that are not committed at all to the language in which the propositions are formulated for the given individual who is responding.

There is a tension between philosophical and psychological methodologies that needs explicit attention. Either in the case of beliefs or responses, psychologists describing detailed data about beliefs or responses would feel called upon to record the actual sentence types that were used as tokens in eliciting responses from individuals. The form of indirect discourse used in the paradox about belief or the paradox about responses would not be regarded as methodologically acceptable. On the other hand, all speakers of English recognize the indirect discourse idiom, understand its meaning in an intuitive way, and have little difficulty with it. Also, ordinary speakers of English understand Church's point that the indirect discourse does not contain information about which language was used in expressing the proposition, either in the case of responses or beliefs. I am lingering over this point because it is possible someone would try to drive a wedge between the belief case and the response case by saying that only in the latter case are the actual sentences used critical.

It is also worth noting that statements about both beliefs and responses are easily constructed. For example:

(3) Jones responded immediately when asked whether he believes that Cicero was bald, but did not respond immediately when asked whether he believes that Tully was bald.

Or the more explicit sort of formulation used above:

(4) Jones responded affirmatively in less than 150 milliseconds when asked whether he believes that Cicero was bald, but in more than 150 milliseconds when asked whether he believes that Tully was bald.

Given differences in response time, one way of putting the matter is that Jones' beliefs about Cicero are more accessible than his beliefs about Tully, but of course this sounds paradoxical when put in this fashion. We might put it still another way, but this would involve an explicit commitment to the names.

(5) Jones responds to beliefs about Cicero more quickly when Cicero is denoted by 'Cicero' than when Cicero is denoted by 'Tully' .

The examples given have involved proper names but the puzzle about responses is not so restricted as the following example similar to (1) shows:

(6) Jones responds more quickly when asked whether he believes that Newton was a bachelor than he does when asked whether he believes that Newton was an unmarried man.

The response examples I have given are obviously meant to argue for a more complicated concept of assent than is ordinarily used in discussions only of beliefs. From a psychological standpoint, it seems apparent that assent is a complex phenomenon of many dimensions. Here I have only mentioned one new psychological variable, that of latency of response, but there are a host of others, ranging from heartbeat to galvanic skin reaction. I see no principled argument for drawing a line in any definite and final way so as to exclude any of the great variety of psychological variables that indicate the differential status of words, expressions, ideas, or emotions in the mind of a given individual. These many different variables define what I call a profile of assent.

Let me put the puzzle in an explicit conceptual fashion. The premises are these:

(7) There is a single fixed concept M of sameness of meaning for expressions.

(8) This concept M of sameness of meaning holds between expression tokens that are not identical, i.e., sameness of meaning is not just the trivial relation of identity.

(9) Expression tokens that stand in the relation M generate the same profile of assent.

(10) But for any individual there are expression tokens that stand in the relation M and yet have distinct profiles of assent.

Premises (7) and (8) are familiar claims about sameness of meaning. Premise (9) corresponds to the claim that expressions that stand in the relation M of sameness of meaning have identical cognitive significance. Premise (10) rests on elementary and widespread psychological evidence. It is obvious that these four premises are mutually inconsistent.

Various moves can be made formally to resolve the inconsistency. One is to deny that the profile of assent should include a variety of psychological variables. But this move would seem to emasculate the concept of assent and make it a highly abstract philosophical concept. The response variable of latency, for example, is widely used as a sensitive measure of degree of mastery of a concept or skill. Cognitive studies using this measure are legion. The commonsense basis of its relevance to cognition is also evident.

A variety of other variables that would naturally be included in a psychologically rich profile of assent can also be defended. There is one variable, however, that has not yet been mentioned but that should be accepted as relevant by everyone for testing sameness of meaning. The variable is that of *strength of belief*, which can be measured behaviorally in different ways, the most popular being by means of real or hypothetical bets at different odds. (It is important to emphasize that numerical bets are not required to infer a very good quantitative estimate of strength of belief, which is often also called degree of belief or subjective probability. Purely qualitative methods can be used. For reviews of the extensive theoretical and experimental literature, see (Luce and Suppes, 1965; Krantz, Luce, Tversky, & Suppes, 1971.)

Relevant examples are easy to construct. Because Jones is not quite sure that Tully is Cicero, the following is true:

(11) Jones' strength of belief in the assertion that Cicero was bald is greater than his strength of belief in the assertion that Tully was bald.

This kind of example can also be applied to the paradox of analysis. Given the usual view that strength of belief is a continuous variable, we might want to claim that most if not all cases of the paradox can be explained away by it. Smith is as certain as he can be that Cicero = Cicero, but just slightly less so that Tully = Cicero. The same analysis applies to the familiar example about female foxes and vixens.

In my own view the argument for the cognitive significance of a rich profile of assent is substantial, and I would not want to reduce the profile just to strength of belief. If that were insisted on, I would argue that the other behavioral measures mentioned not only define a profile of assent but are highly correlated with strength of belief. As is evident, I have not tried to set forth here a detailed conception of the relation between the psychological variables mentioned or alluded to. Some are more theoretical than others, and strong correlations between them would be expected.

The second and more promising move in dealing with the contradiction that follows from premises (7)-(10) is to deny there is any fixed, context-independent concept of sameness of meaning that must be held to through the thick and thin of all possible puzzles or situations. The next section is focused on this approach.

As we go beyond simple ideas of assent to the full range of psychological response variables, it is clear that the assigned differentiations we can make strain the line between direct and indirect discourse. But pursuit of this point is not possible.

CONGRUENCE OF MEANING

For a number of years (Suppes, 1973a) I have been advocating a geometrical approach to the theory of meaning. The geometrical idea is to use various strong and weak concepts of congruence to get varying degrees of closeness of meaning. The idea is not to be caught in the search for a single concept of synonymy, just as in modern geometry we are not caught in a single concept of congruence as were the geometers of ancient Greece and Alexandria. We have in affine geometry, for example, a weaker sense of congruence than in Euclidean geometry but it is also easy to get a commonsense notion of congruence that is stronger than the Euclidean one, namely congruence that requires sameness of orientation.

To continue this analogy with geometry, we would anticipate that extensional uses of language would require a relatively coarse congruence whereas the expression of propositional attitudes, as exemplified in Mates' puzzle, or the even stronger puzzle about responses, would require very strong congruence relations. In fact, due to the continuous character of the response data we would ordinarily think of the probability being zero that response times or, as psychologists would put it, the latency of response, would be the same for two distinct lexical items. Insofar as we want to account for the puzzle about responses the data would suggest that only the trivial congruence relation of identity, the strongest one possible, will suffice. But I hasten to add that it is not really identity here, but only abstraction at a certain level. For example, if we treat in the ordinary sense two printed tokens of the same type as identical we are abstracting. If we look at the ordinary continuous production by sound-pressure waves of two tokens of the same spoken word-type, then the sense of identity in the sense of linguistic identity commonly used, is indeed a very gross abstraction from the detailed acoustical facts. The two sound-pressure waves will not be physically the same for the two tokens and in fact it is an intellectual problem of considerable magnitude to identify what are the invariant features in the two tokens that make possible the abstraction as two occurrences of the same type. Moreover, it is not just the sound-pressure wave but the context, including the prosodic features, the nonverbal features of the speaker and listener, etc., which also influence the richness of congruence we consider. It is only in an abstract axiomatic system that congruence can be brought down to the level of identity in any simple way. It would be part of my claim that there is no final or ultimate level of congruence. In actual language we have ever stronger concepts of congruence and there is no realistic bound to the number of levels.

Almog (1984) gives an excellent analysis of the three levels of what I shall call public meaning: namely, extensions, intensions, and characters. What I am urging is that above these three levels is an infinite hierarchy of stronger congruence relations. Mates' puzzle can be solved at the level of congruence corresponding to our conventional talk about identity for two tokens of the same type, but it is the point of my puzzle about responses to emphasize that it is easy to generate stronger puzzles that require us to go beyond this conventional identity of two printed tokens of the same type. Beyond the examples considered in the preceding section we could easily generate two tokens of the same linguistic word but which have slightly different stress. We would find it easy to relate circumstances in which we could differentiate the responses to the two tokens with slightly different stress. A similar exercise could be engaged in by considering for spoken words the familiar parameters of duration and intensity. The possibilities of variation here are properly infinite because of the naturally continuous character of the phenomena. I am not suggesting, of course, that there are conceptually interesting congruence relations for every possible continuous variation, but rather emphasizing that in principle there is a continuum of possibilities open to us.

The main point really is that there is no natural cutoff point in the concept of congruence of meaning at which we have no finer possibilities of congruence available to us. This is a point that I have not sufficiently emphasized in previous discussions, although I have made the point that we need to include congruence relations for speech acts (Suppes, 1980).

A familiar example that directly involves the intensity of a spoken utterance is repeatedly seen in a parent's instructions to a child. There are many circumstances in which a child does not respond until the intensity of the request from the parent reaches a certain decibel level. A representation of what is taking place here by simple written transcription of what has been said orally would be utterly unfaithful to the facts, and thus not have the appropriate congruence relation. It is in fact surprising that the intricate and subtle aspects of spoken speech have entered so little into the large literature on sameness of meaning. I hope that my point about the infinite hierarchy of congruence of meaning is clearly understood to refer to and to provide an apparatus for dealing with the significant continuous variations of spoken speech.

Let me put the matter another way. Each token at whatever level we define it—sound-pressure wave, speech act with physical expression etc.—is identical to itself but the theory is not really interesting at this level of identity. For all purposes we want to abstract so that types contain more than single tokens. There is an infinite hierarchy of types between the public types of extension, intension and character, on the one hand, and identity at the level of tokens on the other. This is a familiar problem of scientific theories, but not one that is dealt with in detail in ordinary model theory. The concept of individual in standard model theory is unanalyzed. There is no fixed concept of individual in the sense of model theory that is usable in the conceptual analysis of natural language. We should not be discontented with this state of affairs but simply put it on the table as a fact of life. Depending upon the purposes at hand we will abstract to relatively finer or relatively more coarse degrees of congruence. For printed scientific and philosophical texts the requirements of congruence are ordinarily relatively coarse. Analysis of the speech interaction between mother and child is quite another story. Prosodic nuances and shifts in stress may initially be more important than the extensional abstraction in ordinary printed language of what has been said. In principle, for each of the continuous points at which we can fix a level of congruence, a puzzle focused on identification of type at a lower level in the hierarchy is always possible. In practice, only certain points in the hierarchy will be of interest. I believe that the puzzle about responses shows that the consideration of such additional psychological variables does provide a natural way of identifying more refined congruences of interest than are reflected in propositional attitudes about beliefs alone.

Indirect discourse. In considering the puzzle about responses, Mates' puzzle or Kripke's puzzle about beliefs, it is always natural to try to eliminate the idiom of indirect discourse, especially as a direct method of solving the puzzles. In my view, Church's arguments of many years ago (e.g., 1950, 1954), mentioned earlier, remain valid. No simple scheme for replacing indirect discourse by direct discourse is going to work. Rather than review his arguments I want to make some related points that reinforce the case for indirect discourse.

The first is this. When we examine individual sentences like any of (1)-(4) or (6), there is an almost irresistible tendency for many to seek a direct-discourse replacement. But this move focused on individual sentences misses an important point. Deep uses of language are totally dependent on indirect discourse. Any adequate conceptual analysis of natural language must be able to deal correctly and in detail with indirect discourse. Examples of this essential dependence on indirect discourse lie immediately at hand. Any report of a long conversation depends on indirect discourse: She said that so and so, but I said that what really mattered was the following... In a conversation of two hours or so easily 10,000 words can be spoken, and nobody can remember even a small percentage of the sentences spoken—even those spoken by oneself.

Exacting and detailed as legal standards of evidence are, reports by witnesses of conversations must depend on indirect discourse. In all these cases the reason is obvious. Human memory and cognition function beautifully at paraphrasing, but are exceedingly limited in the exact and explicit recall of sequences of words spoken. It is essential to understand the semantics of indirect discourse because its continual use is an essential feature of the human mind.

My second point constitutes a move away from Church insofar as he argues for a single concept of synonymy (see especially Church 1954), for then the concept of proposition is not really explained. The introduction of an infinite hierarchy of congruences permits the concept of proposition to be relativized and, correspondingly, appropriately fine distinctions to be introduced into the theory and practice of paraphrase. The formal theory cannot be worked out here, but it will be useful to sketch some of the main ideas. On the view of congruence I am advocating there is no single fixed proposition that a sentence-token expresses. Rather, a proposition is expressed by a sentence modulo a given congruence relation. Any other sentence standing in the given congruence relation to the given sentence expresses the same proposition—again, modulo the congruence relation. On my view that there is an infinite hierarchy of congruence relations, a given sentence-token expresses a potentially infinite number of different propositions.

In accepting a report in indirect discourse, we naturally make use without explicit acknowledgment of a *Principle of Trust in Partial Truths*. The congruences imposed by the paraphrasing reporter do not distort or leave out facts or nuances essential to the main thrust of the conversation being reported. Contrary to the oath administered to witnesses, we never really expect to hear the whole truth, and in most cases it would be intolerable if we had to. What we hope for is the right set of partial truths with the choice of the level of congruence left to the wisdom and good taste of our reporters, sensitive to how much we really want to know.

COMMENTS ON ALMOG

I am in general agreement with the views set forth by Almog in his article (1984). As should be evident, his move toward privacy is one that I very much favor. From a different standpoint but a congenial one I have emphasized privacy in my conception of procedural semantics (Suppes, 1980). My object here is to go over some points of detail on which we are not in complete agreement or that perhaps need further analysis.

Dictionaries. As indicated, I like the move toward privacy that is explicit in his concept of individual dictionaries but I do not think he has gone far enough. The infinite hierarchy of congruences of meaning discussed in the preceding section shows how rich I think the internal apparatus can be. In particular, dictionaries as such do not seem to me to be sufficient. We need idiosyncratic private procedures. My position would be that individuals differ in their procedures for recognizing a given object or holding that a property applies to an object. These individual procedures are part of the infinite hierarchy of congruences of meaning. A way of putting it is that I think the internal processing of language is a much richer and more idiosyncratic affair than is suggested just by the concept of private dictionaries.

Uniqueness of language. Associated with the point about dictionaries is also a point about the uniqueness of language. There are various ways in which one can claim that two individuals are speaking different languages. One familiar claim is that the rules of grammar, that is, the structural descriptions, must be the same, but it seems to me very likely that this is not the case and so in a strictly literal sense different individuals speak different idiolects of English and thus in some precise sense different languages. On the other hand, by appropriate abstraction at the right level we can show they are speaking the same language. But I also want to hold a stronger thesis than this, which I set forth in somewhat more detail elsewhere (Suppes, 1986). This is the thesis that the creative use of language is not just a matter of using rules but also one of continually creating new rules. Individual rules of grammar are created by speakers and listeners as required and are not a matter of something that is learned once for all at one's mother's knee. So the rules of grammar I use are ones that I generate often in new situations and very likely on many occasions forget, to be relearned and recreated as needed on new occasions. Of course, many rules that are used continuously attain a stable character and do not change from occasion to occasion. My point is just to insist that the rich variety of each individual's language can be differentiated from any one else's. Any two individuals speak different idiolects at the finest level of analysis and in a literal sense their languages are different.

Linguistic truth. I am not sure that Almog really believes in it but he does make use in various places of the concept of linguistic truth, as for example in his proposition (A) toward the end of the paper. I am skeptical of any fixed and definite notion of linguistic truth. The notion is at best relative to context and purpose. Engineers constructing a new highway and the bridges for it take as linguistic truths the classical and fundamental laws of statics, but other scientists working on the fundamental theory of elasticity do not take these as linguistic truths at all but as fallible approximations that are literally false. Words float around in ordinary discourse and get pushed in one direction and then another. Take that old chestnut about its being a linguistic truth that bachelors are unmarried men. This certainly does not apply to talk about bachelor girls. Then, too, there is that archaic meaning of young knight, and also that usage for those who received a Bachelor of Arts degree, as in the possible litany of a graduation ceremony: Will all doctors now stand... now all masters... now all bachelors. I am skeptical of linguistic meaning as having any hard and fixed sense. It floats about from one context to another and does not have the definiteness too often claimed. In the terms I use, different congruences are called for by different contexts and often even in the same public context.

Intersubstitutability. From what I have said already it should be apparent that I would be skeptical of Almog's characterization of expressions being intersubstitutable. His requirement is essentially that two expressions are intersubstitutable when they share completions in all the variants in the neighborhood of evaluation, where his concept of neighborhood as defined for dictionaries is the one being used. It should be apparent from what I have said about congruence of meaning I would reformulate this, to say that two expressions that are intersubstitutable in the sense of extensions, intensions, and characters will not be intersubstitutable at some level of the hierarchy of congruence of meaning, given that the two expressions are not identical tokens.

3

CONGRUENCY THEORY OF
PROPOSITIONS

The main ingredients of the theory I propose are these: the concrete token utterance, which should in general be thought of as a sound-pressure wave uttered in a given context; an infinite hierarchy of congruence relations between utterances; and the creative definition of identity for propositions. Two propositions are identical just when the utterances from which they are ⟨abstracted⟩ are congruent. This means that the concept of identity of propositions is relative to a congruence relation, as in the standard condition of identity for congruence classes in algebra.

The important point is that an utterance does not assert a single proposition but an infinite hierarchy of propositions. The choice of the proposition that is asserted depends upon the congruence relation under consideration or of interest. Formally, the creative definition of identity for propositions has the following form:

(I) $[u] = [u']$ iff $u \simeq u'$

In (I), u and u' are two concrete utterances, and $[u]$ is the proposition expressed by u, or more explicitly, $[u]$ is the proposition expressed by u under the congruence relation $\simeq$.

Comparison with geometry. It will be useful to make some detailed comparisons with geometry in thinking about how this theory of propo-

---

*Reprinted from *Mérites et Limites des Méthodes Logiques en Philosophie*, Paris: Librairie Philosophique J. Vrin, 1986.

sitions is to work. There are certain points about axiomatic geometry that could be confusing and need clarification. In the first place, are the axioms of geometry about concrete physical objects or about abstract objects like propositions? It is fair to say that in a straightforward sense the axioms are about abstract objects. Thus, for example, affine geometry is about affine figures, but saying that affine geometry is about affine figures is also not quite correct. Triangles that are characterized in terms of betweenness, the single necessary primitive concept in affine geometry, are not specifically affine triangles, for the same definition of triangle also works in Euclidean geometry. What is different in Euclidean geometry is that the notion of congruence changes.

Therefore, the right thing to say is that affine geometry provides a formulation of affine relations. It gives the axioms for such relations between points. In particular, the standard axioms of affine geometry are entirely about the ternary relation of betweenness for points because this is the only nonlogical relation that needs to be used in the axioms.

Another way of putting the matter is this. Affine geometry is concerned to axiomatize and prove those propositions that are affine invariant. Thus we can see how there is a parallel to what I want to say about concrete utterances and propositions in this special case of geometry. We are given a concrete utterance about geometric figures; for example, these two lines are parallel. We can ask whether it expresses a proposition that is affine in character or is the congruence relation under which the proposition is invariant of a different character.

It is important to note that the parallel is not exact. As we ordinarily think of it there is one natural proposition expressed by a given eternal sentence of a geometrical character. This single natural proposition is invariant under a given congruence relation. On the basis of this given congruence relation we then will say that the utterance is affine, Euclidean, etc. In the case of propositions and utterances, I want to say something different. The claim is that a given concrete utterance corresponds in geometry to a given figure, not to an utterance about that figure. This is important in carrying through the parallel. A given concrete utterance expresses a variety of propositions, just as a given geometrical figure has a variety of properties which are invariant under different congruence relations. (The comparison is developed further in Suppes, 1973a.)

INVARIANCE AND CONGRUENCE

To discuss the relation between invariance and congruence, it will be useful to continue using geometrical analogies. From school geometry, we are all familiar with the Euclidean concept of congruence, but there is another approach to the foundations of geometry, first made famous by Felix Klein in his Erlangen program of 1872. The central idea of Klein's program is that a geometry is characterized not by axioms on particular primitive notions such as that of congruence of line segments but rather by the group of transformations of space onto itself which leave the relevant geometrical properties invariant. Thus, for example, the appropriate group of transformations of ordinary Euclidean space is just the group of what are called rigid motions, that is, the transformations that can be composed of translations, rotations, and reflections. Such transformations are called rigid motions, because any motion of a rigid body in Euclidean space can be characterized by such a transformation. It is easy to show that familiar geometrical properties of Euclidean space, for example, the shape and size of triangles, are preserved by such rigid motions, and also that some properties we associate with Euclidean space are not preserved by any wider group of transformations.

Given the importance and power of this geometrical concept of invariance under a group of transformations, it is natural to ask whether the same ideas can be applied to language to replace what has been said thus far about congruence. I believe that the first application of these ideas of invariance to logic, and thus to language, is to be found in Lindenbaum and Tarski (1935). The first theorem of their article states that every relation between objects expressible by purely logical means is invariant with respect to every one-one transformation. What is important here is the generality of the transformations. There are no restrictions on the one-one mappings. In the case of all the geometrical transformations that arise as part of Klein's Erlangen program, there is, of course, some additional restriction. As Lindenbaum and Tarski's theorem shows, the standard concept of logical equivalence is, in the sense of the Klein Erlangen program, equivalent to invariance under arbitrary one-one transformations.

There are some further consequences of the Lindenbaum and Tarski theorem that are worth discussing in the present general context. It follows from their theorem, and also from intuitive considerations on the nature of one-one transformations that:

(i) no two individuals are distinguishable by purely logical means;

(ii) only the universal class and the empty class can be defined by purely logical means.

Another consequence is that only four binary relations between individuals are definable by purely logical means, namely, the universal relation, the empty relation, identity, and nonidentity.

It is evident enough that in the ordinary use of language we want to move in the direction of geometry and put some additional conditions on the concept of invariance, that is, additional conditions on the transformations under which we expect a concept to remain invariant. One might even maintain that the distinction between formal logic and the logic of natural language consists precisely in restricting the permissible class of transformations. It is, for example, unintuitive to permit arbitrary one-one transformations of the individuals denoted by given proper names in the ordinary use of language. One of the virtues of the direct theory of reference is to play off of this fact. It is worth saying something more about this point. To introduce a standard piece of terminology, the trans- formations that satisfy the constraints of a given theory are called *automorphisms* of that theory. Let us now restrict the transformations considered by requiring that individuals who are assigned proper names in the fragment of language we are concerned with are only mapped into themselves. We can, in fact, make this what we might call the weak theory of identity of individuals. The automorphisms of this theory are just ordinary one-one transformations of the domain of individuals, with the restriction that each reference of a proper name is only transformed into itself. As is evident, this more restricted notion of transformation also gives us a wider notion of logical truth.

There is one severe limitation of the Erlangen program as applied to what is being said here about congruence. Congruency relations that depend directly on the syntactic form of utterances, and not merely on their semantics, are needed. It is evident that the Erlangen program is aimed just at transformations at the semantic level, that is, transformations on the domain of individuals. No matter how such transformations are restricted, we cannot express by such means the kind of syntactic congruence relations or combined syntactic and semantic congruence relations required for solving various standard puzzles. It is in this respect that the ordinary concept of invariance in geometry, and as extended by Lindenbaum and Tarski to logic, is not an adequate notion for utterances. We must combine invariance of semantics with invariance of syntactic form as well in order to obtain results that are psychologically and computationally the desired ones.

LOGICAL AND METAPHYSICAL APPLICATIONS

I turn now to applications. This section is restricted to logical and metaphysical contexts, and the next section to epistemic rules. The various congruences considered are, with some obvious exceptions, arranged in order of increasing strength.

Equal probability. Consider:

(1) It will rain tomorrow.

(2) There will be gusty winds in the afternoon.

(We are thinking always of concrete utterances.) For John (1) and (2) are congruent in the sense of being equally probable for him at a given point in time. Note that even weaker senses of congruence are easily given. Thus we can have the sense of congruence for two sentences that are both contingent, but it is generally the stronger senses that are of interest and that I shall concentrate on here.

Classical extensional congruence. The following two utterances are congruent in the sense of both being true:

(3) The sun is larger than Earth.

(4) Palo Alto is a smaller city than San Francisco.

Because this is a familiar sense of congruence, I move on without further comment.

Intensional congruence (in one classical sense). This sense of congruence is just that of logical equivalence. A typical example of logical equivalence is this:

(5) It is raining.

(6) It is raining, and it is the case that either protons are heavier than electrons or protons are not heavier than electrons.

Before we go further it may pay to make explicit the concept of proposition relative to the congruence relation of logical equivalence. From what has been said already it should be obvious that relative to intensional congruence two utterances that are logically equivalent express the same proposition. (I shall use continually the standard phrase 'express the same proposition', but of course the appropriate explicit phrasing should be 'express the same proposition relative to the congruence relation of. . .') Thus (5) and (6) express the same proposition relative to intensional congruence. This means that we have the familiar result at this level, namely, there is just one logically true proposition, and also just one logically false proposition. Of course, there is still an infinity of different propositions that are neither logically true nor logically false.

As in this example, I shall be somewhat casual about referring to the truth of propositions or the truth of concrete utterances. In any case, the primary concept of truth is for utterances because some propositions do not have unique truth values, e.g., the case of equal probability discussed above. A restricted theory of congruency could easily be developed that would require identity of truth value of u and u' in (I), but I think such a restriction is a mistake, in spite of the fact that uniqueness of truth value for propositions is an idea dear to the hearts of many philosophers.

If we compare intensional congruence of utterances to topological congruence of figures, there is a similar viewpoint in topology but a different language. One way of talking about such matters in geometry is the search for a structural representation theorem. Such a theorem classifies all figures, for example, by showing how each of them is topologically equivalent to a particular object in a designated class. The conditions on identity for propositions given are not used but the effect is the same. What is shown is that, for example, every geometrical surface is topologically equivalent to a canonical figure of a given genus in the case of topology and with other results for other geometries.

What I have to say about indirect discourse later has a corresponding formulation in one restricted sense for propositional identity in the sense of logical equivalence. We may call any two utterances that are logically equivalent, *logical paraphrases* of one another. One of the more demanding senses of indirect discourse is that the paraphrasing be logically equivalent to what has been said. Of course, such a requirement is often not satisfied in practice but it can be a useful idealization for discussing some of the features of indirect discourse.

The standard classical concept of logical equivalence has been used in the preceding discussion, but variant notions of equivalence from intuitionistic logic, quantum-mechanical logic, Church's intensional logic, and the like, can obviously be the basis of related but distinct concepts of intensional congruence.

M-congruence. There lies between extensional and intensional congruence an important concept of congruence, namely, congruence with respect to a fixed class M of models closed under isomorphism. For example, one may want to consider only models in which the laws of arithmetic, or the laws of classical physics, hold. For example, let M be such a class of models in which the laws of Euclidean geometry hold. Then (5) above and (7) below would be extensionally congruent and M-congruent but not intensionally congruent:

(7) It is raining, or no two lines in the plane are parallel.

I shall not linger over this example because it is of such a familiar type.

EPISTEMIC APPLICATIONS

I turn now to some epistemic puzzles.

Simple puzzles about belief sentences. Without considering complicated cases at all, the semantics of belief sentences seem necessarily devious because we can certainly assert for some individual John the following two sentences, the first of which is true and the second of which is false:

(8) John believes that Cicero was bald.

(9) John believes that Tully was bald.

There are two warnings about the formulation of (8) and (9), namely, both beliefs are stated in the usual form of indirect discourse, a matter which I shall examine in more detail later, and both are given in schematic form, that is, as printed statements. with no attempt to symbolize the niceties of the actual spoken utterance. (The latter reservation is seldom expressed in philosophical writings about these matters.)

In order to analyze the structure of someone's beliefs, we need a concept of congruence that is weaker than identity but stronger than any of those introduced in the preceding section. The analogy in geometry is clear. If we consider congruence in Euclidean space, identity will correspond to formal identity of figures rather than Euclidean congruence. What we want for expressing the structure of someone's beliefs is something closer to Euclidean congruence, which means that we want to build up congruence of utterances from claims about the congruence of parts of those utterances. Thus we may want to claim that for Mary, in contrast to John, the proper names 'Cicero' and 'Tully' are belief-congruent, which means, subject to some technical restrictions that I shall not go into here, that we can substitute one for the other in statements about Mary's beliefs. The absence of belief-congruence of these proper names for John does not permit such a substitution. Thus, we explain the difference in truth value of (8) and (9) in describing John's beliefs by the principled explanation that the two proper names in question are not belief-congruent for John.

What has been said here about belief-congruence is not at all restricted to proper names. Consider the following two attributions of belief to John, the first of which is true and the second of which is false:

(10) John believes that Peter is a rabbit.

(11) John believes that Peter is a hare.

The difference in truth-value of (10) and (11) is the absence of belief-congruence of 'rabbit' and 'hare'.

On the basis of what has been said, it is possible to sketch a theory of coherent beliefs where the beliefs of a person are reported in standard indirect discourse. It is not appropriate here to lay out the general theory, but a sense of developments can be given by considering several examples. Let us suppose the following about Mary's beliefs:

(i) Mary's beliefs are coherent (which operationally here means we can make simple inferences if not complicated ones—I certainly do not want to insist on full closure under logical consequence).

(ii) Mary believes that Peter is a rabbit.

(iii) The common nouns 'rabbit' and 'hare' are belief-congruent for Mary.

(iv) Therefore, Mary believes that Peter is a hare.

To make these ideas more definite but to keep the theory simple, let me illustrate how we should be able to build a theory of assertions about someone else's beliefs from the concept of belief-congruence of individual words and elementary probability considerations. I do not suggest that this is nearly enough for a general theory of cohesion of beliefs, for certainly we want a stronger net of deductive relationships. We can in the present formulation go beyond consideration of terminal words to include phrases as well, so that, for example, we can speak about the belief-congruence of a proper name and a definite description. We may take the probability of the correctness of each belief-congruence as a way of absorbing the context and the variability it introduces.

The elementary theory we can set forth rests upon the theorem that if each of the premises $A_1, \ldots, A_n$ has probability of at least $1 - \epsilon$, and these premises logically imply B, then $P(B) > 1 - n\epsilon$. (This theorem is proved in Suppes, 1966.) The application of the theorem is as follows. Let our initial assertion about a belief of someone have, in our judgment, probability at least $1 - \epsilon$. Let each of the belief-congruences (expressed as identities) required to infer another statement about which we desire to make an assertion have probability at least $1 - \epsilon$. Then we may infer for a person whose beliefs are coherent that the desired new statement has probability at least $1 - n\epsilon$, where n is the number of premises altogether that we have used. In the general theory of such matters we want to take account of the length of the derivation as well as the number of premises, but in the present case I am assuming very simple substitutions are all we are concerned with and therefore complexity of derivation does not enter into the computation of the lower bound on the conclusion.

As is apparent, the concept of belief-congruence takes us outside the framework of traditional model-theoretic semantics, and to a psychological concept of congruence whose actual content will vary from one individual to another. I agree with Saarinen (1982) that there is no hope of solving the puzzles about belief sentences within standard semantics. If the theory of belief is not a part of psychology it is hard to imagine what is.

Puzzle about informativeness. Perhaps the oldest of the puzzles, certainly at least one of the most familiar, is the following. How do we account for the informativeness of 'Cicero $\equiv$ Tully' as opposed to the uninformativeness of 'Cicero $\equiv$ Cicero'? One strong condition of congruence that could be used for the kind of identity statement typical of the paradox of analysis is this. Utterances u and u' are *orthographically congruent* if and only if they consist of the same sequence of written words. Note that this is not actual identity for utterances, for nothing is said about prosodic features, acoustical characteristics, and other features of concrete utterances that will differ between any two speakers or on different occasions of use by the same speaker. We might call orthographic congruence the condition of identity of the written word. It may be said that the solution given in terms of orthographic congruence is too easy. It is obvious that a difference is established between 'Cicero = Tully' and 'Cicero = Cicero'. But the difference that has been established by the principle is a surface one that everyone would accept, and it does not constitute the appropriate principled basis for establishing the cognitive difference between the two utterances.

A deeper approach is one based upon what is surely the fundamental point, the different ways in which we process 'Cicero = Tully' and 'Cicero = Cicero'. In the first case, we have to search for information about the denotation of the two different names. In the second, in standard cases we do not have to pay any attention to the name at all but just the syntactic form of the identity[1]. The cognitive processing required for asserting a truth claim about each of the identities is quite different. The absence of orthographic congruence is the most prominent signal of this difference. The peculiar, pure syntactic form of the trivial identity 'Cicero = Cicero' makes orthographic congruence central to understanding the standard cases, just because of the very special nature of the psychological processing.

This brings out a more general point about orthographic congruence. Extensional or intensional congruence as defined in the previous section

---

[1]Kripke's 'Paderewski is Paderewski' is nonstandard and requires a different analysis.

makes no claims about the close similarity of the syntactical form of two congruent utterances. On the other hand, orthographic congruence puts a very strong constraint on syntactic similarity. There is no doubt in my mind that the puzzle about informativeness requires considering not simply the semantics of an utterance but also matters of syntactic form. Such form is not just a formal grammatical condition but is a surrogate for subtle conditions on computation, that is, on the character of the psychological processing of an utterance.

Puzzle about responses. I formulated this puzzle in the following way in Suppes (1984):

(12) John responds.more quickly in judging the truth of the proposition that Cicero was bald than he does in responding to the proposition that Tully was bald.

Let us assume for the purposes at hand that this assertion is true. The basis of distinction in the indirect report of John's responses goes beyond considerations of belief-congruence to a finer analysis of John's cognitive apparatus. Difference in latency of responses is one of the most well-attested facts in psychological research.

A similar formulation can be given that makes the measures of response latency directly involve beliefs. Here is the example I used in the earlier article:

(13) John responds more quickly when asked whether he believes that Newton was a bachelor than he does when asked whether he believes that Newton was an unmarried man.

Let us assume for this purpose that in the terminology I have been using the common noun 'bachelor' and the noun-phrase 'an unmarried man' are belief-congruent for John, but it is still appropriate to expect a difference in response latency.

Without going all the way to orthographic congruence, it is clear how we can introduce a concept that is a refinement of belief-congruence, namely, that of *latency-congruence*. There is one problem about the continuous measurement of latency. We need to establish a small interval such that if the latency response is nearly the same the two words or phrases are judged latency-congruent. It might be reasonable to make the interval one of ten milliseconds. Notice, of course, that once we introduce such an interval concept the notion of congruence is no longer strictly transitive, but ways of dealing with this fact are familiar in the theory of measurement. Now in the case of many persons, I am sure we would find that their response latencies to simple utterances differentiated by the use of ' Cicero' or 'Tully' would differ by more than ten milliseconds because of the relative unfamiliarity with the proper noun 'Tully'. What we would anticipate is that as a matter of practice such individuals would easily move to a state of latency-congruence for these two proper names, as long as the latency interval is as great as ten milliseconds.

Notice that we get at this level a rather refined concept of proposition. Latency-congruence and belief congruence together require that two utterances expressing the same proposition in this sense be very close computationally for a speaker or listener.

Puzzle of prosodic types. The various types of congruence distinguished thus far have been at the level of type rather than token, although this has not always been made completely explicit and some greater specification of details would be needed to make clear how the treatment of latency-congruence is to be thought of for types rather than for tokens— the natural approach is to speak in terms of mean latencies rather than of individual latencies. At the level of orthographic types, we cannot get finer congruence than that of orthographic congruence, but it would be a mistake to think that there was any difficulty of making further distinctions among cognitive states of individuals which call for more refined concepts of congruence. The absence of latency-congruence of two tokens of the same orthographic type is an obvious example. Another natural class of examples concerns variation in the prosodic features of individual words uttered on different occasions. A prototypical example is the difference between '*I* love you' with the implication of the accent on '*I*' that the person speaking, in contrast to some other person, loves the person to whom the sentence is addressed; and, on the other hand, the orthographically congruent utterance 'I love *you*' where the emphasis is that the person loved is the person addressed rather than some other person. The change in stress changes at once the conception of the cognitive state of either the speaker or the listener. Standard theories of demonstratives do not account for the intuitively obvious difference in meaning of the two utterances. On the other hand, we can show noncongruence, as we have here, by schematically indicating which word is accented or stressed. In talking about prosodic types there is an ambiguity, because the conventions for types in the case of prosodic features are not nearly as well defined and agreed upon as in the case of orthographic representation, but, setting that difficulty aside, we can, I think, still speak in a meaningful way of orthographic-and-prosodic congruence to resolve puzzles about meaning generated by prosody.

Token congruence. Even when the orthographic-and-prosodic type of a phrase is fixed, it is of course still possible—in fact, probable—that systematic differences in various psychological response variables can be obtained to occurrences of a token of a given type on different occasions. (More than mere difference in latency is at issue here.) What this means for cognitive states is clearly related to the stationarity of the cognitive states called up on a given occasion by a given utterance. Thus, for example, let us suppose that John has learned and knows very well the proper name 'Cicero' but is just learning the proper name 'Tully'. Then if he is asked 'Was Cicero bald?' he will respond in approximately the same number of milliseconds on different days to this question—the fine differences from day to day will show no systematic trend. But in the case of the proper noun 'Tully', John's sequence of cognitive states is not stationary but reflects changes due to learning, and so his response latency on one occasion is slower than on the next occasion, and this change is significant. The fundamental concepts back of token congruence are those of stability and stationarity of cognitive states, but an account of the way these concepts can be used to characterize the psychological nature of token congruence must be left for another occasion.

After examining a number of congruence relations, I reiterate my opening claim that there is an infinite hierarchy. As we ascend this hierarchy there is no natural stopping place to select *the* concept of synonymy or sameness of meaning. Correspondingly, there is no natural point at which to abstract *the* proposition that expresses the meaning of an utterance. There is not one natural concept of meaning but many, with the choice to be determined by context and purpose. This acceptance of many distinct concepts of meaning should be just as straightforward as the acceptance of many different geometries. As yet, this is not the case, but the history of geometry is more advanced than that of meaning, and pluralists like myself must be patient.

INDIRECT DISCOURSE AND TRANSLATION

It seems apparent that the implicit use of a concept of congruence occurs most frequently in ordinary discourse in reporting something that someone else said or that we ourselves said sometime in the past. Such reports almost always use indirect discourse. Only in unusual and special circumstances do we actually quote what was previously said by ourselves or someone else.

As I have emphasized before (Suppes, 1984), any serious theory of language must give a detailed account of indirect discourse, how we judge it appropriate, and when we judge it inappropriate. It is also important to realize that what was actually said can in no sense be recovered. There cannot be a direct confrontation between the indirect paraphrase and what was actually said because the record has permanently disappeared. Our judgment of correctness of the paraphrase depends upon our views of the person making it and also on the context and purpose for which the paraphrase was made. An essential aspect of good indirect discourse is the omission of inessential details. What we are striving for is an appropriate congruence between what was actually said and the paraphrased report. The character of this relation of congruence will vary drastically with the circumstance. In almost all cases the relation of congruence that is implicitly used is a coarser one than any of those introduced in the preceding section to deal with epistemic distinctions.

Here is a passage from Harry Truman's *Memoirs* concerning the final decision to dismiss General MacArthur (1956, p. 448):

> On Sunday, the eighth of April, I sent for Acheson to come to Blair House, and I discussed the situation further with him. I informed him that I had already that morning consulted with Snyder. I then told Acheson that I would be prepared to act on Monday, when General Bradley made his report on the recommendations of the Joint Chiefs of Staff.

> At nine o'clock Monday morning I again met with Marshall, Bradley, Acheson, and Harriman. General Bradley reported that the Joint Chiefs of Staff had met with him on Sunday, and it was his and their unanimous judgment that General MacArthur should be relieved.

> General Marshall reaffirmed that this was also his conclusion. Harriman restated his opinion of Friday. Acheson said he agreed entirely to the removal of MacArthur.

> It was only now that I answered that I had already made up my mind that General MacArthur had to go when he made his statement of March 24.

Notice the many different idioms used for indirect discourse by Truman: *I discussed, I informed, I then told, General Bradley made his report, General Bradley reported, General Marshall reaffirmed, Harriman stated, Acheson said he agreed, I answered.* It is nearly impossible to imagine a serious political memoir being written without extensive use of indirect discourse. We could not stand the tedium of the actual conversations that took place, even if they were available and could be recovered, which they most certainly cannot. This brief passage from Truman's *Memoirs* about those tense days of 1951 leading to the dismissal undoubtedly summarizes conversations that would, if reproduced in full, occupy a substantial number of pages. The condensation here is drastic. The congruence relation is very crude but appropriate. Unless Truman is misleading us, for which I think there is no positive evidence, the concurrence in his decision by a number of other individuals is properly reported, even if in summary form.

What can we say about the role of propositions in indirect discourse? Using the creative definition of propositions given earlier, we can easily show that there are propositions common to this brief passage and the much longer discourse that actually took place. This commonality of proposition does not stand in any precise orthographic relation to either the printed passage I have reproduced or the actual conversations that took place. The drastic summarizing that has been engaged in gives us a sense of congruence that, in its independence of syntax, is what we are familiar with from the relation of intensional congruence.

In the article mentioned earlier, I introduced the governing principle of indirect discourse, the principle of trust in partial truths. Without this principle of trust, we would be unwilling to depend in the way we do on indirect discourse. Our acceptance of it varies with our acceptance of the speaker and the circumstances. We are on occasion skeptical but it is not a part of experience in which wholesale skepticism is practical in any sense. We all must accept and live with this principle of trust if we are to engage in normal communication with other persons, and even if we are to deal in a realistic way with our own memories of past conversations.

Remark on translation. Once a theory of congruence is introduced, it is easy to apply the apparatus to a detailed theory of translation. Two sentences of two different languages that are said to be translations of each other express under an appropriately chosen congruence relation the same proposition. Our judgment of the faithfulness of a translation depends upon the strength of the congruence relation that is mainly used in the translation. A poor translation is dominated by a weak sense of congruence and a good one by a strong sense, other things being equal. We also have some clear syntactical judgments of appropriate congruence that make us critical of what appear to be capricious changes in word order or emphasis, especially when we are translating from one language to another that is syntactically rather close.

We tend to be most comfortable when talking about propositions if we are dealing with systematic conceptual material expressed in the sorts of sentences characteristic of the measured discourse of philosophy and science. In this area, talk about the proposition expressed in a passage from Euclid, e.g., is often easily abstracted from its original Greek form and its accepted English translation.

4

THE PRIMACY OF UTTERER'S
MEANING

A central aspect of Grice's theory of meaning is the basic character of utterer's meaning. This feature of his theory has been criticized severely because of its deviation from the conception of semantics as an autonomous discipline independent of such general psychological concepts as speakers' intentions and listeners' recognition of intentions. I believe that Grice is right and his critics are wrong. The purpose of this essay is to offer my reasons for holding this view.

Before getting down to business, there are some preliminary matters to get out of the way. First, concerning the statement of Grice's views I primarily depend upon his three important articles (1957, 1968, 1969). The critics I shall explicitly consider are Chomsky (1975), Yu (1979), and Biro (1979).

I also want to make clear at the beginning that it is not my purpose here to give a detailed analysis of Grice's fundamental concept of utterer's occasion-meaning. As readers of Grice will remember, his program is to use this basic notion to explicate at the next level of abstraction the con-

---

*Reprinted from *Philosophical Grounds of Rationality: Intentions, Categories, Ends.* R.E. Grandy and R. Warner (Eds.), Oxford: Clarendon Press, 1986, pp. 109-129. It is a pleasure to dedicate this paper to Paul Grice, who over the years has patiently instructed me on more philosophical points than I can hope to remember. I am indebted to Dagfinn Follesdal and Howard Wettstein for a number of useful criticisms of an earlier draft.

cept of utterance-type occasion-meaning. At the next higher level is the analysis of the concept of the applied timeless meaning of an utterance-type (complete or incomplete) on a particular occasion of utterance. Finally, we reach the timeless meaning of an utterance-type. Because the criticisms of Grice have focused almost entirely on the nature of his programme rather than on the details, my intention is also to focus on the programme and try to explain why I think it is in principle sound.

Grice's own formulation and reformulations of basic concepts are technical and intricate. It is a surprising feature of the critics I mentioned above that they do not enter into real details of these analyses. In order to make my discussion more or less consonant with those of the critics, I select one rather informal version from Grice (1969). Let p be a proposition and let $*\psi$ be a mood marker. As Grice puts it ψ is 'an auxiliary correlated with a propositional attitude ψ from a given range of propositional attitudes'. Grice's basic concept of meaning is then defined by him along the following lines.

U means by uttering x that $*\psi p = U$ utters x intending

(1) that A should actively ψ that p

(2) that A should recognize that U intends (1) and . . .

(3) that the fulfillment of (1) should be based on the fulfillment of (2). [p. 171.]

CHOMSKY'S CRITICISM

Chomsky (1975, pp. 54-77) discusses Grice's theory of meaning along with a rather detailed discussion of related views of Searle and Strawson. I shall concentrate on what Chomsky says about Grice, but a number of his comments are of a general nature—in fact, most of them are general rather than specific and technical, and consequently are not necessarily aimed at Grice in particular. Also, I shall not go into some of the details of Chomsky's remarks, for a good many of them are specific replies to Searle's criticisms of Chomsky.

There are three central issues I have abstracted from the pages in Chomsky's book cited above. The first is the most important, but the other two bear on Chomsky's discussion of Grice. I do not expect Grice to agree entirely with me in my disagreements with Chomsky. On all three of the conceptual issues I mention I think that Chomsky is wrong. The three are these. First, is the concept of literal meaning required in the definition of utterer's meaning? Second, can we meaningfully talk about the rules of language? Third, is Grice a behaviorist?

Literal meaning. Chomsky's position is summarized in the following passage.

> The notion 'literal meaning,' or some equivalent, again intrudes, and no way has been offered to escape the 'orbit of conceptual space' that includes the suspect abstract notions 'linguistic meaning' and the like, even if the utterer happens to have the postulated intentions with regard to a hypothetical audience, as is by no means necessary in the normal use of language.
>
> One can imagine modifications of the proposed definition that would not involve incorrect claims about intentions, but not, so far as I can see, without introducing some notion like 'linguistic meaning.' [p. 68.]

Another pertinent passage a few pages later is the following:

> We must distinguish between the literal meaning of the linguistic expression produced by S and what S meant by producing this expression (or by saying that so-and-so, whatever expressions he used). The first notion is the one to be explained in the theory of language; I can just as well ask, in the same sense of 'meaning,' what S meant by slamming the door. Within the theory of successful communication, we can, perhaps, draw a connection between these notions. The theory of meaning, however, seems quite unilluminated by this effort. [p. 76.]

These two passages state conclusions that are argued for in several different ways by Chomsky. I want to examine what appear to me to be the more important arguments he offers. One claim he returns to on several occasions is that speakers sometimes fail to have appropriate Gricean intentions, especially when there appears to be no intended audience. Chomsky cites various cases where the speaker has 'no intention of getting the hearer to know anything or to recognize anything, but what I say has its strict meaning, and I mean what I say' (pp. 63-4). Now, it seems to me there are two separate points to be made about what Chomsky repeats in several ways. First, there is a problem to be dealt with concerning the possible absence of an audience. It seems to me this is not a very serious problem and should be set aside at this point—I return to it in the next section on Yu. What is more important is to dig deeper into the concept of intention. Chomsky's counterexamples seem to be riding very much on a superficial and surface notion of intention, in fact, a notion that seems very behavioristic. If I write in my diary or if I write some research notes to myself, it does not do, it seems to me, to say that I write something that has a strict meaning but that it does not make sense to talk about my 'intention to communicate'. It would certainly seem odd if someone asked me what I was doing, to say that I was writing something with strict meaning but of course it is not supposed to communicate anything. Another way of putting the matter is that communication is the primary act and meaning is an aspect of that primary act.

I can certainly agree that we do not have in Grice's writings or in Chomsky's criticisms of Grice or Searle, or in Searle's writings either, a really detailed theory of intention that we can bring to bear in this discussion in a precise way. But it seems to me that the kind of view of intention that Grice has is certainly outlined in general terms rather clearly, and it is not the rather simple view that Chomsky attributes to him. It should be mentioned, by the way, that the competing primary notion of the literal or linguistic meaning that Chomsky uses is similarly lacking in detailed specification.

A second objection of Chomsky's is that communication theorists, as he calls Grice, Searle, and Strawson, are not really concerned to build up the theory of meaning of an utterance from its component parts, and thus to have a principled account either of utterer's or linguistic meaning. All sides are guilty of this. Chomsky too does not provide a theory for building up meaning from an analysis of parts or in any way from a knowledge, let us say, of syntax. There is an attempted sketch for a much too simple formal language in Schiffer (1972), but it is clear from various things that Grice says that his attention to utterer's word meanings is meant to sketch how these matters are to be approached .

It seems to me, however, that there is a genuine issue here that we can discuss without requiring from either side a detailed theory of how we can determine the meaning of complex utterances or sentences. The communication theorists such as Grice argue that the framework of communication influences greatly the meaning of an utterance. Chomsky and others on his side take the opposite view. Some recent good examples of how even literal utterances are undetermined in terms of their strict meaning or literal meaning are to be found in Searle (1980). What I think we could grant Chomsky is that there are lots of sentences in scientific treatises and articles that have the kind of pleasing attributes he would like to see, but that these sentences are, from the standpoint of the primary use of language, highly non-standard. Even to this claim I will not grant very much. It is true perhaps of the theoretical parts of science but, as I have argued in Suppes (1982a), matters are very different when one looks at the language of experimental science. The language is esoteric, context-dependent, and impenetrable from those outside the particular discipline. The real place that is context-dependent and, if you will, communication-dependent, is in the kind of casual give and take so characteristic of our daily conversations. The detailed analysis of most conversations will not get very far with consideration only of the literal meaning of words used. We must, over and over again, involve the speakers and listeners and their intentions in the conversation being analyzed after the fact.

One of Chomsky's central arguments about the primacy of literal meaning is that revisions of Grice's original characterization of utterer's meanings have moved more and more toward implicit use of 'rules' and 'conventions', which are ways of dragging in, illicit or otherwise, a concept of literal meaning. I do not buy this argument at all.

In another article, Grice (1982) has, in general terms, sketched the sense in which his approach to meaning provides a kind of proto-theory of how language came about and came to be used. It seems to me that an argument that this is not the correct order of development can scarcely be taken seriously. An account of the genesis of language that supposed that first came literal meaning and then, as a derivative from that, utterer's meaning, seems hard to conceptualize even in the barest and thinnest sort of outline. Surely, language must have begun from attempts at communication between a few individuals. At first these efforts at communication did not have very much stability of literal meaning. Only slowly and after much time did a stable community of users lead to the abstract concept of literal meaning. In fact, 'abstract' is exactly the right term, taken in its primitive sense. There is no hard and fast platonic literal meaning that utterer's meanings attach themselves to and play upon in their need for dependence and shelter. The story surely is exactly the other way around. Utterers develop similar meanings, but not identical meanings. The commonality of experience of utterers is responsible for the possibility of abstract meaning, not the converse, but more on this in the section on congruence of meaning.

Some rules versus the rules of language. Chomsky repeatedly refers to *the* rules of language, reflecting in such passages once again his commitment to what is essentially a platonic and abstract theory of language. I shall not argue about platonic metaphysics or ontology. My point is rather that Chomsky's conception of language as being embodied in a fixed set of rules used by speakers of that language seems to me an essentially mistaken notion. His arguments, stated in many different places, for the autonomy of syntax, affirm his beliefs on such matters, and are repeatedly given emphasis by his use of the phrase *the rules of language*. It seems to me important to challenge this notion as fundamentally incorrect. Certainly there are some rules of language that speakers and listeners share. We can begin with agreed-upon lists of words, some rules of grammar, some acoustical properties, etc. These matters are unexceptionable and easily stipulated by all parties. What is mistaken is to make the much stronger assumption that there is a fixed and complete set of rules that speakers and listeners share. A more defensible weaker thesis is that individual speakers and listeners have individually different rules. The rules they use are similar enough for them to understand each other and communicate with each other, but they are not using the same rules. It is only abstractions of their actually full-blown rules that lead to a concept of sameness. But this concept of sameness is a weak one, as weak as the concept of congruence in affine geometry that makes any two triangles congruent, a point that I expand on later.

Let us start with the hypothesis that individual speakers and listeners can be characterized by a set of rules. What we notice at once when we begin to study these individual speakers in detail is that the same rules do not apply to them. Perhaps the easiest way to see this is in any attempt to characterize the prosody or rhythm of their speech, and surely anyone not committed to the written word as the final real embodiment of language will want to argue that rhythm and prosody of speech affect the meaning of speech and, therefore, utterer's meaning. There is another way to put the matter dramatically: the ease with which we all recognize individual speakers' voices. The differentiation we establish so readily between speakers is proof enough that if they are using rules to generate their spoken speech the rules are certainly different. I do not begrudge Chomsky his desire for a very generalized abstract theory of meaning, but he needs to recognize it for what it is—an abstraction that gets identity of rules across speakers only because of the coarseness of the abstraction. As in the case of triangles in affine geometry, Chomsky seems to have a kind of affine theory of meaning: we take a theory sufficiently weak and general to make the rules being used the same in a given linguistic community. But in real life we have a much more vivid and concrete geometry of meaning that we use continually, from the recognition of different speakers' voices to the recognition of an individual speaker's intention, rhythm, and prosody.

More radical argument. Let me in this same context turn to a more radical argument, which Grice himself might not accept. It is this. It is a mistake to suppose we can characterize the speech of even a single speaker by a complete set of rules. If we follow the discrete line of the Alexandrian grammarians, passing through Dionysius Thrax to Donatus and on to Chomsky, it might seem that we could talk about language being wholly rule-governed. I do not deny that of course there are partial rules, just as there are partial rules of walking or chewing. But when we look at the acoustical complexity of real speech, when we think about the features we all recognize intuitively without being able to identify acoustically or by rule, varying features of prosody, rhythm, individual quirks of grammar, etc., it seems hopeless to think that this marvelous complexity can be caught in any set of rules. Moreover, the attempts that we now have are so pitiful in character, so totally unsatisfactory, and so crude in approximation, that scepticism at the very idea of being able to capture language in rules is easily supported. Even so natural and obvious a property of a particular speaker's speech as the cadence of his individual rhythms is not discussed in the long treatise on the sounds of English by Chomsky and Halle (1968), and is certainly not discussed with any sophistication that is both mathematically and empirically satisfactory in any place that I know of. Chomsky likes to emphasize the creative use of language—his emphasis here I certainly agree with—but he speaks of this creative use as being generated by finite means and consequently by a finite set of rules. My point is that, once we leave the discreteness of syntax and deal with the continuous properties that we recognize in actual speech, it is a bold thesis that these can be parameterized in a finite way and do not contain complex elements distinctive of a given individual which can in no principled way be reduced to a fixed set of rules.

Many persons might agree with this negative argument about the possibility of having a complete set of rules for actual speech, but still maintain that such completeness is possible for syntax. This, too, I deny. Even at the regimented level of written language there is nothing like an adequate grammar of any natural language. Let me mention a personal example. Two students of mine have written dissertations on the grammar and semantics of the written language of elementary mathematics used in teaching children of about ten years of age. The grammars were far from complete even for this highly restricted topic, but when we examined the written language of mathematical textbooks for children of thirteen years it was not simply a matter of incompleteness, but a deeper sense of hopelessness at ever being able to approach grammatical completeness. Compared to the rhetoric of a Saintsbury or a Churchill these texts in term seem simple.

My own current conjecture, which is not essential to the rest of my argument, is this. Chomsky has told us only half the story. We are not only able to use a fixed set of rules to generate a potential infinity of utterances, but we are also as speakers and listeners continually creating new grammatical rules (not to speak of other aspects of language). These new rules, so I think, are ordinarily harmonious extensions of ones we are already using, but the constraints on their creation I cannot begin to characterize. I should emphasize here that I have in mind the creation of rules within the framework of what we would regard as a more or less homogeneous style, not new rules generated in the trail of an obvious stylistic metamorphosis. Here is a concrete example of what I mean. Let us write a grammar that gives a detailed analysis of every other sentence in the novels of Dickens, contains other general rules we might justify, but not by examining the omitted sentences, and does not permit any sentences we judge ungrammatical. My claim is that this grammar will not adequately parse the half of Dickens's sentences not considered, and still additional rules would be needed. Moreover, I think that speakers engage in such rule creation all the time. Both as speakers and listeners we are continually creating and learning new rules, engaging, if you will, in new practices.

But even with the newly created set of rules it is unlikely that we have grammatical rule-completeness. *Ad hoc* rules for single sentences scarcely count. Let me give a much simpler example to illustrate the point. For a variety of reasons there is and has been a strong interest in giving spelling rules for English, but in even such a relatively simple subject there is no complete set of rules, but sets of rules together with lists of exceptional individual words that account for varying percentages of whatever large population of English words are chosen. So, I claim, it is with sentences. We can and do speak and understand sentences that do not conform to any rules we have in our heads. The grammatical rules of our speech are not at all like the rules of chess. They are like the rules of a children's game that is not codified and is continually changing.

Is Grice a behaviorist? Chomsky claims that Grice is a behaviorist and that consequently his programme suffers all the defects that Chomsky has alleged on numerous occasions are characteristic of empiricist theories about language. Here is what Chomsky says:

> As for the reversion to behaviorism, it seems true of the most care-
> ful work within the theory. In what is, to my knowledge, the most
> careful and comprehensive effort to explain the meaning of linguis-
> tic expressions within this framework, Grice presents a system of
> definitions that rest not only on intentions but also on the speaker's

'policy', 'practice', and 'habit', on the idea of a 'repertoire of procedures'. To have a procedure in one's repertoire is to have 'a
standing readiness (willingness, preparedness), in some degree to
. . . ,' where 'a readiness (etc.) to do something [is] a member
of the same family . . . as an intention to do that thing'. Grice
recognizes the inadequacy of this analysis, but gives only some 'informal remarks' as to how a proper definition might be constructed.
[p. 73.]

He continues a few lines later:

> Grice's final case is intended to deal with the problem that a speaker
> may be 'equipped' to use expressions properly but have no readi-
> ness to do so. He suggests that a person may have a 'procedure
> for X' in the required sense if 'to utter X in such-and-such circum-
> stances is part of the practice of many members of' the group to
> which the person belongs. That is, other members of the group '*do*
> have a readiness to utter X in such-and-such circumstances'. But
> for familiar reasons, this analysis is useless. There are no practices,
> customs, or habits, no readiness, willingness, or preparedness, that
> carry us very far in accounting for the normal creative use of lan-
> guage, whether we consider the practices of a person or of a group.
> [p. 74.]

It seems to me that Chomsky is badly off the mark in the passages
I have quoted, and I want to try to explain why in some detail. Grice
has used words like 'practice' and 'habit' and even the more technical
word 'procedure' in their ordinary senses as they are used in ordinary
discussion. He has not made technical concepts out of them as one might
expect of some behavioral psychologists. There is nothing in any strong
sense that is behaviorist about such talk—it is just ordinary talk about
behavior. There is also nothing exceptional in talking about practice,
customs, or habits of language use. Grice certainly does not intend that
these notions, as he has used them, give anything like a detailed account
of the creative use of language. What Chomsky has to say is essentially a
diatribe against empiricism, secondarily against behaviorism, and in the
third place against Grice. In terms of more reasoned and dispassionate
analyses of the matter, it seems to me that one would ordinarily think of
Grice not as a behaviorist but as an intentionalist.

Yu's criticisms

A rather recent comprehensive review of the literature on Grice's theory of meaning, along with a claim to give an analysis that brings out the nature of the Gricean mistakes 'in a perspicuous way' has been given by Yu (1979). In formulating his criticisms, Yu acknowledges that his greatest debt is to Chomsky's analysis and thus there is some overlap in what they have to say.

Minor points aside, Yu makes three criticisms of Grice. In my view, all three criticisms are mistaken. The first concerns the nature of explication or explanation and in particular whether Grice's theory of meaning is reportive or stipulative. The second concerns the case of intention in communication when there is no audience present. The third criticism makes the claim that sentence meaning is prior to utterer's meaning.

Before making these criticisms, Yu introduces a preliminary distinction with which I agree. He points out that there are two kinds of general theses about language that we can be concerned with. One is to give an account of the genesis of language in the sense of how it developed in the course of human history. The second is to give an account of what it means for an organism or, more particularly, a person to have knowledge or possession of a language. Yu believes that Grice's programme is mainly concerned with the latter thesis, and with this I agree, although his sketch of how language came about in Grice (1982) has already been mentioned.

Nature of explanation. Within this framework the first criticism is that Grice or, as Yu puts it— to make the reference more general, the Griceans claim the following: (i) they can give necessary and sufficient conditions for sentence meaning in terms of speaker-meaning and also necessary and sufficient conditions for speaker-meaning in terms of intention; (ii) the concept of intention is logically prior to the concept of speaker-meaning, and correspondingly, the concept of speaker-meaning is prior to that of sentence-meaning[1]. Yu introduces objections at this point on the basis of very general and rather bad arguments from the philosophy of science. One is that we do not know what *logically prior* means. Another closely related one is that we do not have any very precise notion of explication or explanation. In the case of explication, he wants to distinguish between explanations that are 'entirely stipulative, introducing thereby

---

[1]To follow Yu's terminology I use here the phrase speaker's meaning by which I mean the same thing as Grice does by utterer's meaning. In the same way I do not intend to distinguish in any definite way here between the concept of literal meaning, as used by Chomsky, and the concept of sentence meaning, as used by Yu.

a novel and technical notion', and reportive stipulations where 'the explicans has to characterize . . . correctly a pre-existing notion.' In my judgement this artificial dichotomy is as useful in the theory of explanation as is Aristotle's distinction between violent and natural motion in classical mechanics.

Any attempt to have a simple dichotomous characterization of explanations in this fashion is bad philosophy and bound to fail. Even relatively superficial reflection on any one of a number of conceptual examples in the history of mathematics, philosophy, or science bring out the artificial character of the distinction. Let me just mention a few. With the clarification of the difference between kinetic energy and momentum, a classic controversy in the early history of modern mechanics, a new distinction that did not exist before was created, but at the same time it was important to deal with a number of familiar complex phenomena. Any new distinction that did not would not be acceptable. So was this a reportive or stipulative case? Is the extension of the concept of addition from real numbers to complex numbers a reportive or stipulative explication? Is Russell's theory of descriptions reportive or stipulative? It seems evident that in important and interesting cases some aspects of a new concept are required to meet conditions of adequacy, to use Yu's phrase, as set by past experience and theory, while other aspects of a new concept are stipulative. Almost every important concept cuts across the two. It seems to me this is what we would expect of Grice's concept of utterer's meaning. We certainly have some intuitive ideas about utterer's meaning but we also do not have a very well-worked-out theory of the relevant phenomena. It is Grice's virtue to offer a theory that is far from explicit in our ordinary ideas, that may at certain points disturb or go beyond these intuitive ideas, but that in many respects satisfies our intuitions. Like other good proposals, Grice's explication of utterer's meaning is both reportive and stipulative.

Problem of soliloquy. Yu's second criticism picks up on a problem that is discussed by Grice himself, by Schiffer, Searle, and Chomsky. This is the question of how to apply Grice's characterization of utterer's meaning when an utterance is made with no audience present. Here it seems to me that Griceans have been more concerned than they should be with this problem, and have conceded more to their critics than they should have.

The problem is that when uttering something the utterer normally intends that an audience should actively respond to the utterance. It seems to me that Grice's idea is essential and correct. The primary use of language is for such communication, and it is hard to imagine language having been developed for any other major purpose. It is thus appropriate that utterer's meaning have its primary account in terms of intentions to influence an audience, but it by no means requires that such a complicated and extended skill should always be used only in its primary sense. Most complicated skills that we have can be used in ways other than the ways for which they were primarily developed. It is easy to think of some simple examples from among the repertoires of physical skills. Suppose that Jones is very interested in basketball and becomes very good at 'shooting baskets'. He develops his skill so as to do well in playing the game, but he also practices a great deal by himself and develops a true taste for shooting baskets alone. He develops a method of scoring and has a daily score based on the percentage of baskets shot out of those attempted in his backyard. The primary meaning of the skill makes sense only in the context of the game of basketball, but his additional use of that skill for pleasure and further training is derivative from that and is easily understood even though it is not exercised in the context of an actual game.

Smith is an excellent football-kicker. When held in an enemy prison camp he gets an important message out by kicking it in a can over the wall of the prison. His fellow prisoners tell him afterwards, 'Thank God you can kick like hell.'

And so it goes with a good talker. He has a complicated, useful, and powerful skill. He naturally uses it in supplementary ways to help himself remember things, to express his feelings even when alone, or to summarize his thoughts. The normal cases of speaking are addressed to an audience and have intentions with respect to the audience. It seems simple enough to extend the characterization to include those cases without an audience. I would expect a complicated skill like talking to be no more rigidly circumscribed in its meaningful use than any other such skill. Moreover, I would expect the noncentral uses to have no single, simple characterizations.

Primacy of sentence meaning. Yu's third argument, one that recurs in various forms in earlier criticisms of Grice, is that Grice's characterization of utterer's meaning is essentially circular in so far as it claims to be the basis of giving an account of the meaning of sentences, because the notion of the meaning of sentences is required in order to characterize that the intentions of the speakers are of the right kind. Yu's criticism seems to be based on the following two points. Sentence meaning is prior to utterer's meaning. Secondly, language can be used for many purposes, one of which is communication. Grice's proposal is one aimed at an account of communication, not of language. Such an account of communication must presume already and as logically prior an account of language and therefore of sentence meaning. The next section is devoted to this issue.

Running through the criticisms of Chomsky and Yu, often explicitly, is an appeal to the idea of sentence meaning, but nothing very definite is said about this complicated and subtle notion. Given the many analyses of the concept of synonymy in work of several decades ago by Carnap, Church, Mates, Quine, and others, it is a little surprising to have the concept of sentence meaning referred to so casually by these critics of Grice's theory. (A good review of this earlier work is given in Quine, 1960.) Similar difficulties arise for saying when two proofs are 'the same', or even more recently, when two computer programmes are 'identical'.

I have argued earlier (1973a) that the search for synonymy of sentences or, as often put, identity of propositions is mistaken, and that what we should have is what I have termed a geometrical theory of meaning. By this I mean that we replace the search for any fixed concept of synonymy by a hierarchy of concepts of congruence as is familiar in modern geometry. Thus, for example, we do not have in geometry one single notion of congruence, but one notion for Euclidean geometry, another for affine geometry, and another, say, for topology. In the same way, we have natural weaker and stronger senses of congruence of two sentences, and it is this notion of congruence of meaning that should be introduced and used in talking about sentence meaning. The rather casual paraphrases of meaning that are often used by Chomsky do not constitute a proper concept of sentence meaning, but only the rather coarse kind characteristic of paraphrase congruence.

It is not my purpose here to go into the technical details of my earlier ideas about congruence of meaning, but I want to use these ideas to develop some further remarks about the primacy of utterer's meaning. To do this it will be sufficient simply to give some examples of the different senses of congruence. The basic idea is that the syntactic structure enters into congruence as well as the referential character of a sentence. Thus, the following two sentences are congruent in a strong sense because their trees are syntactically isomorphic and denotationally identical. (By denotation I literally mean denotation, and not some peculiar sense of denotation one might find in generative semantics.)

> *All men are mortal.*
> *Every man is mortal.*

A second sense of congruence is that two sentences are permutationally congruent in meaning and form, but are not congruent in the sense of a strong congruence because the trees are not syntactically and denotationally isomorphic. Here are a pair of simple sentences illustrating permutational congruence:

John and Mary are here.
Mary and John are here.

The permutation of the order of proper names from one sentence to the other breaks apart the strong sense of congruence and leaves us with something weaker. A still weaker sense of congruence is that of paraphrase, mentioned earlier. In this case, only the denotation of the root of the tree for the entire sentence need be the same as its paraphrase.

To the extent that the kind of apparatus of congruence I have introduced for sentences is at all natural, it should be apparent that it has a direct extension to utterances. We now widen the concept of congruence to include features of the speech-act of utterance, and as we bring in an increasing number of factors we get absolute uniqueness, just as we do in geometry, namely, in the strongest sense of identity each utterance is only congruent with itself; that is, it is only identical with itself.

When we think about this natural progression of senses of congruence it seems to me absurd that Yu explicitly, and Chomsky perhaps less so, claim that sentence meaning is implicit in Grice's concept of utterer's meaning. I find this as ridiculous as saying that in any interesting sense affine congruence of triangles, for example, is somehow prior to Euclidean congruence. Certainly, affine congruence is weaker. After all, there is just one triangle in the affine plane up to congruence, but it is certainly not in any interesting way assumed as part of the concept of Euclidean congruence. What does seem to me obvious is that the richer and more concrete notion of utterer's meaning, when looked at from the standpoint of congruence, in no realistic sense whatsoever assumes a notion of sentence meaning. Let me make clear how the argument goes. There is no definite concept of sentence meaning. As in the case of geometry, the only systematic sense of sentence meaning is some particular sense of congruence of sentence meaning, but congruence of sentence meaning is clearly a weaker and more general concept than that of congruence of utterer's meaning. The particular facts and the particular acts of utterance form the basis of a stronger, more concrete, and more definite sense of meaning. It is confusion about sentence meaning that has misled Chomsky and Yu into thinking that there is a serious argument for the priority of sentence meaning over utterer's meaning.

In fact, to pursue this point a bit further it might be desirable to draw still another geometrical analogy. It might be said in response to what I have just said that I have put the shoe on the wrong geometry. It is

Euclidean geometry that corresponds to what Chomsky and Yu have in mind in talking about sentence meaning, namely, the kind of geometry that has been around for a long time, just as talk about sentence meaning has been around for a long time. But it is easy for us to introduce a geometry stronger than Euclidean geometry, for example, a geometry that is sensitive not only to Euclidean geometry but also to orientation in space. Such a geometry in no way depends upon, and must assume as logically prior, the classical and traditional concept of Euclidean geometry. Let us call this concept that of oriented congruence. This is the kind of geometry that goes with much ordinary talk about the location of objects and events in daily experience.

It might still be objected that the fundamental feature of Euclidean geometry that is also characteristic of the idea of sentence meaning is present in oriented geometry but not correspondingly in utterer's meaning. This is the independence of context. In Euclidean geometry, oriented geometry, or affine geometry, a triangle is a triangle no matter what the context of the other points or figures. In fact, the very idea of other points or figures being present or absent is not a coherent concept in classical geometry. The same is implicitly the case for classical ideas of sentence meaning. The context of utterance should not affect the meaning. But all we need to do is to move from geometry to physics to pick a new analogy that is closer still to that of utterer's meaning. Physics is nothing but context. The motion of a particle is entirely different once a new particle comes close by. And so it is with utterer's meaning. The context as determined by the audience, the anxieties of the speaker, and so forth can have a significant and critical effect on utterer's meaning. I mean by this that the congruence of the utterance in the deepest and most detailed sense will depend upon these features as well as the features so characteristic of sentence meaning in the traditional sense.

In this sense my talk about a geometrical theory of meaning is mistaken. It is only in terms of the concept of congruence that I have talked about geometry. At the level of meaning itself, the analogy I would want to insist on as we move from sentence meaning to utterer's meaning is closer to physics than to geometry. It is a virtue of Grice's approach to bring out the importance of context and the importance of the concreteness reflected in utterer's meaning.

Because these matters have been so controversial, let me repeat once more my straightforward line on these matters. It is absurd to charge Grice with using implicitly a concept of sentence meaning once any systematic concept of sentence meaning is set forth. The reason is simple. Sentence meaning is going to entail a rather weak sense of congruence between utterances. The virtue of Grice's ideas is to require a strong sense of congruence. Perhaps the meek and the weak shall inherit the earth, but the strong shall not depend on them. Strong congruence of utterances does not depend on weak congruence in the sense of logical or conceptual dependence. Obviously, strong congruence implies weak congruence, and thus congruence of utterances implies congruence in the sense of sentence congruence, not conversely, but this we would expect and is completely unexceptionable.

BIRO'S CRITICISM OF INTENTIONALISM

Grice's reduction, or partial reduction anyway, of meaning to intention places a heavy load on the theory of intentions. But in the articles he has written about these matters he has not been very explicit about the structure of intentions. As I understand his position on these matters, it is his view that the defense of the primacy of utterer's meaning does not depend on having worked out any detailed theory of intention. It is enough to show how the reduction should be thought of in a schematic fashion in order to make a convincing argument.

I do think there is a fairly straightforward extension of Grice's ideas that provides the right way of developing a theory of intentions appropriate for his theory of utterer's meaning. Slightly changing around some of the words in Grice (1968), we have the following example. U utters ' "Phido is shaggy", if "U wants A to think that U thinks that Jones's dog is hairy-coated." ' Put another way, U's intention is to want A to think U thinks that Jones's dog is hairy-coated. Such intentions clearly have a generative structure similar but different from the generated syntactic structure we think of verbal utterances' having. But we can even say that the deep structures talked about by grammarians of Chomsky's ilk could best be thought of as intentions. This is not a suggestion I intend to pursue seriously. The important point is that it is a mistake to think about classifications of intentions; rather, we should think in terms of mechanisms for generating intentions. Moreover, it seems to me that such mechanisms in the case of animals are evident enough as expressed in purposeful pursuit of prey or other kinds of food, and yet are not expressed in language. In that sense once again there is an argument in defense of Grice's theory. The primacy of utterer's meaning has primacy because of the primacy of intention. We can have intentions without words, but we cannot have words of any interest without intentions.

In this general context, I now turn to Biro's (1979) interesting criticisms of intentionalism in the theory of meaning. Biro deals from his own standpoint with some of the issues I have raised already, but his central thesis about intention I have not previously discussed. It goes to the heart of controversies about the use of the concept of intention to explain the meaning of utterances. Biro puts his point in a general way by insisting that utterance meaning must be separate from and independent of speaker's meaning or, in the terminology used here, utterer's meaning. The central part of his argument is his objection to the possibility of explaining meaning in terms of intentions.

Biro's argument goes like this:

1. A central purpose of speech is to enable others to learn about the speaker's intentions.

2. It will be impossible to discover or understand the intentions of the speaker unless there are independent means for understanding what he says, since what he says will be primary evidence about his intentions.

3. Thus the meaning of an utterance must be conceptually independent of the intentions of the speaker.

This is an appealing positivistic line. The data relevant to a theory or hypothesis must be known independently of the hypothesis. Biro is quick to state that he is not against theoretical entities, but the way in which he separates theoretical entities and observable facts makes clear the limited role he wants them to play, in this case the theoretical entities being intentions. The central idea is to be found in the following passage:

> The point I am insisting on here is merely that the ascription of an intention to an agent has the character of an *hypothesis*, something invoked to explain phenomena which may be *described* independently of that explanation (though not necessarily independently of the fact that they fall into a class for which the hypothesis in question generally or normally provides an explanation). (pp. 250-1.) [The italics are Biro's.]

Biro's aim is clear from this quotation. The central point is that the data about intentions, namely, the utterance, must be describable independently of hypotheses about the intentions. He says a little later to reinforce this: 'The central point is this: it is the intention-hypothesis that is revisable, not the act-description' (p. 251). Biro's central mistake, and a large one too, is to think that data can be described independently of hypotheses and that somehow there is a clean and simple version of data that makes such description a natural and inevitable thing to have. It would be easy enough to wander off into a description of such problems in physics, where experiments provide a veritable wonderland of seemingly arbitrary choices about what to include and what to exclude from the experimental experience as 'relevant data', and where the arbitrariness can only be even partly understood on the basis of understanding the theories being tested. Real data do not come in simple linear strips like letters on the page. Real experiments are blooming confusions that never get sorted out completely but only partially and schematically, as appropriate to the theory or theories being tested, and in accordance with the traditions and conventions of past similar experiments. (Biro makes a point about the importance of convention that I agree with, but it is irrelevant to my central point of controversy with him.)

What I say about experiments is even more true of undisciplined and unregulated human interaction. Experiments, especially in physics, are presumably among the best examples of disciplined and structured action. Most conversations, in contrast, are really examples of situations of confusion that are only straightened out under strong hypotheses of intentions on the part of speakers and listeners as well.

There is more than one level at which the straightening-out takes place through the beneficent use of hypotheses about intentions. I shall not try to deal with all of them here but only mention some salient aspects. At an earlier point, Biro says:

> The main reason for introducing intentions into some of these analyses is precisely that the public (broadly speaking) features of utterances—the sounds made, the circumstances in which they are made and the syntactic and semantic properties of these noises considered as linguistic items—are thought to be insufficient for the specification of that aspect of the utterance which we call its meaning. [p. 244.]

If we were to take this line of thought seriously and literally, we would begin with the sound pressure waves that reach our ears and that are given the subtle and intricate interpretation required to accept them as speech. There is a great variety of evidence that purely acoustical concepts are inadequate for the analysis of speech. To determine the speech content of a sound pressure wave we need extensive hypotheses about the intentions that speakers have in order to convert the public physical features of utterances into intentional linguistic items. Biro might object at where I am drawing the line between public and intentional, namely, at the difference between physical and linguistic, but it would be part of my thesis that it is just because of perceived and hypothesized intentions that we are mentally able to convert sound pressure waves into meaningful speech. In fact, I can envisage a kind of transcendental argument for the existence of intentions based on the impossibility from the standpoint of physics alone of interpreting sound pressure waves as speech.

Biro seems to have in mind the nice printed sentences of science and philosophy that can be found on the printed pages of treatises around the world. But this is not the right place to begin to think about meaning, only the end point. Grice, and everybody else who holds an intentional thesis about meaning, recognizes the requirement to reach an account of such timeless sentence meaning or linguistic meaning. In fact, Grice is perhaps more ready than I am to concede that such a theory can be developed in a relatively straightforward manner. One purpose of my detailed discussion of congruence of meaning in the previous section is to point out some of the difficulties of having an adequate detailed theory of these matters, certainly an adequate detailed theory of *the* linguistic meaning or *the* sentence meaning. Even if I were willing to grant the feasibility of such a theory, I would not grant the use of it that Biro has made. For the purposes of this discussion printed text may be accepted as well-defined, theory independent data. (There are even issues to be raised about the printed page, but ones that I will set aside in the present context. I have in mind the psychological difference between perception of printed letters, words, phrases, or sentences, and that of related but different nonlinguistic marks on paper.) But no such data assumptions can be made about spoken speech.

Still another point of attack on Biro's positivistic line about data concerns the data of stress and prosody and their role in fixing the meaning of an utterance. Stress and prosody are critical to the interpretation of the intentions of speakers, but the data on stress and prosody are fleeting and hard to catch on the fly. Hypotheses about speakers' intentions are needed even in the most humdrum interpretations of what a given prosodic contour or a given point of stress has contributed to the meaning of the utterance spoken. The prosodic contour and the points of stress of an utterance are linguistic data, but they do not have the independent physical description Biro vainly hopes for.

Let me put my point still another way. I do not deny for a second that conventions and traditions of speech play a role in fixing the meaning of a particular utterance on a particular occasion. It is not a matter of interpreting afresh, as if the universe had just begun, a particular utterance in terms of particular intentions at that time and place without dependence upon past prior intentions and the traditions of spoken speech that have evolved in the community of which the speaker and listener are a part. It is rather that hypotheses about intentions are operating continually and centrally in the interpretation of what is said. Loose, live speech depends upon such active 'on-line' interpretation of intention to make sense of what has been said. If there were some absolutely agreed-upon concept of firm and definite linguistic meaning that Biro and others could appeal to, then it might be harder to make the case I am arguing for. But I have already argued in the discussion of congruence of meaning that this is precisely what is not the case. The absence of any definite and satisfactory theory of unique linguistic meaning argues also for moving back to the more concrete and psychologically richer concept of utterer's meaning. This is the place to begin the theory of meaning, and this theory itself rests to a very large extent on the concept of intention.

PART II

PSYCHOLOGY OF CHILDREN'S LANGUAGE

5

YOUNG CHILDREN'S COMPREHENSION OF LOGICAL CONNECTIVES

The development of children's understanding of logical connectives has been discussed by a number of people over the past decade and a half. Without attempting to review this literature in detail, we cite Furth and Youniss (1965), Hill (1961), Inhelder and Matalon (1960), Inhelder and Piaget (1964), McLaughlin (1963), Piaget (1957), Suppes (1965), and Youniss and Furth (1964, 1967). Nevertheless, none of these studies reports the extent to which children of preschool age show comprehension of the meaning of the logical connectives in a well-defined experimental situation.

The importance of understanding the extent and limitations of children's mastery of the logical connectives is evident for any cognitive theory of development. The recent work in psycholinguistics, emphasizing the complex nature of the grammar and semantics of the language of children, has provided further impetus for seeking such understanding.

It seems clear that the development of a better theory about children's behavior and the changes in that behavior with age requires much more detailed information about their linguistic habits and competence than

*Reprinted from *Journal of Experimental Child Psychology*, 1971, **21**, 304-317. Written with Shirley Feldman.

we now have. The present study, which consists of two closely related experiments, is meant to contribute to the accumulation of such systematic information.

The data of the experiments have been analyzed in terms of several specific regression models to provide a deeper insight into what aspects of comprehension of sentential connectives are most difficult.

The formal relations between various English idioms expressing conjunction, disjunction, and negation, and the set-theoretical operations of intersection, union, and complementation are not deeply explored in this paper, but our assumptions about these connections are obvious and uncontroversial. Deeper investigation of these linguistic and semantical matters seems desirable as part of any further extensive study of children's comprehension of logical connectives.

EXPERIMENT 1

The primary aim of the first experiment was to investigate the extent to which children between the ages of 4 and 6 comprehend the logical connectives of conjunction, disjunction, and negation. It was also anticipated that the exact formulation of the idiom in terms of which the connectives were expressed would affect the results. Consequently, a second aim was to investigate the relative ease or difficulty of various idioms used to express the connectives. A third, subsidiary aim of the experiment was to examine the effects of sex, age, and socioeconomic status on the performances of the children in comprehending the meaning of the connectives.

METHOD AND PROCEDURE.

Experimental design. The differences in performance as a function of the type of logical connective and idiom were examined in a within-subject design. A $2 \times 2 \times 2$ factorial design was used to examine the between-subject effects of age, sex, and socioeconomic status (SES).

Subjects. Sixty-four subjects participated in the experiment. Thirty-two kindergarten children between the ages of 5.7 and 6.7 years were drawn from two sources: a middle-class elementary school and a school in a disadvantaged area. The other 32 children were between the ages of 4.5 and 5.4 years and attended either a preschool headstart class or a middle-class nursery school. Eight boys and 8 girls were tested from each of the four sources. The children from the preschool headstart class and from the school in a disadvantaged area were considered culturally deprived by the standards of the Office of Economic Opportunity.

Experimental materials. Eighteen wooden blocks were used. Each block had two salient properties: shape (star, circle, or square) and color (red, green, or black). Each combination of color and shape was represented by two blocks. The blocks were approximately $3\frac{1}{2}$ inches square and $\frac{1}{2}$ inch deep.

Procedure. The children were pretested to ensure that they could identify the elementary properties (color and shape) of the blocks. Three children were eliminated at this stage, but were replaced by others so that 64 subjects were tested.

Each subject was tested individually. After some preliminary commands, the subjects received 12 test commands to hand various blocks to the experimenter. The subjects were told to give all the blocks asked for, and none of the others. When the subject stopped, *E*, who had been recording responses without looking at the *S*, turned to the *S* and asked, "Have you finished? Have you given all the ...(command repeated)?"

The commands were stated with as much inflection as possible. For example, command 11 was expressed as "the things that are green-or-square," with the hyphenated words spoken as a coherent unit. Words were stressed and pauses were used to heighten the effect of the logical connectives. Each command was repeated several times.

The commands were as follows:

1. Give me the green stars.

2. Give me the red things and the square things.

3. Give me the things that are black, but not round.

4. Give me all the red things, and then everything else, but not the stars.

5. Give me all the things that are black and square.

6. Give me the green things, or, the round things.

7. Give me the stars that are red.

8. Give me the things that are black and not square.

9. Give me all the things that are green, and then everything else but not the stars.

10. Give me the black things that are round.

11. Give me the things that are green or square.

12. Give me the things that are not round but are red.

TABLE 1

SUMMARY OF SIGNIFICANT VARIABLES FROM FIVE THREE-WAY
ANALYSES OF VARIANCE ON CORRECT RESPONSES IN EXPERIMENT 1

Analysis	Significant variables	MS	df	F
1. Total commands	SES	76.6	1	33.0**
	(Error)	2.3	56	
2. Conjunction commands	SES	34.5	1	28.3**
	Age	15.1	1	12.3**
	(Error)	1.2	56	
3. Disjunction commands	SES	5.1	1	10.5**
	Age×Sex×SES	2.3	1	4.7*
	(Error)	0.5	56	
4. Negation commands	SES	40.6	1	35.6**
	Age	8.3	1	7.2**
	(Error)	1.1	56	
5. Exclusive-Or Commands	–			

$*p < .05.$
$*p < .01.$

Seven commands—1, 3, 5, 7, 8 10, and 12—tested the conjunction or the intersection of two sets. Three of these, namely, commands 3, 8, and 12, also used negation; i.e., they asked for the intersection of sets when one of the sets was a complement. To investigate disjunction or the union of sets, four alternate forms of the commands were given. These were 2, 4, 9, and 11; of these, commands 4 and 9 involved negation or complementation. One command, 6, used the "exclusive-or" connective. The commands not using negation will be called *positive* commands; the commands using "not" will be called *negative* commands.

RESULTS AND DISCUSSION

Three types of analyses were performed: one on the differences in performance between the various groups of subjects, one on the types of responses made to the different connectives and the different idioms used to express the connectives, and one on the predictive worth of a regression model.

Group differences. To evaluate the contribution of age, sex, and socioeconomic status (SES), five three-way analyses of variance on the number of correct responses were carried out: one each on the total score, the score to conjunction commands, to disjunction commands, to negation commands, and to the exclusive-or command. In Table 1, the significant results from these analyses are presented. In 4 of the 5 analyses, SES was a significant variable with children from culturally deprived homes consistently making fewer correct responses than children from advantaged homes. Age also was important in comprehending the connectives of conjunction and negation, with the older children making more correct responses than the younger children. However, it should be noted that the connectives of conjunction and negation were not independent. Sex did not affect performance differentially. Finally, only 1 of a possible 20 interactions was significant. It tentatively may be concluded that the 3 main effects are independent of one another. The fact that socioeconomic status was a uniformly more significant variable than age is to be emphasized.

Response distributions. The number of correct responses to a logical connective is an estimate of the difficulty of the operation. The rank-order of the difficulty of the binary connectives from least to most difficult is as follows: conjunction (71% correct), exclusive-or (67%), and disjunction (11%). Significant differences are found between conjunction and disjunction ($z = 9.1, p < .001$), between exclusive-or and disjunction ($z = 8.2, p < .001$), but not between conjunction and exclusive-or. For the combined connectives negation substantially increases the difficulty of the commands ($z = 3.8, p < .01$). However, it does not affect the rank-order of the different connectives, and from least to most difficult the order is as follows: positive conjunction (81% correct), exclusive-or (67%), conjunction-negation (56%), positive disjunction (18%), and disjunction-negation (6%).

The errors that the children made to the commands indicate the source of difficulty in understanding connectives. In Table 2 the notation used to describe the responses is presented. In Table 3 the response distribution for the 12 commands is shown. For the positive conjunction commands, 3 of the 4 commands (1, 7, and 10) have similar distributions. The responses to the three conjunction-negative commands (3, 8, and 12) also show a similar distribution to one another. The distribution of the responses to the two positive disjunction commands (2 and 11) are not alike, a difference probably due to the different idioms used.

TABLE 2

LEGEND OF NOTATION USED TO DESCRIBE SUBJECTS' RESPONSES IN
BOTH EXPERIMENTS

Symbol	Definition	Example $\begin{array}{l}X = red \\ Y = square\end{array}$
X	The set of elements with attribute X.	All the red blocks.
$X \cap Y$	Conjunction. The intersection of sets X and Y. Each object has both attributes X and Y.	The red squares.
$X \cup Y$	Disjunction. The union of sets X and Y. Each object has at least one of the attributes X and Y.	The red blocks and the square blocks.
X or Y	The exclusive-or (All members of the set X or all members of the set Y, but not both).	The set of red blocks or the set of square blocks.
$\overline{X}$	Negation. The complementary set of X. The not-X objects.	Green blocks and black blocks.
$(1/n)X$	The incomplete set of X objects.	Five or less (of the six) red blocks.
$(1/n)(X \cup Y)$	The incomplete set of blocks belonging to the union of X and Y, where members of both X and Y are represented.	Five or less of the red *and* five or less of the square blocks.
$(1/n)\overline{X}$	The incomplete complementary set where members of both subsets in the complementary set are represented.	Some, but not all of the green blocks and black blocks.
Misc.	Miscellaneous—any response not defined by the above categories	

In general, an inverse relationship exists between number of blocks for a correct response and performance.

When the command was for the set $X \cap \overline{Y}$, giving the intersection of one set with only a part of the complementary set was the most frequent error. It is not clear whether the difficulty was in identifying the extension of the complementary set or in the operation of intersection. Some recent evidence (Feldman, 1972) indicates that 4–6 year olds have difficulty in being exhaustive with the complementary set, which seems to suggest that the complementation caused the difficulty in these commands rather than the intersection. Another frequent error was to give the first-mentioned set, as may be seen in Table 3.

The negative disjunction commands (4 and 9) were difficult for the subjects, and many errors were made. The first-mentioned set appears in 9% of the responses. Observations of the children revealed that many of them had genuine conflict over where to place the blocks that belonged to $X \cap Y$; for example, in command 4, placement of the red stars when the red things and the not-stars were requested. Many children first included the red stars (in response to command 4) with the objects they gave to the experimenter, but then verbalized "But these are stars, and you said the red things and the things that are not stars", and with this comment removed the red stars. Although an order of selection clearly was suggested by the phrase "and then everything else ..." very few children selected their blocks in this manner. Most children picked up each block as it came to hand and apparently tested it against a memorized version of the command.

For the exclusive-or command the correct response category is probably inflated, for the first-mentioned set is a highly probable component of the response irrespective of the connective used.

Idiom. Table 3 shows that the form of the idiom used to express a particular logical connective affected the difficulty of the command for the subjects. In the case of conjunction, the idiom of command 5, "Give me all the things that are X and Y" was especially difficult. The other three (commands 1, 7, and 10) were quite easy, as reflected in the high proportion of correct responses. As for disjunction, only one idiom was understood with any success and that was "Give me the X things and the Y things" (command 2). The idiom of command 11 was obviously very difficult for the children.

Regression models. The discussion of regression models follows Suppes, Hyman, and Jerman (1967). The main task is to identify the factors that contribute to the difficulty of the commands. Factors to be examined include variation in the connective, the idiom, and the order of the properties. As a matter of notation, the jth factor of command i in a given set of commands is denoted by f_{ij}. The statistical parameters to be estimated from the data are the weights α_j attached to each factor. We emphasize that the factors identified and used here are not abstract constructions from the data. Rather, they are always objective factors identifiable by the experimenter in the commands themselves, independent of any data analysis. Which factors turn out to be important is a matter of the estimated weights α_j. Let p_i be the observed proportion of correct responses to command i for the group of subjects. The central

TABLE 3

DISTRIBUTION OF RESPONSES TO THE 12 COMMANDS OF
EXPERIMENT 1 (DATA EXPRESSED AS PERCENTAGES)

Connective	Command	Response				
		$X \cap Y$	$X \cup Y$	X	Y	Misc.
$X \cap Y$	1	97*	0	0	0	3
	5	42*	13	22	11	12
	7	96*	0	2	2	0
	10	92*	0	3	2	3
$X \cup Y$	2	11	33*	33	0	23
	11	47	3*	25	6	19
X or Y	6	9	6	45*	23*	17

Connective	Command	Response						
		$X \cap Y$	$X \cup Y$	$X \cap (1/n)\overline{Y}$	$X \cap Y$	X	Y	Misc.
$X \cap \overline{Y}$	3	56*	0	23	2	14	0	5
	8	56*	0	25	3	8	0	8
	12	56*	0	30	3	5	0	6
$X \cup \overline{Y}$	4	30	5*	2	0	12	43	8
	9	42	3*	5	0	6	38	6

*Correct response.

task of the model is to predict these observed proportions. The natural linear regression model in terms of the factors f_{ij} and the weights α_j is simply

$$p_i = \sum_j \alpha_j f_{ij} + \alpha_0.$$

All the factors f_{ij} used are 0.1-variables that take the value 1 when present and 0 when absent. The 4 connective factors were C_1 = disjunction, C_2 = conjunction, C_3 = negation, and C_4 = exclusive-or. The second type of factor considered was the form of the idiom used. Four idiom factors were used, namely, I_1 = Give me the things that are X ..., I_2 = Give me all the X things and everything else ..., I_3 = Give me the X things and/or the Y things ..., and I_4 = Give me the X (things) that are Y. This classification included 11 of the 12 commands. The command not included was the first one, for it did not fit any of the 4 categories I_i. The final factor used was an order variable, D_i, which took the value 1 when shape was the first-mentioned dimension.

A standard stepwise, multiple linear regression program was used to

obtain regression coefficients, multiple correlation R, and R^2.
For the regression equation

$$p_i = 0.89 - 0.31C_1 + 0.0SC_2 \quad +0.13C_3$$
$$-0.55I_1 - 0.65I_2 - 0.25I_3 -$$
$$0.25I_4 + 0.03D$$

the multiple R is 0.995, with a standard error of 0.0203. Figure 1 shows the predicted and observed success ratios. Although the fit is good, it must be remembered that 9 parameters—the regression coefficients—are being estimated (and thus 8 structural variables are being used) to make 11 predictions.

If we reduce the number of variables in the regression equation, the problem of interpreting the coefficients is made easier and the reduction in multiple R and R^2 is not very great. Considering only the first 4 variables that entered in the stepwise regression, the equation becomes

$$p_i = 0.64 - 0.26C_1 + 0.29C_2 - 0.39I_1 - 0.32I_2$$

with a multiple R of 0.991, and a standard error of estimate of 0.0579.

Several features of the regression coefficients should be noted. Disjunction commands are difficult, and conjunction commands are easy. Negation does not enter into this regression equation, and the predictions are satisfactory without this variable. Figure 2 shows the predicted and observed success rations.

EXPERIMENT 2

Both regression analyses in Experiment 1 show the significance of connective and idiom variables. In order to investigate further the role of idioms in children's understanding of sentential connectives, we performed a second experiment with a new group of subjects in which the connectives and idioms were standardized in a manner described below.

METHOD AND PROCEDURE

Experimental design. The subjects were divided into 4 groups, with age and sex equated across the groups. Each group was given the same set of 12 commands, with the order of the commands different for each group. Thus, type of connective and type of idiom were within-subject variables and order of commands was a between-subject variable. Each subject was tested individually.

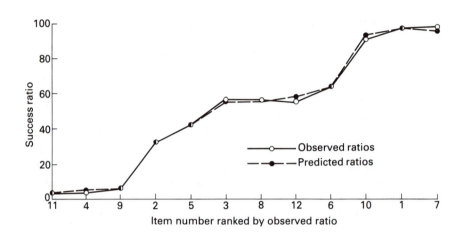

Figure 1. PREDICTED AND OBSERVED SUCCESS RATIOS WITH 8 VARIABLES IN THE REGRESSION EQUATION. EXPERIMENT 1.

Subjects. The 112 subjects between 4.6 and 6.0 years of age were drawn from the Stanford Nursery School and from the kindergarten classes of local elementary schools.

Experimental materials. These were the same as in Experiment 1.

Procedure. The task and the instructions were similar to those described in Experiment 1. However, variation in idioms and connectives was reduced. Three forms of idioms were used. They were:

1. Give me the things that are X and/or Y.

2. Give me the X things and/or the Y things.

3. Give me the X and/or Y things.

The operations included 6 disjunction commands, 4 conjunction commands, and 2 exclusive-or commands. Half of the commands within each connective-type involved negation.
The commands were as follows:

1. Give me the things that are red and square.

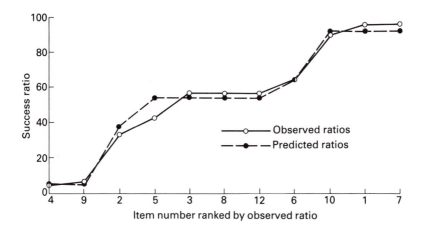

Figure 2. PREDICTED AND OBSERVED SUCCESS RATIOS WITH 4 VARIABLES IN THE REGRESSION EQUATION. EXPERIMENT 1.

2. Give me the round and black things.

3. Give me the things that are round or green.

4. Give me the black things and the square things.

5. Give me the red or star things.

6. Give me the stars or the green things.

7. Give me the things that are stars and not black.

8. Give me the red and not round things.

9. Give me the things that are red and not square.

10. Give me the round things and the not green things.

11. Give me the square or not green things.

12. Give me that black things or the not star things.

Four different orders of commands were given.

RESULTS AND DISCUSSION

Response distributions. An analysis of the responses made to the 12 commands is presented in Table 4. The most striking finding for the 6 positive commands is that irrespective of the connective and the idiom used the distribution of responses for different commands is similar; the most frequent response was the intersection of 2 sets, followed in frequency by one of the mentioned sets. However, the connective influenced the responses, for in 3 of the 6 commands the most frequent response was the correct one. Furthermore, an examination of the intersection response over all 6 positive commands revealed that the most frequent intersection response was to an intersection connective. Similarly, the most frequent union response was to a union connective.

The responses to the commands using negation showed the same general trend, with similar distributions of responses even though different idioms and different connectives were used. Unlike the responses to the positive commands where the first- and second-mentioned sets were given with approximately the same frequency, for the negative commands, the first-mentioned set was given significantly more frequently than the second-mentioned set ($z = 6.6, p < .01$). However, since the second-mentioned set was always the complementary set, it is likely that the preference was less a primacy effect than an avoidance of the complementary set.

To test sequence effects, chi-square tests were performed on each of the 12 commands over the 4 different orders of administering the commands. None of the 12 chi-squares was significant, which indicated that the order of the commands did not affect the number of correct responses.

Regression models. The 4 regression models tested were these: a connective model with conjunction, disjunction, negation, and exclusive-or as the variables; an idiom model with one variable corresponding to each of the idioms used; a connective-idiom model with all the idioms and all the connectives of the first two models included; and a connective-interaction model with variables of conjunction, disjunction, exclusive-or, conjunction-negation, disjunction-negation, and exclusive-or-negation. The results of these 4 models are summarized in Table 5. The column headed *Number of Variables* gives the number of variables that entered the stepwise regression with significant effect.

Although the connective-interaction model had the greatest predictive power, it used 5 variables to predict 12 items. For a very small reduction in predictive power, we may use a two-variable connective model, the variables being disjunction and negation. The results for this connective model are shown in the first line of Table 5. Note that R^2 is 0.867 for this

Connective	Command	$X \cap Y$	$X \cup Y$	X	Y	$(1/n)(X \cap Y)$	$(1/n)(X \cup Y)$	$(1/n)X$	$(1/n)Y$	All	Misc.
							Responses				
$X \cap Y$	1	42	10	5	7	1	2	12	3	4	14
	2	34	10	9	13	0	4	7	2	2	19
	3	30	7	16	17	0	2	4	5	6	13
$X \cup Y$	4	21	14	21	3	0	2	13	2	1	23
	5	34	6	19	17	0	0	9	1	4	10
X or Y	6	21	6	21	13	0	4	13	7	4	11

Connective	Command	$X \cap \overline{Y}$	$X \cap (1/n)$ $X \cap Y$	$\overline{Y}$	$X \cup \overline{Y}$	X	$\overline{Y}$	$(1/n)Y$	Y	All	Misc.
							Responses				
$X \cap \overline{Y}$	7	34	6	24	0	15	4	1	3	1	12
	8	26	4	28	0	10	4	2	4	1	21
	9	13	2	28	0	18	4	4	6	3	22
$X \cup \overline{Y}$	10	17	7	24	0	17	4	2	5	1	23
	11	8	12	17	0	15	6	6	4	3	29
X or $\overline{Y}$	12	19	4	24	0	21	6	5	3	1	17

TABLE 5

SUMMARY OF FOUR REGRESSION MODELS BUILT TO PREDICT CORRECT
RESPONSE TO 12 COMMANDS

Model	R	σ_e	R^2	Number of variables*
Connective	0.931	0.354	0.867	2
Idiom	0.067	0.918	0.005	1
Connective-Idiom	0.936	0.417	0.877	5
Connective Interaction	0.992	0.154	0.983	5

*This refers to the number of variables which entered into the model with significant effect.

TABLE 6

OBSERVED AND PREDICTED PROBABILITIES OF AN ERROR USING THE
TWO-VARIABLE CONNECTIVE MODEL, EXPERIMENT 2

Command	Obs.	Pred.	Command	Obs.	Pred.
1	0.58	0.47	7	0.66	0.83
2	0.66	0.47	8	0.74	0.83
3	0.93	0.95	9	1.00	0.99
4	0.86	0.95	10	1.00	0.99
5	0.94	0.95	11	1.00	0.99
6	0.66	0.47	12	0.73	0.83

two-variable model, which represents a surprisingly good fit for a model with only 3 parameters and contrasts sharply with the very bad fit of the idiom model. In the idiom case, only one variable entered the stepwise regression; the remaining variables did not significantly improve the fit.

Although R^2 is 0.867 for the connective model, discrepancies still existed between the predicted and observed probabilities as shown in Table 6.[1]

---

[1]To avoid problems about the conservation of probability, i.e., to guarantee the predicted p_i always lie between 0 and 1, in Experiment 2 the standard transformation

$$z_i = \log[(1 - p_i)/p_i]$$

was used, and the regression analysis was made in terms of z_i, not p_i. The reported R^2 is for z_i.

CONCLUSIONS

The two experiments reported here lead to results that must be regarded as preliminary in character. More extensive and more detailed studies, especially of the language in which logical connectives are embedded, are required before any general conclusions about the comprehension of logical connectives can be drawn. On the other hand, the results of the 2 experiments, especially the results embodied in the several linear regression models presented in the paper, show that we can account for a large part of the variance in responses of the children by looking at the particular connectives used in a command and also by examining the idiom in which these connectives were expressed. When the idioms are standardized as in the second experiment, the analysis of the connectives alone is sufficient to account for more than 85% of the variance in the behavior. It is to be noted of course that this remark applies to the mean probabilities of response, not to individual responses. Considering the results that have been reported in a wide variety of literature, it is not surprising that negation enters as an important variable in the second experiment. From the studies of Eifermann (1961), Feldman (1972), Wason (1959, 1961), Wason and Jones (1963), and others, it might have been predicted that in a regression analysis of comprehension, negation would be a salient connective in terms of difficulty of comprehension. On the other hand, it was unexpected that negation would not be a significant variable in the first experiment. This is probably the result of a considerable dependence between negation and idiom variables, with the idiom variables being somewhat better predictors.

It is easy enough to characterize additional lines of research needed in terms of the comprehension of logical connectives. We have not been able to present in this paper any picture of the developmental sequence in terms of age. It would be desirable to know more about how comprehension changes with age and with linguistic exposure, and also to have a deeper understanding of why particular sorts of errors were made.

6

THE SEMANTICS OF
CHILDREN'S LANGUAGE

Interest in language, especially that of children, has become a central concern of contemporary psychology. This interest is somewhat surprising, because everyone recognizes the enormous complexity of language use and language development in the child. In spite of a widespread recognition that there is little hope of having a complete theory of these matters at any time in the near future, a general air of activity and in some cases of optimism prevails about the progress being made. For example, it is now possible to cite a fairly large number of references in the literature on almost any aspect of language development in the child, ranging from phonology to semantic comprehension, with probably the largest number of studies being on the syntactical or grammatical development of children's language. It is surely in this area that the most progress has been made over the past decade or decade and a half.

I have been involved in several such grammatical studies myself (Suppes, 1970; Suppes, Smith, and Léveillé, 1972), and I believe in the intrinsic merit of the diversified work that is going on all over the world. On the

*Reprinted from *American Psychologist*, 1974, **29**, 103-114. This article was delivered as a Distinguished Scientific Contribution Award address presented at the meeting of the American Psychological Association, Montreal, Canada, August 1973. The research reported here draws upon collaborative work with a number of younger associates, especially Elizabeth M. Gammon, Madeleine Léveillé, Freeman Rawson, Robert L. Smith, Jr., and Peter Wu.

other hand, I do feel that too great an emphasis has been placed on grammar or syntax, and too little on semantics. I want to try to help redress the balance by making the case for an intensive study of the semantics of children's speech. I shall be especially concerned to argue that there are as many conceptual and technical tools available for semantical analysis as there are for syntactical analysis, but as yet these tools are less familiar to psycholinguists and to psychologists in general then is the concept of a generative grammar. Moreover, psychologists have developed a habit of listening to the latest word from linguists on syntactical matters, and to some extent this has transferred to semantics. Part of my thesis is that while linguists have had little of interest to say about semantics, there is a deep and conceptually rich tradition in logic and philosophy that can be used for the semantical analysis of children's speech and that can provide a body of methods and concepts appropriate to the task. It is not my objective to be controversial and dialectical in this lecture, but I want to emphasize from the beginning my conviction that when it comes to semantical matters, the tradition of model-theoretic semantics that originated with Frege (1879) in the nineteenth century is *the* serious intellectual tradition of semantical analysis, and the recent offshoots by linguists, to a large extent conceived in ignorance of this long tradition, have little to offer in comparison.

LOGICAL TRADITION

The tradition I identify as beginning with Frege—although it has an informal history that runs back at least to Aristotle—is concerned with providing a precise and explicit analysis of the meaning of an utterance. This is not the place to give a history of these developments, but I do want to sketch the central concepts that are particularly relevant to the analysis of children's language. It came to be recognized fairly early that one way to analyze the meaning of an utterance is to state under what conditions the utterance is satisfied. In the case of declarative sentences, this amounts to giving truth conditions; in the case of questions, conditions on a correct answer; and in the case of commands, conditions on a response that satisfies the command.

Perhaps the most important step after Frege was the explicit analysis of the concept of truth by Tarski (1935) in his celebrated monograph. Tarski's analysis of the concept of truth is restricted to formal languages, and much of the development of semantics in logic and philosophy since the 1930s has been concerned with formal languages. No doubt the preponderance of emphasis on formal languages has put off deeper perusal

of these matters by psycholinguists who might otherwise be attracted to
the theoretical developments. What has come to be called the theory of
models in logic, which is really the semantical theory of formal languages,
has been relatively inaccessible to outsiders until fairly recently.

As I have already indicated, it is my contention that the concepts developed in this logical tradition are of central relevance to the semantics
of children's language. I want to sketch why I think this is so, but also
to emphasize that I do not claim that all the intellectual problems that
must be faced in giving an adequate theory of the semantics of children's
language can be solved by any simple and direct application of the concepts taken from the logical theory of models. I shall have more to say
about this later.

The basic semantical notion is that of a sentence or a collection of
sentences being satisfied in a model. The intuitive idea of such satisfaction
is close to the intuitive concept of truth.

Thus, when Nina (one of the children I shall be quoting extensively
in this article) says "Bring me some more candy canes," the semantics
of satisfaction of that command is, it seems to me, as straightforward as
satisfaction of the simple mathematical command "Add 5 and 7." We
all have a clear intuitive understanding in both cases of what satisfaction
of the command is and what the appropriate state of affairs would be
in which either command would make sense with its satisfaction being
describable in relatively simple terms.

To make these intuitions explicit is much easier in the case of elementary formal languages. Their syntax is restricted to sentential connectives,
predicates, variables, the universal and existential quantifiers, and parentheses for punctuation. A model for a sentence of such an elementary
formal language consists just of a nonempty domain, a subset of that domain for each one-place predicate, a binary relation for each two-place
predicate, and so forth. A simple, but explicit, formal definition of what
it means for a sentence to be satisfied in such a model is then easy to give.

Once a concept of a model is introduced for an elementary formal
language, the most important semantical relation between sentences, that
of logical consequence, is easily defined. One sentence of the language is
a logical consequence of a second just when the first sentence is satisfied
in any model in which the second is satisfied.

Direct application of these ideas to a child's language encounters at
least three sorts of difficulties. First, the syntax of the child's language
is more complicated than that of elementary formal languages, even in
the case of a child between the age of two and three years. Second, the
idea of considering *any* model of a child's utterance seems on occasion
too broad and leads to a notion of consequence that seems too general.

Third, the sentences of an elementary formal language are self-contained in their meaning relative to a model that can be easily described. In the case of much of a child's speech there is a vagueness of context and at the same time an apparent high dependency on context that is not easily dealt with by any explicit notion of model. I want to say something about each of these difficulties in turn.

SEMANTICS OF CONTEXT-FREE GRAMMARS

The approach to the first problem of syntax is to restrict initial analysis to that part of the child's language for which a context-free grammar can be written. The semantics of such context-free languages or context-free fragments then consists essentially of two parts. The first part is the assignment of a denotation to individual words or phrases occurring in the child's speech. In many instances, this assignment of denotation would of course vary from one context of use to another, but this variation merely corresponds to using different models on different occasions. Thus, when Nina says "Get big ball," we assign the denotation of a certain two-place relation to *get*, we assign the set of balls in the immediate environment as the denotation of the word *ball*, and we assign a denotation to the adjective *big* that is not simply the set of big things in the environment, but something more complicated that I shall discuss later in a more detailed consideration of adjectives.

The second part of the semantics is to provide rules for putting individual denotations together in a way that fits hand and glove with the syntactic structure of the utterance by assigning a semantic function for combining denotations to each production rule of the grammar. This may sound somewhat abstract and complex, but the intuitive idea is simple, as may be illustrated in some examples drawn from a second corpus, a group of six-year-old black children talking to each other (these children were born and live in Southern California). One of the children said "Black cats could climb up a ladder." Let us look at the subject noun phrase *black cats*. Our grammar for noun phrases contains the production rule $NP \to Adj + N$. As shown in the tree in Figure 1, the semantic rule attached to the grammatical rule is simply that of intersection for this simple noun phrase. On the left-hand side of each node we show either a terminal word or a grammatical category, and to the right of the colon in each node, the denotation of that node. Thus, in the present case the denotation of *black* is the set B of black things, and the denotation of *cats* is the set C of cats. Using the semantic rule of intersection, we see that the denotation of NP as shown in the tree is simply $B \cap C$.

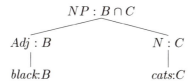

Figure 1. SEMANTIC TREE FOR THE ENGLISH NOUN PHRASE *black cats.*

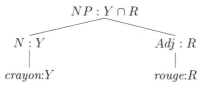

Figure 2. SEMANTIC TREE FOR THE FRENCH NOUN PHRASE *crayon rouge.*

A French sample of a similar sort, taken from the corpus of Philippe, a young Parisian child, indicates that the semantic tree for a noun phrase looks very similar, even when the adjective follows the noun, due to the fact that intersection of sets is commutative (see Figure 2). In the simple case under consideration, similar semantic trees can be found in languages quite different from English. Here is an example drawn from the spoken speech of Lingling, a two-year-old child whose language is Mandarin and who lives in Taiwan. The semantic tree for *hong2 mao2yi1* (red sweater) is shown in Figure 3[1].

The three examples I have given are exceedingly simple. It is no triumph for any theory to be able to give an analysis of them. On the other hand, it is not appropriate here to undertake a full-scale systematic analysis of the speech of any of the children referred to. Extensive technical reports already exist for several of the corpora, and some of the analysis is so detailed and massive that I wonder if the reports will have any readers besides the authors themselves (Smith, 1972; Suppes, 1973b; Suppes and Gammon, 1973; Suppes, Smith and Léveillé, 1972).

To provide illustrations that I think are suggestive of the direction

---

[1] Examples drawn from the Lingling corpus are written in pinjin notation for Mandarin with tones indicated by the numerals 1–4 to make possible linear processing of computer input and output.

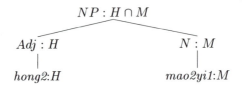

Figure 3. SEMANTIC TREE FOR THE MANDARIN NOUN PHRASE *hong2 mao2yi1*.

taken by the full-scale analysis, I would like to consider four topics: the definite article, adjectives, quantifiers, and the expression of propositional attitudes in children's speech.

THE DEFINITE ARTICLE

In English the definite article is not used at the very beginning of connected speech by young children but it does appear early. In the case of Nina, shortly after she was two years old frequent uses are found: *the little boat, the little baby, I want the next page, I don't want the finger, I want the lion.*

The use of the definite article is even more common in spoken French at the age of two or shortly thereafter. Here are some of Philippe's examples: *pas chercher les voitures, dans la main, tombé le nours, la voiture, va chercher l'avion, tombé sur la bête, de l'eau, plein sur la cuisse, mangé le yaourt, le train, le métro, la valise, les chaussons là, chercher les livres, faire de la musique sur le nôtre.*

Because there is no exact equivalent of the definite article in spoken Mandarin, I shall only consider the semantics of English and French. This does not mean that there is no way of giving definite descriptions in Chinese; rather, it means that different semantical and syntactical methods are used.

There is a familiar story in logic and philosophy about the analysis of definite descriptions and the introduction into formal logic of an explicit notation for the definite description operator. One of the classics of twentieth-century philosophy is Bertrand Russell's (1905) famous article on definite descriptions in which he shows how such descriptions can be eliminated in favor of more primitive logical concepts. His classic example is "The present king of France is bald." For analyzing children's speech or the informal talk of adults, the kind of analysis provided by Russell and the subsequent logical literature on definite descriptions does not seem to provide exactly the right approach, because the objective of the kind of analysis that deals directly with the spoken language is, as I have indicated, to provide a semantics that fits hand and glove with the syntax.

For this purpose, I have found that in many cases, but perhaps not all, it is useful to let the definite article *the* in English (and usually the corresponding definite article in French, for example) denote a set C that is the union of the set of objects in the perceptual surround with the set of objects denoted by phrases in immediately preceding sentences in the conversation, and in some cases, also the set of objects denoted by images or symbolic storage in long-term memory. Thus, when Nina said, "I want the lion," the set C denoted by *the* is intersected with the set of lions both real and toy, and if everything is in good order, the set intersection consists of a unique object. The set C as I have described it might in some cases be too large and thus the intersection would be too large. One device by which we can narrow the set C is to use a sequence of sets C_1 with each element of the sequence being contained in the preceding member. The C that is appropriate in a given case is the first one that leads to a unique object when intersected with the set denoted by the remainder of the noun phrase. Without entering into technical details, I do want to remark that in the case of the definite article the correct semantic function for the production rule is not simply intersection, but intersection only in the case when everything is normal. When it is not, some Fregean or Russellian device is used. Obviously, also, the analysis must change when the definite article is used with a plural noun phrase, as when Nina says "I want the big boxes." In this case, the semantic function places a different cardinality requirement. Rather than a unique object in the intersection there must be at least two objects for the normal meaning to go through.

Whether the explicit decision is taken to let the definite description denote when the proper number of objects is not found in the intersection is really a technical decision and not an important conceptual one. One alternative is to treat the phrase as meaningless and nondenoting, and another is to introduce some arbitrary abstract object as Frege suggested. What is interesting is that the decision here is about as arbitrary and conventional as it is in the case of highly formalized languages, for example, as in a formalized language for axiomatic set theory.

To give you a crude idea of how the set C works, in the analysis of the spoken language of the Southern California black children I mentioned earlier, Elizabeth Gammon and I looked at 4,300 noun phrases in the corpus (Suppes and Gammon, 1973). It was our approximate judgment after we examined the 265 uses of the definite article that in 126 cases the set C could be restricted to the perceptual surround. In 99 cases the C could be restricted to objects denoted in immediately preceding sentences, and in 28 cases familiar objects like the moon, whose image or symbolic description was stored in long-term memory, seemed appropriate. In 12 cases the object referred to seemed to be in the mind of the speaker alone, and there was no easy extraction of the appropriate set C.

To give a sense of the frequency of occurrence of the definite article in the case of Nina, her speech recorded periodically from the age of 23 months to 39 months, with a corpus consisting of 102,230 tokens, contains 4,144 occurrences of *the*. Thus, a requirement of any systematic semantics of Nina's speech is to provide an analysis of the definite article.

In the case of Philippe's spoken French, running from the age of 25 months to 39 months, there are 56,982 tokens: *le* occurs 1,641 times; *la*, 1,457; *l*, 619; and *les*, 777 times.

Of course, the semantics of the demonstrative adjectives is very close to the semantics of the definite article. I shall not consider the ways in which we think they should be given a somewhat different semantics from that of the definite article to indicate continuing focus (*this* in English) or change of focus (*that*). In the case of Nina, there are 2,075 occurrences of *that*, 1,497 occurrences of *this*, 246 occurrences of *these*, and 341 occurrences of *those*.

SEMANTICS OF ADJECTIVES

I turn now to some semantic subtleties involved in the use of adjectives. Native speakers of English will say almost without exception big red book, little blue box, and so forth, but not red big box, or blue little box. There is a good semantic explanation of this fixed order, and the order is found almost without error in young children's speech from the very beginning of the production of phrases that use an adjective of size as well as an adjective of color or some other adjective of simple classification. In the case of Nina, there are 370 occurrences of *big*, and 674 occurrences of *little*. Here are all the instances in which either big or little is combined with an adjective of classification (there are other instances of intensifiers, for example, *great big*, that I shall not examine): *big black; and a big white one; and there a big white one; big black seal; big dirty in her big mouth; big tiny mousie; yeah my big blue dog; I want the little tiny baby; little tiny stones; the little tiny one; and my little soft monkey; I got this pink little blanket* (the only case of reversal of the fixed order mentioned above); *I want my little white blanket; little green table; Mrs. Wood's little green chair; that's yellow little yellow house; where's the little tiny one?; where's the more little green chairs?; where's the little green chair fall down?; yup, that's my little washing machine like you have a washing machine downstairs.*

In the case of standard spoken French, the proper order is the adjective of size preceding the noun, which is followed by the adjective of classification. Here are a few samples from Philippe's speech: *cherchez deux petites cabines bleues; où il est le petit filet jaune?; une petite vitre carée; une petite fenétre ronde; après il a mangé le petit chaperon rouge; et un petit nez noir; le petit bitonniau blanc; les petits bouts ronds là; le petit bitonniau blanc où il est?; la voiture elle fait tomber la petite machine verte; c'est quoi ces petits bouts ronds?; c'est quoi ces petits bouts ronds là?; tu vois les petits points jaunes?; tu veux un petit raisin séqué? (pour sec); mais je prépare des petites cabines bleues.*

In the case of Lingling's Mandarin, the word order is similar to that of English, that is, the adjective of size or of some other characteristic of variable intensity precedes the simple adjective of classification. Again, as in the case of Philippe, I have not attempted to present a full listing, but only to give some samples: *xiao3 zhen1 want2zio* (small real prince), *xiao3 zhen1 lao3shu3* (small real rat), *xiao3 ai3 ren2* (small short man), *xiao3 bai2 tu4* (small white rabbit), *da4 bai2 e2* (big white goose), *da4 ye3 lang2* (bit wild wolf), *da4 mu3 ji1* (big female chicken).

The same regularity is exhibited almost without exception in the speech of the six-year-old children from Southern California. What is impressive in these four sample corpora is the uniformity with which the standard usage is reflected even in quite early stages of a child's speech. It might be argued that the problem is simpler in French. Still impressive is the way in which Philippe uniformly puts *grand* or *petit* before the noun and adjectives of color like *bleu* or *jaune* after the noun.

Let me illustrate with an artificial example what I think is a reasonable explanation of the underlying semantics, and why we place the adjective of variable intensity prior to the adjective of classification. In Figure 4 we see a set of dots in the top row marked *G* for green *R* for red. If we ask for the denotation of *big dot* we get the next row, the single large green dot. If we ask for the denotation of the *red big dot* we get a nonexistent denotation, because we first start with *big dot*, which is green, and then ask for red, but there is no big dot that is red. On the other hand, if we start the other way and ask for the denotation of *red dot*, we get the two red dots. Then if we ask for the big red dot we apply the intensive adjective *big* and select the larger of the red dots.

The idea behind this can be expressed in abstract terms in the following way: First, we intersect the set denoted by the noun with the set denoted by the adjective of classification. We order this set according to

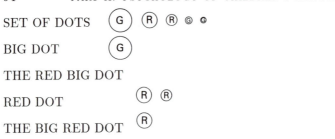

SET OF DOTS

BIG DOT

THE RED BIG DOT

RED DOT

THE BIG RED DOT

Figure 4. DENOTATIONS OF VARIOUS NOUN PHRASES ILLUSTRATING THE ORDER OF MODIFYING ADJECTIVES.

the ordering relation denoted by the adjective of intensity, in the present case, the adjective *big*. If we are talking about the upper end of the ordering, we then select as the denotation of the noun phrase the single largest object or something close to the single largest object, for example, a small subset. It is easy to make all this quite precise in terms of a few mathematical symbols, but that is not my objective here.

For those who are somewhat uneasy about the absolute definiteness of my example in terms of dots, they can substitute *biggest* for *big* and obtain a quite unambiguous analysis. Thus, in the second line we talk about the *biggest dot*, in the third line the *red biggest dot*, which is most unusual English, and so forth. I should mention that I have not analyzed the example in terms of the completely semantically unambiguous superlative, because the use of the superlative in children's language is relatively rare. As already mentioned, there are 370 occurrences of *big* in the Nina corpus and 674 occurrences of *little*. In contrast, there are just five occurrences of the comparative *bigger* and three of the superlative *biggest*, and just three of *littler*, none of *littlest*, none of *smaller*, and one of *smallest*. When I have spoken of the ambiguity of *big* I mean that exactly what initial segment of the objects ordered by size is selected as the denotation will vary from one circumstance to another. I do think the analysis in the present case that sharply differentiates the semantic function associated with an adjective like *red* as opposed to an adjective like *big* is in first approximation correct and represents a useful insight into the subtleties of the use of adjectives in English. Let me mention also that there are cases, and they are proper cases, of usage in English in which the order is reversed. For instance, if someone is looking at two large chairs among a collection of chairs and one of them is green and one of them is red, it is appropriate to say, Give me the green big chair.

Further complex things about the semantics of adjectives are encountered in children's speech. For example, there are 260 occurrences of *another* in the Nina corpus and 227 occurrences of *other*. The semantics of these two adjectives is obviously not in any sense the simple intersection function. Cardinal numbers and their different usages and positions raise additional problems, but here there is a longer tradition and therefore a more straightforward sense of what is correct.

As fascinating as these further details about adjectives can be, in order to give a survey I move on to the special case of quantifiers, which can be treated as adjectives, but in my own analysis should not be.

QUANTIFIERS

To keep the story simple I restrict myself only to classical quantifiers *all* and *some*. And here is Nina at her classical best: *all colors, all of they gonna go in here; all the animals did; all the ducklings going to the California; all these and these children are gonna eat; mommy I need all the pieces cut; and I got some lambs; and I want some people; and I made some pancakes; and some snakes were wrapped up together.*

It is my contention that the meaning of *some* and *all* in these examples from Nina's speech is almost without change the same as in classical mathematical language when we say *All even numbers are divisible by two* or *Some prime numbers are twin primes*, or as another parallel from the classical examples of Aristotle: *All men are mortal, some men are tall.* At the age of 30 months Nina was handling quantifiers with beautiful precision. Compare this fact. It was not until 1879, upon the publication of Frege's *Begriffschrift*, than an explicit theory of quantifiers was formulated. Today, the theory of quantification, in the sense of the theory of the universal and existential quantifiers, is taken to be at the heart of general logic. I have even heard one paper by a philosopher in which the theory of predication and quantifiers was taken to be the most distinguishing characteristic of human as opposed to nonhuman, animal thinking. I am pleased to report that Nina and other children like her seem to have these matters under good control at a very early age.

There are two aspects of Nina's use of quantifiers that I think are representative of the use of a large number of children, but which receive no treatment in Aristotle and very little in the logical tradition from Frege onward.

The first is that both the existential and universal quantifiers, but especially the existential quantifier, occur more in object position than in subject position. The object position for quantifiers is especially natural in stating commands or expressing wants or needs, and it is exactly the logic of such statements that has been ignored until recently in the development of explicit logical theory. Three examples that have not yet been cited, but that would be typical of Nina's use of the existential quantifier in object position would be these: *I want some diaper pins; I will get some blocks; I want some more toys.*

The second point is that the universal quantifier is so often used in conjunction with the definite article. There is a kind of concreteness and contextualism about this, which is especially reinforced by the earlier analysis given of the definite article, that makes this the natural way to talk, rather than using the universal quantifier in unrestricted form. Thus when Nina says *all the animals did*, she is referring to the toy animals in the immediate context, and the definite article *the* makes that clear. The same kind of remark applies to her statement about all the ducklings. An example in which she may use a demonstrative adjective rather than the definite article is this: *All these clothes are getting off.* The force of the definite article or the demonstrative adjective is to restrict the universal quantification to the contextual set at hand, and this is where a restriction properly belongs. Aristotle's or Frege's unrestricted universal quantifier can be defended in terms of logical simplicity, but for working purposes the canonical use of quantifiers is *all the xs*, not *all xs*. This has been too little remarked upon in logical theory, but is evident enough in Nina's speech.

One final remark is needed on Nina's use of *all* and *some*. I have not covered the many different uses of these words as adverbs or parts of adverbial phrases, but in relative frequency these uses are as common as the direct use of quantifiers. In almost all cases, however, the semantical function of the words is similar to their straight function as quantifiers. I have deliberately avoided defining explicitly the semantic functions associated with the production rules by which quantifiers are introduced, not because I think the subject is unmanageable, but because the explicit treatment is rather technical. At least I do not yet understand how to present it in a way that is not technical. The semantics is simplest in my judgment when quantifiers enter at a high level in the derivation tree, and not at the level of adjectives that are part of noun phrases.

PROPOSITIONAL ATTITUDES

There is an important and fundamental distinction in logic that is not needed for the classical development of the foundations of mathematics, but that is essential for obvious distinctions in the use of ordinary language. This is the distinction between language that is purely extensional and language that is intensional. The most obvious way in which language is used intensionally is in the expression of necessity, possibility, or propositional attitudes. Examples of the expression of propositional attitudes are statements about beliefs, needs, wants, expectations, or fears. They are expressed by a wide variety of verbs in every natural language.

Because of the importance and interest in these matters in any complete analysis of the semantics of natural language, let me give one example that is classical in the philosophical literature, but is not directly pertinent to Nina's speech or that of other children her age. The example concerns the non-truth-functional or nonextensional character of belief statements. Thus, from knowing that the statement *The earth is flat* is false, we can infer neither the truth nor falsity of the statement *John Jones believes the earth is flat*. Similarly, from the truth of the statement *The sun is larger than the earth* we can infer neither the truth nor the falsity of the statement *Aristotle believed that the sun was larger than the earth*. I have no direct analogues to these examples in the speech of Nina, because no form of the verb *believe* or the noun *belief* occurs in our extensive sample of her speech. As you would also expect, there are no instances of statements of possibility or necessity. There are, however, numerous instances of the expression of propositional attitudes, especially expressions of wants or needs, and there are many expressions of *because* or *-cause*.

The case of the various forms of *want* for example, *wanna*, is striking. Of the large corpus of over 100,000 words, somewhat over 1% are occurrences of some form of *want* (*want*, 883; *wanna*, 359; *wants*, 60; *wanted*, 6).

One useful distinction in the use of terms or noun phrases in the expression of propositional attitudes occurs already in Nina's speech. This is the distinction between attributive and referential use of terms, a distinction already recognized by medieval logicians who characterized the referential reading as giving us a statement *de re* as opposed to the attributive reading which yields a statement *de dicto*. Both attributive and referential uses occur in the Nina corpus. Here are some examples of attributive uses: *He don't want a Band-aid on; I want milk; I want some more toys; I want another story OK;* and here are some examples of the referential use: *I want the next page* (the next page, of course, having a definite reference or denotation); *I want this* (with *this* having reference to a particular object in the environment); *I want her to wear the blue dress* (where the phrase *her to wear the blue dress* refers to a definite concrete act).

In the examples I have cited there seems to be little ambiguity between attributive and referential use of the noun phrases in object position. In the philosophical literature on these matters there has been considerable discussion of the kinds of examples that do give rise to ambiguity. A typical instance would be: John wants to marry a French girl. Given only this sentence, it is ambiguous whether the reference is to some one particular girl or whether John is looking for a wife, does not have a definite person in mind, but wants her to be a woman who is French. Such examples can also occur with the use of the definite article as well as the indefinite article. For example, Hintikka (1973) cited "John believes that the richest man in town is a Republican." It is ambiguous whether John has in mind some particular individual or simply believes it true that whoever is the richest man in town, he will turn out to be a Republican.

I have examined Nina's use of *want* for the same kind of ambiguity. It exists with the indefinite article, but so far as I can see not with the definite article. Here are several examples with the indefinite article: *Do you want a pink balloon?; her don't want a cup; her want a blanket OK; I don't want a jersey on; I want a toy.* In all these cases, as Hintikka rightly remarked in his own analysis of a different range of examples, additional factual information, in our case the kind of information available in the corpus from preceding sentences or comments on the situation, makes clear whether the usage is attributive or referential.

The question of theoretical interest is what uniform account semantically is to be given of these matters. For example, can the kind of model theory characteristic of elementary formal languages, which are normally extensional, be extended to the kind of language expressing propositional attitudes as found in Nina's speech? If I had asked this question 30 years ago, the answer would almost certainly have been pessimistic and rather negative, because the semantics of modal concepts or propositional attitudes had scarcely been developed. Fortunately, an intense concern with these matters within logic proper in the past three decades has created a considerable logical apparatus, and a deep understanding of the semantical problems involved has developed. In saying this I do not mean to suggest that all the conceptual problems are solved or that the application of current theory to children's speech is simple or straightforward. I do mean to suggest that many powerful and subtle methods are available and can be applied.

The most important theoretical point in these developments is that the semantics of sentences expressing propositional attitudes can be given a precise treatment in terms of the concept of a set of possible worlds.

To illustrate the idea of a set of possible worlds, let me first consider some classical modal concepts before turning to Nina's speech. If I say "It is possible that it will rain tomorrow," then the semantics of this statement is that there is a possible world in which it will rain tomorrow.

If on the other hand I say "It is necessary that an object that is red is colored," then I mean that in every possible world this state of affairs must hold. On the other hand, if I say "It is contingently true that Bertrand Russell lived to be more than 90 years old." I mean that in some possible worlds this assertion would be true and in others it would be false. When Nina says "I don't want a jersey on," one interpretation of the semantics of this is that there is a possible world in which Nina does not put a jersey on, and it is in this world that she wants to be. (When I say "one world," I mean usually a set of worlds having this characteristic.) In general when Nina says "I want X," the semantics can be given a precise interpretation in terms of her desire for the actual world to be drawn from a certain set of possible worlds, and she is asking for actions that will make this take place.

(A technical remark is in order about these matters. A tradition exists in the logical and philosophical literature that defines a proposition as a function from possible worlds to truth values. This, for example, was the definition preferred by the late Richard Montague. On the basis of this kind of analysis, we would say that Nina's statement of a want or need expresses a proposition that is a function from possible worlds in which the want is satisfied to truth values. For various reasons, I do not like this analysis. For instance, one of the difficulties of Montague's view is that any two logically equivalent sentences express exactly the same proposition. Rather, I prefer that the structural characteristics of a sentence be an integral part of its expression of meaning. The identification of an utterance expressing a want with the function mapping possible worlds into truth values ignores the grammatical structure of the utterance. On the other hand, I emphasize that in the semantic analysis of such utterances expressing wants the simple theory of denotation discussed earlier is not satisfactory, and a more complicated theory building on the theory of possible worlds is required. For example, once we pass from a single fixed world or model to a set of models or worlds, simple adjectives like *red* no longer denote a set, but at the very least a set in each possible world or, put another way, a function that is a mapping from possible worlds into sets of objects in that world, in each case the set of objects being the set of red objects in that world.)

At this point many of you may feel that I have pulled you a long way from psychological questions to philosophical questions that seem to have little relevance to Nina's thoughts, actions, and language. I wish to urge upon you the thesis that this is not at all the case. Psychologists have mainly ignored the complexities and subtleties of the expression of propositional attitudes by young children even at their earliest stages. There may be a simpler way of giving a full-scale analysis of these matters, but if there is, it is not known to me, and it is certainly not widely available in the current relevant literature on these matters. What I have hoped to convince you of, and I think in the limited space available I have not been able to do the job adequately, is that already a host of methods and subtle distinctions are available, which we may effectively use for a better understanding of the explicit semantics of children's speech. What I have tried to make evident in my discussion of propositional attitudes is this: Even from the very beginning of a child's speech, in the age from two to three years, the whole battery of semantical problems associated with propositional attitudes, a set of problems among the most subtle in current semantical theory, arise in providing a detailed and accurate theory of children's speech.

CONSEQUENCE AND PARAPHRASE

In my introductory remarks I mentioned the desirability of changing the classical logical notion of consequence, and I now turn to this topic. In order to give the discussion a focus, I shall relate my remarks about logical consequence and a wider concept of consequence to psycholinguistic discussions of paraphrase and how problems of paraphrase arise in the analysis of the semantics of children's speech.

Frege's definition of paraphrase is that two sentences are paraphrases of each other just when the have the same logical consequences. If we use the characterization of propositions stated above, that is, a proposition is a function from possible worlds to truth values, then we may also characterize in equivalent fashion two sentences as being paraphrases of each other just when they express the same proposition. It is surprising to find this semantical characterization of paraphrase essentially unreferred to in the psycholinguistics studies on the paraphrasing ability of children or adults.

For example, in the careful and extensive study of Gleitman and Gleitman (1970), *paraphrase* is characterized as a notion that is properly thought of as a part of generative grammars, but this seems to me a clear error. Gleitman and Gleitman emphasized that transformations of a sentence can express paraphrases, but in the standard semantical Fregean sense, two sentences that have totally unrelated derivational histories can be logical paraphrases of each other. In practice, moreover, what is used in experimental tests of paraphrasing ability is really a semantic and not a syntactic criterion. The explicit use of model-theoretic semantics would put the experimental studies in this area on a sounder conceptual basis.

Nevertheless, I think there is adequate ground for changing the Fregean definition, which is too stringent. When Nina says things that are ungrammatical to our adult ears, it is usually easy for us to paraphrase what she has said, even without knowledge of the context. Consider the following: *No, I wanna go to what that thing and see if I'm tall; no more presents he doesn't give me; now let me try other Rachel's sunsuit, mommy; I feel better my diaper rash.* On the other hand, the following sentence of Nina's might present some difficulty even within context: *I want to save this on with the same time.*

In paraphrasing Nina's speech or someone else's, we almost always assume without question certain background information and knowledge that is not included in Frege's strict definition of paraphrase in terms of logical consequence. As I mentioned earlier, within model-theoretic semantics it is easy to give a characterization of logical consequence; namely, one sentence is a logical consequence of another if the first sentence is satisfied in any model in which the second is satisfied. In other words, we consider all possible models. But, we can get a less strict notion of consequence by reducing the set of possible models to some smaller set in which basic intuitive knowledge is held rigid across all the models in the set. Two sentences can then be said to be paraphrases relative to this reduced set of models if they both are satisfied in exactly the same models of the reduced subset.

This reduced notion of consequence, which I shall call R-consequence, has other uses than in the treatment of paraphrase. It is also the appropriate concept, in my judgment, for the analysis of questions and answers in children's speech. In the age range I have been mainly discussing, children primarily answer questions by adults, and it is only a year or so later that the tables are turned and they begin asking the questions and expecting answers. For this early stage of answers or the later stage of questions, the concept of R-consequence provides the proper concept for characterizing semantically correct answers to a question. (Notice that I do not say *the* semantically correct answer, because in general any one of an indefinite number of paraphrases will be accepted as correct.) I return to the importance of questions and answers in children's speech when I discuss problems of verification.

I conclude this article with a discussion of three types of problems: problems of context, problems of process, and problems of verification.

PROBLEMS OF CONTEXT

When Nina says "I need some more" or "I want some too," it is clear that a full semantical account of these utterances is dependent on the context of utterance. This dependence on context is characteristic not only of children's speech, but of much casual adult talk as well. It stands in sharp contrast to sentence tokens of a formal language that are self-contained and timeless in character, or even to mathematical statements or other scientific statements in ordinary language in formal textbook or treatise mode. The way in which the kind of model-theoretic semantics I am advocating can be extended to cover such matters of context has already been indicated in the treatment described for definite articles. I see nothing standing in the way of similar extensions to other problems of interpretation, as in the case of the two examples just cited.

On the other hand, elaboration of the context to give an adequate account of what Nina was perceiving or remembering at the time she was speaking is to extend in quite substantial ways the framework of classical semantics to include concepts and requirements that have been investigated in all their complexity for many years by psychologists. Putting together what we know about remembering and perceiving with the kind of semantic structure for language I have outlined is a formidable theoretical task that has yet hardly begun. It seems to me, however, that this is the direction in which we should try to take account of context and, in the doing, build a much richer psychological model of Nina's and other children's language behavior.

PROBLEMS OF PROCESS

Building such a model of remembering and perceiving takes us at once to the consideration of process. A proper criticism of the semantic theory I have outlined is that there are no serious considerations of processing. There is no temporal analysis of the machinery children or adults use for semantic processing of sentences they speak or hear.

This absence of an explicit analysis of process has been brought home to me in a salient way in some of our own research at Stanford University in the past year or so. In attempting to understand these problems of process and how model-theoretic semantics can be applied to actual production of speech, we have turned to the problem of implementing an ongoing question-answering system for our computer system. We have chosen a domain that has no requirements of context, namely, elementary mathematical language—with an emphasis on the natural language and not on the elementary mathematics. But even here we have found that substantial theoretical extensions have had to be made to the model-theoretic semantics as described here or as found in the standard logical literature in order to have a workable computer program for actual question answering. My younger colleagues, Robert L. Smith and Freeman Rawson, have now advanced this analysis of process a fair distance (see Rawson, 1973). Space does not permit me to compare this work with earlier work by William Wood, Terence Winograd, or other computer scientists concerned with creating computer programs of a similar sort.

One way of describing the situation is similar to what I said about the problem of context. It is not that model-theoretical semantics as such is wrong, but rather that it has to be extended in order to obtain a working model. Just as a theory of remembering and perceiving must be built into an adequate model of a child in order to give a full account of his speaking and listening, so the model-theoretic semantics of even so definite a subject as elementary mathematics must be extended to fixed and definite dynamic ideas about the order in which functions are called, the precedent procedure for processing of given functions, and in general, the many kinds of considerations that enter into the construction of a compiler or interpreter for a computer language.

PROBLEMS OF VERIFICATION

As in psychological theorizing and experimentation in all areas, it is seldom the case that we can construct a theory that is adequate to account for all aspects of the psychological process under investigation. This widespread fact of theoretical incompleteness doubly holds for phenomena as complex as those of language. Without providing a full theory of remembering, perceiving, or internal processing we can still ask for empirical tests or verification of theoretical concepts such as those of model-theoretic semantics that I have been discussing.

What must be faced is that the verification of a semantic theory is more difficult and less direct than the verification of grammatical theory. For instance, if one writes a grammar for the corpus of a child's speech, it is possible in a direct way to say what percentage of the utterances in the corpus the grammar parses, and if probabilistic criteria are imposed additionally how well it generates utterances with approximately the same frequency as the frequencies observed in the corpus. Verification that the denotations assigned to terminal words or the semantic functions assigned to production rules of the grammar are correct is not amenable to such straightforward and direct attack. It is of course the case that in testing any theory there are areas of intuitive judgment that cannot be reduced to a formal algorithm of verification, and in many cases the semantic analysis given the utterances of young children by the kind of apparatus I have described can receive widespread intuitive agreement as to the correctness of the analysis. All the same, the central problem of verification is a subtle one and is not easily handled. For example, in his dissertation, Robert L. Smith (1972) gave an extensive semantic analysis of the corpus of Erica. The Erica corpus consists of 27,922 words. Erica was about 32 months old at the time the corpus was collected and thus fits within the range of the corpora of Nina, Philippe, and Lingling. Smith has written a completely systematic model-theoretic semantics for Erica, assigning a semantic function to each production rule of the generative grammar he also wrote for the corpus. The total system is complex and difficult to comprehend in any simple way. The problem arises of how to test in a systematic way that his semantical analysis is correct. Intuition can be tested on each rule, but it is a strain on the viability of intuition when the number of rules is large and some of them are complex. So far as I can see, we have at the present time no direct way to test the correctness of such a systematic semantics. It is a genuine theoretical construction, and we must use classical methods of indirect analysis to test its validity. The difficulty of providing such a direct test is one of the reasons we have been involved in writing a question-answering computer program for elementary mathematical questions and commands, because the intuitive agreement and understanding of such questions and commands is absolutely sharp and objective in character, and so the correctness of the underlying semantics is subject to a universally agreed upon test. To some extent, this same approach can be extended to the corpus of speech of a young child when the adult speech is recorded as well, for the question-answering pairs can be analyzed in similar fashion, and in many cases a highly objective criterion is possible for evaluating the semantic analysis of the question-answer pairs. All the same, a fair portion of the question-answering between adult and child is not subject to the same sharp test that obtains for elementary mathematical questions.

The other route is to carry only so far the analysis of spontaneous speech and to turn to experimentation for the detailed verification of semantical concepts and theories. It is my present view that this step is essential, and we shall not be able to collect the evidence to persuade the skeptic until comprehensive experiments that adequately test the kind of semantical ideas I have discussed today are performed. Such experimentation is not hopelessly complex and does seem feasible. There is already a useful tradition of experimentation with three- and four-year-old children, especially in the form of the creation of toy or puppet characters that talk and perform simple actions, and it seems possible to build reasonably sharp tests of comprehension into such situations. On the other hand, designing adequately structured experiments that elicit speech from two-year-olds to provide a clear test of their underlying understanding of what they are saying is not a simple matter. It is an area of methodology that badly needs development, and I call on those of you who are interested for support and help.

7

ON THE GRAMMAR AND MODEL-THEORETIC SEMANTICS OF CHILDREN'S NOUN PHRASES

I had originally intended to prepare for this colloquium a detailed analysis of noun phrases used by children in English, French, and Chinese. That program of work is well under way, but is not sufficiently complete to offer a systematic and summary presentation of results at this time. However, in view of the difficulties I have encountered on other occasions in communicating the ideas of model-theoretic semantics to linguists or psychologists not primarily interested in or familiar with the work in the theory of models in modern logic, I think a discursive and informally organized explanatory paper may actually serve a useful purpose.

At the Institute for Mathematical Studies in the Social Sciences at Stanford we have under way a detailed analysis of several large corpora. Two of them are extensive recordings of children whose first language is English and whose ages are between two and three years. We have 20 hours recorded for one girl and more than 40 hours for a second, with the second still continuing. A third corpus is that of a young French boy, whose age is in the same range as that of the two American girls. With more than 16 hours recorded and transcribed, the data collection for the

*Reprinted in *Colloques Internationaux du C.N.R.S.*, No. 206 – Problèmes Actuels en Psycholinguistique.

French boy continues at the rate of one hour per week. Finally, we have recordings from two Mandarin-speaking children, who are also between two and three years of age.

The corpora of all the children are recorded on tape and then transcribed and input into our computer system at the Institute for extensive analysis by a variety of programs. This work is being conducted in conjunction with a number of younger colleagues, and detailed results of the work will be presented in collaborative publications with them. The work in French is being conducted in collaboration with Madeleine Léveillé of the Laboratoire de Psychologie in Paris, the Chinese corpus is being collected and analyzed in collaboration with Dr. Teresa Cheng of the Phonology Laboratory, University of California at Berkeley, and the analysis of the two English corpora, together with all of the computer programming, is being done in collaboration with Mr. Robert Smith of the Institute.

Our objective is to provide a relatively complete grammar and model-theoretic semantics of these corpora. In previous papers (Suppes, 1970, 1973b) I have elaborated on the technical details of the work. The first of these papers describes the methods we are using for constructing probabilistic grammars and the second the model-theoretic approach to semantics. Further application of the notion of probabilistic grammar was made in Elizabeth Gammon's dissertation (1973).

I shall not try to recapitulate the technical details but rather try to explain in an informal way the underlying ideas and their sources.

In the case of the grammar, the analysis is done within a generative framework. The line of attack is to write a generative grammar and to attach to each production rule of the grammar a conditional probability of its use, given that a rewrite occurs of the nonterminal symbol that is the first half of the rule. The applications thus far have been in terms of context-free grammars, but the basic idea is not restricted to context-free grammars. It is certainly applicable in direct fashion to indexed grammars that are context-sensitive but not context-free, and also to optional transformations. Once such grammars are constructed for a corpus and the probabilities for the use of a given rule are estimated by standard statistical methods, an ordinary criterion of goodness-of-fit test can be performed in order to compare one grammar with another for the same corpus. The idea that is new is the introduction of probabilities and the application of standard goodness-of-fit tests to evaluate the grammar. There is more to be said here than this sketch conveys, and I know from previous discussions that a detailed clarification of what is involved in constructing the probabilistic part of such a grammar would be desirable.

However, making a generative grammar probabilistic is a minor affair compared to the difficulties and subtleties involved in adding a model-theoretic semantics to that generative grammar. I therefore want to spend most of my time here discussing in the framework of generative grammars the approach to semantics that grows out of the main thrust of work in mathematical logic.

The technical apparatus of contemporary model theory in logic is substantial, but the underlying ideas, which go back to Frege in the 19th century, are completely intuitive and straightforward. The idea is to have a clear and definite procedure for assigning a meaning to an utterance, and to do this, one must be able to show how each word in a sentence performs a definite function. I admit at once that this statement sounds far too vague and uninformative, but the word *function* means something more here.

As a first recast of this idea, we can begin by saying that we shall use standard techniques of modern mathematics to give a set-theoretical account of the meaning of a sentence. This means that we talk about objects as set-theoretical objects, and thus, we talk about individuals, classes of individuals, classes of classes of individuals, relations between individuals, relations between classes and individuals, etc., functions of individual functions of classes, etc. All of these objects are built up in a natural way into a hierarchy of sets, with of course in the classical view, relations and functions being particular kinds of sets, so that when we talk about the meaning of a sentence we must assign to each word a set-theoretical object. In the case of a noun like *men* we assign the class of men; in the case of an adjective like *green* we assign the class of green objects. Thus, fairly simple ideas of reference work. Already, however, there are adjectives that create problems. If we think of the phrase *alleged dictators*, it would not do to assign to the adjective *alleged* the class of *alleged things*, or, at least, this already seems to be somewhat strange. Once we leave adjectives and nouns, the picture can become complicated rather quickly. For example, ordinary and simple-minded ideas of reference do not give us any clues of what object to assign to the definite article *the*, or what object to assign to a preposition like *of*. It is for situations like this that set theory was created. The definite article or a preposition do not designate a simple set of individuals, but are more complicated set-theoretical functions or relations. We shall look at some examples shortly.

Another point that needs to be clarified early is that in first approximation it is often easier to assign a meaning that is a set-theoretical object to a phrase rather than to individual words. Let me give an example from some recent work I have been doing in another context. In a variety of computer applications and as a focal point of much research in computer science, there is a desire to develop question-answering systems so that when a question is input the computer can give back the correct answer. In analyzing a typical example much looked at because of its simplicity, namely, the geography of a set of countries, we might ask the question, "Does X have diplomatic relations with Y?" Now, if we take the simple approach that each single word designates a set-theoretical object, then the word *relation* in this context has a quite abstract set-theoretical object as its denotation. But, if instead, we take the phrase *diplomatic relations* as a denoting phrase, the parts of which do not denote, then a much simpler and more concrete set-theoretical object can be assigned to that phrase, namely, just what we expect as the ordinary binary relation between countries.

For some people the talk about set-theoretical objects will already seem somewhat abstract and perhaps obscure. It should be kept in mind that by set-theoretical object I ordinarily mean a fairly simple object like a class of individuals, a binary relation between individuals, etc. In ordinary talk anyway it is unusual to have set-theoretical objects of any really great complexity denoted by words or phrases occurring in the talk.

The next point of importance about the application of model-theoretic semantics to natural languages, as well as to formal languages, is that we cannot give an adequate account of meaning by assigning a denotation to individual words or phrases, or, as we would tend to say in grammatical context, by assigning denotations to the terminal words. Set-theoretical functions now enter in a second way, namely, in telling us how denotations of the various parts of the sentence are related. The analysis of how the various parts of a sentence are related in terms of meaning, that is, to put it explicitly now, what set-theoretical functions relate the denotations of the words occurring in the sentence, constitutes one important part of our intuitive idea of meaning.

Again, as in the case of the denotations of individual words, the set-theoretical functions that relate the denotations of individual words are ordinarily relatively simple in character. If I use the phrase *red books*, for instance, then the natural set-theoretical function for this phrase is the intersection of the set of red things and the set of books. The subtle thing about the semantical functions relating the various parts of a sentence is that the surface evidence for the choice of these semantic functions is considerably less evident than is the choice of the denotations of individual words or phrases. As far as I can see there is no escaping this difficulty. In one genuine and obvious sense, the semantic functions that represent the structure of meaning of a sentence are theoretical in character. The correctness of a given choice cannot be settled by any direct observational procedure, but rather only by indirect procedures of confirming predic-

(1)

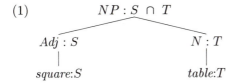

$$NP : S \cap T$$

$Adj : S$ $N : T$

square:S   table:T

tions, as for example, confirming a variety of predictions about responses to questions, executing actions taken in response to commands, etc. On the other hand, using a weaker standard of introspection, in many cases the selection of a particular set-theoretical function, seems obvious and natural to any native speaker of the language. It seems to me, for example, that this is the case with the selection of intersection in the case of *red books*. However, an example already given shows that this selection of function will not work uniformly with adjectives, namely, in the phrase *alleged dictators*.

If we look at a sentence of any complexity, it is natural to ask how the semantic functions that express the structure of the sentence, that is, the relationships between the denotations of the individual sentences or phrases, are to be built up. Fortunately, a straightforward answer is available to this question. With each production rule of the grammar there is associated a semantic function, and thus, we may convert each derivation tree for a given terminal utterance to a *semantic tree* by attaching not only labels to the nodes of the tree, but also denotations generated by the semantic functions.

Let us illustrate these ideas with some simple examples. Consider first the rewrite rule

$$NP \rightarrow Adj + N$$

The simple semantic function associated with this production rule is intersection of sets, as already discussed above. Using this production rule, let us construct the semantic tree for the phrase *square table*, (1). Let S be the set of square shaped things and T the set of tables. The denotation of each node of the tree is shown after the colon following the label of the node.

The semantic tree for the corresponding phrase in French, (2), looks very similar, except that a left-right reflection is made; however, the denotation of NP is left undisturbed, because intersection of sets is commutative.

I would like to say that an analogous use of intersection as the semantic function attached to the generating rule for simple noun phrases will

(2) $NP : S \cap T$

$N : T$ $Adj : S$

| |

table:T   carrée:S

suffice in a wide variety of languages. However, it is doubtful that this is the case, mainly because the grammatical structure of noun phrases is different in other languages. Consider an example from our Chinese corpus, written in pinyin notation with tones indicated by the numerals 1–4 to make possible linear processing of computer input and output. The example is *hong2 de hua1*, literally, *red of flower*, and more idiomatically, *red flower*. Because of the extensive use of the particle *de* (or *te*), restraint seems required in classifying *hong2* (*red* or *redness*) as an adjective. The semantical structure of this Chinese phrase is much like the English *capital of France* or the French *capitale de la France*.

To draw the semantic tree of the Chinese phrase, we need some notation. Let MOD be an adjective-or-adverb-forming particle. For sets A, B and f, where f intuitively is a function, let Ψ be the set-theoretical function defined as:

$$\Psi(A, B, f) = f_A(B),$$

and f is a choice function such that for each A, $f_A(B) \subseteq B$[1].

The tree is as shown on the following page.

Note that A is the set of red things, B is the set of flowers, and f is a function that selects a set of red flowers from the set of flowers. In other words, $f_A(B)$ is the set of red flowers.

---

[1]Such choice functions arise early in children's speech; I used them in Suppes (1973b) in the analysis of Roger Brown's classic corpus Adam I. In the earlier article I required that $f_A(B) \in B$, which makes f a standard set-theoretical choice function. I have come to feel that the better choice is that $f_A(B) \in PB$, i.e., in the power set of B, which is the set of all subsets of B, and for this purpose, we may write, as I have in the text, $f_A(B) \subseteq B$. In the present case we end up with

$$f_A(B) = A \cap B,$$

and it might be asked why not dispense with the function f and not let *de* denote at all? My present view of the matter is that we assign the semantic function Ψ to the rule

$$NP \rightarrow NP + MOD + NP.$$

We may want to replace the first NP not by an adjective, or an adjective-like word, but by a noun expressing possession as in *gelgel de shu1 (brother's book)*. Then intersection is totally inappropriate. Here $f_A(B)$ is the set of members of B possessed by A.

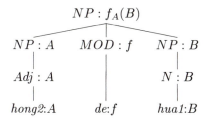

NUMERICAL ADJECTIVES

That the model-theoretic semantics can determine a choice between the generative or production rules of the grammar constructed for a corpus is nicely illustrated by the simple attributive use of numerical or cardinal concepts in children's speech. Let us begin with English and then look at some corresponding French and Chinese phrases. An example as good as any is *two red flowers*. A part of our noun-phrase grammar, very close to the one I developed earlier for Adam I in Suppes (1973b), might look like the following:

(3)

$$NP \rightarrow AdjP + N$$
$$AdjP \rightarrow AdjP + Adj$$
$$AdjP \rightarrow Car$$
$$AdjP \rightarrow Adj.$$

Here "$AdjP$" is a nonterminal symbol used to obtain a simple recursion for building up adjective phrases, and "Car" is a nonterminal symbol for cardinal number names. The last two rules of this grammar would most naturally have the identity function as its semantic function: each set is mapped into itself, and in the simple case the first two rules would have set intersection as the appropriate semantic function. Both identity and intersection functions have been used already; in trees (1) and (2) the lexical rules replacing *Adj* by *square*, etc., have the identity function as the semantic function. The semantic tree for *two red flowers* according to the grammar (3) would look like the tree of (4).

I have written "?" for the denotation that is not assignable at the node labeled "$AdjP$." The notation for the denotation of the root of the tree may look formidable, but its intuitive meaning is simple. I use the Frege-Russell concept of cardinal number: 2 is just the set of all pair sets.

(4)

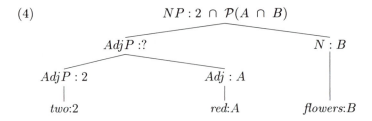

$NP : 2 \cap \mathcal{P}(A \cap B)$

$AdjP :?$ $N : B$

$AdjP : 2$ $Adj : A$

two:2   red:A   flowers:B

(To avoid standard paradoxes of set theory, I only consider members of sets a certain distance up the hierarchy of sets, functions, and relations—this is a technical problem of no real concern here.) The set $A \cap B$ is, as before, just the set of red flowers and $\mathcal{P}(A \cap B)$ is the power set of $A \cap B$, i.e., the family of all subsets of $A \cap B$.

It is important to realize that I am not suggesting that a speaker or listener of English is examining in any sense the entire set 2 or the large set $\mathcal{P}(A \cap B)$. A model of language is being provided within a standard set-theoretical framework. To provide a psychological theory of how the child comes to understand these denotations is a matter that in my judgment requires *still more* set-theoretical machinery, not a different sort of mathematical framework from the set-theoretical one I am using.

There is a simple solution to our problem of the grammar of *two red flowers*. It is to let the semantics guide the construction of the tree, and thus of the generative rules. The tree we want is something close to the tree of (5).

(5) $NP : 2 \cap \mathcal{P}(A \cap B)$

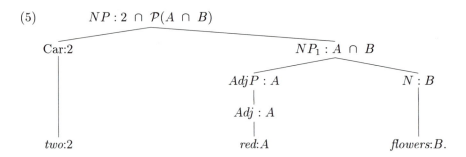

Car:2 $NP_1 : A \cap B$

$AdjP : A$ $N : B$

$Adj : A$

two:2   red:A   flowers:B.

And the partial grammar (3) should be revised to:

(6)

$$NP \rightarrow NP_1$$
$$NP \rightarrow Car + NP_1$$
$$NP_1 \rightarrow AdjP + N$$
$$AdjP \rightarrow AdjP + Adj$$
$$AdjP \rightarrow Adj.$$

In (5) and (6) the subscript "1" on "NP" has been introduced to impose a restriction that blocks a recursion of cardinal number names. At any simple and straightforward level, we do not want phrases such as *two three red flowers*.

The French phrase corresponding to *two red flowers* is *deux fleurs rouges*, even though it is much more uncommon in French to omit the definite article than it is in English. The semantic tree of (7) is the same as (5), except for the sort of left-right reflection that occurred in going from (1) to (2).

The corresponding Chinese semantic tree that includes a noun classifier (NC) and the particle *de* (MOD) is more complicated on the surface than the English or French trees, but the underlying semantics is similar. (Later we shall look at some children's phrases in Chinese that omit the noun classifier or particle, thus making them closer in surface structure to the English or French examples.)

Teresa Cheng and I currently feel that the simplest semantics for the noun classifiers is to let them denote the union of all the sets of objects denoted by the nouns they modify. (When an NC is used as a mechanism of pronominal reference something more must be said.)   On this assumption, our semantic tree for *liang3 duo3 hong2 de hua1* (two red flowers) is as shown on the following page.

(7)

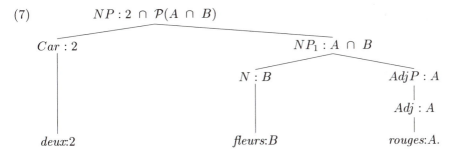

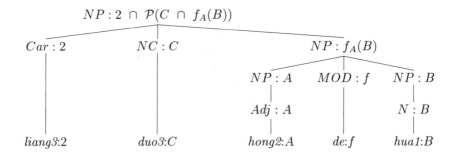

SAMPLE DATA

To show that the semantic functions I have been discussing are to be found in children's speech under the natural interpretation of what they are saying, I give some examples from Nina (English), Philippe (French) and Chi-Chi (Chinese).[2]

I begin with the intersection function for *Adj + N*. In the Chinese examples the particle *de* does not occur. Instances in which it does are listed below.

INTERSECTION FUNCTION

red fish	*aiguille rouge*	*hong2 hua1er1 (red flower)*
big bird	*grosse raquette*	*bai2 yi1shang (white dress)*
big kitty-cat	*bon côté*	*xiao3 yang2la4 (little candle)*
big moussie	*petits ronds*	*da4 gong1dian4 (big palace)*
tiny rabbit	*pauvres voitures*	*jin1 jildan4 (golden egg)*
tiny guitar	*petite aiguille*	*hei1 mian2yang2 (black lamb)*

In the case of French the position of the adjective does not change the semantic function, but a preliminary scan of the corpus does show a greater frequency of adjectives before nouns than the reverse in the early recordings of Philippe. The somewhat greater sophistication of the Chinese examples is at least partly a reflection that Chi-Chi is about six months older than Nina and Philippe.

---

[2]The recording and transcribing of Nina's speech has been done by Mrs. Florence Yager of the Institute's staff.

Next, let us look at the choice function as the semantics of possession.

CHOICE FUNCTION FOR POSSESSION

Mommy eyes	*raquette de papa*	*mian2yang2 de mao2*
		(lamb's hair)
rabbit splinter	*cordes de la raquette*	*ma1ma1 de hua4*
		(mother's talking)
horse feet	*trains de tracteurs*	*Qi3qi3 de shu1*
		(Chi-Chi's book)
dolly dress	*peau de Philippe*	*ge1ge1 de shu1*
		(brother's book)
		ba4ba4 de shu1
		(father's book)

The same uninflected patterns of possession in English are exhibited in Adam I. Analysis in terms of a choice function is given in Suppes (1973b) and will not be repeated here, except to note that for the English grammar, one production rule is

$$NP \rightarrow NP + NP$$

and the semantic tree is as seen below.

Use of cardinal number names in noun phrases as already discussed above is illustrated in the following examples

NUMBER FUNCTION

one rabbit	*une deux trois*	*wu3 ge4 xiao3toui, (five thieves)*
three ball		
two ladies		

In the Chinese example, the particle *de* does not occur, only the noun-classifier *ge4*. I emphasize that the frequency of cardinal number names is low in all three corpora.

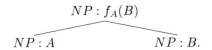

$$NP : f_A(B)$$

$$NP : A \qquad\qquad NP : B.$$

CONCLUDING REMARKS

Within the confines of this paper I have restricted myself to some of the simplest examples of semantic functions in the speech of young children. I believe the more complete identification of the set of such functions, and especially their sequence of appearance in the language of the child, will provide a new and significant way of looking at language acquisition. The relation of such functions to the linguistic concept of "deep structure" is apparent, but for a number of reasons that I cannot develop here I am not inclined to identify the two approaches.

An equally important aspect of model-theoretic semantics in the analysis of children's language is comparison of semantic functions across languages. The examples I have given bring out semantic similarities of English, French and Chinese, but they are really meant only to exhibit the methodology. More detailed and more quantitative comparisons are needed to assess the similarities and differences in a serious way.

Finally, I reiterate the main purpose of this paper. It is to show in an informal way how model-theoretic semantics may be used to give a straight-forward analysis of the meaning of children's language. Such an analysis is an essential element of any empirically adequate theory of language or language acquisition. That a systematic account of meaning is lacking in most discussions of language acquisition is surprising, at least on any common-sense view of what aspects of language are important. The methods I have outlined, which derive from the formal work of Frege in the 19th century and Tarski in the 1930's, can help to fill this lacuna.

8

SYNTAX AND SEMANTICS OF CHILDREN'S LANGUAGE

In this article I take a retrospective look at work in which I have been engaged with younger colleagues for a number of years. We now have at hand several large corpora of spoken English, one of French, and a smaller one of Mandarin Chinese. All of the speech is by young children, in the age range from 22 months to approximately 50 months, and by persons with them at the time, usually their parents. Previous reports of the work are to be found in Smith (1972), Suppes, (1974a, 1974b), Suppes, Léveillé, and Smith (1974), and Suppes, Smith and Léveillé (1972, 1973).

The first part describes the steps taken in the analysis, ending with the test of different developmental models of grammar. In the second part, I discuss various questions and issues that have currency in the continuing controversies about the nature of language acquisition. The matters addressed in the second part are related to the concrete details of the work outlined in the first part.

STEPS OF ANALYSIS

I have broken the process of analyzing the syntax and semantics of a child's speech into six steps, but there is nothing magical about the number six

*Reprinted from S.R. Harnad, H.D. Steklis, & J. Lancaster (Eds.), *Origins and evolution of language and speech. (Annals of the New York Academy of Sciences,* 1976, **280**, 227-237.) New York: New York Academy of Sciences, 1976.

and it would be easy to subdivide further or even to coalesce certain steps for some purposes. The six steps I have used are record, transcribe, write grammar, test probabilistic fit of grammar, construct semantics, and test developmental models.

Recording. The first step is to select a child and some part of his environment and to record his speech and that of the other persons around him for a selected number of hours. In our largest corpus, that of the speech of a young girl, Nina, recordings were made periodically from the time she was 23 months until she was 39 months; the resulting corpus of her speech alone consists of 102,230 tokens. In the case of Philippe's spoken French, running from the age of 25 months to 39 months, there are 56,982 tokens. A great deal of work in linguistics, psycholinguistics, and the philosophy of language does not depend in any way on the collection of a corpus; it seems to me, however, that the empirical study of children's speech must depend, at least partially, on the collection of data, and especially for the study of developmental models, a corpus collected over an extended period of time seems desirable.

Transcribing. After recordings have been made there remains the massive problem of transcribing the speech. The exact method of transcription will depend upon the interest of the investigator. For example, if the interest is primarily syntactical or semantical, a detailed transcription emphasizing either phonetic or prosodic features will probably not be made, in order to reduce somewhat the amount of effort required to obtain a workable transcription. This is the procedure we followed, and we have used normal word boundaries where possible. Thus, our transcriptions are not satisfactory for studies of the development of phonology or prosody. On the other hand, we have directly entered the transcriptions into the files of the Institute's PDP-10 computer system, and we are able to investigate the edited transcriptions in great systematic detail; the superb assortment of sophisticated programs written by Dr. Robert L. Smith for this purpose has been especially helpful.

Writing the grammar. The objective of this step is to write a generative grammar for the entire corpus of the child's speech. By and large we have attempted to write context-free grammars with transformations entering only where absolutely required. The level of complexity of children's speech in the age range mentioned above is sufficiently low that most of the spoken speech fits rather naturally into a context-free grammar, but we have no ideological position against transformations and believe they should be used whenever simplifications of the grammar results.

The initial measure of success is the percentage of the utterances of the corpus that are parsed by the grammar, but already the use of such an evaluation measure has to be treated with care. It would, for example, be trivial in every case to write a universal grammar in terms of the vocabulary such that any concatenation of the child's vocabulary would be a well-formed utterance and thus the grammar would properly parse any utterance whatsoever. What is to be regarded as a natural restriction on the grammar in the case of a young child's speech is not obvious, although in practice what is done by a great many investigators is to write a grammar that deviates from the standard adult usage only when necessary. Of course, with this approach the grammar is simpler than one concerned with adult usage but corresponds rather closely to a fragment of adult usage with certain notable exceptions. In broad terms, this is the strategy adopted by Suppes, Smith and Léveillé (1973) for the spoken French of Philippe.

Excellent examples of the construction of such grammars are to be found in the books and articles of Roger Brown and his collaborators (1970, 1973).

Testing the probabilistic fit of the grammar. For persons with a background in mathematical models in the social sciences, especially probabilistic models, a natural further step to take to tighten the criteria for goodness of fit of the grammar is to introduce probabilistic parameters for each production rule and to estimate these parameters from the data. On the basis of the estimated parameters, a straightforward goodness-of-fit test in standard statistical terms can be applied to the grammar. Psycholinguists who are not familiar with parametric models or linguists who abhor statistical linguistics find this step from writing a grammar to testing its probabilistic fit a difficult one to accept. I have engaged in polemics on this matter several times in the past (1970, 1973b), and so I shall not engage in a further defense here. I can say from experience that the attempt to fit a grammar probabilistically can lead to insightful and important changes in the details of the grammar. What it especially affects is the level at which various production rules are introduced. A common effect of fitting a probabilistic grammar is to raise in the hierarchy of rules the position of those that generate holophrastic utterances, that is, single-word utterances that seem to have the semantic content of complete utterances but not the grammatical form.

Constructing semantics. The next step is to put a semantic hand into the syntactical glove and show that it fits snugly. The approach in this case is to assign to each production rule of the grammar a semantic function and to build in an appropriate way a model-theoretic semantics for the child's speech. This approach is outlined in Suppes (1974a), and a detailed working out for the corpus of Erica is to be found in Smith (1972). If the grammar is fully written before the semantics is begun, in all likelihood the working out of the semantics will cause a revision in the grammar. If space permitted I would illustrate this point with examples of grammatical production rules that are often suggested by linguists but that cannot lead to a reasonable semantics. Examples of this character and a detailed discussion of such matters as the semantics of propositional attitudes in children's speech are discussed in Suppes (1974b).

I shall have something more to say about model-theoretic semantics below and so I shall not attempt a further explication at this point. I do, however, want to make the point that model-theoretic semantics for children's speech and for natural language in general is a natural outgrowth of the long tradition of semantics in logic and philosophy, a tradition that has been too much ignored, at least until recently, by most linguists and psycholinguists.

Testing of developmental models. With a systematic syntactical and semantical apparatus at hand it is then possible to test specific developmental models of children's language. The overview of development does not have to be restricted to consideration of a few salient instances of speech, but can be examined in a more systematic and global way. From the standpoint of development of grammar it is a virtue of the probabilistic approach that it provides a natural tool for studying grammatical development. In Suppes, Léveillé, and Smith (1974), specific alternative models of an incremental or discrete-stage sort are tested, and I shall have something later to say about what I term the myth of stages.

Roughly speaking, the methodology is this. The grammar, and if desired the semantics as well, can be written to cover the entire range of the corpus, but then probabilistic parameters can be estimated for each block of time. The changes in the parameters directly reflect changes in the uses of grammatical rules, some of the more complex rules, for example, having probability zero in the early period. Alternative models then deal with the conceptual way in which the changes in usage of rules take place. The two natural and simple polar opposites are a continuous incremental model versus an all-or-none stage model. In the data we have analyzed thus far, the continuous incremental model is supported more by the data, although, as is not surprising, neither model, given its simplicity, has as good a fit as one would like.

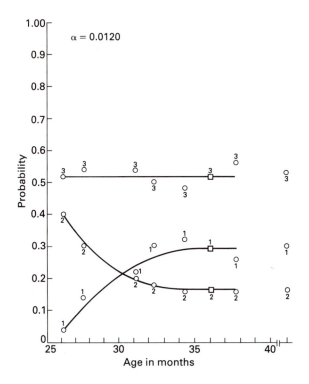

Figure 1. FIT OF INCREMENTAL MODEL FOR PRODUCTION RULES AT THE HIGHEST LEVEL.

These ideas about developmental models may be illustrated by drawing on the data and analysis given in Suppes, Léveillé, and Smith (1974). The basic assumptions of the all-or-none stage model are two. First, development is discontinuous and may be represented by a relatively small number of stages. Second, within each stage there is a constant probability of a rule being used. The specific assumption appropriate to this situation is that the probabilities of rules being used within a given stage constitute a multinomial distribution, and thus satisfy assumptions of independence and stationarity. In the data reported in Suppes, Léveillé, and Smith (1974), six distinct time sections were analyzed. Thus, by having six stages, a perfect fit to the data would be obtained. In order to have a reasonable test and also because of the relatively restricted time span, a two-stage model was tested against a linear incremental model. From rather natural qualitative assumptions the following equation is de-

rived for the incremental model in the report (1974). The exponential
distribution occurring in the model is a natural generalization for the
continuous-time assumption of the usual geometric distribution characteristic of discrete time processes. The equation is:

$$p(t, r) = \pi_r - (\pi_r - p_r)e^{-\alpha(t - t_1)}$$

where t is the time parameter, r is a given grammatical rule, π_r is the
asymptotic probability of r's being used, p_r is the initial probability of
the rule being used at the beginning of time t_1 in which observations were
made of Philippe's beginning French, and α is the learning parameter
estimated from the data.

As remarked, the fit of the incremental model was considerably better.
I exhibit in several figures the sense of that fit. In these figures, Philippe's
age in months is plotted on the abscissa, and the ordinate shows the
probability of use of the rules. The rules are divided into subgroups, and
thus the probabilities are conditional probabilities of use within a given
subgroup. The curves, labelled in square boxes, show the theoretical
functions predicted by the incremental model. The data points of the
individual rules are numbered; for example, the numeral 1 in a circle
indicates a data point for rule 1 of the group, etc.

Figure 1 shows data for the highest level rules in the grammar, for
example, production rules for sentences. The production rules, beginning
with the start symbol S of the grammar, divide the types of utterances
into: first, short utterances consisting primarily of adverbs, locutions,
interjections, and numerals; second, utterances consisting of noun phrases
and adjective phrases that stand as utterances without a verb; and, finally,
utterances in which a verb is present or questions that occur with or
without a verb.

Figure 2 shows the data and theoretical curves of top-level rules that
produce incomplete utterances. Figure 3 shows the data and theoretical curves for the rules that generate object noun phrases, that is, noun
phrases that occur as objects and not as subjects of verbs. The rules for
incomplete utterances mainly generate terminal nodes directly to which
it is then only necessary to apply lexical rules. The rules for producing
object noun phrases have the form one would expect, but they also have
some special features that will not be examined here for noun phrases in
object position.

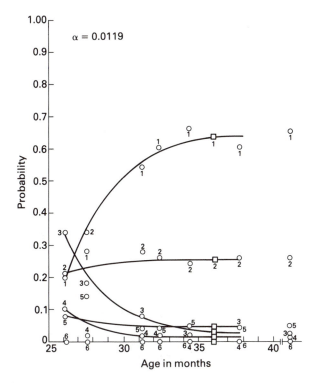

Figure 2. FIT OF INCREMENTAL MODEL FOR HIGH-LEVEL PRODUCTION RULES GENERATING INCOMPLETE UTTERANCES.

Figure 4 shows data and theoretical curves for rules that produce verb phrase structures. The 15 rules of this group have been generated into seven subgroups in order to consolidate the data. The first subgroup consists of the single main rule represented by Curve 1, which generates simple verb phrases. (What I mean by *simple* will be clear from the description of the other subgroups.) Subgroup 2 generates verb phrases that begin with a preposition or a personal pronoun. Subgroup 3 introduces auxiliaries, and Subgroup 4 generates several sorts of verb phrases that include an auxiliary or a modal. Subgroup 5 generates verb phrases with a modal followed by a verb phrase that begins with a preposition or a personal pronoun. Subgroup 6 generates verb phrases with a modal followed by a simple verb phrase, that is, one governed by Subgroup 1. Finally, Subgroup 7 generates verb phrases with a personal pronoun before the modal or the auxiliary. As can be seen and as would be expected, the simple verb phrases generated by Subgroup 1 dominate Philippe's usage

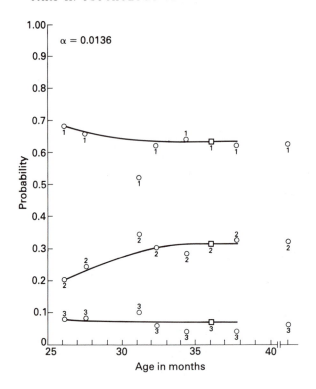

Figure 3. FIT OF INCREMENTAL MODEL FOR PRODUCTION RULES GEN-
ERATING OBJECT NOUN PHRASES.

of verb phrase structures. The fit of theory to data is especially good
for Figure 4. It is to be emphasized that what I have given is a very
brief description of a considerably more complicated analysis in Suppes,
Léveillé, and Smith (1974).

QUESTIONS AND ISSUES

Size of grammar. I have in the past characterized the present stage of
our knowledge of how to construct grammars of children's speech as the
pre-Ptolemaic stage. What I have in mind is that we do not yet seem
to have even the degree of fundamental insight characteristic of Greek
astronomy with respect to the subtle and complicated data it faced. One
way of expressing this concern is by considering the large size of all of the
grammars I know of that have attempted to encompass a corpus in com-

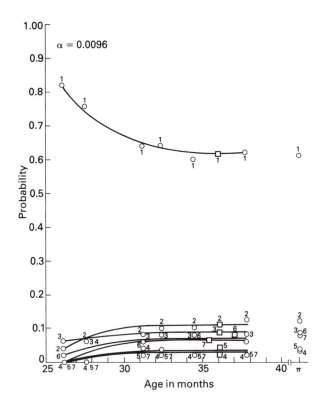

Figure 4. FIT OF INCREMENTAL MODEL FOR PRODUCTION RULES GEN-
ERATING VERB PHRASE STRUCTURES.

plete detail. The grammar, for example, that we have written for Philippe
(1974) is already extremely large, consisting of more than 300 rules, and
yet the grammar does not reflect all of the requirements of inflection nor
does it fit more than about 75 percent of the utterances in the corpus.
This might be thought to be a part of the irregularity and spontaneity of a
young child's first speech, but something like the same situation obtains
when we turn to what should be one of the most regimented domains
one can think of: written language of elementary mathematics. The dissertation of Nancy Smith (1974) was directed at the problem of writing
a grammar for the written language of elementary-school mathematics.

This seems like a simple, relatively artificial fragment of English, but in fact it turns out to be as full of difficult and subtle problems as the corpus of any of the children's speech we have discussed. It is awe inspiring to contemplate what must be the full set of rules required to describe the speech of a young child from the age of 24 months to 48 months. I suspect we are not approaching the problem in the correct way, but what I do not have is a good insight as to how to change the approach and I see no reasonable alternatives available to us in the work of others.

Nature of semantics. It is a commonplace that constructive production of speech as meaningful commentary in a given perceptual and social context could scarcely proceed simply on the basis of model-theoretic semantics as a complete theory of meaning. There are many ways of stating the difficulty. One way is that it will not do to talk about the set of red objects as the extension of the concept *red* in the world as it is. Other more constructive methods of computing along intensional lines are surely required. The model-theoretic semantics we have used in our analyses is meant to provide an analysis of semantics and correspondingly to provide a theory of meaning of children's speech at the level of abstraction characteristic of set theory in general.

I have come to recognize what I feel is the root of misunderstanding on the part of many psycholinguists and some linguists about the nature of model-theoretic semantics. It is characteristic of a great deal of empirical work in psycholinguistics that is concerned with the acquisition of meaning of individual words. The problem of how children acquire the meaning of individual words is an important and central one, but it is only one part of an adequate theory of meaning. What has been the primary concern in logic and philosophy has been the development of a theory to account for the meaning of a complex utterance as built up from the meaning of its parts. This is the problem that Frege recognized as central to a theory of meaning, and it was first given a constructive and concrete formulation in Tarski's famous monograph on truth (1935). Model-theoretic semantics is addressed to the problem of giving an account of how the meaning of the whole is built up from the meaning of its parts—I here use *meaning* in a way that includes the theory of reference and the theory of truth or satisfaction. What goes on in the child's head will need more detailed constructive characterization. The many sophisticated efforts currently under way to characterize procedural semantics for computer programming languages provide perhaps one of the best lines of attack on this problem. I do want to emphasize that out of the tradition of psycholinguistics proper, or linguistics itself, there has been as yet no really serious competitor to model-theoretic semantics and there is no evidence that either psycholinguists or linguists will offer on their own a serious theory of meaning. The chances do seem good that within the framework of computer science the proper constructive extension of model-theoretic semantics is being put together and will be ready for appropriate mutation as a theory of the semantics of natural language. Development of procedural semantics for children's language is, in my judgment, the most important next step in the theory of children's language.

Myth of stages. The developmental models described earlier, in which we tested the two alternative hypotheses of incremental change or all-or-none change by stages, decisively supported the incremental change, even though the detailed fit of neither model was as good as could be expected. The talk about stages has affected the conceptual apparatus of psycholinguistics to such an extent that the myth of the reality of stages will not be easily eradicated. On another occasion (1973c) I have criticized the myth of stages in Piagetian theory. The ubiquitous use of the concept of stages by Piaget has encouraged a similar use in psycholinguistics. In view of the lack of serious tests in almost all cases of alternative hypotheses, the presumed existence of stages has exactly the epistemological status reserved for myths. From the evidence I know about, language development at the level ordinarily discussed by psychologists proceeds by continuous change and not by stages. The case for stages is to be found in the microlevel of the learning of individual items of great simplicity. At this microlevel, evidence for stages can be found, as was demonstrated amply in the early 1960s in the enormous literature on this subject in mathematical learning theory. There is, in contrast, no serious evidence in support of stages on the scale of a child's language performance between the ages of 18 months and 36 months, if we have in mind grouping his development within five or six stages, and not at the level of calling the learning of each new word a stage.

On the other hand, it is clearly an open research problem for the future to characterize in a more precise and satisfactory manner the actual development of children's language. The models and theories we have at hand at present are clearly too simplistic and too simple to do an adequate job.

Nativism and rationalism. The strongly empirical tone I have adopted might lead to the conclusion that I advocate some simple empiricism as the appropriate framework for a detailed theory of children's acquisition of language. This is not the case. A simple *tabula rasa* theory seems to me as much out of place as a correspondingly simple rationalistic theory. Platitudes about these matters are easy. A child obviously comes to the age of language learning with an enormously flexible apparatus for perception and learning, much of it clearly fine tuned to what he will hear. We have, it seems to me, as yet too little theoretical definiteness about the way in which children acquire language to parcel out the variance between genetic endowment and environmental influences. The extensive empirical work we have done on children's language over the past seven years seems to weigh very little on either side of the issues, except perhaps to discourage premature closure on any simple theoretical position.

There is one amusing point of numerical comparison that I sometimes like to use when engaged in dialogue with nativists. Elementary computations on the corpora we have collected indicate that a child between the ages of 24 months and 36 months will produce a half a million utterances and will hear from his parents and other persons almost a million utterances. This is just in the one-year span. In contrast, a child who is learning elementary-school mathematics will ordinarily work at most about 4,000 exercises a year for a total of 24,000. In gross terms, these data suggest that the more developed innate potential really present in children is arithmetic and not linguistic. All children do not learn arithmetic simply because they do not get the few thousand trials needed to activate the rationalist potential. Given similarly limited exposure to language, certainly the same would be true. Perhaps arithmetic should replace language as the new nativist stronghold.

Theses about expressive power. In other papers in this volume there has been considerable dispute about the relative expressive power of various natural languages. Keenan, for example, has defended the thesis that natural languages vary greatly in their expressive power. Katz, on the other hand, has essentially advocated the thesis that all natural languages have the same expressive power. To make the discussion interesting, additional distinctions are needed. There is, for example, a large literature in logic coming at the problem of expressive power from a number of different directions, and a variety of interesting results has been established. I am not suggesting for a moment that the results in logic can be interpreted in any direct way as bearing on the issue of what is the expressive power of a given natural language. What that tradition does suggest, however, is that it is important to think in terms of appropriate kinds of distinctions and to settle the issue not once and for all but in terms of a particular aspect of the general and vague concept of expressive power. For example, the many interesting results established by Tarski (1953) for the interpretability of one theory expressible in first-order logic in terms of another introduces a number of concepts that seem applicable with appropriate changes to the current controversy. I restrict myself to one other example, a more recent one. In general discussions of elementary logic it is standard dogma to make the point that definitions play no essential role if they are proper, that is, if they satisfy the standard criteria of eliminability and noncreativity. Working practice in logic and mathematics shows very well that this is far from the case. Any substantial mathematical theory requires the introduction of a succession of definitions to be manageable, to have, in other words, the right expressive power. One thesis lurking in the background in discussing the expressive power of natural languages is that one can always define new concepts by the resources available in the language. Thus, if we take a primitive language, the claim would be we could bring it up to the standards of modern science by appropriate introduction of new terms by definition. The plain man would, of course, regard this much-extended language as a new language, and so claims about the expressive power of the thus extended language would not amount to the same thing as claims about the original language. The rationalist who believes in the quality of the expressive power of all natural languages might want to report that he can in principle dispense with the new terms by using their definitions and by expanding any scientific language back into the original language. I do not believe that any rationalist precisely holds that such explicit expansion into the original natural language of all scientific terminology is possible, but approximations to this thesis seem to be present and sufficiently close to make the point I want to make. The point is that the expressive power of languages with or without explicit definitions is of quite a different character. This can be shown in several ways, but let me just cite one interesting recent example. Statman (1974) has shown that if we consider mathematical argument or proofs as an example of expressive power, and if we use the genus of the graph of a proof as the measure of its complexity, then there is no upper bound on the genus of proofs that result from eliminating the use of explicit definitions. In other words, if the genus of a proof that uses explicit definitions is n, then a proof of unbounded complexity is in some cases required of the same theorem once explicit definitions are eliminated. Clearly the case of mathematical proofs is rather special, but it is exactly around issues of complexity that the more detailed discussion of expressive power should center; and it would be my conjecture that as the discussion becomes more definite and specific, examples can be constructed of conceptual importance that support Keenan's thesis.

In contrast, in examining the grammar and semantics of English, French, and Chinese that we have constructed for the children's speech available to us, we have found no significant differences in expressive power; or if they do exist in the corpora we are not sensitive to them.

On the basis of what evidence I have seen, fragmentary though it may be, I could imagine myself believing a thesis of approximately uniform expressive power for most natural languages as used by very young children, but being skeptical that such a uniformity thesis can be maintained as we move up the scale to older and more sophisticated speakers and listeners.

9

STEPS TOWARD A VARIABLE-FREE SEMANTICS OF ATTRIBUTIVE ADJECTIVES, POSSESSIVES, AND INTENSIFYING ADVERBS

In this article we attempt to give a model-theoretic semantics for some adjectives and noun phrases drawn from a corpus of speech collected from 15 black children ranging in age from 6 to 7 years. The fact that the children are black has little to do with the grammar and semantics. The speech of the children is very close to standard English. What we have tried to do is give a semantics that applies in almost all standard contexts to the kind of noun phrases exhibited here. Details about the corpus are given in the Appendix.

It is not possible to review the extensive and subtle literature on adjectives in linguistics and philosophy, but we do want to comment on some of the issues that have been discussed and that are most pertinent to our own analysis. In the heyday of transformational approaches to grammar (e.g., Chomsky, 1957), it was often claimed that predicative adjectives

*Reprinted from K. Nelson (Ed.), *Children's Language*, Vol. 1. New York: Gardner Press, 1978, pp 81-115. Written with Elizabeth Macken.

were primary and that attributive uses of adjectives were derived from predicative. Thus, for example, a relative clause construction would be used for the underlying deep structure to express *a tall man* as a *man who is tall*. Criticisms of this viewpoint have come from many quarters and for many different reasons. Perhaps the best is the existence of many attributive adjectives that cannot be expressed in any straightforward way as predicative, for example, *the corporate officer, the main speaker*, and that old chestnut, *alleged dictator*. Good discussions of these matters are to be found in Bolinger (1967) and Sussex (1974), as well as in the dissertation of Siegel (1976) which provides an excellent review of many of the issues we will mention, even though we do not agree with her on the way in which they should be resolved in all cases. In line with the more recent views just mentioned, we have treated attributive adjectives as capable of grammatical and semantical construction, independent of predicative use of many of the same adjectives.

A second issue that is closer to the core of the present article and a difficult one is the absence of any agreed-upon classification of attributive adjectives in the literature. What we have called *classifying* adjectives are often called absolute adjectives or intersective adjectives because of their simple semantic properties. Examples, at least that we have so classified, from our corpus are *bald, black, brave,* and *fancy* (a longer list is given in Table 1).

TABLE 1

CLASSIFYING ADJECTIVES

(a) African house	(a) green one
American ship	Indian boat
(his, these) baggy pants	Indian guide
(a) bald head	Indian house
(this) black cat	Indian war
black cats	Japanese bee
(this) blue one	Japanese sticks
(the) brave men	(the) poor people
(a) brown puppy	skinny legs
Chinese food	skinny one
Chinese sticks	(a) strange kind
(the) Disneyland submarine	(a) white girl
(a) Eskimo house	(that, a) white house
fancy pants	white people
(a) German plane	(a) wiggly bike
(his) gold one	(a) yellow airplane
green grass	(the) yellow house

Another classification that is used is that of measure adjectives, for example, *tall* or *heavy*, which we have called intensive adjectives. We have called such adjectives *intensive* rather than *measure* adjectives to reflect the fact that, in many cases, only a qualitative ordering rather than a cardinal measure underlies the meaning of the adjective. In fact, we would maintain that this is the case even for the use of intensive adjectives that have a proper physical theory of measurement, for example, *big* or *old*, because the quantitative theory is usually not assumed in the qualitative semantics of ordinary talk (this point will become clear in the analysis we give later). The issue of whether to call such adjectives intensive adjectives or measure adjectives is not a serious one. A more difficult issue is that of classifying a variety of instances about which there seems to be little agreement. Siegel (1976), for example, wants to exclude from the class of intensive adjectives many comparatives. Her basic test is that such comparatives do not permit a *for a* interpretation. By this she means that one can say such sentences as *Sally is tall* (for a girl). It seems to us that the priority of argument is incorrect here. The ability to form a comparative is better evidence for an adjective being intensive than the *for a* interpretation. This is not the place to make the argument in detail but it does provide a way of formulating how our classification disagrees with hers. We say more about this issue later, once the semantics we consider for intensive adjectives is introduced. Our semantics is different from hers and justifies in a more detailed way the remark we just made about comparatives. In this connection, we have also introduced a distinction between intensive adjectives and comparison adjectives. Thus, *tall* is an intensive adjective, but *taller* is a comparison adjective. Comparatives as such did not really occur in our corpus, but superlatives did and the exact semantic meaning of a superlative is not the same as that of the related intensive adjective. It could be said that comparison adjectives constitute a proper subset of intensive adjectives in our treatment, but they do need to be singled out as a separate subset with special properties of their own.

We have called certain adjectives *function* adjectives; they are discussed by almost everybody, but not always with exactly the same definition in mind. Typical instances are such adjectives as *alleged*, and also nouns that play the role of adjectives, as in *birthday party*, *train ride*, and *fire engines*, all of which occur in our corpus. The disagreement with Siegel in this case is that she would require the use of intensions to give a proper account of such function adjectives in general.

This last remark takes us to the third issue we consider, that of intensionality. To avoid any misunderstanding, let us emphasize at the very beginning that we do not deny the necessity of recognizing intensional contexts. Some theory of intensionality is required for any adequate theory of propositional attitudes, and, furthermore, such expressions of propositional attitudes occur with high frequency very early in a child's development of language. For example, as reported in Suppes (1974b), expressions of the propositional attitude of wanting, as in *I wanna cookie*, constitute somewhat over 1 percent of a large corpus of a young child from the age of 2 to $3\frac{1}{2}$ years. On the other hand, we are not at all persuaded that the proper distinction between extensional and intensional context is drawn in Siegel (1976), for she makes this distinction the fundamental distinction in two kinds of adjectives. Thus, in her example *Marya is a beautiful dancer*, under one reading *beautiful* is a classifying adjective that is absolute and extensional, and in the other reading it is relative, intensional, and, as she puts it, nonintersective, because the basic semantic function is not intersection. She claims that "the meaning of a nonintersective adjective is always relative to that of the common noun it modifies" (p. 3). This view, which is central to her intensional claim, is not thoroughly defended in any sense at all, and it is one that we are skeptical of. We very much agree on the existence of nonintersective adjectives, that is, ones that are not simply classifying adjectives, but there is no agreement about the intensionality claim she makes, and, in fact, the theory of meaning that seems to underlie the quotation just given is far from clear. We allude to various intensional contexts in the body of our article, but the general semantical ideas we advance do not require an intensional commitment to any one class of adjectives and we doubt that such a claim can be made to stick.

We take up some other issues, especially that of logical form, in the context of setting forth our own viewpoint toward semantics. Our approach has been to write a context-free grammar and to associate with each rule of the grammar a semantic function. (The restriction to a context-free grammar is not essential.) Let us illustrate these ideas with a simple example. Consider the following production rule, where NP = Noun Phrase, $CAdj$ = Classifying Adjective, and N = Noun:

$$NP \rightarrow CAdj + N.$$

The simple semantic function associated with this production rule is intersection of sets, as already discussed above. Using this production rule, let us construct the semantic tree for the phrase *black cat*, which occurs in our corpus. Let B be the set of black things and C the set of cats. The denotation of each node of the tree is shown in Figure 1 after the colon following the label of the node. Once the denotation of terminal words or phrases is fixed, then the denotation of each labelled node of a derivation tree is fixed recursively by the semantic functions associated with the production rules. This approach has been described in detail in Suppes

Figure 1. SEMANTIC TREE FOR *black* CAT.

(1970, 1973b); an extensive example of such an application to a corpus is provided in Smith (1972). The present article, along with Suppes (1976), extends this earlier work in several substantive ways.

The general assumptions underlying our analysis need to be made explicit, in order that the viewpoint from which we approach the task will be clear to the reader. First, the analysis is set-theoretical, not procedural, in character. This does not mean that we are negative about procedural semantics, but rather that we have selected for the present level of analysis the simpler methods of a set-theoretical sort. Second, the analysis is extensional rather than intensional, a point already discussed above and to be returned to later.

Third, the set-theoretical semantics has been restricted still further by the elimination of variables, including either free or bound variables. This approach, via extended relation algebras using only a notation of constants and operations on constants, has already been set forth in Suppes (1976). The viewpoint is further developed in this article. In many of the analyses of the semantics of natural language, there has been a commitment to expressing the "meaning" of English sentences in first-order (predicate) logic. Several of the more subtle philosophical articles about adjectives (e.g., Parsons, 1970; Wheeler, 1972) are committed to this view that the logical form of natural-language expressions should be put in first-order logic. We find such a commitment to first-order logic as unwieldy a restriction in the case of natural language as it is in many other domains to which we want to apply formal mathematical analysis. In fact, perhaps the central weakness of the work of Parsons and Wheeler is the absence of apparatus to account for the actual structure of natural-language utterances. In many ways, we believe that the framework of relation algebras without variables, further extended in this article, is a more suitable one.

Fourth, we emphasize that not every node of a semantic tree denotes, but that semantic information is carried from one node to another only by the denotation. A liberalization needed to handle intensifying adverbs is discussed in the last part of this article. The viewpoint extends the one developed earlier, for example, in Suppes (1973b).

Fifth, an explicit remark about denotations is useful. We have mentioned the use of extended relation algebras, but it is perhaps worthwhile to make explicit the commitment behind this use. The denotations of nodes of semantic trees that do denote are restricted to either individuals, sets of individuals, or relations among individuals. The relation-algebraic viewpoint restricts the further use of denotations so that, for example, control structure or function words like *of* or quantifiers like *all* or *some* do not denote.

Our original intent was to give a rather complete model-theoretic semantics for all the noun phrases from our corpus. But we found that our efforts created more questions than we could adequately answer. What we will cover here are primarily the semantics of attributive adjectives and possessives, either singly or in various combinations. We also consider at the end the complications introduced by intensifying adverbs. We will not include here the semantics of quantifiers, articles, or demonstratives, but in our examples of noun phrases containing descriptive adjectives, we have included noun phrases that may be headed in our corpus by an article or a demonstrative. We assume that the semantic functions for articles or demonstratives operate on the remaining noun phrase essentially as a unit, so that whatever semantics we give for the adjectives will apply in the same way whether or not the unit is preceded by an article or demonstrative. In the same spirit of simplification, we have omitted the ultimately necessary distinction between singular and plural noun phrases.

Before turning to the details of our analysis, we would like to comment on a disparity that is apparent between the philosophical and logical literature on meaning and the linguistics literature that depends on it, on the one hand, and, on the other, the psycholinguistic literature that grows out of the long tradition of dictionary construction. The concern in the logical literature is to give an analysis of semantics in terms of how the parts of an utterance are put together to determine the meaning of the entire utterance. The concern in psycholinguistics, however, has primarily been the meaning of individual words. Brown (1973) has a good deal to say about the meanings of individual words and even about the meanings of verb inflections, e.g., imperatives, but he does not face at any point the Fregean task of trying to understand how children put the meanings of individual words together to construct the meaning of a complex utterance. Without this constructive putting together of individual meanings, there can be no serious theory of meaning—as the enormous literature in logic and philosophy has surely demonstrated by this time. We recognize, however, that the attention given to the meanings of individual words and how children acquire them represents an important and necessary part of the picture. We have introduced this distinction to emphasize that the present article is almost entirely concerned with the Fregean task of analyzing how the semantics of the whole is built up from the parts.

We have organized the detailed analysis into four main sections. The first deals with the semantics of the various types of attributive adjectives already briefly discussed above. The second is concerned with possessives, both adjectives and nouns, which occur in noun phrases. The third deals with combinations of adjectives (including possessives) in the formation of longer noun phrases. And finally, the last main section addresses the subtle problems generated by intensifying adverbs. We return in the summary section at the end to some of the general issues raised in this introduction.

ATTRIBUTIVE ADJECTIVES

As indicated earlier, we have divided descriptive adjectives into four categories—classifying adjectives, intensive adjectives, comparison adjectives, and function adjectives. We will sketch briefly the semantic function of each category using examples in which the noun phrase consists of one adjective plus the noun. We will then discuss problems that arise when more than one adjective precedes the noun.

Classifying adjectives. Table 1 (presented earlier) shows all of the singleton classifying adjective noun phrases we found in the corpus. Examples include *a yellow airplane, a wiggly bike,* and *the brave men.* The classifying adjectives have the simplest set-theoretic function—just that of intersection. For example, if Y is the set of yellow things and A is the set of airplanes, then their intersection, $Y \cap A$, gives the set of yellow airplanes.

Siegel (1976) has advanced what she terms a doublet theory of adjectives which requires that what we have called classifying adjectives also have, in her terms, an intensional interpretation, and in our terms an intensive interpretation. From our standpoint this is illustrated by the ability to form comparatives out of many classifying adjectives as, for example, *John is redder than Bill.* We do not have any examples from our corpus and will not explore the matter here, but we do agree with her about the possibility of two interpretations. Where we disagree is in the manner in which she construes such examples as being intensional in character. It seems evident that there is a strong tendency to convert classifying adjectives into intensive adjectives and to apply intensifying adverbs to these adjectives as, for example, in *Bill is very red.*

TABLE 2
INTENSIVE ADJECTIVES

(a,that) bad boat	(a) little baby	long hair
(these) bad boats	(a) little bear	(the) long hand
(the) bad guys	(a) little bit	long sideburns
(a,that) bad jet	(a) little body	(a) new bike
bad mags*	(a) little boy	(the) old days
bad natural	(a) little brother	(that) old horn
(that) bad one	little cars	old house
(a) bad plane	(a) little dog	(the) old kind
(a) big building	(a) little duck	(a) old lady
(a) big dog	(the) little hand	(a) old man
(a) big Great-Dane	(a) little head	old men
(that) big hand	little houses	(the) old one
(a) big one	(a) little one	(that) old put-put
big people	little puppies	(the) old timers
funny airplane	(a) little ship	(that) old train
(that) funny bike	(a) little table	(a) old woman
(those) funny bikes	little teeth	(a) tiny one
(those) funny elephants	(a) little thing	(the) skinny one
funny hopscotch	(a) little tire	ugly planes
(the) good guys	(a) little way	
(the) good part	(a) little wheel	

*Reference, in slang, to a jazzy decoration on a bicycle

Intensive adjectives. Singleton intensive adjective phrases are listed in Table 2. At first glance, it might appear that intersection is appropriate for these adjectives too. To assign a semantic function to a *little bear*, for example, one might try intersecting the set of little things with the set of bears. The well-known problem with this analysis is that the set of little things, that is, little things relative to all things in the universe, might not include any bears at all, in which case the intersection would be empty.

We have called such adjectives *intensive* because there is often an implied scale of measurement—at least an ordinal scale and usually a stronger sort—underlying their use. From the standpoint of the theory of measurement, it would be more natural to call them *ordinal* adjectives, so as to include ordinal scales that are not interval or ratio scales, but this usage seemed ruled out by the linguistic tendency to think of ordinal adjectives as the ordinal number names *first, second,* etc. Interval scales are instances of *intensive* measurement, and so we have moved up to this level for terminology, although our semantic theory is much weaker and more general than that of interval scales. From a measurement stand-point some intensive adjectives, e.g., *long,* designate ratio scales, i.e., they imply procedures of extensive measurement, but the distinction between intensive and extensive measurement does not seem especially salient in the ordinary use of adjectives and so we have ignored it.

Our semantical approach is to have an intensive adjective denote an irreflexive, strict partial ordering relation—in the case of *little,* an order-ing by size. The noun phrase consisting of the adjective and a noun then denotes an initial segment of the set denoted by the noun and ordered by the relation. For example, let L denote an ordering relation that or-ders objects by size with the smallest first, and let B denote the set of bears. We assume that the dimension of the ordering—area, volume, and so forth—is selected by the context. Then the denotation of *little bears* is $IS(B, L, c) = \{y : y \in B \& yLc\}$ where c is a criterion object selected to use in evaluating the relative size of bears. (The letters IS are mnemonic for initial segment.) If we extended our extensional semantic approach to a procedural semantics, the criterion object c would be replaced by a procedure to determine whether an object met the appropriate size crite-rion. We believe that such a procedural semantics is psychologically more realistic than our extensional approach, but—and this is the important point—clarity about the extensional theory is a necessary prerequisite for clarity about the richer and more complicated procedural approach.

Wheeler (1972) has used, instead of a criterion object, a reference class. Thus, in his theory, an attributive is a two-term relation between an individual and a class of individuals. Our basic view is that the analysis should be procedural and a choice of a criterion object is a move in that direction away from the full extensionality of a class. Actually, the matter is probably very complicated psychologically. In some cases, indeed, it is likely that a person using an intensive adjective has in memory an ideal case of the given attribute, and anything that lies beyond this ideal case or near to it satisfies the noun phrase in which the intensive adjective occurs. The child who uses the noun phrase *a little tire* may remember a small tire he thinks of for comparison and judge the tire in question to be smaller than that criterion object held in memory. In other cases, a purely procedural, not directly referential criterion could well be used. It would be our conjecture that both kinds of cases are fairly frequent, but we cannot offer any evidence in the present context for this conjecture.

A possible objection to the use of a strict partial ordering is that ordering judgments of an exact character are required. It is easy to meet this objection by using a semiorder rather than a strict partial order. The intuitive idea is that objects in the ordering beyond the criterion object c must be at least a threshold away. We shall not enter further into details about semiorders here. Some references are Luce (1956), Scott and Suppes (1958), and Suppes and Zinnes (1963).

It should now be clear why, although we agree with Siegel's (1976) nonintersective view of what we have termed intensive adjectives, we do not require an intensional theory to account for them. The general theory of partial orderings we have used, together with the semantic function represented by the initial segment operation, is our alternative to the Montague-type analysis she gives. Thus, our production rule and associated semantic function for intensive adjectives has the following form where the criterion object c is as discussed above:

Production Rule   *Semantic function*

$$NP \to IAdj + N \quad [NP] = IS([N], [IAdj], c)$$

A further remark, however, is needed about this criterion object. In many cases it will be selected by the nonverbal context of the utterance when an explicit linguistic reference is not made. (Note that, in the statement of the semantic function for general purposes, we have shown the denotation of a nonterminal symbol by using square brackets. Thus, the denotation of N is $[N]$.)

Comparison adjectives. Comparison adjectives are mainly the comparatives and superlatives. No comparatives occurred in noun phrases in our corpus, but examples of superlatives are the adjectives in *the best car*, *the first grade*, and *the funniest bus*. The complete list of comparison adjectives in our corpus is shown in Table 3. We again let the adjective denote an irreflexive, strict partial ordering relation; then the denotation of the combination of the comparison relation with the set denoted by the noun is the R-first element, if one exists, and null otherwise. Consider *the funniest bus*. Let F be an ordering relation which orders according to funniness, and let B be the set of buses. Then x is the F-first element of B if and only if for all y, if $y \in B$ and $x \neq y$, then $x F y$. That is, x is the funniest bus if x is the first element of the set of buses ordered according to funniness.

In general, a context restriction is needed to select the correct R-first element. The general means of fixing the context, developed earlier but in the spirit of the present article, is to let the definite article *the* denote the set of objects in the context appropriate to the utterance (Suppes, 1974b). In the present context, this set C would be intersected with B,

TABLE 3
COMPARISON ADJECTIVES

(the) baddest one	(the) first one
(the) best kind	(the) first grade
(the) best car	(the) funniest bus
(the) biggest one	(the) mostest money

and thus the denotation of *the funniest bus* would be the F-first element of $B \cap C$.

We recapitulate some of the details of this approach. For various reasons, the classical logical notation for definite descriptions does not seem right for spoken language, especially as a method of providing a semantics that fits hand in glove with the syntax. The approach we have used is to let the definite article denote a set C that is the union of the set of objects in the perceptual surround with the set of objects denoted by phrases in immediately preceding sentences in the conversation and, in some cases, also the set of objects denoted by images or symbolic storage in long-term memory. Thus, in our case, when a child says, "See the yellow house," the set C denoted by *the* is intersected with the set of yellow houses, both real and pictured in the immediate surround, and, if everything is in good order, the set intersection consists of a unique object.

Appropriate description of the set C is a somewhat delicate matter. In some cases, what would first come to mind would be too numerous and thus the intersection would be too large. We can narrow the set C by using a sequence of sets C_i with each element of the sequence being continued in the preceding member. The C that is appropriate in a given case is the first one that leads to a unique object when intersected with the set denoted by the remainder of the noun phrase. It should be clear how to convert these informal remarks into a formal characterization of the appropriate semantic function. (It should also be apparent how the definition of the semantic function is affected by use of a plural noun phrase.) To give an approximate idea of how the set C works, we looked at all the noun phrases in the corpus. There were 265 uses of the definite article. In 126 cases, we judged that the set C could be restricted to the perceptual surround. In 99 cases, C could be restricted to objects referred to in immediately preceding sentences, and in 28 cases, familiar objects like the moon, whose image or symbolic description was stored in long-term memory, seemed appropriate. In 12 cases, the object referred to seemed to be in the mind of the speaker alone, and there was no easy extraction of the appropriate set C.

Function adjectives. Function adjectives (sometimes abbreviated $F Adj$) in our corpus are either participles or words that are ordinarily used as nouns. Examples include *a magnifying glass, the fire engines, tire marks,* and *a punching ball.* The function adjectives found in our corpus are shown in Table 4. In our semantical approach they denote functions defined on the set indicated by the noun. In the phrase *the fire engines,* for example, *fire* maps the set of engines into the set of fire engines. What we have to say about these matters is more or less standard. Like others, we leave the substantive theory of the semantics of such function adjectives in an undeveloped state.

TABLE 4

FUNCTION ADJECTIVES

(an) army boat	(a) flying airplane	(a,no) rain hat
(a) baby bird	flying airplanes	(a) ratio gear
(that) baby buggy	(no) girl ones	(a) rifle gun
bath room	(a) Greyhound bus	sail boat
BB gun	gun boats	(a) secret door
(a) birthday party	(the) honey hunt	(a) soda truck
(a) boat balloon	(the) ice-cream cone	(a) steam boat
(the) boat junk	(that) jaguar thing	(a) stick shift
(a) boat ride	(that,the) machine gun	(a) sting bug
(a) boat slide	(a) magnifying glass	(a) stop sign
(a) bread shop	(a) motor car	(a,the) swimming pool
cave men	(a) motorcycle race	tire marks
cave people	(a) number thing	(a) train horse
(a) computer face	(a) nut head	(a) train ride
cowboy vests	(the) pencil marks	training wheels
diving boards	(that,a) pig boat	(a) vampire picture
fairy tales	play day	viking ship
(the) fire boat	(a) punching ball	(a,no) war one
(a) fire car	race cars	(that) water thing
(the) fire engines	(no, some) race cars	(the) work airplanes
(some) fish blood	(a) racing boat	

POSSESSIVES

With the exception of one type, all of the possessive noun phrases we found in our corpus are shown in Table 5. We found 247 possessive noun phrases in which a single possessive adjective is followed by a noun, and so we show only a representative sample in the table.

Possessives fall into two classes, possessive adjectives and possessive nouns (including proper nouns–PPn in the table stands for possessive proper noun). Because of the close semantic affinity of possessive adjectives and possessive nouns, we treat them together in this section, although certain features of iteration can apply only to the nouns and not to the adjectives. This matter will be discussed below.

Our first inclination was to assign a very simple semantic function to both kinds of possessives, just that of intersection. Consider, for example, *your hand*. Let H be the set of hands and Y the set of things belonging to the referent of *your*. (The referent of *your*, of course, varies from one context to another as is the case with all the possessive adjectives.) Then the denotation of *your hand* would be $Y \cap H$, the intersection of the set of hands and the set of the possessions of the referent of *you*. Similarly, in *Jessie's bike*, the denotation of *Jessie's* would be the set of possessions of Jessie which, when intersected with the set of bikes, would give the bike that belongs to Jessie.

Iterated possessives. To see that the choice of intersection as the semantic function of possessives is not correct, consider the following phrase from our corpus: *Candy's mother's name*. Let C be the set of things that belong to Candy, M the set of things that belong to mother, and N the set of names. Then the use of intersection would give as the denotation of this phrase the set $c \cap (m \cap n)$ or $(c \cap m) \cap n$, depending on the structure of the syntactic rules. since intersection is commutative and associative, both representations must denote the same set as $m \cap (c \cap n)$ denotes. but, of course, *candy's mothers' name* $((c \cap m) \cap n)$ has a different referent than *mother's candy's name* $(m \cap (c \cap n))$.

A more complicated treatment of possessive nouns was given in Suppes (1973b). The method used a choice function ϕ that operates in the following fashion. Again, consider *Jessie's bike*. Let J be the unit set consisting of Jessie and B be the set of bikes. Then the choice function $\phi(J, B) = f_J(B) \in B$. In this case, f_J is a standard set-theoretical choice function, and it is a choice function belonging to the set of objects of J, that is, Jessie, that selects Jessie's bike from the set of bikes. An extension of this treatment to *Candy's mother's name* would begin as follows. Let C be the unit set consisting of Candy, M the set of mothers, and N

TABLE 5

POSSESSIVE NOUN PHRASES

PossAdj + Adj + N	PossAdj + N	PossAdj + PosN + N
his baggy pants	her earrings	her mother's name
his big head	his back	my brother's name
his gold one	my brains	my father's name
his jewelry box	my cousin	my mama's father
his whole body	my daddy	my nurse's name
my baby brother	my mother	my sister's book
my baby sister	my park	our father's house
my bad car	nobody's name	our father's name
my bad jet	your finger	our friend's house
my bad truck	your hand	our grandmother's house
my bald head	your hands	our mother's car
my big boat	your mouth	your daddy's house
my library book	your shoes	your mama's father
my little brother	your sideburns	your mother's father
my little sister	your toes	
my other brother		**Car + PosN + N**
my other father	**PPn + N**	Two donkey's heads
my other uncle	Jessie's bike	
my own paper	Paulette's name	**Poss Adj + IAdj + PosN + N**
my race car	Stacy's house	my big brother's house
our baby brother		
our next-door neighbor	**PossAdj + CAdj IAdj + N**	**PossAdj + PosN + FAdj + N**
your bad breath	my big old ship	your father's gas station
your little jeans		
your little sister	**PPn + PosN + N**	
your little teeth	Candy's mother's name	
your own chair		

the set of names. Then $f_c(M)$ selects Candy's mother. Now $f_N(f_C(M))$ must select Candy's mother's name, but $f_c(M)$ is not the set of possessions of Candy's mother, but simply Candy's mother, so the function f_N is not operating on the set of names and the resulting set must be null. In other words, the choice-function approach is not satisfactory for iterated possessives.

The analysis which we originally believed to be correct uses the notion of the image of a set under a relation. Let P be the relation that assigns each object to its owner; examples of members of P include ⟨Jessie,bike⟩, ⟨you, hand⟩, ⟨Candy, mother⟩, and ⟨mother (i.e., a particular mother), name⟩. Consider the expression $(P``J) \cap B$, where $J$ is the singleton set consisting of Jessie, $B$ is the set of bikes, and $P``J$ is the image of J under the relation P. Then $P``J$ is the set of Jessie's possessions including her bike, and the intersection of $(P``J)$ with B is Jessie's bike.

This interpretation seems to extend correctly to *Candy's mother's name*. The denotation is $((P``(P``C) \cap M)) \cap N$, where C is the singleton set consisting of Candy, M is the set of mothers, and N is the set of names. Then $P``C$ is the set of Candy's possessions which, when intersected with $M$, is Candy's mother. Then $P``((P``C) \cap M)$ is Candy's mother's possessions, and the intersection with N is Candy's mother's name. While we do not have an example of a further extension in our corpus, it is useful to see that the interpretation would seem to extend indefinitely. Consider an example that is not from our corpus, *Tom's mother's aunt's kitten*. If T, M, A, and K stand for the obvious sets, the semantic interpretation is $(P``(P``((P``T) \cap M)) \cap A) \cap K$.

It is clear that the same treatment could be given to possessive adjectives. Consider *our father's house*. Let O be the set of objects possessed by the referent of *our*, F the set of fathers, and H the set of houses. Then the semantic interpretation is $(P``((P``O) \cap F)) \cap H$. The only difference between possessive adjectives and possessive nouns is that with adjectives the referent varies more drastically with the context.

The problem with this analysis arises when we try to generate the semantics with standard trees. We will return to the problem and suggest a possible solution in the next section on combinations of adjectives.

COMBINATIONS OF ADJECTIVES

We now consider the set-theoretical functions for the semantics of noun phrases containing more than one adjective. We must use for each adjective category the function assigned for noun phrases consisting of the single adjective plus a noun, but we must determine how and when the several functions are combined. It is at this point that the rules for generating syntax are affected; incorrect rules create nodes to which it is not possible to assign a semantic function that is within the set-theoretical framework we have established. We use several examples to demonstrate this.

The most frequent combinations of adjectives in our corpus are two intensive adjectives or an intensive adjective followed by a classifying adjective. The complete list of nonsingleton adjective phrases is shown in Table 6.

Intensive adjective followed by classifying adjective. We first take up combinations consisting of an intensive adjective and a classifying adjective. In these combinations, the need for the syntactic rules to be controlled by the semantic functions is particularly apparent. Consider *a little brown dog*. The semantic function for *little brown dog* is defined as follows. Let B be the set of brown things and D the set of dogs. *Brown* is a classifying adjective, so the set-theoretical function for *brown dog* is intersection. *Little* is an intensive adjective, and its denotation is the ordering relation L defined earlier. The semantic function for *little brown dog* is then $IS(B \cap D, L, c)$, where c is a criterion object for ordering of dogs according to size.

To see how the semantic interpretation affects the generation of the syntax, consider the following partial grammar for the generation of noun phrases containing an intensive adjective followed by a classifying adjective.

Rule	Semantic function
$N \rightarrow AdjP + N$	?
$AdjP \rightarrow IAdj + CAdj$	?

We need to identify the set-theoretical functions to be associated with each rule, but the close association in the tree of the various types of adjectives leads to disastrous results in terms of having a simple semantics. In particular, we do not have a natural set-theoretic denotation to be assigned $AdjP$ in the second generation rule, and we do not know which function to use to combine $AdjP$ and N in the first rule.

The natural partial grammar to replace the semantically incorrect rules is the following:

$$NP \quad \rightarrow IAdj + NP'$$
$$NP' \quad \rightarrow CAdj + N$$

Semantic functions can now be assigned to the rules which lead to the analysis presented at the beginning of this section. In particular, the functions are:

TABLE 6
NONSINGLETON ADJECTIVE PHRASES

IAdj + IAdj + N

(that) big old donkey	(that) big old submarine
(a) big old hump	big old toes
(a) big old 'mustache	(a) little old elephant
(a) big old place	little teensy teeth

IAdj + CAdj + N

(the) big round moon	(that) little Chinese baby
(that) big yellow boat	(a) little steel thing
(a) little brown dog	

IAdj + FAdj + N

(this) bad motor car	(the) old drums set
(those) little star cookies	

IAdj + IAdj + CAdj + N

(that) big old wild bear

CAdj + CAdj + N

green fresh grass

IAdj + IAdj + FAdj + N

little tiny BB shots

IAdj + IAdj + IAdj + IAdj + N

(a) big old giant giant world

IAdj + IAdj + IAdj + IAdj + IAdj + IAdj + N

(them) big big big big big
big cars

$$\begin{array}{ll} \text{\textit{Rule}} & \text{\textit{Semantic function}} \\ NP \rightarrow IAdj + NP' & [NP] = IS([NP'], [IAdj], c) \\ NP' \rightarrow CAdj + N & [NP'] = [CAdj] \cap [N] \end{array}$$

where the denotation of a nonterminal symbol is shown in square brackets, as mentioned earlier.

Notice how, by using the semantics, we can also establish that the order of the adjectives is correct. If we try to give the semantic analysis along the lines just indicated for *brown little dog*, we first take the set of dogs ordered according to smallness, and from that we take the set of brown dogs. But the set of little dogs might not include any brown dogs, and so the intersection would be empty. On the other hand, what we want to do is to take the set of dogs restricted to the set of brown dogs and then order the restricted set of brown dogs according to smallness. Occasionally, we do invert the standard order, and when we do the semantic difference is correctly reflected in our analysis. For instance, faced with several small dogs, we may refer to the brown one.

Two classifying adjectives. When we consider two classifying adjectives preceding a noun, as in *green fresh grass*, the order of the adjectives does not affect the semantic interpretation. That is, *green fresh grass* and *fresh green grass* denote the same set. However, the syntactic rules must again generate the adjective preceding the noun and the noun as a unit and then combine that unit with the second adjective, or else we run into the same problem of having no denotation for two adjectives—for *green fresh*. Our analysis of classifying adjectives seems defective because in actual speech we do seem to have a preferred order. For instance, we would usually say *fresh green grass* and not *green fresh grass*. A more subtle classification of attributive adjectives than we have given is required to catch this distinction.

Two or more intensive adjectives. We now turn to noun phrases containing two intensive adjectives, as in *little teensy teeth* or *a little old elephant*. Here, again, the order of the adjectives affects the semantic interpretation, and this interpretation must be preserved through a correct interaction of the syntactic rules and the semantic functions. In *a little old elephant*, we first want to select the old elephants and then choose a little elephant from the old elephants. If, on the other hand, we first choose little elephants from the set elephants, we probably would not select any old elephants at all. Similarly, if we first choose teensy teeth and from those choose the little teeth, we may well end up with smaller teeth than if we first choose little teeth and from those, teensy ones. In each case, the syntactic rules

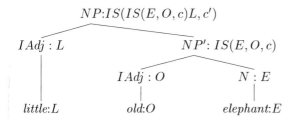

Figure 2. SEMANTIC TREE FOR *little old elephant.*

must associate the adjective preceding the noun with the noun and then associate that unit with the next preceding adjective. Otherwise, we encounter the problem we illustrated earlier of having no semantic function for the combination of two adjectives—for *little teensy* and *little old.*

The appropriate partial grammar is written below with the semantic function following each rule.

Rule	Semantic function
$NP \to IAdj + NP'$	$[NP] = IS([NP'], [IAdj], c)$
$NP' \to IAdj + N$	$[NP'] = IS([N], [IAdj], c)$

To see explicitly how the rules are applied, consider, for example, *a little old elephant.* Let E denote the set of elephants, and let L and O denote strict, partial, irreflexive orderings—one according to size and one according to age. Using the partial grammar written above, the semantic tree for *a little old elephant* is shown in Figure 2.

We first order elephants according to age and obtain the set consisting of those older than the criterion c. Then we order that set according to size and obtain the subset smaller than the criterion c'. Any member of the resulting set can then be described as a little old elephant. We note that *old* is often used in another sense to denote familiarity or affection. In that case, the semantics we have given would not be appropriate, and a different ordering would apply.

It is easy to see how to extend this argument to noun phrases containing any number of intensive adjectives, such as *a big old giant giant world* and *these big big big big big big cars.* We can also extend the argument to account for phrases containing a series of intensive adjectives, a classifying adjective, and a noun, as in that *big old wild bear.* Let Br be the set of bears, W the set of wild things, and B and O the obvious strict partial orderings. The denotation of *big old wild bear* is $IS(IS(W \cap Br, O, c), B, c')$.

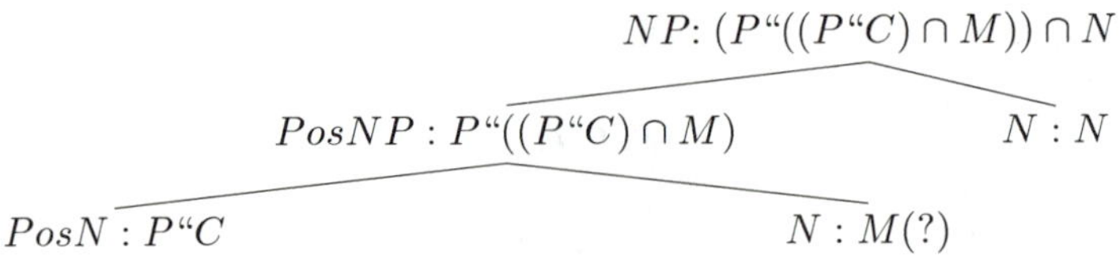

$$NP: (P^{"}((P^{"}C) \cap M)) \cap N$$

$$PosNP: P^{"}((P^{"}C) \cap M) \qquad\qquad N: N$$

$$PosN: P^{"}C \qquad\qquad\qquad N: M(?)$$

Figure 3. INCORRECT SEMANTIC TREE FOR *Candy's mother's name.*

Possessives reconsidered. We now return to the problem of reiterated possessives. While the analysis we gave above seems to be correct for the noun phrase taken as a whole, we have not yet discussed the individual syntactic rules and semantic functions that generate the phrase. Here again, certain restrictions on the form of the syntactic rules are imposed by the semantics.

The rule which would seem to be the best choice for simple possessive noun phrases such as *Jessie's bike* is the following:

$$\begin{array}{cc}
\textit{Rule} & \textit{Semantic function} \\
PosNP \rightarrow PosN + N & [PosNP] = (P^{"}[PosN]) \cap [N]
\end{array}$$

An extension of the application of this rule to more complicated possessive noun phrases is shown in the following incorrect tree of Figure 3 for *Candy's mother's name.* The associated syntactic rules and semantic functions are as follows:

$$\begin{array}{cc}
\textit{Rule} & \textit{Semantic function} \\
NP \rightarrow PosNP + N & [NP] = [PosNP] \cap [N] \\
PosNP \rightarrow PosN + N & [PosNP] = P^{"}([PosN]) \cap [N]
\end{array}$$

The error here is in the denotation of *mother's* as the set M of mothers rather than as $P^{"}M$, the set of possessions of mother. If *Candy's* denotes $P^{"}C$, then to be consistent, *mother's* should denote $P^{"}M$. But if we let *mother's* denote $P^{"}M$, we have the set of possessions of all mothers, and we have no way to first select Candy's mother.

The analysis is improved if we rewrite the rules in the following fashion:

$$\begin{array}{cc}
\textit{Rule} & \textit{Semantic function} \\
NP \rightarrow PosNP + N & [NP] = [PosNP] \cap [N] \\
PosNP \rightarrow PosNP + PosN' & [PosNP] = P^{"}([PosNP] \cap [PosN']) \\
PosNP \rightarrow PosN & [PosNP] = P^{"}[PosN]
\end{array}$$

In the second rule we indicate through the prime that a possessive noun following a possessive noun phrase is of a different sort than a possessive

noun used by itself. When a word is marked as PosN', it does not denote
the set of possessions, but rather it denotes the set of objects indicated by
the word without the inflection. We rely then on the *PosNP* rule (Rule 2)
to both intersect the set denoted by *PosN* with another set and to select
the set consisting of the possessions of the members of the restricted set
resulting from the intersection.

We can make the analysis more consistent by introducing a rule for
inflection, thereby treating the inflection as a separate word. Now we are
dealing in a direct way with the fact that a possessive noun serves two
functions—first to denote a set and then to denote objects possessed by
the set. Appropriate syntactic rules and associated semantic functions for
this analysis are the following.

Rule	*Semantic function*
$NP \rightarrow PosPh + N$	$[NP] = [PosPh] \cap [N]$
$PosPh \rightarrow N + Inf$	$[PosPh] = P\text{“}[N]$
$PosPh \rightarrow NP' + Inf$	$[PosPh] = P\text{“}[NP']$
$NP' \rightarrow PosPh + N$	$[NP'] = [PosPh] \cap [N]$

The application of these rules to *Candy's mother's* name is shown in
the tree of Figure 4.

The most interesting feature of this tree is the relatively large separation of the noun and its inflection. The noun denotes a set which may
be restricted to a smaller set by a preceding modifier. The inflection is
then applied to this reduced set. In our example, the set of mothers, M,
is restricted to the set consisting of Candy's mother at the third level of
the tree. Not until the second level is the inflection on mother used to

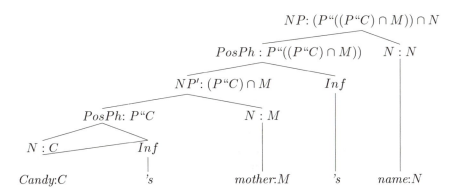

Figure 4. SEMANTIC TREE FOR *Candy's mother's name.*

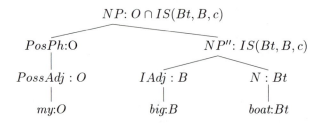

Figure 5. SEMANTIC TREE FOR *my big boat.*

denote the set of possessions of Candy's mother.

More complex phrases. Finally, we must consider examples in which an adjective precedes the noun or the possessive noun, as in *my big boat* and *my big brother's house.* A partial grammar for these more complicated phrases is shown below:

Rules	Semantic function
$NP \rightarrow PosPh + N$	$[NP] = [PosPh] \cap [N]$
$NP \rightarrow PosPh + NP''$	$[NP] = [PosPh] \cap [NP'']$
$PosPh \rightarrow NP' + Inf$	$[PosPh] = P''[NP']$
$PosPh \rightarrow PossAdj$	$[PosPh] = [PossAdj]$
$NP' \rightarrow PosPh + NP''$	$[NP'] = [PosPh] \cap [NP'']$
$NP'' \rightarrow IAdj + N$	$[NP''] = IS([N], [IAdj], c)$

Note that the denotation [*PossAdj*] is the set of possessions of the person (or other object) to whom the possessive adjective refers. This difference in the semantics of *PossAdj* reflects its inability to express reiterated possession.

The resulting semantic trees for *my big boat* and *my big brother's house* are shown in Figures 5 and 6, where the denotation of *my* is shown as O, the set of things owned or possessed by the speaker.

We note that this analysis is not always correct. According to our analysis, we first select big boats or big brothers and then intersect that set with the set of possessions of the referent of *my.* The resulting set may be mistakenly null—for example, if what the referent of *my* owns is a collection of small model ships, none of which is a big boat as such.

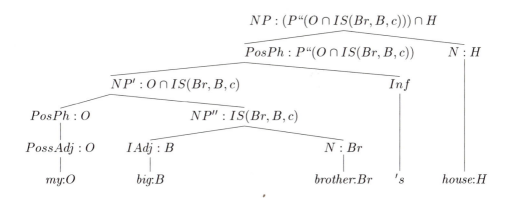

Figure 6. SEMANTIC TREE FOR *my big brother's house.*

Adverbs that modify adjectives are often used in ordinary speech, and they occur with reasonable frequency in our corpus. Two examples are *a real real real big one* and *a very good face*. The adverb *real* is not used in standard written English as an intensifier, but it occurs frequently in our corpus, considerably more so than *very*, and represents a widely used idiom. In the semantic treatment we present here, we shall treat these adverbs as if they functioned identically, and we shall restrict our analysis to their modification of intensive adjectives.

Ignoring for the moment the problem of syntactic production rules and their associated semantic functions, we give what we think is the most plausible initial candidate for the denotation of an entire phrase, in line with our earlier analysis of intensive adjectives. We follow this with an analysis of difficulties. Recall that the semantic analysis of *little baby* is the initial segment of the ordering L of objects by size restricted to babies (the set B) and using a certain baby c as a norm for defining the initial segment, i.e.,

(1) $$[little\ baby] = IS(B, L, c).$$

The natural extension of this analysis to *real little baby* (which did not occur in the corpus) seems to be iteration of the operation of taking the initial segment:

(2) $$[real\ little\ baby] = IS(IS(B, L, c), L, c').$$

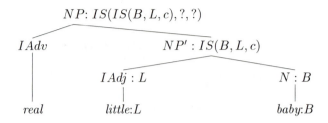

Figure 7. INCORRECT SEMANTIC TREE FOR *real little baby*.

Roughly speaking, we represent the intensifier *real* by taking an initial segment of the initial segment—under the same size ordering L, of course. This representation seems plausible, but the trouble begins when we attempt to draw an appropriate semantic tree. Even if we follow the semantic "bracketing" of (2) by an unrealistic grouping of *little* with baby, we are confronted with problems, as is apparent in Figure 7. At the top level of the tree—the denotation of NP—we have lost the relation L, for the denotation of NP' is purely a set without any ordering, an initial segment of the relation L. Looking at the other side of the tree, it is implausible that the relation L is part of the intensifier, and, in fact, in the analysis attempted by the tree, the adverb *real* does not denote at all but serves as a function or control-structure word.

If we group *real* and *little*, the same sort of problem arises, as shown in Figure 8. So, we do not have a reasonable candidate for the denotation of $IAdjP$, the intensive adjective phrase. The failures of the semantic analyses represented by these two trees might be taken as a strong argument for expanding the restricted framework of extended relation algebras we have adopted. However, we think there are good semantic and psychological intuitions behind the view that the denotations of words and phrases in much of ordinary speech should be representable within such a restricted and computationally efficient setting.

Geometrical analogy. There is a natural analogy to geometrical constructions in the semantic constructions we have been considering. This analogy provides a way out of the difficulties we have been encountering. The way out will call for some loosening of the restricted semantical framework within which we have been operating, but a loosening that is not very severe and has a rather natural interpretation. Let us recall the situation in geometric constructions. If we represent these constructions set-theoretically, then the sequence of operations leading to the desired

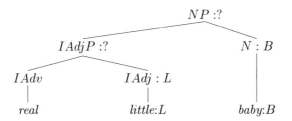

Figure 8. SECOND INCORRECT SEMANTIC TREE FOR *real little baby*.

figure does not carry along the auxiliary points used in the construction. For example, if we follow the familiar construction for finding the midpoint of a line segment, the formal representation of this construction has at the end only the midpoint explicitly represented, and the auxiliary points constructed by intersecting arcs of circles do not remain in the formal representation. On the other hand, in the auxiliary figures or illustrations that are always used to show how the constructions are made, the auxiliary points constructed do remain and are a salient part of one's memory of the constructions. More particularly, once one has made a number of such constructions, there is then even considerable memory for the dynamic sequence in which the auxiliary points are constructed.

The suggestion to follow out in the case of our semantic trees is to use a similar approach. At each node of a tree the denotation is represented as before, but the denotations of all subnodes are also carried along and remain accessible for subsequent use if so desired. There is no need to change the notation, but the framework has been definitely enlarged, because now it is possible to use a relation, for example, that has occurred in a subnode and that has been used in the construction of a particular set above it. Using this approach, we represent reiterated uses of the intensifying adverb *real* by the semantic tree shown below in Figure 9. The semantic function corresponding to the production rule

$$NP \rightarrow IAdv + NP$$

has the following form

$$[NP] = IS([NP], R([NP]), c([NPI]),$$

where $R([NP])$ is the relation occurring as the denotation of a descendant node of NP—in the case of Figure 9, the size relation L—and $c([NP])$ is the criterion object selected for the set $[NP]$ and the relation $R([NP])$.

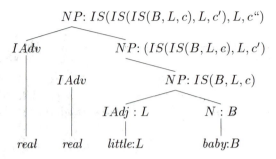

Figure 9. SEMANTIC TREE FOR *real real little baby.*

The conceptual importance of this shift to being able to access denotations that occurred in a descendant node should be emphasized. It is a very definite strengthening of the apparatus available to us in constructing semantic trees. At the same time, bearing in mind the familiar images of constructions, it seems a natural step and one that has at least a prima facie psychological plausibility in terms of short-term memory. A plausible restriction is that there is a continual elimination from memory of the denotations of earlier nodes, but that various salient ones remain as needed as part of the framework of discourse which extends beyond the level of an individual sentence. In fact, the clear claims of semantic connectivity between the sentences of a given piece of discourse make all the more plausible the holding in short-term memory of the denotation of descendant subnodes in a given tree.

It should be clear that we have not attempted to give a full formal treatment of the matters just introduced. The approach has an intuitive appeal, but more systematic work is needed to complete the intended extension of the semantic apparatus.

SOME FINAL REMARKS

We have tried to provide an analysis for the main types of adjectives, possessives, and intensifying adverbs encountered in our corpus. It should be obvious, however, that, even within the restricted framework of our corpus of 6- and 7-year-old children talking, there remain a reasonable number of unresolved problems. On the other hand, we feel that the line of attack we have taken lies in the proper direction, and we want to amplify this view in some concluding remarks.

We mentioned at the beginning our skepticism about the logical form of natural-language expressions being given in terms of first-order logic. Another place to express this skepticism lies in the analysis of adverbs just given. By considering the case of adverbs, our views about logical form can be given sharper formulation. Parsons (1970) provides a good example of a strong contrast to our own approach. He represents adverbs as operators; in ordinary first-order logic the operators precede well-formed formulas and, thus, have the character of sentential operators. In those cases in English where adverbs have a prefix position in a sentence, as in *Slowly but surely, he turned around*, there seems to be a case for a sentential analysis. This is also true of some postfix adverbs, but the kind of variable-free semantics used in our approach is especially appropriate for analyzing adverbs in infix position as modifiers of verb phrases or noun phrases. It seems especially unwieldy to treat intensifying adverbs that modify adjectives or noun phrases as sentential operators. It seems to us that no simple way can be given of making the semantics fit with the syntax of noun phrases when such a viewpoint is adopted, and we also feel this problem of fit arises for most adverbs that modify verbs, as in *He drove slowly down the street*. Along this line, the semantics of negation given in Suppes (1976) provides an example of how we would propose to handle such adverbs in infix position.

Thomason and Stalnaker (1973) introduce a distinction between adverbs that are sentence modifiers and those that are predicate modifiers— a move in the right direction, but they work primarily within the framework of first-order logic in terms of explicit theory, and they do not discuss the logic of adverbs that modify adjectives or noun phrases. As in the case of Parsons, much of what they have to say seems subtle and accurate but not directly helpful in our attempt to analyze the semantics within the syntax of natural language.

This consideration of adverbs leads to the more general point that we have emphasized from the beginning by billing this article as developing *a variable-free semantics*. We characterized such a semantical theory earlier as one that restricted itself to constants and operations on constants. The many examples considered should have made the central point of this kind of semantics. It is aimed at fitting in a detailed and exact way the syntax of natural-language utterances. The words and phrases of natural language that denote have been restricted to a classical conception of objects as individuals, sets of individuals, and relations between individuals, although we concede that there may be cases requiring extension. What is most important is the elimination of any use of variables in expressing the "meaning" of the parts of natural language we have considered.

Such a variable-free semantics runs contrary to the popular trends at the moment, but these trends reflect the present attitude toward first-order logic as the primary intellectual tool for the analysis of the semantic structure of English. We feel that there are so many limitations to first-order logic when used for this purpose, and it itself is so far removed in structure from the syntax of natural language, that the kind of relation-algebraic viewpoint we have adopted has a reasonable chance of proving useful.

As we have continually emphasized, our primary argument for the use of relation algebra, with notation only of constants and operations on constants to represent semantics, is that this provides an elegant approach to matching semantics to the syntax of natural language. To avoid the claim, however, that this is a very special mathematical viewpoint, it seems desirable to mention that the development of formal systems without variables has received a fair amount of attention within logic itself. Perhaps the most extensive example is that of combinatory logic, either in the early form of Schönfinkel (for a recent discussion, see Quine, 1974) or in the extensive development of such logic by Curry and his collaborators—a definitive exposition is Curry, Hindley, and Seldin (1972). There is also a very general tendency in computer programming languages to avoid the use of variables, and it is common practice at the level of assembly language. In other words, there is a broad intellectual basis for the use of a semantical language without variables, and a good many more conceptual alternatives are available than we have examined in the present context.

What we have aimed at in this article is to provide a sense of how even the simplest use of attributive adjectives and some of their modifying adverbs generates difficult semantical problems. The constructive suggestions for partial solutions we have made seem plausible, at least to us, but a more systematic and technical development is needed to make a deeper evaluation possible, and further study will no doubt require modification of the proposals we have made.

APPENDIX

We summarize here the details of the collection of the corpus—the subjects, the recording procedures, and the transcription.

Subjects. The subjects were 15 black children in the first grade at a public school in southern California; they ranged in age from 6 to 7 years. The recordings were made in the spring of 1970. The children were members of a classroom of 29 students—19 black children, 6 Mexican-American children, and 4 Caucasian children. Eleven of the subjects were born in California—9 within a 20-mile radius of their school. Of the others, one was born in North Dakota, one in Texas, and one in Alabama; the school had no record of the birthplace of the 15th. All of the subjects had attended both kindergarten and first grade in southern California; 11 had attended kindergarten and first grade at the same school. Ten children lived with both parents, one only with his father, and four only with their mothers. All of the fathers living at home were blue-collar workers, with the exception of one who was serving in the Air Force. Two of the mothers living at home were nurses; the rest were housewives. The average number of children per family was 3.6.

Recording procedure. The recordings were made in a small room separate from the classroom with groups of three to five children at a time; each recording session lasted about 15 minutes. The children were seated around a small table with the tape recorder in the center. We had participated with the children in their regular classroom activities before attempting to record their speech, so we were not strangers when we began recording.

In the first session, each group had an opportunity to experiment with the tape recorder; they recorded and listened to their own voices and any other sounds they could produce. In the remaining sessions, the children were given some activity designed to elicit discussion. We sat off to one side seemingly engrossed in some unrelated activity. We attempted to remove the teacher-figure from the situation as much as possible so that the children would talk to each other naturally rather than in language geared to adults.

We provided a variety of activities, but the activity that elicited the most discussion was looking through books together. The favorite among the boys was a book showing many modes of transportation; both boys and girls enjoyed books containing large pictures of family and school situations. The pictures often reminded the children of their own experiences, which they would then discuss with each other.

All members of the class participated in several recording sessions, so it was not obvious to the students that any particular members were being observed. At first there were only two restrictions on the selection of the recording groups: the children were to be of the same race, so that, in transcription, it would be possible to distinguish the speech of different racial groups, and the children were to be chosen from those students who, at that moment, were not directly involved with the classroom teacher. It soon became evident, however, that certain combinations of children produced more discussion than others; thus, in the later recording sessions, children who appeared to work best together were recorded together.

A total of 11.5 hours of speech were recorded. From this sample, the 10 sessions (2.5 hours of conversation) that seemed the best in terms of naturalness, amount, and clarity were selected for analysis in this article. The resulting corpus contains approximately 4,300 utterances.

Transcribing conventions and grammatical categories. In transcribing the recordings the end of an utterance was determined by several indicators: another speaker starting to talk, a drop in pitch or a pause when the context indicated the end of a thought, or a rise in pitch indicating a question. Words were spelled according to their standard English spelling unless a different pronunciation was used consistently; for example, *gonna* was written for *going to*. Pauses within utterances and unfinished thoughts were marked, and speakers were identified. Memorized phrases, such as lines from songs, were transcribed but were not included in this analysis.

Each utterance was coded as an ordered n-tuple according to the grammatical category of each word in order of occurrence. The grammatical categories were those commonly used in English grammars (see Table A). Ordinary parts of speech were assigned to words even when the child used them in a nonstandard way. For example, *a Japanese* in the utterance *I saw a Japanese* was coded as article plus adjective, and the utterance was then marked as nonstandard.

Subscripts were added to category notations when necessary to make the particular usage clear. Subscripts indicated number, person, and case for pronouns; number for demonstrative pronouns; number and case for nouns; and number, person, tense, and contraction (e.g., *I've*) for verbs. We do not show the subscripts in Table A because we have not used them in this article.

TABLE A

CATEGORIES USED IN THE CODING OF UTTERANCES

Verbs

Aux	auxiliary verb	IV	intransitive verb
BV	to be	TV	transitive verb
CV	copulative verb		
AuxI		AuxInf	
BVI		BVInf	
CVI	imperative form	CVInf	infinitive form
IVI		IVInf	
TVI		TVInf	
AuxP		BVPP	
BVP		CVPP	
CVP	present participle	IVPP	past participle
IVP		TVPP	
TVP			

Other Parts of Speech

Adv	adverb	P	personal pronoun
AP	impersonal pronoun	PN	proper noun
CAdj	classifying adjective	PosN	possessive noun
Car	cardinal number	PosP	possessive pronoun
CC	coordinating conjunction	PossAdj	possessive adjective
Count	numerical description	Prep	preposition
CompAdj	comparative adjective	Qu	unrestricted quantifier
DAdj	demonstrative adjective	QuN	negative quantifier
DP	demonstrative pronoun	QuR	restricted quantifier
E	exclamation	R	rejoiner
FAdj	function adjective	RAdj	relative adjective
Ger	gerund	RP	relative pronoun
IA	indefinite article	SC	subordinating
IAdj	intensive adjective		conjunction
IAdv	interrogative adverb	T	definite article
IP	interrogative pronoun	To	"to" used with
K	vocative		infinitives
L	locative	ToC	"to" contracted with
N	common noun		preceding verb
Neg	negative	U	uh,um
NegP	negative pronoun		

PART III

VARIABLE-FREE
SEMANTICS

10

SEMANTICS OF CONTEXT-FREE FRAGMENTS OF NATURAL LANGUAGES

The search for a rigorous and explicit semantics of any significant portion of a natural language is now intensive and far-flung—far-flung in the sense that wide varieties of approaches are being taken. Yet almost everyone agrees that at the present time the semantics of natural languages are less satisfactorily formulated than the grammars, even though a complete grammar for any significant fragment of natural language is yet to be written.

A line of thought especially popular in the last couple of years is that the semantics of a natural language can be reduced to the semantics of first-order logic. One way of fitting this scheme into the general approach of generative grammars is to think of the deep structure as being essentially identical with the structure of first-order logic. The central difficulty with this approach is that now as before how the semantics of the surface

*Reprinted from Hintikka et al. (Eds.), *Approaches to Natural Language*, 370-394. Copyright 1973 by D. Reidel Publishing Company, Dordrecht-Holland. I am indebted to Pentti Kanerva for help in the computer analysis and organization of the data presented in the section on noun-phrase semantics, and I am indebted to Elizabeth Gammon for several useful ideas in connection with the analysis of the data. D.M. Gabbay and George Huff made a number of penetrating comments on the third section, and Richard Montague trenchantly criticized an unsatisfactory preliminary version.

grammar is to be formulated is still unclear. In other words, how can explicit formal relations be established between first-order logic and the structure of natural languages? Without the outlines of a formal theory, this line of approach has moved no further than the classical stance of introductory teaching in logic, which for many years has concentrated on the translation of English sentences into first-order logical notation. The method of translation, of course, is left at an intuitive and ill-defined level.

The strength of first-order logic approach is that it represents essentially the only semantical theory with any systematic or deep development, namely, model-theoretic semantics as developed in mathematical logic since the early 1930s, especially since the appearance of Tarski (1935). The semantical approaches developed by linguists or others whose viewpoint is that of generative grammar have been lacking in the formal precision and depth of model-theoretic semantics. Indeed, some of the most important and significant results in the foundations of mathematics belong to the general theory of models. I shall not attempt to review the approaches to semantics that start from a generative-grammar viewpoint, but I have in mind the work of Fodor, Katz, Lakoff, McCawley and others.

My objective is to combine the viewpoint of model-theoretic semantics and generative grammar, to define semantics for context-free languages and to apply the results to some fragments of natural language. The ideas contained in this paper were developed while I was working with Hélène Bestougeff on the semantical theory of question-answering systems. Later I came across some earlier similar work by Knuth (1968). My developments are rather different from those of Knuth, especially because my objective is to provide tools for the analysis of fragments of natural languages, whereas Knuth was concerned with programming languages.

Although on the surface the viewpoint seems different, I also benefited from a study of Montague's interesting and important work (1970) on the analysis of English as a formal language. My purely extensional line of attack is simpler than Montague's. I adopted it for reasons of expediency, not correctness. I wanted an apparatus that could be applied in a fairly direct way to empirical analysis of a corpus. As in my work on probabilistic grammars (Suppes, 1970), I began with the speech of a young child, but without doubt, many of the semantical problems that are the center of Montague's concern must be dealt with in analyzing slightly more complex speech. Indeed, some of these problems already arise in the corpus studied here. As in the case of my earlier work on probabilistic grammars, I have found a full-scale analytic attack on a corpus of speech a humbling and bedeviling experience. The results reported here hopefully chart one possible course; in no sense are they more than preliminary.

This paper is organized in the following fashion. In the next section, I describe a simple artificial example to illustrate how a semantic valuation function is added to the generative mechanisms of a context-free grammar. The relevant formal definitions are given in the following section. The reader who wants a quick survey of what can be done with methods, but who is not really interested in formal matters, may skip ahead to the section which contains the detailed empirical results. On the other hand, it will probably be somewhat difficult to comprehend fully the machinery used in the empirical analysis without some perusal of the section on denoting grammars, unless the reader is already quite familiar with model-theoretic semantics. How the results of this paper and the earlier one on probabilistic grammars are meant to form the beginnings of a theory of performance is sketched in the last section.

A SIMPLE EXAMPLE

To illustrate the semantic methods described formally below, I use as an example the same simple language I used in Suppes (1970). As remarked there, this example is not meant to be complex enough to fit any actual corpus; its context-free grammar can easily be rewritten as a regular grammar. The five syntactic categories are IV, TV, Adj, PN and N, where IV is the class of intransitive verbs, TV the class of transitive verbs or two-place predicates, Adj the class of adjectives, PN the class of proper nouns and N the class of common nouns. Additional nonterminal vocabulary consists of the symbols S, NP, VP and $AdjP$. The set P of production rules consists of the following seven rules, plus the rewrite rules for terminal vocabulary belonging to one of the five categories.

	Production Rule	*Semantic Function*
1.	$S \rightarrow NP + VP$	Truth-function
2.	$VP \rightarrow IV$	Identity
3.	$VP \rightarrow TV + NP$	Image under the converse relation
4.	$NP \rightarrow PN$	Identity
5.	$NP \rightarrow AdjP + N$	Intersection
6.	$AdjP \rightarrow AdjP + Adj$	Intersection
7.	$AdjP \rightarrow Adj$	Identity

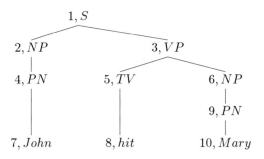

Figure 1.

If Adj^n is understood to denote a string of n adjectives, then the possible grammatical types (infinite in number) all fall under one of the following schemes.

Grammatical Type

1. $PN + IV$
2. $PN + TV + PN$
3. $Adj^n + N + IV$
4. $PN + TV + Adj^n + N$
5. $Adj^n + N + TV + PN$
6. $Adj^m + N + TV + Adj^n + N$

What needs explaining are the semantic functions to the right of each production rule. For this purpose it is desirable to look at an example of a sentence generated by this grammar. The intuitive idea is that we define a valuation function v over the terminal vocabulary, and as is standard in model-theoretic semantics, v takes values in some relational structure.

Suppose a speaker wants to say 'John hit Mary'. The valuation function needs to be defined for the three terminal words 'John ', 'hit' and 'Mary'. We then recursively define the denotation of each labeled node of the derivation tree of the sentence. In this example, I number the nodes, so that the denotation function Ψ is defined for pairs (n, α), where n is a node of the tree and α is a word in the vocabulary—see Figure 1 for the tree.

Let I be the identity function, $\check{A}$ the converse of A, i.e.,

$$\check{A} = \{\langle x, y \rangle : \langle y, x \rangle \in A\},$$

and $f``A$ the image of A under f, i.e., the range of f restricted to the domain A, and let T be truth and F falsity. Then the denotation of each labeled node of the tree is found by working from the bottom up:[1]

$$\Psi(10, Mary) = v(Mary)$$
$$\Psi(9, PN) = I(v(Mary))$$
$$\Psi(8, hit) = v(hit)$$
$$\Psi(7, John) = v(John)$$
$$\Psi(6, NP) = I(v(Mary))$$
$$\Psi(5, TV) = I(v(hit))$$
$$\Psi(4, PN) = \underbrace{I(v(John))}$$
$$\Psi(3, VP) = I(v(hit)) \text{``} I(v(Mary))$$
$$\Psi(2, NP) = I(I(v(John)))$$
$$\Psi(1, S) = f(\Psi(2, NP), \Psi(3, VP)) = \begin{cases} T & \text{if } \Psi(2, NP) \subseteq \\ & \Psi(3, VP) \\ F & \text{otherwise.} \end{cases}$$

Clearly, the functions used above are just the semantic functions associated with the productions. In particular, the production rules for the direct descendants of nodes 2, 4, 5 and 6 all have the identity function as their semantic function.

One point should be emphasized. I do not claim that the set-theoretical semantic functions of actual speech are as simple as those associated with the production rules given in this section. Consider Rule 5, for instance. Intersection is fine for *old dictators*, but not for *alleged dictators*. One standard mathematical approach to this kind of difficulty is to generalize the semantic function to cover the meaning of both sorts of cases. In the present case of adjectives, we could require that the semantic function be one that maps sets of objects into sets of objects. In this vein, Rule 5 would now be represented by

$$\Psi(n_1, NP) = \Psi(n_2, AdjP) \text{``} \Psi(n_3, N).$$

Fortunately, generalizations that rule out the familiar simple functions as semantic functions do not often occur early in children's speech. Some tentative empirical evidence on this point is presented later.

DENOTING GRAMMARS

I turn now to formal developments. Some standard grammatical concepts are defined in the interest of completeness. First, if V is a set, V^* is the set of all finite sequences whose elements are members of V. I shall often refer to these finite sequences as *strings*. The empty sequence, 0, is in V^* ; we

---

[1] I have let the words of V serve as names of themselves to simplify the notation.

define $V^+ = V^* - \{0\}$. A structure $G = \langle V, V_N, P, S \rangle$ is a *phrase-structure grammar* if and only if V and P are finite, nonempty sets, V_N is a subset of V, S is in V_N and $P \subseteq V_N^* \times V^+$. Following the usual terminology, V_N is the nonterminal vocabulary and $V_T = V - V_N$ the terminal vocabulary. S is the start symbol or the single axiom from which we derive strings or words in the language generated by G. The set P is the set of production or rewrite rules. If $\langle \alpha, \beta \rangle \in P$, we write $\alpha \rightarrow \beta$, which we read: from α we may produce or derive β (immediately).

A phrase-structure grammar $G = \langle V, V_N, P, S \rangle$ is *context-free* if and only if $P \subseteq V_N \times V^+$, i.e., if $\alpha \rightarrow \beta$ is in P then $\alpha \in V_N$ and $\beta \in V^{+2}$. These ideas may be illustrated by considering the simple language of the previous section. Although it is intended that N, PN, Adj, IV, and TV be non-terminals in any application, we can treat them as terminals for purposes of illustration, for they do not occur on the left of any of the seven production rules. With this understanding

$$
\begin{aligned}
V_N &= \{S, NP, VP, AdjP\} \\
V_T &= \{N, PN, Adj, IV, TV\}
\end{aligned}
$$

and P is defined by the production rules already given. It is obvious from looking at the production rules that the grammar is context-free, for only elements of V_N appear on the left-hand side of any of the seven production rules.

The definition of derivations is as follows. Let $G = \langle V, V_N, P, S \rangle$ be a phrase-structure grammar. First, if $\alpha \rightarrow \beta$ is a production of P, and γ and δ are strings in V^*, then $\gamma\alpha\delta \Rightarrow_G \gamma\beta\delta$. We say that β is *derivable* from α in G, in symbols $\alpha \Rightarrow_G \beta$ if there are strings $\alpha_1, \ldots, \alpha_n$ in V^* such that $\alpha = \alpha_1$, $\alpha_1 \Rightarrow_G \alpha_2, \ldots, \alpha_{n-1} \Rightarrow \alpha_n = \beta$. The sequence $\Delta = \langle \alpha_1, \ldots, \alpha_n \rangle$ is a *derivation* in G. The language $L(G)$ generated by G is $\{\alpha : \alpha \in V_T^* \,\&\, S \Rightarrow_G^* \alpha\}$. In other words, $L(G)$ is the set of all strings made up of terminal vocabulary and derived from S.

The semantic concepts developed also require use of the concept of a derivation tree of a grammar. The relevant notions are set forth in a series of definitions. Certain familiar set-theoretical notions about relations are also needed. To begin with, a *binary structure* is an ordered pair $\langle T, R \rangle$ such that T is a nonempty set and R is a binary relation on T, i.e., $R \subseteq T \times T$. R is a *partial ordering* of T if and only if R is reflexive, antisymmetric and transitive on T. R is a *strict simple ordering* of T

---

[2]As Richard Montague pointed out to me, to make context-free grammars a special case of phrase-structure grammars, as defined here, the first members of P should be not elements of V_N but one-place sequences whose terms are elements of V as belong to V^*. Consequently, to avoid notational complexities, I treat elements, their unit sets and one-place sequences whose terms are the elements, as identical.

if and only if R is asymmetric, transitive and connected on T. We also need the concept of R-immediate predecessor. For x and y in T, xJy if and only if xRy, not yRx and for every z if $z \neq y$ and zRy then zRx. In the language of formal grammars, we say that if xJy then x *directly dominates* y, or y is the *direct descendant* of x.

Using these notions, we define in succession *tree, ordered tree* and *labeled ordered tree*. A binary structure $\langle T, R \rangle$ is a *tree* if and only if (i) T is finite, (ii) R is a partial ordering of T, (iii) there is an R-first element of T, i.e., there is an x such that for every y, xRy, and (iv) if xJz and yJz then $x = y$. If xRy in a tree, we say that y is a *descendant* of x. Also the R-first element of a tree is called the *root* of the tree, and an element of T that has no descendants is called a *leaf*. We call any element of T a *node*, and we shall sometimes refer to leaves as *terminal nodes*.

A ternary structure $\langle T, R, L \rangle$ is an *ordered tree* if and only if (i) L is a binary relation on T, (ii) $\langle T, R, \rangle$ is a tree, (iii) for each x in T, L is a strict simple ordering of $\{y : xJy\}$, (iv) if xLy and yRz then xLz, and (v) if xLy and xRz then zLy. It is customary to read xLy as 'x is to the *left* of y'. Having this ordering is fundamental to generating terminal strings and not just sets of terminal words. The *terminal string* of an ordered labeled tree is just the sequence of labels $\langle f(x_1), \ldots, f(x_n) \rangle$ of the leaves of the tree as ordered by L. Formally, a quinary structure $\langle T, V, R, L, f \rangle$ is a *labeled ordered tree* if and only if (i) V is a nonempty set, (ii) $\langle T, R, L \rangle$ is an ordered tree, and (iii) f is a function from T into V. The function f is the labeling function and $f(x)$ is the *label* of node x.

The definition of a derivation tree is relative to a given context-free grammar.

DEFINITION 1. *Let $G = \langle V, V_N, P, S \rangle$ be a context-free grammar and let $\mathcal{F} = \langle T, V, R, L, f \rangle$ be a labeled ordered tree. $\mathcal{F}$ is a derivation tree of G if and only if*

(i) If x is the root of $\mathcal{F}, f(x) = S$;

(ii) If xRy and $x \neq y$ then $f(x)$ is in V_N;

(iii) If $y_1, \ldots, y_n$ are all the direct descendants of x, i.e.,

$$\bigcup_{i=1}^{n} \{y_i\} = \{y : xJy\} \neq 0, \text{ and } y_iLy_j \text{ if } i < j,$$

then $\langle f(x), \langle f(y_1), \ldots, f(y_n) \rangle \rangle$

is a production in P.

We now turn to semantics proper by introducing the set Φ of set-theoretical functions. We shall let the domains of these functions be n-

tuples of any sets (with some appropriate restriction understood to avoid set-theoretical paradoxes).

DEFINITION 2. *Let* $\langle V, V_N, P, S \rangle$ *be a context-free grammar. Let* Φ *be a function defined on* P *which assigns to each production* p *in* P *a finite, possibly empty set of set theoretical functions subject to the restriction that if the right member of production* p *has* n *terms of* V, *then any function of* $\Phi(p)$ *has* n *arguments. Then* $G = \langle V, V_N, P, S, \Phi \rangle$ *is a* potentially denoting context-free grammar. *If for each* p *in* P, $\Phi(p)$ *has exactly one member then* G *is said to be* simple.

The simplicity and abstractness of the definition may be misleading. In the case of a formal language, e.g., a context-free programming language, the creators of the language specify the semantics by defining Φ. Matters are more complicated in applying the same idea of capturing the semantics by such a function for fragments of a natural language. Perhaps the most difficult problem is that of giving a straightforward set-theoretical interpretation of intensional contexts, especially to those generated by the expression of propositional attitudes of believing, wanting, seeking and so forth. I shall not attempt to deal with these matters in the present paper.

How the set-theoretical functions in $\Phi(p)$ work was illustrated in the preceding section; some empirical examples follow in the next section. The problems of identifying and verifying Φ even in the simplest sort of context are discussed there. In one sense the definition should be strengthened to permit only one function in $\Phi(p)$ of a given number of arguments. The intuitive idea behind the restriction is clear. In a given application we try first to assign denotations at the individual word level, and we proceed to two- and three-word phrases only when necessary. The concept of such hierarchical parsing is familiar in computer programming, and a detailed example in the context of a question-answering program is worked out in a joint paper with Hélène Bestougeff. However, as the examples in the next section show, this restriction seems to be too severe for natural languages.

A clear separation of the generality of Φ and an evaluation function v is intended. The functions in Φ should be constant over many different uses of a word, phrase or statement. The valuation v, on the other hand, can change sharply from one occasion of use to the next. To provide for any finite composition of functions, or other ascensions in the natural hierarchy of sets and functions built up from a domain of individuals, the family $\mathcal{H}'(D)$ of sets with closure properties stronger than needed in any particular application is defined. The abstract objects T (for truth) and F (for falsity) are excluded as elements of $\mathcal{H}'(D)$. In this definition $\mathcal{P}A$ is the power set of A, i.e., the set of all subsets of A.

DEFINITION 3. *Let D be a nonempty set. Then $\mathcal{H}'(D)$ is the smallest family of sets such that*

(i) $D \in \mathcal{H}'(D)$,

(ii) *if $A, B \in \mathcal{H}'(D)$ then $A \cup B \in \mathcal{H}'(D)$,*

(iii) *if $A \in \mathcal{H}'(D)$ then $\mathcal{P}A \in \mathcal{H}'(D)$,*

(iv) *if $A \in \mathcal{H}'(D)$ and $B \subseteq A$ then $B \in \mathcal{H}'(D)$*

We define $\mathcal{H}(D) = \mathcal{H}'(D) \cup \{T, F\}$, with $T \notin \mathcal{H}'(D), F \notin \mathcal{H}'(D)$ and $T \neq F$.

A model structure for G is defined just for terminal words and phrases. The meaning or denotation of nonterminal symbols changes from one derivation or derivation tree to another.

DEFINITION 4. *Let D be a nonempty set, let $G = \langle V, V_N, P, S \rangle$ be a phrase-structure grammar, and let v be a partial function on V_T^+ to $\mathcal{H}(D)$ such that if v is defined for α in V_T^+ and if γ is a subsequence of α, then v is not defined for γ. Then $\mathcal{D} = \langle D, v \rangle$ is a model structure for G. If the domain of v is exactly V_T, then $\mathcal{D}$ is simple.*

We also refer to v as a *valuation function* for G.

I now define semantic trees that assign denotations to nonterminal symbols in a derivation tree. The definition is for simple potentially denoting grammars and for simple model structures. In other words, there is a unique semantic function for each production, and the valuation function is defined just on V_T, and not on phrases of V_T^+.

DEFINITION 5. *Let $G = \langle V, V_N, P, S, \Phi \rangle$ be a simple, potentially denoting context-free grammar, let $\mathcal{D} = \langle D, v \rangle$ be a simple model structure for G, let $\mathcal{F}' = \langle T, V, R, L, f \rangle$ be a derivation tree of $\langle V, V_N, P, S \rangle$ such that if x is a terminal node then $f(x) \in V_T$ and let ψ be a function from f to $\mathcal{H}(D)$ such that*

(i)   *if $\langle x, f(x) \rangle \in f$ and $f(x) \in V_T$ then $\psi(x, f(x)) = v(f(x))$,*
(ii) *if $\langle x, f(x) \rangle \in f, f(x) \in V_N$ and $y_1, \ldots, y_n$ are all the direct descendants of x with $y_i L y_j$ if $i < j$, then $\psi(x, f(x)) = \phi(\psi(y_1, f(y_1))), \ldots, \psi(y_n, f(y_n))$, where $\phi = \Phi(p)$ and p is the production $\langle f(x), \langle f(y_1), \ldots, f(y_n) \rangle \rangle$.*

Then $\mathcal{F} = \langle T, V, R, L, f, \Psi \rangle$ is a simple semantic tree of G and $\mathcal{D}$.

The extension of Definition 5 to semantic trees that are not simple is relatively straightforward, but is not given explicitly here in the interest of restricting the formal parts of the paper. The empirical examples considered in the next section implicitly assume this extension, but the simplicity of the corpus makes the several set-theoretical functions ϕ attached to a given production easy to interpret.

The function Ψ assigns a denotation to each node of a semantic tree. The resulting structural analysis can be used to define a concept of meaning or sense for each node. Perhaps the most natural intuitive idea is this. Extend the concept of a model structure by introducing a set of *situations*. For each situation $\sigma\langle D_\sigma, v_\sigma\rangle$ is a model structure. The meaning or sense of an utterance is then the function Ψ of the root of the tree of the utterance. For example, using the analysis of *John hit Mary* from the first section, dropping the redundant notation for the identity function and using the ordinary lambda notation for function abstraction, we obtain as the meaning of the sentence

$$\Psi(1, S) = (\lambda\sigma)f(v_\sigma(John), \overbrace{v_\sigma(hit)} \; {}^{\omega}v_\sigma(Mary)),$$

but this idea will not be developed further here. Its affinity to Kripke-type semantics is clear.

NOUN-PHRASE SEMANTICS OF ADAM I

In Suppes (1970), I proposed and tested a probabilistic noun-phrase grammar for Adam I, a well-known corpus of the speech of a young boy (about 26 months old) collected by Roger Brown and his associates—and once again I wish to record my indebtedness to Roger Brown for generously making his transcribed records available for analysis. Eliminating immediate repetitions of utterances, we have a corpus of 6109 word occurrences with a vocabulary of 673 different words and 3497 utterances. Noun phrases dominate the corpus. Of the 3497 utterances, I have classified 936 as single occurrences of nouns, another 192 as occurrences of two nouns in sequence, 147 as adjective followed by noun, and 138 as adjectives alone. The context-free grammar for the noun phrases of Adam I has seven production rules, and the theoretical probability of using each rule in a derivation is also shown for purposes of later discussion. From a probabilistic standpoint, the grammar has five free parameters: the sum of the a_i's is one, so the a_i's contribute four parameters and $b_1 + b_2 = 1$, whence the b_i's contribute one more parameter. To the right are also shown the main set-theoretical functions that make the grammar potentially denoting. These semantic functions, as it is convenient to call them in the present context, are subsequently discussed extensively. I especially call attention to the semantic function for Rule 5, which is formally defined below.

Noun-phrase grammar for Adam I

	Production Rule	Probability	Semantic Function
1.	$NP \to N$	a_1	Identity
2.	$NP \to AdjP$	a_2	Identity
3.	$NP \to AdjP + N$	a_3	Intersection
4.	$NP \to Pro$	a_4	Identity
5.	$NP \to NP + NP$	a_5	Choice function
6.	$AdjP \to AdjP + Adj$	b_1	Intersection
7.	$AdjP \to Adj$	b_2	Identity

As I remarked in the earlier article, except for Rule 5, the production rules seem standard and an expected part of a noun-phrase grammar for standard English. The new symbol introduced in V_N beyond those introduced already in the first section is *Pro* for pronoun; inflection of pronouns is ignored. On the other hand, the special category, PN, for proper nouns is not used in the grammar of Adam I.

The basic grammatical data are shown in Table 1. The first column gives the types of noun phrases actually occurring in the corpus in decreasing order of frequency. Some obvious abbreviations are used to shorten notation: A for Adj, P for Pro. The grammar defined generates an infinite number of types of utterances, but, of course, all except a small finite number have a small probability of being generated. The second column lists the numerical observed frequencies of the utterances (with immediate repetition of utterances deleted from the frequency count). The third column lists the theoretical or predicted frequencies when a maximum-likelihood estimate of the five parameters is made (for details on this see Suppes, 1970). The impact of semantics on these theoretical frequencies is discussed later.

The fourth column lists the observed frequency with which the 'standard' semantic function shown above seems to provide the correct interpretation for the five most frequent types. Of course, in the case of the identity function, there is not much to dispute, and so I concentrate entirely on the other two cases. First of all, if the derivation uses more than one rule, then by *standard interpretation* I mean the derivation that only uses Rule 5 if it is necessary and that interprets each production rule used in terms of its standard semantic function. Since none of the derivations is very complex, I shall not spend much time on this point.

The fundamental ideas of denoting grammars as defined in the preceding section come naturally into play when a detailed analysis is undertaken of the data summarized in Table 1. The most important step is to identify the additional semantic functions if any in $\Phi(p)$ for each of the seven

TABLE 1

PROBABILISTIC NOUN-PHRASE GRAMMAR FOR ADAM I

Noun phrase	Observed frequency	Theoretical frequency	Stand. semantic function
N	1445	1555.6	1445
P	388	350.1	388
NN	231	113.7	154
AN	135	114.0	91
A	114	121.3	114
PN	31	25.6	
NA	19	8.9	
NNN	12	8.3	
AA	10	7.1	
NAN	8	8.3	
AP	6	2.0	
PPN	6	.4	
ANN	5	8.3	
AAN	4	6.6	
PA	4	2.0	
ANA	3	.7	
APN	3	.1	
AAA	2	.4	
APA	2	.0	
NPP	2	.4	
PAA	2	.1	
PAN	2	1.9	

production rules. A simple way to look at this is to examine the various types of utterances listed in Table 1, summarize the production rules and semantic functions used for each type, and then collect all of this evidence in a new summary table for the production rules.

Therefore I now discuss the types of noun phrases listed in Table 1 and consider in detail the data for the five most frequently listed.

Types N and P, the first two, need little comment. The identity function and no other function, serves for them. It should be clearly understood, of course, that the nouns and pronouns listed in these first two lines—a total of 1833 without immediate repetition—do not occur as parts of a larger noun phrase. The derivation of N uses only $P1$ (Production Rule 1), and the derivation of P uses only $P4$.

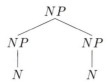

The data on type NN are much richer and more complex. The derivation is unique; it uses $P5$ then $P1$ twice, as shown in the tree. As before, the semantic function for $P1$ is just the identity function, so all the analysis of type NN centers around the interpretation of $P5$. To begin with, I must explain what I mean by the choice function shown above as the standard semantic function of $P5$. This is a set-theoretical function of A and B that for each A is a function selecting an element of B when B is the argument of f. Thus

$$\varphi(A, B) = f_A(B) \in B.$$

I used 'A' rather than an individual variable to make the notation general, but in all standard cases, A is a unit set. (I emphasize again, I do not distinguish unit sets from their members.) A standard set-theoretical choice function, i.e., a function f such that if B is in the domain of f and B is non-empty then $f(B) \in B$, is a natural device for expressing possession. Intuitively, each of the possessors named by Adam has such a function and the function selects his (or hers or its) object from the class of like objects. Thus *Daddy chair* denotes that chair in the class of chairs within Adam's purview that belongs to or is used especially by Daddy. If we restrict our possessors to individuals, then in terms of the model structure $\mathcal{D}=\langle D, v \rangle$, $\phi(A, B)$ is just a partial function from $D \times \mathcal{P}(D)$ to $\mathcal{D}$.[3]

---

[3]Other possibilities exist for the set-theoretical characterization of possession. In fact, there is an undesirable asymmetry between the choice function for *Adam hat* and the intersection function for *my hat*, but it is also clear that *v(my)* can in a straightforward sense be the set of Adam's possessions but *v(Adam)* is Adam, not the set of Adam's possessions.

TABLE 2

SEMANTIC CLASSIFICATION

OF NOUN PHRASES OF TYPE NN

Choice function

Adam checker	Adam horn
Adam hat	Adam hat
Adam bike	Adam pillow
Moocow tractor	Moocow truck
Catherine dinner	Car mosquito
Newmi book	Newmi bulldozer
Daddy briefcase	Adam book
Adam book	Adam paper
Daddy chair	Daddy tea
Mommy tea	Tuffy boat
Tuffy boat	Adam pencil
Adam tractor	Tuffy boat
Judy buzz	Judy buzz
Ursula pocketbook	Ursula pocket
Daddy name	Daddy name
Daddy Bozo	Daddy Johnbuzzhart
Daddy name	Adam light
Catherine Bozo	Monroe suitcase
Adam glove	Adam ball
Adam locomotive	Daddy racket
Daddy racket	Adam racket
Adam pencil	Joshua shirt
Joshua foot	Adam busybulldozer
Robie nail	Adam busybulldozer
Train track	Adam Daddy
Daddy suitcase	Cromer suitcase
Adam suitcase	Daddy suitcase
Adam doggie	Adam doggie
Choochoo track	Daddy Adam
Adam water	Ursula water
Ursula car	Adam house
Hobo truck	Doctordan circus
Doctordan circus	Joshua book
Daddy paper	Adam Cromer
Cromer coat	Adam pencil
Adam pillow	Mommy pillow
Adam pillow	Daddy pillow
Dan circus	Doctordan circus
Adam ladder	Adam mouth
Adam mouth	Daddy desk
Doctordan circus	Adam sky
Adam horn	Adam baby
Adam piece	Adam candy

Adam playtoy
Doggie car
Adam book
Adam shirt
Adam ball
Cromer suitcase
Adam letter
Adam firetruck
Bambi wagon
Like Adam bookshelf
Pull Adam bike
Write Daddy name
Hit Mommy wall
Hit Adam roadgrader (?)
Spill Mommy face
Bite Cromer mouth
Hit Mommy ball
Get Adam ball
Write Cromer shoe
Sit Missmonroe car
Walk Adam Bambi
Adam Panda march. (?)
Oh Adam belt
Adam bite rightthere (?)
Fish water inhere
Put Adam bandaid on
Put Missmonroe towtruck (?)
Mommy tea yea
Adam school tomorrow
Daddy suitcase goget it
Take off Adam paper
No Adam Bambi
That Adam baby
Powershovel pick Adam dirt up

Kitchen playtoy
Man Texacostar (?)
Adam paper
Adam pocketbook
Daddy suitcase
Adam suitcase
Adam pencil
Adam firetruck
See Daddy car
Give doggie paper
Read Doctor circus
Write Daddy name
Hit Mommy rug
See Adam ball
Bite Mommy mouth
Bite Ursula mouth
Take Adam car
Sit Adam chair
Sit Monroe car
Walk Adam Bambi
Going Cromer suitcase
Doggies tummy hurt
Yea locomotive caboose
Adam shoe rightthere
Take lion nose off
Pick roadgrader dirt (?)
Put Adam boot
Adam pencil yeah
Becky star tonight
Adam pocket no
Big towtruck pick Joshua dirt up
Look Bambi Adam pencil
Break Cromer suitcase Mommy
Where record folder go

Converse of choice function

Part trailer
Book boy
Ladder firetruck
Part head
Foot Adam

Part towtruck
Name man
Record Daddy
Part game
Track train

Car train

Taperecorder Ursula

Speghetti Cromer

Part basket

Game Adam

Take piece candy

Excuseme Ursula part broom

Part broom

Circus Dan

Part apple

Piece candy

Time bed (?)

Paper kitty open

Choice function on Cartesian product

Pencil paper

Mommy Daddy

Mommy Daddy

Pencil roadgrader (?)

Busybulldozer truck (?)

Jack Jill come

Paper pencil

Towtruck fire

Record taperecorder

Jack Jill

Give paper pencil

Adam wipeoff Cromer Ursula

Intersection

Lady elephant

Lady Ursula

Toy train

Lady Ursula

Lady elephant

Record box

Identity

Pin Game

Daddy Cromer (?)

Doctor Doctordan

Babar Pig

Mommy Cromer (?)

Unclassified

Joshua home

Train train (Repetition?)

Dog pepper

Suitcase water

Doggie pepper

Daddy home (S)

Door book

Pumpkin tomato

Chew apple mouth (2)

Hit door head (2)

Hit head trash (2)

Show Ursula Bambi (2)

Look car mosquito (2)

Pick dirt shovel up (2)

Ohno put hand glove (2)

Pencil doggie

Adam Adam (Repetition?)

Kangaroo bear

Doggie doggie (Repetition?)

Kangaroo marchingbear

Ball playtoy (?)

Pumpkin tomato

Put truck window (2)

Hit towtruck knee (2)

Make Cromer Doctordan (2)

Hurt knee chair (2)

Show Ursula Bambi (2)

Daddy Daddy work (Repetition?)

Mommy time bed

Time bed Mommy

The complete classification of all noun phrases of type NN is given in Table 2. (I emphasize that this classification must be regarded as tentative at this early stage of investigation.) As the data in Table 2 show, the choice function is justly labeled the standard semantic function for $P5$, but at least four other semantic functions belong in $\Phi(P5)$. One of these is the converse of $\phi(A, B)$ as defined above, i.e.,

$$\phi(A, B) = f_B(A),$$

which means the possessor is named after the thing possessed. Here are examples from Adam I for which this interpretation seems correct: *part trailer* (meaning *part of trailer*), *part towtruck, book boy, name man, ladder firetruck, taperecorder Ursula*. The complete list is given in Table 2.

The third semantic function is a choice function on the Cartesian product of two sets, often the sets' being unit sets as in the case of *Mommy Daddy*. Formally, we have

$$\phi(A, B) = f(A \times B),$$

and $f(A \times B) \in A \times B$. Other examples are *Daddy Adam* and *pencil paper*. The frequency of use of this function is low, however—only 12 out of 230 instances according to the classification shown in Table 2.

The fourth semantic function proposed for $\Phi(P5)$ is the intersection function

$$\phi(A, B) = A \cap B.$$

Examples are *lady elephant* and *lady Ursula*. Here the first noun is functioning like an adjective.

The fifth semantic function, following in frequency the choice function and its converse, is the identity function. It seems clear from the transcription that some pairs of nouns are used as a proper name or a simple description, even though each noun is used in other combinations. (By a *simple description* I mean a phrase such that no subsequence of it denotes (see Definition 4).) Some examples are *pin game* and *Daddy Cromer*.

I do not consider in the same detail the next two most frequent types shown in Table I, namely, AN and A. The latter, as in the case of N and P, is served without complications by the identity function. As would be expected, the picture is more complicated for the type AN. Column 4 of Table I indicates that 91 of the 135 instances of AN can be interpreted as using intersection as the semantic function. Typical examples are these: *big drum, big horn, my shadow, my paper, my tea, my comb, oldtime train, that knee, green rug, that man, poor doggie, pretty flower*. The main exceptions to the intersection rule are found in the use of numerical or comparative adjectives like *two* or *more*. Among the 116 *AN* phrases standing alone, i.e., not occurring as part of a longer utterance, 19 have *two* as the adjective; for example, *two checkers, two light, two sock, two men, two boot, two rug*. No numerical adjective other than *two* is used in the 116 phrases.

I terminate at this point the detailed analysis of the Adam I corpus, but some computations concerning the length of noun phrases in Adam I are considered in the next section.

TOWARD A THEORY OF PERFORMANCE

The ideas that developed in this paper and in my earlier paper on probabilistic grammars are meant to be steps toward a theory of performance. In discussing the kind of theories of language wanted by linguists, philosophers or psychologists, I have become increasingly aware of the real differences in the objectives of those who want a theory of ideal competence and those who are concerned with performance. Contrary to the opinions expressed by some linguists, I would not concede for a moment that a theory of competence must precede in time the development of a theory of performance. I do recognize, on the other hand, the clear differences of objectives in the two kinds of theories. The linguistic and philosophical tradition of considering elaborate and subtle examples of sentences that express propositional attitudes is very much in the spirit of a theory of competence. The subtlety of many of these examples is far beyond the bulk of sentences used in everyday discourse by everyday folk. The kind of corpus considered in the preceding section is a far cry from most of these subtle examples.

The probabilistic grammars discussed in the preceding section, and elaborated upon more thoroughly in the earlier paper, clearly belong to a theory of performance. Almost all of the linguists or philosophers interested in theories of competence would probably reject probabilistic grammars as being of any interest to such theories. On the other hand, from the standpoint of a theory of performance, such grammars immediately bring to hand a detailed analysis of actual speech as well as a number of predictions about central characteristics of actual speech that are not a part of a theory of competence. Perhaps the simplest and clearest example is predictions about the distribution of length of utterances. One of the most striking features of actual speech is that most utterances are of short duration, and no utterances are of length greater than 10^4 even though in the usual theories of competence there is no way of predicting the distribution of length of utterance and no mechanism for providing it. A probabilistic grammar immediately supplies such a mechanism, and I would take it to be a prime responsibility of a theory of performance to predict the distribution of utterances from the estimation of a few parameters.

Here for example, are the theoretical predictions of utterance length in terms of the parameters a_i and b_j assigned to the production rules for Adam I noun phrases. In order to write a simple recursive expression for the probability of a noun phrase of length n, I use ℓ_i for the probability of an utterance of length $i < n$. Thus, for example, one of the terms in the expression for the probability of a noun phrase of length 3 is $2a_5\ell_1\ell_2$. By first using Rule 5 (with probability a_5) and then generating for one NP a noun phrase of length 1, which starting from NP has probability ℓ_1, and generating for the other NP a noun phrase of length 2 with probability ℓ_2, we obtain $2a_5\ell_1\ell_2$, since this can happen in two ways. We have in general the following:

Length of noun phrase	Probability of this length
1	$a_1 + a_2b_2 + a_4$
2	$a_2b_1b_2 + a_3b_2 + a_5(a_1 + a_2b_2 + a_4)^2$
3	$a_2b_1^2b_2 + a_3b_1b_2 + 2a_5\ell_1\ell_2$
.	.
.	.
.	.
n	$a_2b_1^{n-1}b_2 + a_3b_1^{n-2}b_2 + a_5 \displaystyle\sum_{\substack{1 \leq i,j < n \\ i+j=n}} \ell_i\ell_j$

Using the maximum-likelihood estimates of the parameters a_i and b_j obtained to make the theoretical predictions of Table 1, we can compare theoretical and observed distributions of noun-phrase length for Adam I. The results are shown in Table 3 for lengths up to 3.

TABLE 3

PREDICTION OF LENGTH OF NOUN PHRASES FOR ADAM I

Length	Observed frequency	Theoretical frequency
1	1947	2027.1
2	436	314.1
3	51	66.9
>3	0	25.9
	2434	2434.0

Because this paper is mainly concerned with semantics, I shall not pursue these grammatical matters further, but turn to the way in which the theory of semantics developed here is meant to contribute to a theory of performance. From a behavioral standpoint it is much easier to describe the objective methods used in constructing a probabilistic grammar, because the corpus of sentences and the classification of individual words into given syntactic categories can be objectively described and verified by any interested person. The application of the theory, in other words, has an objective character that is on the surface. Matters are different when we turn to semantics. For example, it does not seem possible to state directly objective criteria by which the classification of semantic functions as described in the preceding section are made. Clearly I have taken advantage of my own intuitive knowledge of the language in an inexplicit way to interpret Adam's intended meaning in using a particular utterance. If the methodology for applying semantics to actual speech had to be left at the level of analysis of the preceding section, objections could certainly be made that the promise of such a semantics for a theory of performance was very limited.

A first naive approach to applying semantics to the development of a more complete theory of performance might have as an objective the prediction of the actual sentences uttered by a speaker. Everyone to whom this proposal is made instantly recognizes the difficulty, if not the impossibility, of predicting the actual utterance made once the structure of the utterance goes beyond something like a simple affirmation or denial. Frequently the next step is to use this common recognition of difficulty as an argument for the practical impossibility of applying any concepts of probability in analyzing actual speech behavior. This skeptical attitude has been expressed recently by Chomsky (1969, p.57) in the following passage:

> ...If we return to the definition of 'language' as a "complex of dispositions to verbal behavior", we reach a similar conclusion, at least if this notion is intended to have empirical content. Presumably, a complex of dispositions is a structure that can be represented as a set of probabilities for utterances in certain definable 'circumstances' or 'situations'. But it must be recognized that the notion 'probability of a sentence' is an entirely useless one, under any known interpretation of this term. On empirical grounds, the probability of my producing some given sentence of English—say, this sentence, or the sentence "birds fly" or "Tuesday follows Monday", or whatever—is indistinguishable from the probability of my producing a given sentence of Japanese. Introduction of the notion of 'probability relative to a situation' changes nothing, at least if

'situations' are characterized on any known objective grounds (we can, of course, raise the conditional probability of any sentence as high as we like, say to unity, relative to 'situations' specified on *ad hoc*, invented grounds).

One can agree with much of what Chomsky says in this passage, but also recognize that it is written without familiarity with the way in which probability concepts are actually used in science. What is said here applies almost without change to the study of the simplest probabilistic phenomenon, e.g., the flipping of a coin. If we construct a probability space for a thousand flips of a coin, and if the coin is approximately a fair one, then the actual probability of any observed sequence is almost zero, namely, approximately 2^{-1000}. If we use a representation that is often used for theoretical purposes and take the number of trials to be infinite, then the probability of any possible outcome of the experiment in this theoretical representation is strictly zero. It in no sense follows that the concept of probability cannot be applied in a meaningful way to the flipping of a coin. A response may be that a single flip has a high probability and that this is not the case for a single utterance, but corresponding to utterances, we can talk about sequences of flips and once again we have extraordinarily low probabilities attached to any actual sequence of flips of length greater than, say, a hundred. What Chomsky does not seem to be aware of is that in most sophisticated applications of probability theory the situation is the same as what he has described for sentences. The basic objects of investigation have either extremely small probabilities or strictly zero probabilities. The test of the theory then depends upon studying various features of the observed outcome. In the case of the coin the single most interesting feature is the relative frequency of heads, but if we are suspicious of the mechanism being used to toss the coin we may also want to investigate the independence of trials.

To make the comparison still more explicit, Chomsky's remarks about the equal probability of uttering an English or Japanese sentence can be mimicked in discussing the outcomes of flipping a coin. The probability of a thousand successive heads in flipping a fair coin is 2^{-1000}, just the probability of any other sequence of this length. Does this equal probability mean that we should accept the same odds in betting that the relative frequency of heads will be less than 0.6, and betting that it will be greater than 0.99? Certainly not. In a similar way there are many probabilistic predictions about verbal behavior that can be made, ranging from trivial predictions about whether a given speaker will utter an English or Japanese sentence to detailed predictions about grammatical or semantic structure. Our inability to predict the unique flow of discourse no more invalidates a definition of language as a "complex of dispositions to verbal behavior" than our inability to predict the trajectory of a single free electron for some short period of time invalidates quantum mechanics—even in a short period of time any possible trajectory has strictly zero probability of being realized on the continuity assumptions ordinarily made.

Paradoxically, linguists like Chomsky resist so strongly the use of probability notions in language analysis just when these are the very concepts that are most suited to such complex phenomena. The systematic use of probability is to be justified in most applications in science because of our inability to develop an adequate deterministic theory.

In the applications of probability theory one of the most important techniques for testing a theory is to investigate the theoretical predictions for a variety of conditional probabilities. The concept of conditional probability and the related concept of independence are the central concepts of probability theory. It is my own belief that we shall be able to apply these concepts to show the usefulness of semantics at a surface behavioral level. Beginning with a probabilistic grammar, we want to improve the probabilistic predictions by taking into account the postulated semantic structure. The test of the correctness of the semantic structure is then in terms of the additional predictions we can make. By taking account of the semantic structure, we can make differential probabilistic predictions and thereby show the behavioral relevance of semantics. Without entering into the kind of detailed data analysis of the preceding section, let me try to indicate in more concrete fashion how such an application of semantics is to be made.

I have reported previously the analysis of the corpus of Adam I. We have also been collecting data of our own at Stanford, and we have at hand a corpus of some 20 hours of Erica, a rather talkative 30-month-old girl.[4] We have been concerned to write a probabilistic grammar for Erica of the same sort we have tried to develop for Adam I. The way in which a semantic structure can be used to improve the predictions of a probabilistic grammar can be illustrated by considering Erica's answers to the many questions asked her by adults. For the purposes of this sketch, let me concentrate on some of the data in the first hour of the Erica corpus. According to one straightforward classification, 169 questions were addressed to Erica by an adult during the first hour of the corpus. These 169 questions may be fairly directly classified in the following types: *what*-questions, *yes-no*-questions, *where*-questions, *who*-questions, etc. The frequency of each type of question is as follows:

---

[4]The corpus was taped and edited by Arlene Moskowitz.

What-questions	79
Yes-no-questions	60
Where-questions	12
Who-questions	9
Why-questions	4
How-many-questions	3
Or-questions	1
How-do-you-know-questions	1

By taking account of the most obvious semantic features of these different types of questions, we can improve the probabilistic predictions of the kind of responses Erica makes without claiming that we can make an exact prediction of her actual utterances. Moreover, the semantic classification of the questions does not depend on any simple invariant features of the surface grammar. For example, some typical *yes-no*-questions, with Erica's answers in parentheses, are these: *Can you sit on your seat please? (O.K.), You don't touch those, do you? (No), Aren't they? (Uh huh. That Arlene's too), He isn't old enough is he? (No. Just Martin's old enough.)*

It is an obvious point that the apparatus of model-theoretic semantics is not sufficient to predict the choice of a particular description of an object from among many semantically suitable ones. Suppose John and Mary are walking, and John notices a spider close to Mary's shoulder. He says, "Watch out for that spider." He does not say, "Watch out for the black, half-inch long spider that has a green dot in its center and is about six inches from your left shoulder at a vertical angle of about sixty degrees." The principle that selects the first utterance and not the second I call a *principle of minimal discrimination*. A description is selected that is just adequate to the perceptual or cognitive task. Sometimes, of course, a full sentence rather than a noun phrase is used in response to a *what*-question, the sort of question whose answer most naturally exemplifies a minimal principle. Here is an example from Erica: *What do you want for lunch? (Peanut butter and jelly), What do you want to drink? (I want to drink peanut butter).* In answering *what*-questions by naming or describing an object, Erica uses adjectives only sparingly, and then mainly in a highly relevant way. Here are a couple of examples: *What are you going to ride on? (On a big towel), What are those? (Oboe and clarinet. And a flute. Little bitty flute called a piccolo).* Preliminary analysis of the Erica corpus indicates that even a relatively crude probabilistic application of the principle of minimal discrimination can significantly improve predictions about Erica's answers. Presentation of systematic data on this point must be left for another occasion.

I want to finish by stressing that I do not have the kind of imperialistic ambitions for a theory of performance that many linguists seem to have for a theory of competence. I do not think a theory of performance need precede a theory of competence. I wish only to claim that the two can proceed independently—they have sufficiently different objectives and different methods of analysis so that their independence, I would venture to suggest, will become increasingly apparent. A probabilistic account of main features of actual speech is a different thing from a theory-of-competence analysis of the kind of subtle examples found in the literature on propositional attitudes. The investigation of these complicated examples certainly should not cease, but at the present time they have little relevance to the development of a theory of performance. The tools for the development of a theory of performance, applied within the standard scientific theory of probability processes, are already at hand in the concepts of a probabilistic grammar and semantics. Unfortunately, many linguists dismiss probabilistic notions out of hand and without serious familiarity with their use in any domain of science.

Quine ended a recent article (1970) with a plea against absolutism in linguistic theory and methodology. It is a plea that we should all heed.

11

ELIMINATION OF QUANTIFIERS IN THE SEMANTICS OF NATURAL LANGUAGE BY USE OF EXTENDED RELATION ALGEBRAS

A plethora of proposals besieges seekers after an adequate semantics of natural language. The special twist of my proposal is to offer simplicity, not generality. We need, so it seems to me, systematic semantic analyses of restricted but substantive fragments of natural language. Such analyses should have the same broad aims as restricted models in other areas of knowledge: simplicity of formulation, ease of comprehension, and computational efficiency.

The present work is an outgrowth of my earlier work on the semantics

*Reprinted from *Revue International de Philosophie*, **117-118**, 243-259, 1976. The ideas developed here were first outlined in my Stanford course of lectures on mathematical linguistics in the winter term of 1973. They were almost crystallized into their present form in a joint seminar I gave with Paul Grice in Berkeley during the spring term, 1975. He would undoubtedly not wholly agree with everything I say here, although in response to his sharp questions, and those of George Myro and Richard Warner as well, I made a valiant effort at persuasion. I have benefited recently from a lively exchange with Robert Smith and Freeman Rawson. Their trenchant remarks on the next-to-final draft saved me from several blunders and obscurities.

of context-free fragments of natural language (Suppes, 1973b). The arena is narrower, but my intention is to enter more deeply into the details. One egocentric way of putting my objective is that I propose an analysis in terms of what I call *extended relational algebras* of the semantics of a large part of the ordinary-language examples of quantifiers in my logic text (Suppes, 1957). Thus, I want to analyze not only *All men are animals*, but also *Some sophomores date juniors, Every man loves some woman, Some men look at every woman*, or *Every number is less than some number*. It is, of course, easy to construct examples of mathematical sentences that fall outside the intended range of analysis, e.g., *For all distinct points* x, y, *and* u, *if* x, y *and* u *are not collinear, then there is a point* v *such that the line determined by* x *and* y *is parallel to the line determined by* u *and* v[1]. But the extent of ordinary usage covered by the semantic calculus of extended relation algebras is substantial, mainly because complex sequences of quantifiers are rare in natural language.

I hasten to add there are many other important features of natural language that the present theory gives no account of—perhaps the most salient example would be the semantics of adverbs. On the other hand, extensions of what I develop here could handle parts of the semantics of tense in verb systems, and also some essential semantic features of anaphora.

The advantages of not needing a full Zermelo-like hierarchy of sets for the model structures of ordinary sentences are obvious. In a general way the algebraic push for efficiency of computation by avoiding a hierarchy is probably a rather widely acceptable idea.

Other aspects of the "algebraic" semantics proposed here are much more controversial. Linguists especially will not like my insistence that such expressions as *every man, all freshmen,* or *some dogs* are not noun phrases. Furthermore, these phrases as such do not, in my approach, have a denotation, contrary, for example, to the semantic proposed by Grice or Montague. Indeed, the quantifier words *every, all, some,* etc., do not denote at all in my approach but function as *control structure* words—to use a terminology favored by computer scientists[2]. To be more explicit, they control the selection of semantic functions in a way that will be explained in detail later.

My central point is that the fixation of first-order logic as the proper vehicle for analyzing the "logical form" or the "meaning" of sentences

---

[1] From a formal standpoint, a better example, taken from Tarski (1941), that cannot be expressed in the calculus of relations is this: *for every* x,y, *and* z *there is a* u *such that* xRu & yRu & zRu

[2] For a sophisticated discussion of control structures in natural language, see Smith and Rawson (1976).

in a natural language is mistaken. The semantics of first-order logic is ideal for the expressions of that logic. The syntax and semantics fit each other as subtly as could be desired, *pace* Gödel's completeness theorem. The same snug fit of syntax and semantics should be our objective for natural language, but such a fit will not be obtained by rigidly holding to the apparatus of first-order logic to frame the semantics of natural languages. Individual variables do not occur in most natural utterances. A semantical approach that requires their appearance is bound to fit the syntax in an awkward way. Much of what I am saying has been recognized de facto at least in the special case of the standard A,E,I, and O sentences that occur as premises or conclusions of syllogisms. What I attempt to show here is that the algebraic approach can be extended considerably beyond these limited forms to a fairly rich body of natural utterances.

On the matter of the denotation or lack of it of *every man*, and the corresponding linguistic production rules for sentences and noun phrases, we can prove in a simple way that the conventional production rules will not even permit a semantic account of the syllogism at the level of Boolean algebra, i.e., at the level of subsets of the domain, but require what I consider an artificial escalation of type (see the fourth section).

Exhaustive discussion of the variant positions that have been taken toward the denotation or reference of *every man* has been given by Geach (1968), but he passes over, without much analysis, a position close to that advocated here (p. 13). Since the introduction of quantifiers as explicit logical notation by Frege, the separation of semantics from the syntax of natural language seems to have widened. I see no reason for this. The more the logical apparatus of semantical analysis is separated from the actual syntactical forms of natural language, the less reason there is to accept its correctness as an analysis of what has been said.

Although Frege did not develop a closely linked syntax and semantics of natural language—and was indeed suspicious of the logical coherence of natural language—his informal view of the logical role of quantifier words in natural language is close to what I am advocating. Here is a significant passage (Frege, 1960, p. 48) referred to by Geach:

> It must here be remarked that the words 'all', 'any', 'no', 'some', are prefixed to concept-words. In universal and particular affirmative and negative sentences, we are expressing relations between concepts; we use these words to indicate the special kind of relation. They are thus, logically speaking, not to be more closely associated with the concept-words that follow them, but are to be related to the sentence as a whole. It is easy to see this in the case of negation. If in the sentence 'all mammals are land-dwellers' the

phrase 'all mammals' expressed the logical subject of the predicate *are land dwellers*, then in order to negate the whole sentence we should have to negate the predicate: 'are not land-dwellers'. Instead, we must put the 'not', in front of 'all'; from which it follows that 'all' logically belongs with the predicate.

As Frege hints at, some change in a tradition that goes back to the Alexandrian grammarians is required in the linguistic classification of quantifier words. This reclassification is already presaged in the treatment of quantifiers in first-order logic where they are not categorized as terms or parts of terms. By modifying *both* the logical and the linguistic traditions, an approach can be given, so I claim, that brings completely together the syntax and semantics of sentences containing quantifier words—not all such sentences, but many of the garden-variety ones.

I shall proceed in the following fashion. The second section is devoted to a quick overview of my conception of semantic trees for context-free languages. The third section develops the restricted semantics for extended relation algebras. The fourth section is concerned with the proof that the kind of grammatical production rules often used by linguists for quantifiers, in contrast to the ones given here, lead to an undesirable escalation of logical type in the underlying set-theoretical semantics.

SEMANTIC TREES

The ideas central to model-theoretic semantics in mathematical logic go back to Frege. They have been developed extensively by the work of Tarski and his students, but most of the model theory is not concerned with natural language. The semantical approaches developed by linguists or others whose viewpoint is that of generative grammar have been lacking the formal precision of model-theoretic semantics. My objective here and in other writings has been to combine the viewpoint of model-theoretic semantics, on the one hand, and generative grammar, especially the work of Chomsky, on the other.

A number of examples will give an intuitive idea of the intended application of model theory. Let us take as an instance the simple noun phrase *square table*. That noun phrase can be represented by a simple tree (Figure 1), where NP = noun phrase, N = noun, and Adj = adjective.

This grammar has (except for insertion of lexical items) as yet only one production rule: $NP \rightarrow Adj + N$. How is the semantics of this noun phrase to be formalized? With each production rule of the grammar we associate a semantic function, and thus we may convert each derivation tree to a *semantic tree* by assigning a denotation to each node of the tree.

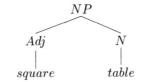

Figure 1.

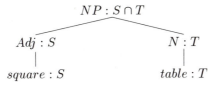

Figure 2.

The denotation of each node of the tree is shown in Figure 2 after the colon following the label of the node.

The semantic tree is obtained by the assignment of (i) denotations to terminal words or phrases, in this case S for the set of square things and T for the set of tables, and (ii) semantic functions to production rules, in this case the identity function for the lexical rules and intersection for $NP \rightarrow Adj + N$. The word order in the corresponding French example *table carrée* (Figure 3) is reversed. The denotation of the root of the tree is just the same. The semantic parts of the French and English trees are more alike than the grammatical parts.

Let us next consider the analysis of a simple sentence. The semantic tree of *John loves Mary* has the form of Figure 4. Note that in this tree L

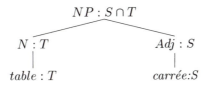

Figure 3.

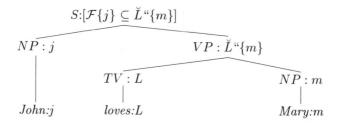

Figure 4.

is the binary relation of loving. Perhaps the most interesting denotation is that of the VP node. The denotation of this node is the set consisting of the image of Mary under the converse of loving ——$\check{L}\text{“}\{m\}$—— or, in more intuitive language, the set of persons that love Mary. The denotation of the root of the tree I take to be what I term the Frege function defined as follows:

$$[_{\mathcal{F}}\phi(A,B)] = \left\{ \begin{array}{l} T \text{ if } \phi(A,B) \\ F \text{ otherwise.} \end{array} \right.$$

I give a brief overview of the systematic ideas back of these examples. First, a structure $G = \langle V, N, P, S \rangle$ is a *phrase-structure grammar* if and only if V and P are finite, nonempty sets, N is a subset of V, S is in N, and $P \subseteq N^* \times V^+$ where N^* is the set of all finite sequences whose terms are elements of N, and V^+ is V^* minus the empty sequence. The grammar G is *context-free* if and only if $P \subseteq N \times V^+$. In the usual terminology, V is the vocabulary, N is the nonterminal vocabulary, S is the start symbol of derivations or the label of the root of derivation trees of the grammar, and P is the set of production rules.

This formal definition of a grammar may be illustrated by an example, call it G_1, that will be useful in the subsequent discussion. Note that G_1 generates, among other things, the classical A, I, E, and O propositions. The set P_1 of production rules, minus the lexical rules for introducing terminal vocabulary, is:

$$
\begin{array}{rl}
S \to & UQ + NP + VP/EQ + NP + VP/NQ + NP + VP \\
NP \to & N \\
VP \to & TV + UQ + NP/TV + EQ + NP/TV + NQ + NP/IV \\
& Cop + NP/Cop + Adj/Cop + Neg + NP/Cop + Neg + Adj.
\end{array}
$$

(The slash '/' is used to present several rules that have the same nonterminal on the left; thus there are 12 rules given above.) The set N_1 of nonterminal symbols consists of $S,NP,VP,UQ,EQ,NQ,N,TV,IV,Cop,Adj,Neg$, each with its nearly classical grammatical meaning—e.g., TV = transitive verb, IV = intransitive verb, Cop = copula, $UQ \to All$, $EQ \to Some$, and $NQ \to No$. I assume as known the standard definitions of one string of V^* being G-*derivable* from another, the concept of a *derivation tree* of G, and the *language* $L(G)$ generated by G. (For a detailed treatment of these concepts, see Hopcroft & Ullman, 1969).

We move from syntax to semantics in two stages. First the grammar G is extended to a *potentially denoting* grammar by assigning at least one set-theoretical function to each production rule of G. Thus, in the example of Figure 2, the set-theoretical function assigned to the single nonlexical rule is intersection. We may show these functions in general by using brackets to show the denotation of a nonterminal. In the case of Figure 2,

$$\begin{array}{ll} Rule & Semantic\ function \\ NP \to Adj + N & [NP] = [Adj] \cap [N] \end{array}$$

The second stage is the characterization of model structures. In the general theory of model-theoretic semantics for context-free languages, I use the concept of a *hierarchy* $\mathcal{H}(D)$ of sets built up from a given nonempty domain D by closure under union, subset, and power set 'operations'. A *model structure* for a given grammar G with a terminal vocabulary V_T is a pair $\langle D, v \rangle$ where D is a nonempty set and v is a partial function from V_T^+ to $\mathcal{H}(D)$. Explicit details are to be found in Suppes (1973b).

Extension of the concept of semantic tree to transformational grammars is in principle conceptually straightforward, but formally complex. Some of the problems are discussed in Suppes (1973a).

EXTENDED RELATION ALGEBRAS

Extended relation algebras enter as highly restricted forms of the hierarchy $\mathcal{H}(D)$ of a model structure $\langle D, v \rangle$. The natural preliminary definition is that of a nonempty family $\mathcal{F}$ of sets closed under the Boolean operations of complementation and union, the relation operations of converse and relative product, and the image $R``A$ of a set A under the relation R. In familiar notation these are just the following conditions:

$E1.$ If $A \in \mathcal{F}$ then $\neg A \in \mathcal{F}$;

$E2.$ If $A, B \in \mathcal{F}$ then $A \cup B \in \mathcal{F}$;

$E3.$ If $A \in \mathcal{F}$ then $\check{A} \in \mathcal{F}$;

$E4.$ If $A, B \in \mathcal{F}$ then $A/B \in \mathcal{F}$;

$E5.$ If $A, B \in \mathcal{F}$ then $A``B \in \mathcal{F}$.

The properties of all these operations are discussed in some detail in Suppes (1960). If D is a domain, then $\mathcal{F}$ is a subset of the power set of $D \cup (D \times D)$. For the classical syllogism we need only that $\mathcal{F}$ is an algebra of sets, i.e., is a subset of the power set of D and satisfies $E1$ and $E2$. The conditions $E1$–$E5$ define a structure that from a purely logical or mathematical standpoint is somewhat unusual, because of $E5$, but as we saw in the analysis of *John loves Mary* in Figure 4, the image of a set under a relation is the natural denotation of a VP node that has a transitive verb as a descendant. More generally, the conditions of closure are required by the semantics of standard S–V–O sentences, except possibly for $C4$, the closure condition on the relative product, which does not seem to be needed very often in the semantic analysis of common sentences. One possible use is in the semantic analysis of adverbs that intensify a property or relation.

To account for all nodes of semantic trees that denote—in particular, to take account of the values T and F of the Frege function, we may enlarge $\mathcal{F}$ to $\mathcal{F} = \mathcal{F} \cup \{T, F\}$ with $T, F \in \mathcal{F}$ and $T \neq F$. However, for the algebraic viewpoint of this paper, it is preferable to make the semantic function at the root of a tree not the Frege function used in Figure 4, but a relational function, i.e., a function that is a mapping from $\mathcal{F}$ to $\mathcal{F}$ in the case of a single argument, from $\mathcal{F} \times \mathcal{F}$ to $\mathcal{F}$ when the function has two arguments, etc. Hilbert and Ackermann's (1950) classic algebraic treatment of the syllogism illustrates the method. Generalizing their treatment we have for the first two production rules of G_1

Rule	Semantic function
$S \rightarrow UQ + NP + VP$	$[S] = \neg[NP] \cup [VP]$
$S \rightarrow EQ + NP + VP$	$[S] = [NP] \cap [VP]$

The functions shown on the right are Boolean functions—the concept is familiar and I shall not give a formal definition. Later I do use the fact that there are 4 Boolean functions of one argument and 16 such functions of two arguments; e.g., in the case of one argument, if A is an arbitrary set of a Boolean algebra of sets and f is a Boolean function of one argument, the $f(A)$ is A, $\neg A$, O, or V, where O is the empty set and V is the universe. The number of extended relational functions of one or two arguments is more complicated to compute and will not be needed in the sequel.

I now turn to the analysis of quantifiers in object position. I begin with existential quantification because of its greater simplicity, the reason for which will soon be evident. In the initial version we shall move outside extended relation algebras.

Clearly, the meaning of the notation "$\cup \breve{D} \text{``} \{j\}_{j \in J}$" takes us beyond a

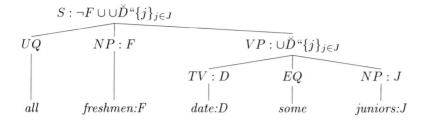

$$S : \neg F \cup \cup \check{D}\text{``}\{j\}_{j \in J}$$

UQ — NP : F — VP : $\cup \check{D}\text{``}\{j\}_{j \in J}$

TV : D — EQ — NP : J

all — freshmen:F — date:D — some — juniors:J

Figure 5.

family $\mathcal{F}$ of sets satisfying $E1$–$E5$, but the following elementary theorem of set theory brings us back within $\mathcal{F}$.

THEOREM 1. *For any sets A and B,*

$$B\text{``}A = \bigcup_{a \in A} B\text{``}\{a\}$$

What this theorem shows is that on the basis of the semantic analysis given here the existential quantifier does not, in standard cases, have any force in object position. Thus the semantic tree of *All freshman date juniors* is identical except for the branch with *EQ* as label off the *VP* node in Figure 5. I would claim that this fact is reflected in idiomatic English by the omission of the existential quantifier. Thus it is natural to say *Some dogs bite people* but pedantic to say *Some dogs bite some people*, as is also true of the pair of sentences about freshmen. I do not consider here those sentences with existential quantifier in object position which, it is often claimed, have at least one reading with the logical force of $(\exists x)(\forall y)\phi(x, y)$ rather than $(\forall x)(\exists x)\phi(x, y)$.

The relational analysis of the universal negative quantifier *no* goes hand in hand with that of the existential quantifier, just as in the classical case of I and E propositions. This can be seen by constructing the semantic tree for the sentence in Figure 6.

If we consider as well the sentence *Some people eat some vegetables*, the *VP* denotations of *eat some vegetables* and *eat no vegetables* are set-theoretic complements of each other: $\check{E}\text{``}V$ and $\neg(\check{E}\text{``}V)$ corresponding exactly to a classical E proposition being the contradictory of the corresponding I proposition.

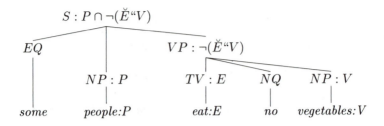

Figure 6.

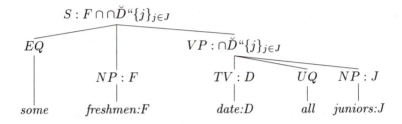

Figure 7.

The analysis of universal quantifiers in the object position is more difficult. Consider the sentence in Figure 7. In the universal case we have

$$\bigcap_{j \in J} \check{D}\text{“}\{j\} \subseteq \check{D}\text{“}J$$

but in general not equality. To account for universal quantifiers in object position we must extend the preliminary definition of extended relation algebras. As far as I know, the method of extension given here is new.

There are two ways of making the extension, the first of which fits in most naturally with conditions $E1$–$E5$, and the other by explicit definition. The first approach requires adding an additional closure condition.

Let us define for any two sets A and B, with B intuitively thought of as a relation:

$$\cap(B, A) = \bigcap_{a \in A} B\text{“}\{a\}.$$

The new closure condition is then just:

E6. If $A, B \in \mathcal{F}$ then $\cap(B, A) \in \mathcal{F}$.

A second approach is to eliminate the closure conditions on $\mathcal{F}$ altogether and to consider all sets in the power set of $D \cup (D \times D)$, where D is the domain of individuals of the model structure. In both approaches I am not entirely happy with the inclusion of sets that are "mixtures" of relations and sets of individuals, so another alternative that does not really affect the formal developments here is to take all sets in the union of the power set of D and the power set of $D \times D$. I assume this latter choice in what follows, and I now define $\cap(B, A)$ in terms of operations closed on this family of sets, which I call $\mathcal{E}(D)$–$\mathcal{E}$ for extended relation algebra of sets. Formally,

$$\mathcal{E}(D) = \mathcal{P}(D) \cup \mathcal{P}(D \times D),$$

where $\mathcal{P}(D)$ is the power set, i.e., the set of all subsets, of D.

For the definition of $\cap(B, A)$, we need the concept of restricting a relation to having a given set as domain. The notation $R|A$ is standard in set theory; it is the relation derived from R by restricting the domain of R to the set A. In other words, in terms of intersection and the Cartesian product, we have:

$$R|A = R \cap (A \times \mathcal{R}(R)).$$

The next step is to define the set $\cap_{a \in A} R\text{``}\{a\}$ in terms of operators closed in $\mathcal{E}(D)$. For this set I use the notation $\cap(R, A)$. For arbitrary sets A, B, and R, $\cap(R, A) = B$ iff

(i) $B \subseteq R\text{``}A$,

(ii) For every C, if $C \neq 0$ & $C \subseteq B$ then $(R|A)\text{``}C = A$,

(iii) For every D, if $D \neq 0$ & $D \subseteq R\text{``}A$ & $D{-}B \neq 0$

then $(R|A)\text{``}(D{-}B) \neq A$.

It is easy to show that $\cap(R, A)$ has the intended properties. We thus may replace the semantic tree of Figure 7 by the tree of Figure 8.

A THEOREM ABOUT QUANTIFIERS

A context-free grammar $G = (V, N, P, S)$ is *unambiguous* if and only if every terminal string in $L(G)$ has exactly one derivation tree (with respect to G). A context-free grammar $G' = (V', N', P', S')$ is a *conservative extension* of an unambiguous grammar $G = (V, N, P, S)$ if and only if (i) $V \subseteq V'$, $N \subseteq N'$, and $P \subseteq P'$, (ii) every terminal string in $L(G)$ has exactly one derivation tree with respect to G'. The concept of conservative

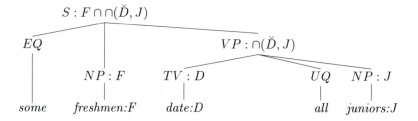

Figure 8.

extension is not standard in the literature—in contrast to the definition just given of *unambiguous*—but is useful for showing why the conventional linguistic treatment of quantifiers leads to an unnecessary escalation of type semantically. A conservative extension of an unambiguous grammar does not open up a new route to avoid semantic escalation of type.

To prove the point at hand, I restrict consideration to a fragment of English for generating plural forms of the standard A, E, I, and O sentences of the classical syllogism. The grammar G_2 will be only partially specified, for I shall omit the terminal English nouns and adjectives that we use to form the ordinary premises and conclusions of syllogisms. The nonterminal vocabulary $N_2 \subseteq N_1$, as given earlier, but the set P_2 of production rules is, of course, not a subset of P_1. (Thus G_2 is not a conservative extension of G_1.) The following are assumed, plus the unstated but necessary lexical rules for nouns and adjectives. The rules given are meant to approximate the conventional linguistic view of quantifiers as it would be developed for this small fragment of English. The rules of P_2, minus the lexical rules, are:

$$
\begin{aligned}
S &\rightarrow & NP + VP \\
NP &\rightarrow & UQ + N/EQ + N/NQ + N \\
VP &\rightarrow & Cop + N/Cop + Adj/Cop + Neg + N/Cop + Neg + Adj \\
UQ &\rightarrow & All \\
EQ &\rightarrow & Some \\
NQ &\rightarrow & No \\
Cop &\rightarrow & are \\
Neg &\rightarrow & not
\end{aligned}
$$

The semantics of the VP rules is classical and not an issue here. In particular,

$$[VP] = [N]/[Adj]/\neg[N]/\neg[Adj],$$

respectively, for the four VP rules given above. Note that the copula, *Cop*, does not denote. In the sequel, I need only the denotation $[VP]$ of VP. I also assume without comment the usual model-theoretic relational structures for proving validity and invalidity.

A model structure $\langle D, v \rangle$ of a grammar G is *Boolean* iff for any string s of V_T^+ for which v is defined, $v(s)$ is a subset of D. The model structure is *relational* iff $v(s)$ is an element of $\mathcal{E}(D)$. A potentially denoting context-free grammar G is *Boolean* iff for any Boolean model structure $\langle D, v \rangle$ of G, every semantic function of G has its value in $\mathcal{P}(D)$ whenever its arguments are subsets of D; the grammar G being *relational* is defined in similar fashion. Making explicit the Boolean semantic functions that make G_1 Boolean is routine based on the examples given and the details shall not be repeated. A Boolean grammar is *semantically correct* iff it has a semantically valid model theory of the syllogism. (The term *semantically valid* as defined here is really too general. It would probably be better to say *syllogistically valid*.) The theorem I want now to prove is a negative one about grammar G_2. I interpret the theorem as being a semantically based argument against the possibility of having both a standard linguistic parsing of quantifiers and an appropriately simple model theory of the syllogism.

THEOREM 2. *The grammar G_1 for the syllogism is Boolean and semantically correct. In contrast, neither the grammar G_2 nor any of its conservative extensions can be both Boolean and semantically correct.*

Proof. The proof for G_1 is obvious. I therefore give only the negative proof for G_2. To begin with, I shall assume that UQ and EQ do not have a denotation. Later it will be apparent that the same argument works when they do denote. Also for the proof it is necessary to consider only two of the three quantifiers and so I omit any consideration of NQ.

In general, for the rule $NP \to UQ + N$ we have a semantic function f such that

$$[NP] = f([N]),$$

on the assumption already made that UQ does not denote. Similarly for the rule $NP \to EQ + N$ we have a semantic function g such that

$$[NP] = g([N])$$

Suppose these semantic functions are Boolean. Then, as remarked earlier, f is one of four possible functions, which we may show for an arbitrary set A of the universe $V : f(A)$ is $A, \neg A, V$, or O. Similarly for g.

Next we suppose there is a Boolean semantic function ϕ for the top-level rule $S \to NP + VP$. We must then have for the universal quantifier.

(1) $\phi([NP], [VP]) = \phi(f([N]), [VP]) = \neg[N] \cup [VP]$

and for EQ

(2) $\phi([NP], [VP]) = \phi(g([N]), [VP]) = [N] \cap [VP].$

Since there are 4 possible functions for f and 4 for g, we must consider 16 possibilities and show in each case that ϕ cannot both be Boolean and evaluate A and I propositions correctly. Put another way, we must show that the Boolean functional equations (1) and (2) do not have a simultaneous solution. It will suffice to consider one case to illustrate the method of argument. Let $f(A) = A$ and $g(A) = \neg A$. Then, to cover the UQ needs, we must have

$$\phi([N], [VP]) = \neg[N] \cup [VP],$$

but then for the I propositions we will have

$$\phi(g([N]), [VP]) = \phi(\neg[N], [VP]) = [N] \cup [VP],$$

which clearly leads to semantically incorrect evaluations, for we should have $[N] \cap [VP]$.

If, on the other hand, UQ and EQ are permitted to denote, $f([UQ], [N])$ can be one of 16 Boolean functions and so can $g([EQ], [N])$ for a total of 256 possibilities, or, also, we have UQ denoting and EQ not, for 64 possibilities, and still another 64 if we reverse matters so that EQ denotes and UQ does not. All the same, it is straightforward but tedious to show that in none of these additional 384 cases can ϕ both be a proper Boolean function and evaluate A and I propositions correctly. The point is that the denotations $[UQ]$ and $[EQ]$ cannot be made to do any real work. Thus we conclude that G_2 cannot be both Boolean and semantically correct. This conclusion also clearly holds for its conservative extensions.

In looking back over this proof it might be thought that the linguistic approach to quantifiers might be saved by rules like

$$S \to NP' + VP$$
$$NP' \to UQ + NP/EQ + NP,$$

and so quantifiers are once again classified as parts of noun phrases. But it is easy to show that this syntactic move cannot be endowed with appropriate Boolean functions (for the case of A, I, E, and O propositions).

The imposition of formal semantic constraints on the kinds of grammars that can be regarded as acceptable or efficient is, as yet, fairly unexplored territory. Indeed, the restriction to extended relation algebras in this paper has not really been justified by an explicit theoretical argument. Broadly speaking, the arguments are the typical ones for seeking an algebraic formulation of a theory, especially when possible a quantifier-free algebraic version. In the case of language, the more detailed argument must surely be in terms of developing algorithms or semi-algorithms for handling certain linguistic structures that are frequently used.

Smith and Rawson (1976) develop a procedural semantics for natural language that provides an attractive alternative that would be compatible with the standard linguistic treatment of quantifiers and yet not lead to an escalation of type. Roughly speaking, they use partial functions and conditional expressions rather than higher types of sets to provide the appropriate semantic encoding. Their approach works well for many features of natural language, but the model theory is not yet explicitly worked out, and so it is not yet clear how the standard theory of validity and logical consequence is to be developed within their framework. As it is developed, it will be of some interest to compare the computational efficiency of their approach to the algebraic one outlined in this paper.

12

VARIABLE-FREE SEMANTICS
FOR NEGATIONS WITH
PROSODIC VARIATION

In several recent publications (Suppes, 1976; Suppes and Macken, 1978) I
have argued for a variable-free semantics of quantifiers, attributive adjectives, possessives, and intensifying adverbs. This work is a specialization
of my earlier efforts at developing context-free fragments of natural language (1973b, 1973a, 1974b). It is also part of my rejection of first-order
logic as the appropriate instrument for the analysis of natural language,
but I shall not digress here to state in any detail my views on this matter.
The central idea is that the syntax of first-order logic is too far removed
from that of any natural language, to use it in a sensitive analysis of the
meaning of ordinary utterances.

In the present note I restrict myself to negation as it occurs in many
simple utterances. I do not claim the analysis is anything like being universally correct, but within the context I have applied it, the intertwining
of semantic and prosodic features works out rather well. For other reasons
and other interests I have recently become interested in prosody, and I
now feel that the ability to incorporate in a faithful way the subtleties of
meaning conveyed by various prosodic features is a reasonable semantic

*Reprinted from E. Saarinen, R. Hilpinen, I. Niiniluoto, and M. Provence Hintikka
(eds.), Essays in Honour of Jaakko Hintikka, 49-59. All Rights Reserved. Copyright
©1979 by D. Reidel Publishing Company, Dordrecht, Holland.

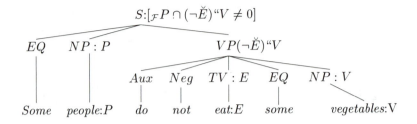

Figure 1.

demand.

In the first section, I sketch the theory of semantics for generative grammars developed in earlier articles. In the second section, I concentrate on the problems of negation.

GENERATIVE GRAMMARS AND THEIR MODEL STRUCTURES

An example will illustrate the framework I have in mind and provide an intuitive introduction to those unfamiliar with the concept of semantic trees for context-free grammars. Consider the tree for the sentence *Some people do not eat some vegetables* shown in Figure 1. On the left of the colon at each node is shown the terminal or nonterminal label. The nonterminal grammatical categories should be obvious: S = sentence, EQ = existential quantifier, NP = noun phrase, Aux = auxiliary, etc. To the right of the colon at a node is shown the denotation of the label if it has one. Thus, in the semantic tree of Figure 1, *people* and its ascendant NP node have the set P of people as denotation; *eat* and its ascendant TV—transitive verb—node have the binary relation E of eating as denotation; *vegetables* and its ascendant NP node have the set V of vegetables as denotation. The VP—verb phrase—node has a denotation composed of set-theoretical operations on E and V. Intuitively the denotation is just the set of people who do not eat some vegetables. The notation $\breve{E}$ is for the *converse* of the relation E; $\neg\breve{E}$ is the *complement* of the relation $\breve{E}$; and $(\neg\breve{E})$"V is the *image* of the set V under the relation $\neg\breve{E}$. I take the root of the semantic tree of a sentence to denote the value T or F in a standard Fregean manner. Most of this notation is standard in elementary set theory (see, e.g., Suppes, 1960). Some subtleties about complementation are discussed below.

I give now a quick overview of the relevant formal concepts. First, a structure $G = \langle V, N, P, S \rangle$ is a *phrase-structure grammar* if and only if

V and P are finite, nonempty sets, N is a subset of V, S is in N, and $P \subseteq N^* \times V^+$ where N^* is the set of all finite sequences whose terms are elements of N, and V^+ is V^* minus the empty sequence. The grammar G is *context-free* if and only if $P \subseteq N \times V^+$. In the usual terminology, V is the vocabulary, N is the nonterminal vocabulary, S is the start symbol of derivations or the label of the root of derivation trees of the grammar, and P is the set of production rules. I assume as known the standard definitions of one string of V^* being *G-derivable* from another, the concept of a *derivation tree* of G, and the language $L(G)$ generated by G. (For a detailed treatment of these concepts, see Hopcroft and Ullman, 1969.) A context-free grammar G is *unambiguous* if and only if every terminal string in $L(G)$ has exactly one derivation tree (with respect to G).

Semantics may be introduced in two steps. First, the grammar of G is extended to a *potentially denoting* grammar by assigning at most one set-theoretical function to each production rule of G. We may show these functions in general by using a notation of square braces; e.g., $[NP]$ is the denotation of NP. In the case of Figure 1,

Production Rule	*Semantic Function*
$S \rightarrow EQ + NP + VP$	$[S] = [\mathcal{F}[NP] \cap [VP] \neq 0]$
$VP \rightarrow Aux + Neg + TV + EQ + NP$	$[VP] = (\neg[TV])^{\backprime\backprime}[NP],$

where the Frege function $[\mathcal{F}\phi]$ is defined for any (extensional) sentence ϕ as follows:

$$[\mathcal{F}\phi] = \begin{cases} T & \text{if } \phi \text{ is true (in the given model)} \\ F & \text{otherwise.} \end{cases}$$

and in the case of the other nodes with only one descendant, the semantic function is identity if there is a denotation. For example,

$$TV \rightarrow eat \qquad [TV] = [eat].$$

The second step is the characterization of model structures. In the general theory of model-theoretic semantics for context-free languages, I use the concept of a *hierarchy* $\mathcal{H}(D)$ of sets built up from a given non-empty domain D by closure under union, subset, and power set 'operations', with T and F excluded from the hierarchy and $T \neq F$. A *model structure* for a given grammar G with terminal vocabulary V_T is a pair $\langle D, v \rangle$ where D is a nonempty set and v is a partial function from V_T^+ to $\mathcal{H}(D)$. Explicit details are to be found in Suppes (1973b). The treatment here is restricted. First, only terminal words, not terminal phrases, are permitted to denote, so that the domain of the valuation function v is V_T, not V_T^+. (The function v remains a partial function because many terminal words, e.g., quantifier words, do not denote.)

The more important restriction is in the hierarchy. In line with my earlier paper (Suppes, 1976), I restrict the model structures to the power set $\mathcal{P}(D)$ of the domain D, i.e., the set of all subsets of D, and the power set of the Cartesian product $D \times D$. Thus, only binary relations are considered. Formally, I define

$$\mathcal{E}(D) = \mathcal{P}(D) \cup \mathcal{P}(D \times D),$$

using '$\mathcal{E}$' for extended relation algebras of sets, a terminology introduced in the earlier paper. The valuation function v is then a partial function from V_T to $\mathcal{E}(D)$.

The 'algebraic' operations on elements of $\mathcal{E}(D)$ have mainly already been mentioned: union, intersection, and complementation on arbitrary sets, the converse of relations, the image of a set under a relation: $R``A$. The image of a set under a relation corresponds to function application in Montague grammars. As always, complementation is relative to some given set. From the standpoint of $\mathcal{E}(D)$ the natural set-theoretical choice is $D \cup (D \times D)$, but conceptually this is not very intuitive. For instance, if L is the relation of loving, then $\neg L$ should be the *relation* of not loving, i.e.,

$$\neg L = (D \times D) - L.$$

Consequently, complementation is here taken to mean with respect to $D \times D$ in the case of relations, and with respect to D in the case of sets that are subsets of D. The only point of ambiguity concerns complementation of the empty set or relation, and the context will make clear which is meant.[1]

NEGATION

Let the stressed word in a sentence be marked by an accent. Then the following two sentences have closely related meanings in spoken English.

(1) *John does nót like Mary.*

(2) *John does not líke Mary.*

---

[1] For some theoretical purposes it is useful to make the Frege function a Boolean function, and thus to replace the value T by the domain D and the value F by the empty set. This algebraic viewpoint simplifies the argument in Suppes (1976) that quantifier words like *all* and *some* not be part of the syntax of noun phrases, in order to keep the set-theoretical entities that are denoted by words or phrases at the level of elements of $\mathcal{E}(D)$, the extended relation algebra of sets for D.

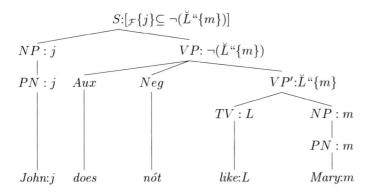

Figure 2.

Yet the semantic trees for (1) and (2) seem different. The critical production rule and the associated semantic function exhibited in Figure 2 is:

(3) $\qquad VP \to Aux + Neg + VP' \quad [VP] = \neg[VP'].$

The corresponding rule for sentence (2) is close to that used in Figure 1, but for present purposes may be written:

(4) $\qquad TV \to Aux + Neg + TV' \quad [TV] = \neg[TV'],$

and thus we have the semantic tree as shown in Figure 3. Some readers may be unhappy with the exact form of the production rules (3) and (4). The trees in Figures 2 and 3 might then be thought of as arising from transformations on different phrase-structure rules. This issue is not critical here. Nor is it critical if (3), for example, were replaced by the two rules:

(5)

$$\begin{cases} VP \to Neg + VP' \\ Neg \to Aux + Neg'. \end{cases}$$

As the many types of negation illustrated in Jespersen (1940, Ch. 23) show, there is no point in insisting on the exact form of production rules or of transformations until a very large variety of cases is considered, and my focus in this article is more semantical than syntactical. Admittedly, I have made syntactical choices that facilitate the semantics; this is a

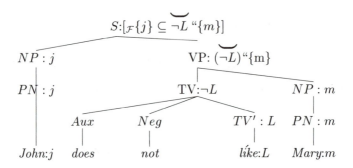

Figure 3.

strategy that is not fortuitous but one I strongly advocate. The point
is that I do not cut much of a syntactical swath in the analysis given
here but hope that enough is done to show the virtues of my variable-
free semantics in fitting snugly to the surface of some standard ordinary
utterances that express negations. If we look more closely at the meaning
of (1) and (2) as expressed in the semantic trees of Figures 2 and 3, we
find that they are equivalent in truth-value for all domains, because it is
easy to prove for any domain D

(6) $$\neg(\check{L}\,"\{m\}) = (\overbrace{\neg L})\,"\{m\}.$$

(I also note that

$$\neg(\check{L}) = (\overbrace{\neg L}),$$

i.e., the order of taking the complement and taking the converse of a
relation does not matter.)

   Equation (6) would seem to argue that change of stress does not change
referential meaning in use of negation, but the constancy of meaning of
(1) and (2) is deceptive. Slightly more complex examples tell a different
story. Consider

(7) *John does nót like some girls.*

(8) *John does not líke some girls.*

In examining (7) and (8) one criticism of the analysis given above is
that the production rules do not seem to be consistent with the general prosodic rule: The last word of an immediate constituent should be

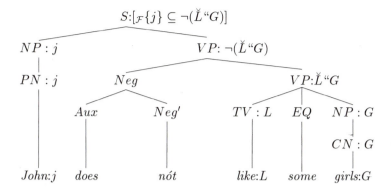

Figure 4.

stressed. The following six production rules (and their associated semantic functions) do this, and I shall use them in analyzing (7) and (8):

Production Rule[2]	Semantic Function
$VP \rightarrow VP'$	$[VP] = [VP']$
$VP \rightarrow Neg + VP'$	$[VP] = \neg[VP']$
$VP' \rightarrow TV + NP$	$[VP'] = [\underline{TV}]\,"[NP]$
$VP' \rightarrow TV + EQ + NP$	$[VP'] = [TV]\,"[NP]$
$TV \rightarrow Neg + TV'$	$[TV] = \neg[TV']$
$Neg \rightarrow Aux + Neg'$	No denotation

The tree for (7) is shown in Figure 4, while the tree for (8) is shown in Figure 5. The following model assigns different truth values to (7) and (8), and thus shows how the difference in stress carries a difference in meaning. The intuitive interpretation of the difference is discussed further below. Let $j =$ John, $m =$ Mary, and $s =$ Susan, with, of course, all three individuals distinct.

---

[2]It is a matter of some controversy to make prosodic features such as primary stress a part of the phrase-structure grammar. Prosodic contours are often added at a later point by many linguists, as Arvin Levine has pointed out to me. For reasons that cannot be gone into here, I much prefer their early introduction on the thesis that the speaker's intention to express a particular meaning should be part of the generation of the utterance from the beginning. Prosodic features that sharply change the meaning, as in some of the examples discussed below, should somehow be marked at an early stage, or at least so I think.

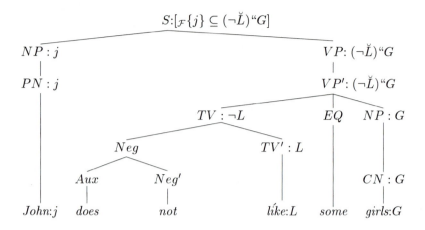

Figure 5.

So the domain $D = \{j, m, s\}$, and we define G as expected and L in a natural way—so the model is not peculiar:

$$G = \{m, s\}$$
$$L = \{\langle j, m \rangle\}.$$

It is then easy to show that

$$\check{L}\,{}^{"}G = \{j\},$$

so

$$[\mathcal{F}\{j\} \subseteq \neg(\check{L}\,{}^{"}G)] = F$$

but

$$(\neg\check{L})\,{}^{"}G = D,$$

so that

$$[\mathcal{F}\{j\} \subseteq (\neg\check{L})\,{}^{"}G] = T,$$

which means that in this model (7) is false and (8) is true.

The intuitive basis of this difference in truth value is brought out by noticing that a somewhat more idiomatic formulation of (7) is:

(7′) *John does nót like girls.*

which is clearly false in the model, since John likes Mary, but (8) is true because he does not like Susan. On the other hand, I emphasize the uniform semantical treatment of the quantifier *some* in both cases—details are to be found in Suppes (1976). The equivalence of (7) and (7′) rests on the set-theoretical identity

$$R``A = \cup_{a \epsilon A} R``\{a\}$$

for any sets R and A.

Matters are somewhat more complicated in the case of *all*. Corresponding to (7) and (8) consider

(9) John does nót like all girls.

(10) John does not líke all girls.

The analysis of *all* in 'object' position in Suppes (1976) is more complicated than it need be. The key to a simpler analysis is to use the set-theoretical analogue of the first-order logic equivalence: $(\exists x)\phi(x)$ iff $\neg(\forall x)\neg\phi(x)$. Letting UQ stand for universal quantifier, a nonterminal to be rewritten as *all*, we add to the fragment of grammar given above:

$$VP' \to TV + UQ + NP \qquad [VP'] = \neg((\neg[\overbrace{TV}])``[NP]),$$

where the 'inside' complementation on the right is with respect to $D \times D$ and the 'outside' complementation is with respect to D. Since the trees for (9) and (10) are very similar to those of (7) and (8) respectively, we can go at once to the Frege functions directly. For (9), we have

$$[\mathscr{F}\{j\} \subseteq \neg\neg(\overbrace{\neg L})``G]$$

and for (10), we have

$$[\mathscr{F}\{j\} \subseteq \neg((\neg\neg\check{L})``G)],$$

but it is obvious that under the usual rule of 'double negation' for complementation, i.e., for any set A

$$\neg\neg A = A,$$

the Frege function for (9) is the same as that for (8), and the Frege function for (10) is the same as for (7).

In the case of either pair, (7) and (8), or (9) and (10), the difference in meaning within the pair can be seen more clearly by thinking of *not-like*, where the stress is on *like*, as a new transitive verb. So, abstractly, we have:

(8′) *John does* TV *some girls.*

(10′) *John does* TV *all girls.*

In contrast, in the case of (7) or (9), *nót* negates the entire verb phrase, *like some girls* or *like all girls.* Because there is a tendency to insist on the need for presuppositions to analyze explicitly many idiomatic utterances, I emphasize that the semantic distinction made in the present instance requires no use of presuppositions.

The analysis shows how by a prosodic shift in stress we obtain logical equivalence of the existential and universal quantifiers, at least within the restricted framework described. As far as I know, this particular intimate relation between semantics and prosody has not previously been explicitly commented upon. It is a virtue, I believe, of the variable-free semantics I have outlined that the dissection of this relation is relatively simple and straightforward, but the relation itself is justified on independent grounds. Indeed, I consider giving an account of it a reasonable constraint on alternative approaches.

13

PROCEDURAL SEMANTICS

The great success of set-theoretical semantics in mathematical logic, and the strong tradition, at least since Frege, against psychologism in logic, have been the basis of good arguments for the same approach to the semantics of natural language. If appropriate limits are clearly recognized, much can be and has been accomplished by this approach. Some of the notable successes are the restricted use of Tarski's definition of truth and the semantic analysis of modal concepts.

As a final account of meaning or reference, however, set-theoretical semantics in its standard form is clearly inadequate. There are several different ways of making the inadequacy explicit. My own favored route is a psychological one. On this point I agree with Chomsky. Linguistics broadly conceived is a part of cognitive psychology. A fully adequate theory of language must postulate mechanisms of at least three broad types:

  (i) learning mechanisms for acquiring language,
 (ii) performance mechanisms for producing and comprehending speech,
(iii) connecting mechanisms that intimately link language to perception and bodily movement.

All of these mechanisms essentially involve aspects of meaning, and set-theoretical semantics is too abstract, general, and noncomputational to

*Reprinted from R. Haller and W. Grassl (Eds.), *Language, logic, and philosophy* (Proceedings of the 4th International Wittgenstein Symposium, Kirchberg/Wechsel, Austria, 1979). Vienna: Hölder-Pichler-Tempsky, 1980.

provide a proper framework at any serious level of detail.

It is a surprising and important fact that so much of the language of mathematics and science can be analyzed at a nearly satisfactory formal level by set-theoretical semantics, but the psychology of users is barely touched by this analysis. Not only logic, set theory, and modern abstract branches of mathematics but also such physically and perceptually intuitive disciplines as Euclidean or projective geometry can be given a formally very satisfactory set-theoretical semantics. Such easily visualized geometric relations as incidence of point and line, intersection of lines, betweenness of points, and congruence of triangles have natural set-theoretical representations. Ordinary verbs of perception or motion do not. Nor do the many nouns and adjectives describing emotional states. If we were able to give adequate set-theoretical representations of these and similar common words and phrases, we might, as in the case of geometry, be at least partially content with an austere, vegetarian-like, set-theoretical diet in spite of our knowledge that 'real' geometry and the discovery of nontrivial geometrical facts depend not at all on set theory.

But in the case of ordinary language the set-theoretical fare does not offer minimal nutritional content. True, we can have a certain amount of logic, but the gruel of quantifiers and connectives is too thin. Not only are the four-letter words missing (in the case of English), but also the much more important high-frequency two-letter words; *to, in, of, on, at, by* and *as*. The set-theoretical semantics of any of these seven two-letter words–or their functional analogues in other languages–is far from being satisfactorily characterized.

At this point it would be reasonable for an advocate of set-theoretical semantics to respond that set-theoretical requirements of analysis are much weaker than procedural requirements—for example, a computable function or relation with a given set-theoretical representation as a set of ordered pairs has ordinarily an unbounded set of procedural representations relative to a given fixed set of procedures. (Anyone who has ever examined student computer programs written to solve a problem of moderate difficulty will recognize the reasonableness of this claim that the set of procedural representations is unbounded.) So if we cannot solve the weaker set-theoretical problem, why tackle the much harder procedural one?

At a general level, the answer is familiar. It is time for a fresh start. Moreover, the formal guidelines for a fresh start are already well laid down by two important lines of research that have been pursued for some time. The earlier line is the identification and definition of the set of computable functions and their representation in terms of Turing machines. The general set-theoretical representation of computable functions is trivial and uninteresting, but their equivalent representations as partial recursive functions, Turing-machine computable, etc., is one of the most important results of 20th-century research in the foundations of mathematics.

The second line of research, that on computer programming, depends to a certain limited extent on the first, but the problems of greatest conceptual interest, for example, the efficiency of compilers or the correctness of operating systems, seem to require new and specialized concepts not found in the general theory of recursion. Above all, set-theoretical semantics seems to have been of little serious use in either practical or theoretical problems of programming. What has been important, indeed fundamental, is the concept of procedure or subroutine, which has been central almost from the beginning to the recent theory of structural programming. Some cognitive psychologists, but perhaps no philosophers, talk about human procedures as if humans were a current IBM computer model nearly ready for the marketplace. As will become clear in what follows, I think there are similarities between human procedures and computer subroutines, but there are also many essential differences. Moreover, it should be clear that starting over with a computer analogy will not in itself solve many of the problems left open in the set-theoretical semantics of natural language, for example, that of providing a proper analysis of the seven two-letter words mentioned earlier. But it does provide a more powerful framework for generating and testing hypotheses about the mechanisms of language learning and performance to which I previously referred.

These general remarks about semantics are sketchy and need to be expanded considerably to be persuasive. Rather than do this, in order to get a more concrete sense of what procedural semantics is intended to be like, I turn now to a number of propositions I am prepared to defend. These propositions are followed by one extended example, which is simple but by no means entirely artificial.

SOME GENERAL PROPOSITIONS ABOUT PROCEDURES AND MEANING.

I begin with the relation between properties and procedures.

Proposition 1. Properties are abstractions of procedures, just as extensions are abstractions of properties.

Two different procedures may test for the same property. For example, we may easily have two different methods for deciding whether or not a certain flower has the property of being hybrid. We do not have a precise constructive theory for abstracting properties from procedures, but we do have a great deal of experience in ordinary contexts in making such abstractions. More on this later.

Proposition 2. In finest detail, the meaning of a word, phrase, or utterance is a procedure, or collection of procedures.

Thus, for me the meaning of the word *red* is the procedure I use in a given context for applying the term. I said *the meaning* and *the procedure*, but this is because I include contextual parameters in the procedure and thus in the meaning. In many ways it is more suggestive to speak of different procedures for applying, using, or understanding a given word or phrase, with the choice appropriate–in most cases at least–to the context, and this is the use I shall favor hereafter.

To go beyond what Chisholm said in his paper, in my view of procedural semantics the meaning of a proper name is a collection of procedures, which in their full complexity will almost certainly be different for speaker and listener. His properties are abstractions of my procedures.

There is, of course, a tendency both in philosophy and in ordinary talk to use a concept of sameness of meaning that is much coarser than the one I am insisting on. Thus, someone asks, "What does it mean to say that a triangle is isosceles?" The answer comes back, "That just means the same as saying that two interior angles of the triangle are equal." But as the endless literature on synonymy and propositional attitudes has repeatedly brought out, the concept of sameness at work in the above example is really that of semantic paraphrase, which is a quite loose sense of sameness. It is my argument that between semantic paraphrase and the very highly individuated sense of meaning given in Proposition 2 there is no natural firm ground on which to stand. It certainly is the case that the definition I advocate will run contrary to much ordinary usage of the sort indicated, but I think the theoretical grounds are extremely good for starting with a highly detailed and private sense of meaning and then abstracting, by appropriate congruence relations, coarser senses. (Such a 'geometrical' theory of meaning that recognizes no single preferred congruence relation–just as there is none in geometry–has been worked out in the set-theoretical case in Suppes (1973a); the theory of congruence of meaning developed there has a natural extension to procedural semantics.)

Proposition 3. In finest detail, the meaning of a word, phrase, or utterance is private for each individual.

The force of this proposition is not to deny the important public aspects of language but to require an explicit theory of communication of how listeners understand speakers and how speakers test for this understanding. Another aspect of the privacy of meaning needs to be stressed. The particular procedure called on a given occasion when a word is spoken or heard is not uniquely determined by the context but often results from current accidental associations that strongly influence the selection. The meaning in this sense is not a matter under conscious control or an object of purely intentional selection.

Proposition 4. High probability of successful communication depends, among other things, on the following factors:

4.1 *Spoken words, phrases, and utterances are identified as "being the same", that is, being appropriately congruent, by speaker and listener.*

4.2 *The procedures called by words or phrases yield for the given context congruent computational results for speaker and listener.*

4.3 *The speaker uses nonverbal as well as verbal cues from the listener to determine if the words he uses are calling result-congruent procedures in him and the listener.*

4.4 *When the speaker judges his words are not calling result-congruent procedures, he uses paraphrases in terms of words he believes will call result-congruent procedures.*

The search for result-congruent procedures must ordinarily terminate successfully for a successful communication to occur.

What I have sketched in Proposition 4 is a theory of communication. It is meant to outline how we are to move from private meaning to public communication. Although I am certainly not able to formulate the theory in anything close to a scientifically satisfactory form, there are some clarifying remarks about the various parts of Proposition 4 that I want to make. First, as to words being perceived the same by speaker and listener, this is a necessary non-trivial condition of communication and, in the central case of spoken language, requires an elaborate theory of how sameness of utterance is perceived. Even several occurrences of the same word in a given utterance can have very different acoustical properties, and it is not easy to identify those invariant features necessary for identification of sameness. In fact, it is fair to say that at a fundamental level the theory of such matters is far from being well worked out.

The focus of 4.2 is the calling of result-congruent procedures by speaker and listener. What I mean by *result-congruent* procedures can be made more explicit by a simple example of a sort already alluded to. Consider two programs written to compute a certain function for a given range of input data. The two programs are clearly not identical; one has 500 lines and the other 550. What is more important, the run time is 95 milliseconds for one and 135 milliseconds for the other. But for any given input selected from the range of input data, the two programs always compute the same result and thus are result-congruent.

Consider now a speaker talking to a listener, say, a pupil he is teaching arithmetic, as in the extended example to be considered later. The speaker

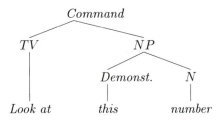

Figure 1.

says, "Look at this number", and simultaneously points his finger at the
number which is at the top of a column of numbers. The procedure called
up by these words of the speaker is not the same for the listener–or at least
would have a low probability of being the same–but the two procedures in
this simple case are result-congruent. Cases of this sort are an important
aspect of good teaching of skills such as those of elementary mathematics
or reading. Just as important, the good teacher uses 4.3 and 4.4 when
4.2 fails.

It also should be apparent that the procedure called by "Look at this
number" can be broken up into components along standard grammatical
lines (see Figure 1). The general *Look at* subroutine is restricted, as it
ordinarily is, to the object of attention, *this number*. The set-theoretical
semantic trees I have used in the past (Suppes 1973b) may be modified to
become procedural semantic trees, where now procedures rather than set
denotations are shown at appropriate nodes of a grammatical derivation
tree like that of Figure 1. But I shall not enter into details here, although
these matters are at the heart of the technical development of procedural
semantics.

My continued focus is 4.2, and I want now to examine cases of casual
conversation or questions where the cognitive fit between speaker and listener is less tight. When this occurs, the sense of result-congruence is
coarse and loose, in line with the 'geometrical' theory of meaning referred
to earlier, for which there is no single sense of synonymy or congruence.
Smith says to Jones, "My wife came home from the hospital yesterday",
and Jones responds, "I'm glad to hear it". The sense of result-congruence
in this exchange is relatively loose and vague. Jones's response, keyed to
his processing of Smith's statement, reflects his feelings as he imagines–
visually or possibly propositionally–Smith's wife coming home. Smith's
procedures are full of details that are missing in Jones's. In the case of
Smith's processing of Jones's response, an even looser match of procedures

is required to catch the sense of gladness. Smith will in fact probably depend as much on the prosodic features of Jones's utterance, and perhaps on his facial expression, as he will on any procedures directly called by *glad*. And this will be almost equally true for Jones's production procedures. The appropriateness of the loose sense of congruence is reinforced by our inability at present to say anything interesting about the semantics of *glad* at the more abstract set-theoretical level.

Suppose, on another occasion, Smith asks Jones, "Why does water almost always run out of basins in a counterclockwise direction?" (Smith lives in the Northern Hemisphere.) Smith is really puzzled by this phenomenon and he is not educated enough to know how to look up the answer in a book on meteorology. All the same, his question evokes a procedure for answering it in his own mind. It is a pictorial matter of the water being twisted around, always in a certain way. He imagines water running out, and an obscure cause is applied to it. He is then satisfied with, and at a qualitative level understands, Jones's explanation of the rotation in terms of the Coriolis force generated by the earth's rotation, because it fits into his own qualitative, pictorial procedure.

I do not want to push these examples too far. There is a variety of psychological evidence that what is evoked by a complicated question can vary enormously from person to person. Some individuals seem to have almost no visual memory and little tendency to visual imagination. In any case, in my casual sketch of Smith's and Jones's internal processing, I have ignored most of what I consider methodologically and theoretically important, namely, the detailed synthesis of complex procedures from simple ones, as reflected either in the processing of complex sentences or in the building up of complex skills from simpler ones. I do want to emphasize that almost always this synthesis is made unconsciously, just as procedures as meanings are ordinarily called up automatically without any deliberate or conscious effort.

At this point, I must abandon further efforts to give a better account of 4.2. I shall also have to leave for another occasion the more detailed spelling out of the procedures outlined in 4.3 and 4.4 for establishing communication when it appears to be absent.

Proposition 5. Classical set-theoretical referential semantics can be obtained, where appropriate, by abstraction from procedural semantics.

This proposition applies particularly to the language of mathematics and theoretical science. There is much that is satisfying and correct about standard model theory. Although it has not been completely and adequately developed for the natural and informal mathematical language of even elementary textbooks, the task does not seem impossible to accomplish.

By keeping in mind that procedures are meant to apply to a range of possible input data, we can also easily see how to derive a set-theoretical possible-worlds semantics for propositional attitudes, intentional verbs, words that designate properties, etc. But the procedural approach, when it is specific, provides at once the opportunity of going beyond the general logic of propositional attitudes and the like to much more specific theories that restrict the possible worlds severely, just as in the classical case of geometry, by using the specific content of the procedures and their restricted ranges of applicable data.

As Proposition 5 indicates, procedural and set-theoretical semantics are not inconsistent with each other. The procedural approach is meant to be almost infinitely more detailed and to ground the theory of meaning in the privacy of each individual's inaccessible mental procedures. To those in search of a bedrock of certainty as a foundation for fundamental concepts, the ground I have selected for meaning seems soft and unstable. But assigning a serious role to the psychology of language forces a view like mine to the fore–at least, so I claim. More detailed supporting arguments must wait another occasion.

To avoid any suggestion that I think procedural semantics leads to a view of persons as rather primitive computers, I end my list of general propositions with the following.

Proposition 6. Human procedures are similar to computer subroutines, but there are notable differences.

6.1 *What corresponds to the underlying machine language of human procedures is radically different from any current computer language; moreover, this underlying language is probably unknowable in complete detail.*

6.2 *Human procedures are subject to continual modification and are much affected by use; computer subroutines are not–they can stay the same for a thousand years.*

6.3 *Human procedures are intrinsically connected to perceptual and motor activities; for computer subroutines these connections are still artificial, awkward, and difficult.*

6.4 *Human procedures are intrinsically continuous rather than discrete or digital in character; prosodic features of speech are a prime example.*

I stressed at the beginning the usefulness of the computer analogy for thinking about human procedures, but a deeper and more detailed theoretical view of the differences is also needed. What I have formulated in Proposition 6 is too general to be of much help and can be of use only in the most preliminary way.

AN EXTENDED EXAMPLE: COLUMN ADDITION

To avoid the sense that everything I have had to say of a general nature is wholly and hopelessly programmatic, I turn to a simple but natural example, children of seven or eight years of age being taught what it means to carry out the teacher's request "Add these numbers", where the numbers are written in a standard column form. (What I say here extends the analysis in Suppes (1973c)).

I first analyze the problem in terms of a pseudo machine-language that has some psychological basis. Then I ask, how can we actually proceed with instruction, and so how do we communicate with the student? My answer is that we build up the complex procedure of adding–the meaning of *Add these numbers*–by using simpler commands whose meaning is already known to the student. We can thus say that our complex procedure of adding numbers is first synthesized for the student by calling up simpler subroutines that are the meaning of commands he already understands.

I now turn to the pseudo machine-language used in the program at the left of Table 1.

For one-column addition, two registers suffice in our scheme of analysis. There is a stimulus-supported register [SS] that holds an encoded representation of a printed symbol to which the student is perceptually attending. In the present case the alphabet of such symbols consists of the 10 digits and the underline symbol '_'. As a new symbol is attended to, previously stored symbols are lost unless transferred to the second register, the non-stimulus-supported register [NSS], which provides longer term storage for making computations.

I drastically simplify the perceptual situation by conceiving each exercise as being presented on a grid with at most one symbol in each square of the grid. For column addition we number the coordinates of the grid from the upper right-hand corner. Thus, in the exercise

$$5$$
$$4$$
$$\underline{7}$$

the coordinates of the digit 5 are (1,1), the coordinates of 4 are (2,1), and the coordinates of 7 are (3,1), with the first coordinate being the row number and the second being the column number (the column number is needed for the general case).

The restricted set of instructions we need for column addition is the following:

Attend (a,b):	Direct attention to grid position (a,b).
$(\pm a, \pm b)$:	Shift attention on the grid by $(\pm a, \pm b)$.
Readin [SS]:	Read into the stimulus-supported register the physical symbols in the grid position addressed by Attend.
Lookup [R1] + [R2]:	Look up table of basic addition facts for adding contents of registers [R1] and [R2] and store the result in [R1].
Copy [R1] in [R2]:	Copy the content of register [R1] into register [R2].
Jump (val) R,L:	Jump to line labelled L if content of register [R] is val.
Outright [R]:	Write (output) the rightmost symbol of register [R] at grid position addressed by Attend.
Deleteright [R]:	Delete the rightmost symbol of register [R].
End:	Terminate processing of current exercise.

Of these instructions, only *Lookup* does not have an elementary character. In our complete analysis, it has the status of a subroutine built up from more primitive operations such as those of counting. It is, of course, more than a problem of constructing the table of basic addition facts from counting subroutines; it is also a matter of being able to add a single digit to any number stored in the non-stimulus supported register [NSS], as, for example, in adding many rows of digits in a given column. I omit the details of building up this subroutine. It should also be obvious that the remaining instructions are not a minimal set.

To illustrate the ideas of how an exact procedural semantics can be given in terms of this pseudo machine-language, the left-hand column of Table 1 shows a program for adding any single column of numbers such that the sum is equal to or less than 99.

By attaching error parameters to various segments of the program, performance models are easily generated. Extensive analysis, using somewhat simpler structural models, of a variety of data that lead to estimation of such error parameters is to be found in Suppes (1969) and Suppes and Morningstar (1972).

I refer to the programming language I have developed as a pseudo machine-language because, as indicated in the previous section, I consider it not simply impractical but, within our present conceptual framework, impossible to identify the actual machine language used for internal programming of even simple cognitive tasks. Given this twilight status of the language I have developed, it might be asked why I consider it at all. I think the important point is to analyze what minimal language can do the job that has some claim to psychological naturalness, that includes a simplified perceptual component, and that has a transparent structure that can be analyzed in terms of actual performance data.

I will not try to report on any actual data analysis in the present context but rather go on to the question of how we can move from this somewhat abstract, pseudo machine-language to the use only of English. After all, as already indicated, the instructor or tutor teaching the young child how to do column addition must be able to talk to him in English and to synthesize, as I have put it, a new procedure from procedures already known to the child. In the right-hand column of Table 1, I have

TABLE 1
EXAMPLE OF ONE-COLUMN ADDITION
FOR SUMS ≤ 99

	Pseudo machine-language program	English-addressable subroutines
	Attend (1,1)	Look at this number.
	Readin	
	Copy SS in NSS	Remember the number.
	Attend (+1,+0)	Now look at this next number.
	Readin	
Opr	Lookup NSS + SS . . .	Add the two numbers and remember the sum.
	Attend (+1,+0)	Move down the column.
	Readin	If there is another number,
	Jump (0–9) SS, Opr	add as before and continue.
	Attend (+1,+0)	If not, move down to the blank space.
	Outright NSS	Write down the number of ones in the answer.
	Deleteright NSS	
	Attend (+0,+1)	Now look at the space to the left.
	Outright NSS	Write down the number of tens in the answer (unless it is zero).
	Deleteright NSS	
	End	

written down an English version of the program and have called the various commands *English-addressable subroutines*. The semantics of these individual phrases, for example, "Look at this number" or "Remember the number", have a direct procedural interpretation and also a direct relation to corresponding parts of the pseudo machine-language program. It is, I think, characteristic of the kind of task being considered that a procedural viewpoint is very much more fruitful than a set-theoretical one. General set-theoretical semantics for the various English phrases shown on the right in Table 1 is unlikely to be very useful. The use of such English phrases to call subroutines whose machine-language code is unknown to us also helps emphasize the point that I think this is the correct way to think about procedural semantics. We build up from English complex routines out of simpler routines, and the attempt to get very much deeper into the structure of the processing will not be highly successful. I do not mean to suggest that all avenues of approach are fenced off. For example, with younger colleagues I am now in the process of rather extensively studying eye movements in the context of such procedures, and a good deal more can be learned from such data. But it is still the case that the main tools are English (or another natural language) and the behavioral responses to the natural language by the child as well as his own spoken queries and comments.

It should be apparent from this quite simple example that the procedural semantics of such a simple phrase as "Add these numbers" is not to be given a simple set-theoretical interpretation but involves complicated matters of perception and memory as well as elementary computation. It is easy enough to think of other, more complex and sophisticated examples that also require a procedural approach to achieve any sort of psychological realism.

If time permitted, I would go on to give a rather detailed theory of learning for this and related elementary mathematical procedures. For this restricted subject, a rather thorough development can be given for procedural semantics and the associated learning and performance mechanisms. Even if the claims of my general propositions seem fanciful when left unrestricted, I am confident that the kind of procedural semantics I have described is actually applicable to the talking and listening characteristic of much elementary teaching and learning.

14

VARIABLE-FREE SEMANTICS WITH REMARKS ON PROCEDURAL EXTENSIONS

In earlier publications (Suppes, 1976, 1979; Suppes & Macken, 1978), I have emphasized the development of a model-theoretic semantics for English sentences, which uses neither quantifiers nor variables, but only constants denoting given sets and relations, and operations on sets and relations. I first want to survey these developments and then consider some extensions to procedural semantics.

The set-theoretical apparatus is that of what I call *extended relation algebras*. To the ordinary concept of a relation algebra with Boolean operations and operations on relations such as converse and relative product, the standard operation of forming the image of a set under a relation is added. (There are important features of natural language that this framework does not easily account for. A good example would be the semantics of prepositional phrases.)

There is one strong computational advantage of the kind of "algebraic" semantics I am proposing. A full Zermelo-like hierarchy of sets is not needed for the model structure as it is, in principle, for Montague semantics. Some aspects of the analysis run contrary to many standard

*Reprinted from T.W. Simon and R.J. Scholes (Eds.), *Language, Mind, and Brain.* Hillsdale, N.J.: Lawrence Erlbaum, 1982.

linguistic ideas. This is perhaps especially true of my insistence that such expressions as *every man, all sophomores*, and *some lovers* are not noun phrases. As should be evident from what has been said, the English quantifier words *every, all, some*, etc., do not denote at all but function as control structure words.

In the matter of the denotation or lack of it of *every man*, or *all men*, we can prove in a simple way that the conventional production rules will not permit a semantic account of the syllogism at the level of Boolean algebra, that is, at the level of subsets of the domain, but require what from a semantical or set-theoretical standpoint is to be regarded as an artificial escalation of type. This proof, which is meant to be a strong substantive argument against assigning a denotation to *every man*, is given at the end of the next section. (Arguments in favor of this viewpoint and the proof of the theorem are given in Suppes, 1976, but I amplify here some of the details in order to make the proof more explicit.)

GENERATIVE GRAMMARS AND THEIR SEMANTICS

A couple of examples will illustrate the framework I have in mind and provide an introduction to the concept of semantic trees for context-free grammars.

Consider the tree for the sentence *Some people do not drink some wines*, shown in Figure 1. On the left of the colon at each node is shown the terminal or nonterminal label. The nonterminal grammatical categories should be obvious: S = sentence, EQ = existential quantifier, NP = noun phrase, Aux = auxiliary, etc. To the right of the colon at a node is shown the denotation of the label if it has one. Thus, in the semantic tree of Figure 1, *people* and its ascendant NP node have the set P of people as denotation; *drink* and its ascendant TV (transitive verb) node have the binary relations D of drinking as denotation; *wines* and its ascendant NP node have the set W of wines as denotation. The VP (verb phrase) node has a denotation composed of set-theoretical operations on D and W. Intuitively the denotation is just the set of people who do not drink some wines. The notation $\check{D}$ is for the *converse* of the relation D, $\neg\check{D}$ is the *complement* of the relation $\check{D}$, and $(\neg\check{D})\text{``}W$ is the *image* of the set W under the relation $\neg\check{D}$. At this point I take the root of the semantic tree of a sentence to denote the value T or F in a standard Fregean manner; an explicit Boolean function is introduced later. Most of this notation is standard in elementary set theory (see, e.g., Suppes, 1960). Some subtleties about complementation are discussed later. I give now a quick overview of the relevant formal concepts. First, a structure

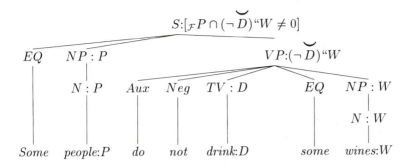

Figure 1.

$G = (V, N, P, S)$ is a *phrase-structure grammar* if and only if V and P are finite, nonempty sets; N is a subset of V; S is in N; and $P \subseteq N^* \times V^+$, where N^* is the set of all finite sequences whose terms are elements of N and V^+ is V^* minus the empty sequence. The grammar G is *context-free* if and only if $P \subseteq N \times V^+$. In the usual terminology, V is the vocabulary, N is the nonterminal vocabulary, S is the start symbol of derivations or the label of the root of derivation trees of the grammar, and P is the set of production rules. I assume as known the standard definitions of one string of V^* being *G-derivable* from another, the concept of a *derivation tree* of G, and the language $L(G)$ generated by G. (For a detailed treatment of these concepts, see Hopcroft & Ullman, 1969.) A context-free grammar G is *unambiguous* if and only if every terminal string in $L(G)$ has exactly one derivation tree (with respect to G).

Semantics may be introduced in two steps. First, the grammar G is extended to a *potentially denoting* grammar by assigning at most one set-theoretical function to each production rule of G. We may show these functions in general by using a notation of square braces; for example, $[NP]$ is the denotation of NP. In the case of Figure 1,

Production Rule	Semantic Function
$S \rightarrow EQ + NP + VP$	$[S] = [_{\mathcal{F}}[NP] \cap [VP]] \neq 0]$
$VP \rightarrow Aux + Neg + TV + EQ + NP$	$[VP] = (\neg[\underbrace{TV}])\text{``}[NP],$

where the Frege function $[_{\mathcal{F}}\phi]$ is defined for any (extensional) sentence ϕ as follows:

$$[_{\mathcal{F}}\phi] = \begin{cases} T & \text{if } \phi \text{ is true (in the given model)} \\ F & \text{otherwise.} \end{cases}$$

(This definition is slightly reformulated below, in order to make it explicitly Boolean.) And in the case of the other nodes with only one descendant, the semantic function is identity if there is a denotation. For example,

$$TV \rightarrow drink \qquad [TV] = [drink].$$

The second step is the characterization of model structures. In the general theory of model-theoretic semantics for context-free languages, I use the concept of a *hierarchy* $\mathcal{H}(D)$ of sets built up from a given non-empty domain D by closure under union, subset, and power set "operations", with T and F excluded from the hierarchy and $T \neq F$. A *model structure* for a given grammar G with terminal vocabulary V_T is a pair (D, v) where D is a nonempty set and v is a partial function from V_T^+ to $\mathcal{H}(D)$. Explicit details are to be found in Suppes (1973b). The treatment here is restricted. First, only terminal words, not terminal phrases, are permitted to denote, so that the domain of the valuation function v is V_T, not V_T^+. (The function v remains a partial function because many terminal words—e.g., quantifier words—do not denote.)

The more important restriction is in the hierarchy. In line with my earlier paper (Suppes, 1976), I restrict the model structures to the power set $\mathcal{P}(D)$ of the domain D, that is, the set of all subsets of D, and the power set of the Cartesian product $D \times D$—thus, only binary relations are considered. Formally, I define

$$\mathcal{E}(D) = \mathcal{P}(D) \cup \mathcal{P}(D \times D).$$

using "$\mathcal{E}$" for extended relation algebras of sets, a terminology introduced in the earlier paper. The valuation function v is then a partial function from V_T to $\mathcal{E}(D)$.

The "algebraic" operations on elements of $\mathcal{E}(D)$ have mainly already been mentioned: union, intersection, and complementation on arbitrary sets; the converse of relations; the image of a set under a relation, $R``A$. In addition, we need the restriction of the domain of a relation R to a set $A, R|A$, which is defined as:

$$R|A = R \cap (A \times \mathcal{R}(R)),$$

where $\mathcal{R}(R)$ is the range of the relation R.

As always, complementation is relative to some given set. From the standpoint of $\mathcal{E}(D)$, the natural set-theoretical choice is $D \cup (D \times D)$, but conceptually this is not very intuitive. For instance, if L is the relation of loving, then $\neg L$ should be the *relation* of not loving, that is,

$$\neg L = (D \times D) - L.$$

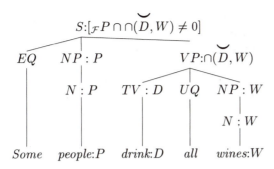

Figure 2.

Consequently, complementation is here taken to mean complementation with respect to $D \times D$ in the case of relations, and with respect to D in the case of sets that are subsets of D. The only point of ambiguity concerns complementation of the empty set or relation, and the context will make clear which is meant.

In the earlier paper on these matters (Suppes, 1976) I introduced the notation

$$\cap(R, A) = \cap_{a \in A}(R``\{a\})$$

for the appropriate denotation when a verb phrase uses a universal quantifier in object position. This use may be seen in the semantic tree (Figure 2) for *Some people drink all wines*. I note that UQ is the non-terminal symbol for the universal quantifier *all*. In direct analogy with O syllogistic propositions being the contradictory of A propositions, we may define $\cap(R, A)$ in the following manner (Suppes, 1979) for $R \subseteq D \times D$ and $A \subseteq D$,

$$\cap(R, A) = (\neg((\neg R)``A)).$$

Note that the "inside" complementation is with respect to $D \times D$ and the "outside" one with respect to D.

I now apply these ideas to prove the theorem mentioned earlier. To prove the theorem we need to define two grammars, one, G_1, that does not assign a denotation to *all men,* etc. The grammar G_2, in contrast, is meant to capture the widely accepted linguistic idea that *all men* is a noun phrase and has a denotation. (In both grammars I use only plural verbs and nouns in order to avoid problems of inflection.)

To keep the grammars simple, I shall restrict them to generating sentences of the standard A, E, I, and O forms used in the classical syllogism.

It is apparent that the results can be generalized to the kinds of relational examples discussed earlier.

Grammar G_1 has the following structure. The set N_1 of nonterminal vocabulary consists of $S, NP, VP, UQ, EQ, NQ, N, Cop, Adj$, and Neg, each with its nearly classical grammatical meaning, for example, NP for noun phrase. Also the lexical production rules for function words are these: $UQ \rightarrow All, EQ \rightarrow Some, NQ \rightarrow No, Cop \rightarrow are, Neg \rightarrow not$. The many lexical rules for N and Adj are left open, and so the set V of vocabulary is left unspecified but will be taken to be the same for both grammars considered.

The set P_1 of production rules, minus the lexical rules, is as follows, where the associated semantic function for each rule is also given, although the semantic functions for the three top-level rules are made explicitly Boolean later:

$$
\begin{aligned}
S & \rightarrow UQ + NP + VP/EQ + NP + VP/NQ + NP + VP \\
[S] & = [\mathcal{F}[NP] \subseteq [VP]]/[\mathcal{F}[NP] \cap [VP] \neq 0]/[\mathcal{F}[NP] \cap [VP] = 0] \\
NP & \rightarrow N \\
NP & = [N] \\
VP & \rightarrow Cop + N/Cop + Adj/Cop + Neg + N/Cop + Neg + Adj \\
[VP] & = [N]/[Adj]/\neg[N]/\neg[Adj]
\end{aligned}
$$

(The slash "/" is used to present several rules that have the same nonterminal symbol on the left; thus there are eight rules given here.)

The grammar G_2 has the same nonterminal vocabulary as G_1, so $N_2 = N_1$, and, as already stated, the same terminal vocabulary. The production rules, however, are different, to reflect the different treatment of quantifiers. No semantic rules are shown for S and NP rules; rather, the possibilities are examined in the proof of the theorem. Because the semantics of the restricted verb phrases permitted by G_1 and G_2 are not at issue, the semantic rules are the same as for G_1. Thus, the set P_2 is specified as follows:

$$
\begin{aligned}
S & \rightarrow NP + VP \\
NP & \rightarrow UQ + N/EQ + N/NQ + N \\
VP & \rightarrow Cop + N/Cop + Adj/Cop + Neg + N/Cop + Neg + Adj \\
VP & = [N]/[Adj]/\neg[N]/\neg[Adj].
\end{aligned}
$$

To state the desired theorem, some additional general concepts are needed.

A context-free grammar $G = (V, N, P, S)$ is *unambiguous* if and only if every terminal string in $L(G)$ has exactly one derivation tree (with respect to G). A context-free grammar $G' = (V', N', P', S')$ is a *conservative extension* of an unambiguous grammar $G = (V, N, P, S)$ if and only if (1)

$V \subseteq V', N \subseteq N'$, and $P \subseteq P'$ and (2) every terminal string in $L(G)$ has exactly one derivation tree with respect to G'. The concept of conservative extension is useful for showing why the conventional linguistic treatment of quantifiers leads to an unnecessary escalation of type semantically. A conservative extension of an unambiguous grammar does not open up a new route to avoid semantic escalation of type.

A model structure (D, v) of a grammar G is *Boolean* if and only if for any string s of V_T^+ for which v is defined, $v(s)$ is a subset of D. A potentially denoting context-free grammar G is *Boolean* if and only if for any Boolean model structure (D, v) of G, every semantic function of G has as its value a subset of D whenever its arguments are subsets of D. Making explicit the Boolean semantic functions that make G_1 Boolean is routine based on the examples given, and the details will not be repeated, but it is worth making explicit the Boolean formulation of the Frege function—rather functions, for we now have different Boolean functions for different top-level rules.[1] In particular, for grammar G_1, using mnemonically U for the universal quantifier function, E for the existential quantifier function, and N for the negative quantifier function, we have for any set A

$$U(A) \; = \begin{cases} D \text{ if } A = D \\ 0 \text{ if } A \neq D \end{cases}$$

$$E(A) \; = \begin{cases} D \text{ if } A \neq 0 \\ 0 \text{ if } A = 0 \end{cases}$$

$$N(A) \; = \begin{cases} D \text{ if } A = 0 \\ 0 \text{ if } A \neq 0, \end{cases}$$

Thus, explicitly, for the top-level rules of G_1

$$\begin{aligned} S & \rightarrow UQ + NP + VP \\ [S] & = U(\neg[NP] \cup [VP]) \\ S & \rightarrow EQ + NP + VP \\ [S] & = E([NP] \cap [VP]) \\ S & \rightarrow NQ + NP + VP \\ [S] & = N([NP] \cap [VP]). \end{aligned}$$

It is important for later purposes to note that for a two-element Boolean algebra

$$U_2(A) = E_2(A) = A$$

---

[1] I am indebted to Barbara Partee for pointing out to me the need for a more explicit treatment of these matters than I gave in Suppes (1976).

and

$$N_2(A) = \neg A,$$

where the subscript has been introduced to denote the number of elements in the Boolean algebra. A Boolean grammar is *semantically correct* if and only if it has a semantically valid model theory of the syllogism. The theorem I want now to prove is a negative one about grammar G_2. I interpret the theorem as being a semantically based argument against the possibility of having both a standard linguistic parsing of quantifiers and an appropriately simple model theory of the syllogism.

THEOREM. *The grammar G_1 for the syllogism is Boolean and semantically correct. In contrast, neither the grammar G_2 nor any of its conservative extensions can be both Boolean and semantically correct.*

PROOF. The proof for G_1 is obvious. I therefore give only the negative proof for G_2. To begin with, I shall assume that UQ and EQ do not have a denotation. Later it will be apparent that the same argument works when they do denote. Also, for proof it is necessary to consider only two of the three quantifiers and so I omit any consideration of NQ.

In general, for the rule $NP \rightarrow UQ + N$ we have a semantic function f such that

$$[NP] = f([N]),$$

on the assumption already made that UQ does not denote. Similarly, for the rule $NP \rightarrow EQ + N$ we have a semantic function g such that

$$[NP] = g([N]),$$

It is required that these semantic functions be Boolean. There also must be a Boolean semantic function ϕ for the top-level rule $S \rightarrow NP + VP$. At this point we specialize to a two-element Boolean algebra to provide a simple counterexample to the semantic validity of G_2. We must then have for the universal quantifier

$$(1) \quad \phi([NP], [VP]) = \phi(f([N]), [VP]),$$

and so in the two-element model we must have the following results for the various possible values of $[N]$ and $[VP]$ in accordance with the standard semantics of A propositions:

$$(2) \begin{cases} \phi(f(0), 0) = 1 \\ \phi(f(0), 1) = 1 \\ \phi(f(1), 0) = 0 \\ \phi(f(1), 1) = 1, \end{cases}$$

and correspondingly we must have for I propositions:

$$(3) \begin{cases} \phi(g(0),0) = 0 \\ \phi(g(0),1) = 0 \\ \phi(g(1),0) = 0 \\ \phi(g(1),1) = 1. \end{cases}$$

We must show that the eight Boolean functional equations of (2) and (3) do not have a simultaneous solution, that is, there are no Boolean functions $\phi, f,$ and g that simultaneously satisfy these equations.

First, we note from the first and third equations of (2) that f cannot be a constant function, that is, we can have neither $f(0) = f(1) = 0$ nor $f(0) = f(1) = 1$. The second and fourth equations of (3) show that g also cannot be a constant function. Next, we note from the first equations of (2) and (3) that $f(0) \neq g(0)$, so f and g must have "opposite" values for the same argument. We are thus left with two possibilities: Either

(4) $$f(0) = 0, f(1) = 1, g(0) = 1, g(1) = 0,$$

or

(5) $$f(0) = 1, f(1) = 0, g(0) = 0, g(1) = 1.$$

Consider, first, (4). Then we must have:

$$\begin{aligned} \phi(f(0),0) = 1 &= \phi(0,0) \\ \phi(g(1),0) = 0 &= \phi(0,0). \end{aligned}$$

which is a contradiction. The same kind of analysis shows (5) cannot lead to a solution, for we have:

$$\begin{aligned} \phi(f(0),0) = 1 &= \phi(1,0) \\ \phi(g(1),0) = 0 &= \phi(1,0). \end{aligned}$$

The conceptual situation is not changed by permitting UQ and EQ to denote, for they would need to be constant denotations, and they could do no more than select functions f and g as just analyzed. Thus we conclude that G_2 cannot be both Boolean and semantically correct. This conclusion also clearly holds for its conservative extensions.

A quite different sort of application of variable-free semantics to prosodic variations of negation is given in Suppes (1979).

PROCEDURAL SEMANTICS

It is obvious to anyone that the kind of set-theoretical semantics described thus far in this chapter cannot hope to offer a direct psychological model of speech production or comprehension. I have recently outlined my approach to procedural semantics, which is meant to move a step toward a more psychologically realistic theory (Suppes, 1980). Without repeating the general themes of that paper here, I want to sketch how I currently view the problems of moving from a set-theoretical to a procedural version of the highly restricted fragment of language encompassed by grammar G_1. Certainly from a psychological standpoint this grammar is not really interesting because it is far too restricted in its range, but it can serve as a kind of toy example for the discussion of the problems of working out in partially satisfactory form a procedural approach.

What is procedural semantics? Without giving a general definition or a systematic characterization of expected properties, I would like in an informal way to describe how I think about procedural semantics. The basic and fundamental psychological point is that, with rare exception, in applying a predicate to an object or judging that a relation holds between two or more objects, we do not consider properties or relations as sets. We do not even consider them as somehow simply intensional properties, but we have procedures that compute their values for the object in question. Thus if someone tells me that an object in the distance is a cow, I have a perceptual and conceptual procedure for making computations on the input data that reach my peripheral sensory system, and as these data change with the shortening of the distance between the object and me, my computations change and I come to a firm view as to whether the object in question is indeed a cow. In the same way, if someone says to me that the sum of 653 and 742 is 1,395, I do not have an abstract, set-theoretical way of deriving the answer but an algorithmic procedure that I learned early in school, and that perhaps I have since modified to some degree but that in essence is similar to an algorithm taught throughout the world to children of about 8 to 10 years of age. Fregean and other accounts of number scarcely touch this psychological aspect of actually determining by application of a specific algorithmic procedure a truth claim about the sum of certain numbers. As a third example, if someone asks me: Have you ever been to Katmandu?, I am able to make a very quick computation and respond almost immediately, "No." On the other hand, if I am asked whether I have ever been to Paris, I can with at least as great an ease compute a positive answer. These three examples certainly do not exhaust the range of computational procedures but they are typical cases, and a psychological theory of computation is required in order to give a serious account of how utterances or parts of utterances are processed either by speakers or by listeners.

In the paper mentioned earlier (Suppes, 1980), I try to give a somewhat detailed account in the final section of how to approach, from a procedural standpoint, the meaning and proof of declarative statements, commands, or questions about elementary arithmetic.

Properties as abstractions of procedures. It has been a familiar point in philosophy since the last century that classes are abstractions of properties. The point relevant here is that properties stand in the same relation to procedures that classes stand to properties. For example, the property of a number being prime can be tested by quite different procedures, and among this indefinitely large number of procedures some will of course be much more efficient or faster than others. It is part of the thesis of the earlier paper on procedural semantics that I have mentioned to claim that the procedures used by each of us in talking and listening, or indeed in perceiving and moving about, are private and individually idiosyncratic. These private procedures are behind public talk about properties. Two of us can agree that a given object has the property of being heavy but we may compute this in quite different ways, for example, by comparison with different reference objects.

In general, intensional logic has made the move from classes to properties but not the additional move from properties to procedures. The line of attack for moving from classes to properties, in terms of the grammar G_1 and its associated semantics, is straightforward and scarcely needs detailed discussion here. I shall restrict myself to sketching one way of approaching this step. Each of the non-functional lexical items, that is, adjectives and nouns, as introduced by the unstated lexical rules of G_1, is represented by a set of properties, based upon some primitive list, perhaps. This list of properties, for example, the list of properties of cows or of numbers, is not something we always consciously know but is part of our psychological—in particular of our linguistic—development. Of course, there are immediate questions that arise about the list of properties that belong to a given adjective or noun. Is the list composed entirely of essential properties or are there also accidental properties? And under what formal operations do we think the list of properties is closed? In other words, what do we maintain is the algebra of properties? Once we start talking about closure properties of the algebra of properties, it is also easy to move away from a psychologically realistic model, just as it is unrealistic to believe that any logical consequence of our beliefs must also be a belief. On the other hand, some kinds of highly constructive closure properties seem natural and psychologically relatively acceptable. Thus, if an object that falls under some noun has two properties, we would ordinarily think of it as having the property consisting of the conjunction of these two properties.

When we are prepared to make an explicit commitment to the list of properties, then the logical structure of sentences and their relationships can be studied in a formal manner, a topic that is rather removed from a psychological model of speech. For example, when the property lists are explicit, then those universal propositions that are necessary are easily identified, namely, just those sentences generated by grammar G_1 for which the properties of the subject are a subset of the properties of the predicate.

The formal generalization of the semantics of the first section to properties is obvious: The denotations of individual lexical items are replaced by functions from possible worlds to subsets of each world in the standard manner of possible-world semantics, and the set-theoretical operations of combination as we move up the semantic tree of a sentence are modified accordingly. The totally unrealistic computational aspects of this procedure make it unreasonable to pursue further in the present context.

Procedures and computations. As we move from properties to procedures, the steps should be obvious. We replace the functions just described, which in turn replace the standard sets, by procedures, and the procedures are combined into a program in accordance with the structure given by the semantic trees considered earlier. But there is now another difficulty. What are the input data for the procedures, and is there more than one way to convert a semantic tree in the sense of the first section into a procedural tree? Both questions have answers that lead to difficulties.

Avoiding these difficulties for the moment, let me try to illustrate in a schematic way how procedural ideas might be developed from the simplest sort of example. Suppose that we are in a room with a fair number of objects and somebody asserts "Some balls are green." The sentence is uttered in such a context that it refers to balls in the room and not to balls elsewhere. We might describe in English the following program or procedure that tests for the truth or falsity of this sentence.

> Look at the first object on the left.
> Is it round? If yes, is it green?
> If yes, stop and answer "true."
> But if not round or not green, look for a next object.
> If there is a next object, proceed as before.
> If there is no next object, stop and answer "false."

Here the assumption is that the predicate *round* has an underlying procedure that provides an adequate test for an object being a ball in the present context, and also there is a perceptual procedure back of the color word *green* that tests whether an ordinary object in direct perception is green or not. Thus, in this example we need two lexical procedures, the one for *round* and the other for *green*. The program then provides a way of determining the truth or falsity of the statement "Some balls are green" in the context in which the statement is made.

This example illustrates several features of my current thinking about these matters. The most important idea is that there is no attempt to spell out a primitive machine language that the individual uses, for it is my claim that this machine language is private and unknowable. Moreover, there is no reason to introduce a technical language. It is very likely that the ordinary use of English is deeply intertwined for speakers of English with their private machine language, and it is better to use English than an artificial language for describing procedures because it is in this language that we give one another instruction on how to construct new procedures. Second, the program that I have written down is meant to be only an example of the way that the ideas are organized, and a given individual will not follow this exact setup, in accordance with my claim of privacy. Third, although English words are used extensively in the giving of instruction and in the putting together of new and more complex procedures from simpler ones, once a complex procedure is learned the English labelled "sub-routines" illustrated in the example are almost surely eliminated and a more efficient internal procedure is used without reference to the kinds of English phrasing I have used. Roughly speaking, this corresponds to compiling into machine language a procedure written in a high-level language in standard computer practice. Fourth, there are no procedures that we describe in English that are primitive. The primitive procedures are in a machine language we cannot get our hands on precisely, although we might make some naive guesses from psychophysiological studies. Thus, any sentence, no matter how simple, can be explained in words we as English-speaking adults already understand. The procedures that are called by English phrases can be used to interdefine appropriate procedures for one another. It is also apparent that I have not really specified a general constructive way in which the objects in the room are scanned. It is certainly an unnecessary convention to begin by looking at the first object on the left.

One thing is evident. In the case of sentences as simple and as qualitative in character as "Some balls are green," much of the computing required is called for by the procedures denoted by lexical substantives, *round* and *green* in the present instance. In other cases the computation can be a good deal more difficult just because of the complexity of the structure of the sentence. Another point is that I have presented the procedure as a linear program rather than as a procedural tree. Just as in the case of grammatical derivations for context-free grammars, there is a natural relation between linear programs and procedural trees, but I shall not pursue technical details here, which do need to be worked out. It seems likely that a realistic computational model of speech processing will be structurally more complex than either linear programs or semantic trees.

Procedures and variable-free semantics. Something needs to be said about the way in which the two main sections of this article are related. The variable-free set-theoretical semantics outlined in the first section is, in my view, a natural abstraction of the procedures sketched earlier. The algebraic character of the semantics of the first section and the highly constructive character of the representations, due to the absence of variables make a computational model already implicit in the formalism. Second, the set-theoretical semantics is meant to fit hand in glove with the structure of the English sentences, and this, too, accords well with the intertwining of the procedural approach I have described to the surface structure of English.

If I were willing to commit to a specific machine language, it would then be straightforward to prove some representations of procedures at an abstract level in terms of the set-theoretical semantics given earlier, but I have come to view such a commitment as a mistake. On the other hand, because of the complexity of working out details of the procedural approach, the greater abstraction and simplicity of the set-theoretical approach will continue to be of value as an intermediate step of analysis. However, I do want to insist on the point that it should be regarded as an intermediate step and not in any sense as providing a fully satisfactory theory of the semantics of language as actually used.

Procedures and meaning. This takes me to my final point. In the paper mentioned earlier (Suppes, 1980) I have defended the thesis that the meaning of a sentence is a procedure or a collection of procedures and that this meaning in its most concrete representation is wholly private and idiosyncratic to each individual.[2] This private representation is the most detailed sense of meaning. Thus, for example, the meaning of a proper name is a procedure—or, better yet, a private collection of procedures— that each of us uses in various contexts for recognizing the person or object denoted by the proper name. Public meaning is obtained by abstraction from the great variety of private meanings. Sufficiently coarse congruence relations take us all the way back to set-theoretical semantics. I have outlined the beginnings of a theory of congruence for set-theoretical

---

[2] I hold a similar thesis about each individual's grammar.

semantics in Suppes (1973a), but a psychologically realistic theory of congruence that takes into account not only procedures but also intentions and emotional states of speakers and listeners is needed as part of any empirically satisfactory theory of communication.

15

LOGICAL INFERENCE IN
ENGLISH: A PRELIMINARY
ANALYSIS

GENERATIVE GRAMMARS AND THEIR MODEL STRUCTURES

A couple of examples will illustrate the framework I have in mind and provide an intuitive introduction to those unfamiliar with the concept of semantic trees for context-free grammars.

Consider the tree for the sentence *Some people do not eát some vegetables* shown in Figure 1 (with the stress on *eat*). On the left of the colon at each node is shown the terminal or nonterminal label. The nonterminal grammatical categories should be obvious: S = sentence, EQ = existential quantifier, NP = noun phrase, Aux = auxiliary, etc. To the right of the colon at a node is shown the denotation of the label if it has one. Thus, in the semantic tree of Figure 1, *people* and its ascendant NP node have the set P of people as denotation; *eat* and its ascendant TV— transitive verb—node have the binary relation E of eating as denotation; *vegetables* and its ascendant NP node have the set V of vegetables as denotation. The VP – verb phrase – node has a denotation composed of set-theoretical operations on E and V. Intuitively the denotation is just the set of people who do not eat some vegetables. The notation $\check{E}$

---

*Reprinted from *Studia Logica*, **38**, 1979, 375-391.

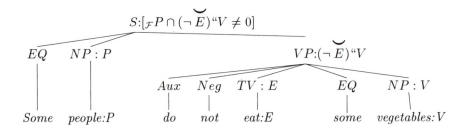

Figure 1.

is for the *converse* of the relation E, $\neg \check{E}$ is the *complement* of the relation $\check{E}$, and $(\neg \check{E})$ "V is the *image* of the set V under the relation $\neg \check{E}$. I take the root of the semantic tree of a sentence to denote the value T or F in a standard Fregean manner. Most of this notation is standard in elementary set theory (see, e.g., Suppes, 1960). Some subtleties about complementation are discussed below, as is the point about stress.

I give now a quick overview of the relevant formal concepts. First, a structure $G = \langle V, N, P, S \rangle$ is a *phrase-structure grammar* if and only if V and P are finite, nonempty sets; N is a subset of V; S is in N; and $P \subseteq N^* \times V^+$, where N^* is the set of all finite sequences whose terms are elements of N and V^+ is V^* minus the empty sequence. The grammar G is *context-free* if and only if $P \subseteq N \times V^+$. In the usual terminology, V is the vocabulary, N is the nonterminal vocabulary, S is the start symbol of derivations or the label of the root of derivation trees of the grammar, and P is the set of production rules. I assume as known the standard definitions of one string of V^* being *G-derivable* from another, the concept of a *derivation tree* of G, and the language $L(G)$ generated by G. (For a detailed treatment of these concepts, see Hopcroft & Ullman, 1969.) A context-free grammar G is *unambiguous* if and only if every terminal string in $L(G)$ has exactly one derivation tree (with respect to G).

Semantics may be introduced in two steps. First, the grammar G is extended to a *potentially denoting* grammar by assigning at most one set-theoretical function to each production rule of G. We may show these functions in general by using a notation of square braces; for example,

$[NP]$ is the denotation of NP. In the case of Figure 1,

Production Rule	Semantic Function
$S \to EQ + NP + VP$	$[S] = [_{\mathcal{F}}[NP] \cap [VP] \neq 0]$
$VP \to Aux + Neg + TV + EQ + NP$	$[VP] = (\neg[\overline{TV}]) \,{}^{\shortmid\shortmid}[NP],$

where the Frege function $[_{\mathcal{F}}\phi]$ is defined for any (extensional) sentence ϕ as follows:

$$[_{\mathcal{F}}\phi] = \begin{cases} T \text{ if } \phi \text{ is true (in the given model)} \\ F \text{ otherwise.} \end{cases}$$

And in the case of the other nodes with only one descendant, the semantic function is identity if there is a denotation. For example,

$$TV \to eat \qquad [TV] = [\text{eat}].$$

The second step is the characterization of model structures. In the general theory of model-theoretic semantics for context-free languages, I use the concept of a *hierarchy* $\mathcal{H}(D)$ of sets built up from a given nonempty domain D by closure under union, subset, and power set "operations," with T and F excluded from the hierarchy and $T \neq F$. A *model structure* for a given grammar G with terminal vocabulary V_T is a pair $\langle D, v \rangle$ where D is a nonempty set and v is a partial function from V_T^+ to $\mathcal{H}(D)$. Explicit details are to be found in Suppes (1973b). The treatment here is restricted. First, only terminal words, not terminal phrases, are permitted to denote, so that the domain of the valuation function v is V_T, not V_T^+. (The function v remains a partial function because many terminal words—e.g., quantifier words—do not denote.)

The more important restriction is in the hierarchy. In line with my earlier paper (Suppes, 1976), I restrict the model structures to the power set $\mathcal{P}(D)$ of the domain D, that is, the set of all subsets of D, and the power set of the Cartesian product $D \times D$—thus, only binary relations are considered. Formally, I define

$$\mathcal{E}(D) = \mathcal{P}(D) \cup \mathcal{P}(D \times D),$$

using "$\mathcal{E}$" for extended relation algebras of sets, a terminology introduced in the earlier paper. The valuation function v is then a partial function from V_T to $\mathcal{E}(D)$.

The "algebraic" operations on elements of $\mathcal{E}(D)$ have mainly already been mentioned: union, intersection, and complementation on arbitrary sets; the converse of relations; and the image of a set under a relation,

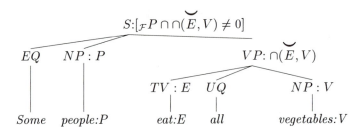

Figure 2.

$R``A$. In addition, we need the restriction of the domain of a relation R to a set A, $R|A$, which is defined as:

$$R|A = R \cap (A \times \mathcal{R}(R)),$$

where $\mathcal{R}(R)$ is the range of the relation R.

As always, complementation is relative to some given set. From the standpoint of $\mathcal{E}(D)$, the natural set-theoretical choice is $D \cup (D \times D)$, but conceptually this is not very intuitive. For instance, if L is the relation of loving, then $\neg L$ should be the *relation* of not loving, that is,

$$\neg L = (D \times D) - L.$$

Consequently, complementation is here taken to mean with respect to $D \times D$ in the case of relations and with respect to D in the case of sets that are subsets of D. The only point of ambiguity concerns complementation of the empty set or relation, and the context will make clear which is meant.

In the earlier paper on these matters (Suppes, 1976), I introduced the notation

$$\cap(R, A) = \cap_{\alpha \in A}(R``\{a\}),$$

for the appropriate denotation when a verb phrase uses a universal quantifier in object position. This use may be seen in the semantic tree (Figure 2) for *Some people eat all vegetables*. I note that UQ is the nonterminal symbol for the universal quantifier *all*, just as in the next section NQ is the nonterminal symbol for the negative universal quantifier *no*. In direct analogy with O syllogistic propositions being the contradictory of A propositions, we may define $\cap(R, A)$ in the following manner (Suppes, 1979) for $R \subseteq D \times D$ and $A \subseteq D$,

$$\cap(R, A) = (\neg((\neg R)``A)).$$

Note that the "inside" complementation is with respect to $D \times D$ and the "outside" one with respect to D.

GRAMMAR G_1 AND ITS SEMANTICS

The grammar G_1, which will be the focus of the remainder of this paper, is left partially unspecified. In particular, the terminal vocabulary of nouns, adjectives, transitive verbs, and intransitive verbs will not be listed. Ones that are used must satisfy the semantics given. There are many that do. On the other hand, use of the nine control words that do not denote is explicitly fixed by nine lexical production rules.

It is my intention that every sentence generated by the grammar be an acceptable English sentence, even if on occasion somewhat awkward or pedantic. Consequently, to avoid what are at this stage uninteresting details, all sentences are meant to be in the plural, as are all verbs and nouns; moreover, all verbs are assumed to be in the present tense, active voice, and indicative mood. Another reason for restricting the grammar at this stage is that the rules of inference are still formulated in a rather inelegant fashion. More use and development will be required to determine what condensations and abbreviations are appropriate.

In spite of the concentration on quantifiers, I have foregone introducing *any* in the same spirit of simplification. In the framework given here, the semantics of *any* seems straightforward but calls for some details not needed for the three quantifier words introduced.

The production rules are followed by the semantic functions on the next line. To reduce the number of lines required for the rules, I use the standard convention of a slash "/" to separate rules given on the same line. Comments are interspersed after each group of rules, for a straight listing of the syntactical rules and associated semantic functions is rather opaque. I begin with the top-level rules for generating sentences.

$$S \to UQ + NP + VP/EQ + NP + VP/NQ + NP + VP$$
$$[S] = [_{\mathcal{F}}\neg[NP] \cup [VP] = D]/[_{\mathcal{F}}[NP] \cap [VP] \neq 0]/[_{\mathcal{F}}[NP] \cap [VP] = 0]$$
$$S \to DA + Cop + NP/DA + Cop + EQ + NP/DA + Cop+$$
$$NQ + NP$$
$$[S] = [_{\mathcal{F}}[NP] \neq 0]/[_{\mathcal{F}}[NP] \neq 0]/[_{\mathcal{F}}[NP] = 0]$$

The first three rules, given in one line, generate standard sentences with initial quantifiers *all, some,* or *no.* The associated semantic functions use the Frege function defined earlier. The set D is, of course, the domain of the extended relation algebra that is the given model. The most important conceptual point about these three rules is the one emphasized in

Suppes (1976), that is, the quantifiers are not parts of the noun phrases but enter at the top level. In the paper just mentioned it is proved that this approach is required if the semantics is to be Boolean for the classical syllogism and, by extension, relational for the sentences of G_1. The semantic functions are familiar from the usual treatments of A, I, and E propositions of the classical syllogism. Propositions of type O, for example, *Some people are not tall*, do not appear in full form at this level, because the negation is buried in the verb phrase.

The next three rules are for generating sentences that begin with the demonstrative adverb *there*, and so the nonterminal symbol is DA. A typical instance of each type in order would be: *There are trees, There are some trees, There are no trees*. Notice that the semantical function is the same for the first two types. This parallels what happens to existential quantifiers in object position. The semantic functions are the same for *Some people eat vegetables* and *Some people eat some vegetables*, but more on this point later.

The next group of rules is for generating noun phrases. The nonterminal symbols have the following intuitive meaning: *Adj* for adjective, N for noun, *RelPr* for the relative pronoun *that*, *PPrep* for the preposition of possession *of*. The semantical notation $[N]_2$ refers to forming a binary relation from the set $[N]$. Consider, for example, *vegetables* and *vegetables of Southern growers*. The denotation of vegetables simpliciter is, let us say, the set V. For V_2 or $[N]_2$, we form the relation pairing each vegetable in V with its properties, such as color, weight, and origin, given extensionally.[1] Let G be the set of Southern growers. Then $\check{V}_2\text{``}G$ is the denotation of *vegetables of Southern growers*.

$$NP \rightarrow \quad N/Adj + N/NP + RelPr + VP/N + PPrep + NP$$
$$[NP] = \quad [N]/[Adj] \cap [N]/NP] \cap [VP]/([N]_2)\text{``}[NP]$$

It should be noted that the rules do not permit iteration of adjectives. This is because rather subtle rules are required to get the adjectives in correct order, and the details would be diversionary in the present context. (For an extensive treatment of adjectives in the present spirit, especially for semantics of nonclassificatory adjectives, see Suppes & Macken, 1978.) Unlimited nesting of relative clauses is permitted. Thus, we can generate *Triangles that cover squares that are projections of cubes are isosceles*.

The next group of rules governs verb phrases. Because they cover the treatment of quantifiers in object position, they require especially detailed comments. Perhaps of equal significance is the semantic analysis of negation, which in the context of a verb phrase—as negation usually is

---

[1] For general application a more subtle theory is needed.

in idiomatic English—is not a sentential connective, but complementation of a verb or a verb phrase.

Quantifiers in object position give rise to forms analogous to $A, I, E,$ and O propositions of the classical syllogism. I illustrate each and its semantic denotation, where E is the binary relation denoted by the verb *eat* and V is the set denoted by *vegetables*.

A :	*eat all vegetables*	$\cap(E,V)$ or $\neg((\neg\breve{E})\,\text{``}V)$
I :	*eat (some) vegetables*	$\breve{E}\,\text{``}V$
E :	*eat no vegetables*	$\neg(\breve{E}\,\text{``}V)$
O :	*do not eat (some) vegetables*	$(\neg\breve{E})\text{``}V$

Analogous to the classical case, it is apparent that A and O verb phrases are complements of each other, as are I and E verb phrases, but the reading of O phrases given above is changed in the following. These four examples also illustrate how quantifiers are eliminated in the underlying semantic analysis; the general method is determined by the semantic functions given below.

There are two semantically distinct readings of negation, for both *some* and *all* in the object position. Different contexts seem to generate a differentially preferred reading, indicated by stress in spoken English. I mark stress by an acute mark over the emphasized word, and the semantic representation is shown immediately following, in accordance with Suppes (1979).

(1)	*do not eát some vegetables* :	$(\neg\breve{E})\text{``}V$
(2)	*do nót eat some vegetables* :	$\neg(\breve{E}\,\text{``}V)$
(3)	*do nót eat all vegetables* :	$\neg\cap(\breve{E},V) = (\neg\breve{E})\text{``}V$
(4)	*do not eát all vegetables* :	$\cap(\neg\breve{E},V) = \neg(\breve{E}\,\text{``}V)$

Thus, (1) and (3) are logically equivalent, and so are (2) and (4). The change in stress semantically equates the uses of *all* and *some*. The semantics underlying the grammar given here permits only (2) and (3), and the semantics of (2) is also used when *some* is deleted, as in *do not eat vegetables*. It is worth noting that (3) calls for a deeper embedding of the negation, semantically expressed by complementation, than does (2), but both contain the semantics of negation firmly within the verb phrase. The readings (1) and (4) can be added with attendant complications in the theory of inference. In fact, a theory ready for realistic use will need

to have such distinctions, and it is my intention in the future to pursue
the link between prosody and inference in some detail—certainly what I
have said here only begins the story.

A simple example shows, by the way, that (1) and (2) are not logically
equivalent. Let

$$D = V = \{1,2\},$$
$$E = \{\langle 2,1 \rangle\}.$$

Then

$$(\neg \overset{\smile}{E})\text{“}V = \{1,2\},$$

but

$$\neg(\overset{\smile}{E}\text{“}V) = \{1\}.$$

The production rules and associated semantic functions for verb phrases
are straightforward except for the complications introduced by negation.
What I propose may need modification, but not in ways that are yet clear
to me. I use the notation $NegVP$ for a high-level nonterminal symbol
introducing verb phrases that contain the negative quantifier *no* in object
position or negations with an existential quantifier; if the second natural reading of *all* in object position with *not* were included, as discussed
above, additional rules of the same sort would be required. The nonterminal $NegVP$ is also used to negate intransitive verbs and the copula. As
usual, IV is a nonterminal symbol for *intransitive verb*, TV for *transitive
verb*. The only terminal form of the copula, Cop, in the grammar G_1 is
are, and the only auxiliary, Aux, is *do*.

$$
\begin{aligned}
VP &\to NegVP \\
[VP] &= [NegVP] \\
VP &\to IV/Cop + NP/Cop + Adj/TV + UQ + NP/ \\
&\quad TV + EQ + NP/TV + NP \\
[VP] &= [IV]/[NP]/[Adj]/ \cap ([\overset{\smile}{TV}],[NP])/[\overset{\smile}{TV}]\text{“}[NP]/ \\
&\quad [TV]\text{“}[NP] \\
NegVP &\to Aux + Neg + TV + UQ + NP/TV + NQ + NP/ \\
&\quad Aux + Neg + TV + EQ + NP/Aux + Neg + TV + NP \\
[NegVP] &= \neg \cap ([\overset{\smile}{TV}],[NP])/\neg([\overset{\smile}{TV}]\text{“}[NP])/ \\
&\quad \neg([TV]\text{“}[NP])/\neg([TV]\text{“}[NP]) \\
NegVP &\to Aux + Neg + IV/Cop + Neg + NP/Cop + Neg + Adj \\
[NegVP] &= \neg[IV]/\neg[NP]/\neg[Adj]
\end{aligned}
$$

Note that in the case of the last line of three $NegVP$ rules, the semantic
functions are identical, as would be expected. This identity in the preceding three cases as well is, on the other hand, evidence for introducing

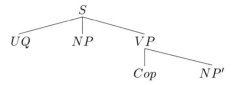

Figure 3.

prosodic differentiation as a basis for needed and often expected semantic differentiation.

The rules of inference introduced are stated in natural deduction form, but there are various preliminary matters of notation to deal with, for the usual notation of sentential and first-order predicate logic is not appropriate. In the first place, there are no sentential connectives. The only possible candidate is *not*, and the semantic rules given above make clear that what is negated is a verb or verb phrase. It is obvious that the language can be extended to include the standard connectives, but it was not done here deliberately to emphasize the differences from the standard formalism of elementary logic.

Secondly, the nonterminal vocabulary of the grammar can play the role usually assigned to metamathematical variables in the explicit formulation of the rules of inference. A minor additional piece of notation is the use of primes to distinguish possibly different noun phrases, as in *All men are animals*. Thus, in accordance with the A, I, E, and O propositions of classical syllogistic theory, a natural notation is $A(NP, NP')$ for a sentence with a tree base of the form shown in Figure 3. (The technical meaning of the *tree base* should be clear from this example and will not be given formally.) Because the grammar is unambiguous, hereafter a linear notation will be used. Thus, we have

$$A(NP, NP') \quad \text{for} \quad UQ + NP + Cop + NP'$$
$$I(NP, NP') \quad \text{for} \quad EQ + NP + Cop + NP'$$
$$E(NP, NP') \quad \text{for} \quad NQ + NP + Cop + NP'$$
$$O(NP, NP') \quad \text{for} \quad EQ + NP + Cop + Neg + NP'.$$

When what is of concern inferentially is only the subject of a sentence, as in

All students like some teachers,
All sophomores are students,
Therefore, all sophomores like some teachers,

some more simplified notation is useful.

$$A(NP) \quad \text{for} \quad UQ + NP + VP$$
$$I(NP) \quad \text{for} \quad EQ + NP + VP$$
$$E(NP) \quad \text{for} \quad NQ + NP + VP.$$

The notation A, I, and E is suggestive of the classical syllogism, but no separate O form is required at this stage. The semantics of each of the three forms is clear:

$$A(NP): \quad [NP] \subseteq [VP]$$
$$I(NP): \quad [NP] \cap [VP] \neq 0$$
$$E(NP): \quad [NP] \cap [VP] = 0.$$

For these semantic relations, it does not matter whether or not the VP includes a negation. Thus, *All men do not like chains* is semantically represented by

$$M \subseteq \neg((\overset{\smile}{L})``C),$$

just as *All men like chains* is represented by

$$M \subseteq \overset{\smile}{L} ``C,$$

where M, L, and C have an obvious meaning. (In these and subsequent semantic representations I omit the notation for the Frege function, but it is implicitly assumed.) Of course, my reading of *All men do not like chains* is not one everyone would agree to. Many would consider this sentence logically equivalent to *It is not the case that all men like chains*, but I shall hold to the reading given above for the restricted grammar G_1 and its associated semantic functions. Also a notation for purely existential sentences of the form *There are unicorns* is desirable, and for the denial of such sentences, for example, *There are no unicorns*.

$$T(NP) \quad \text{for} \quad DA + Cop + NP/DA + Cop + EQ + NP$$
$$N(NP) \quad \text{for} \quad DA + Cop + NQ + NP.$$

In other cases of inference, the structure of the verb phrase is the focus of inference, as in

Some people eat no vegetables.
Therefore, some people eat no raw vegetables.

As already remarked, the classical $A, I, E,$ and O propositions have direct analogues in verb phrases, and so we could introduce abbreviations accordingly by adding V for *verb phrase* after each traditional letter. But additional considerations are important, and some consolidation is also efficient. For inference purposes a distinction must be made between positive and negative quantifiers in subject position. Fortunately, both positive quantifiers *all* and *some* act the same way, in the sense of providing a constant context with the same semantical impact on varying terms in the verb phrase. I use PQ for UQ or EQ, and NQ, as before, for the negative quantifier *no.*

There are five verb-phrase cases with positive quantifiers in subject position and a corresponding five with the negative quantifier in subject position. The five PQ forms are abbreviated as follows:

$$PQAV(NP) \quad \text{for} \quad PQ + NP'' + TV + UQ + NP$$
$$PQIV(NP) \quad \text{for} \quad PQ + NP'' + TV + (EQ) + NP/$$
$$PQ + NP' + Cop + NP$$
$$PQNV(NP) \quad \text{for} \quad PQ + NP'' + TV + NQ + NP$$
$$PQNAV(NP) \quad \text{for} \quad PQ + NP'' + Aux + Neg + TV + UQ + NP$$
$$PQNIV(NP) \quad \text{for} \quad PQ + NP'' + Aux + Neg + TV + (EQ) + NP/$$
$$PQ + NP'' + Cop + Neg + NP$$

The parenthesis around EQ mean that deletion is optional. The five NQ forms follow exactly the same pattern. The only change is to replace the initial PQ in the definiens and the definiendum by NQ.

The semantic relation of one set containing another is exemplified by $A(NP, NP')$, because such an A proposition is true in a model just when $[NP] \subseteq [NP']$ in the model. This relation of inclusion is characteristic of parts of sentences as well, for example,

$$\text{if } NP \rightarrow Adj + NP' \text{ then } [NP] \subseteq [NP'].$$

The relevant cases are embodied in the general notation $C(NP, NP')$, where I have chosen C for expressing syntactically the relation of being contained in.

$C(NP, NP')$ for one of the following:

$$(i) \quad A(NP, NP')$$
$$(ii) \quad NP \rightarrow Adj + NP'$$
$$(iii) \quad NP \rightarrow NP' + RelPr + VP$$
$$(iv) \quad NP \rightarrow NP' + PPrep + NP''$$
$$(v) \quad NP \rightarrow N + PPrep + NP'',$$
$$NP' \rightarrow N + PPrep + NP''',$$
$$A(NP'', NP''')$$

The most complicated of the five cases is the last one. It is exemplified by

$$[NP] = [\text{vegetables of Southern growers}] \subseteq [\text{vegetables of growers}] =$$
$$= [NP']$$

and

$$[NP''] = [\text{Southern growers}] \subseteq [\text{growers}] = [NP'''].$$

The restriction in the grammar to only nouns, not general noun phrases, being modified by a prepositional phrase of possession is an artificial restriction but one that can only be removed by changing the grammar itself. Unlike most classical forms of inference, the use of $C(NP, NP')$ permits many inferences from a single sentence. The inference schemes given below do not necessarily require two sentences even though they seem to have such a form, because $C(NP, NP')$ can express a relation between parts of a sentence, for example,

$$\frac{A(NP), C(NP', NP)}{A(NP')},$$

as seen in

All cows are sick
Therefore, all black cows are sick.

Here, NP is the constituent *cows* and NP' is the constituent *black cows*. Soundness of the rules of inference is easily checked because of the set-theoretical semantic representation that does not use variables. Thus the semantic analysis of the rule just given is:

$$\frac{[NP] \subseteq [VP] \ [NP'] \subseteq [NP]}{[NP'] \subseteq [VP]}.$$

Consider now the rule like the above but with $A(NP)$ replaced by $I(NP)$. The semantic analysis is shown on the right.

$$\frac{I(NP) \ C(NP, NP')}{I(NP')} \qquad \frac{[NP] \cap [VP] \neq 0 \ \ [NP] \subseteq [NP']}{[NP'] \cap [VP] \neq 0}$$

In this case we have $[NP] \subseteq [NP']$ rather than the reverse as in the previous rule. But these two cases exhaust the possibilities for the semantics of $C(NP, NP')$, and so we can form two general rules for the two possibilities: $[NP] \subseteq [NP']$ or $[NP'] \subseteq [NP]$, which embody a number of other cases.

For the abstract generalization of the first rule, we may introduce a new symbol, say J, for which we may substitute one of the following eight cases defined earlier.

$$J \text{ for } A/E/PQAV/PQNV/PQNIV/NQIV/NQNAV/N,$$

where N refers to the form $N(NP)$ for denials of existence. Using the J notation, one general inference form subsuming the earlier example of $A(NP)$ may be written

$$JC \quad \frac{J(NP) \quad C(NP', NP)}{J(NP')}.$$

Without introducing a much more general set-theoretical notation, a direct semantic analysis of this inference form, which I label JC, cannot be given, but it is easy to write down the analysis for the seven remaining cases of J to verify its soundness. To help make the ideas more familiar, I give two more examples—from the seven.

$$\frac{NQNAV(NP) \quad C(NP', NP)}{NQNAV(NP')}$$

$$\frac{[NP''] \cap ((\neg\overbrace{[TV]})\,{}^{\mbox{\tiny“}}[NP]) = 0 \quad [NP'] \subseteq [NP]}{[NP''] \cap ((\neg\overbrace{[TV]})\,{}^{\mbox{\tiny“}}[NP']) = 0}$$

$$\frac{N(NP) \quad C(NP', NP)}{N(NP')} \quad \frac{[NP] = 0 \quad [NP'] \subseteq [NP]}{[NP'] = 0}$$

Some English examples of the eight cases of J that are in the JC rule are the following. The various examples use different types of instances of $C(NP', NP)$. The instance of J is shown on the left.

A: All students like logic
        Therefore, all bright students like logic.

E: No women like boxing
        Therefore, no women of Northern countries like boxing.

$PQAV$:   Some persons hate all vegetables.
        Therefore, some persons hate all white vegetables.

$PQNV$:   Some children eat no vegetables of
        Southern growers.
        Therefore, some children eat no vegetables of red-nosed
        Southern growers.

$PQNIV$:   Some persons do not like books.
        Therefore, some persons do not like travel books.

This last example shows the importance of stress. To my ear, this example seems quite natural, with the stress on *not*. If we add *some* to make the object noun phrase *some books* it no longer seems natural, and the stress moves to *like*, which has the different semantic analysis already given. It is, I think, a clear defect of the grammar G_1 to treat these two sentences, one with and one without *some*, in the same way. The defect is not a logical one, but one that goes against idiomatic usage. In more realistic future versions, this distinction will be incorporated.

Corresponding to the eight cases of J are seven others, which we may represent by L.

$$L \text{ for } I/PQIV/PQNAV/NQAV/NQNV/NQNIV/T.$$

The general inference form that includes the earlier example of $I(NP)$ is then the rule LC:

$$LC \qquad \frac{L(NP) \quad C(NP, NP')}{L(NP')}.$$

Some English examples of this rule follow. The reader may easily supply the formal semantic analysis along the lines already laid down.

$PQNAV$:   Some persons do not read all emergency notices.
            Therefore, some persons do not read all notices.

$NQAV$:   No persons read all books of modern British authors.
            Therefore, no persons read all books of modern authors.

$NQNV$:   No persons drink no nutritious liquids.
            All nutritious liquids are caloric foods.
            Therefore, no persons drink no caloric foods.

T: There are white elephants.
            All white elephants are rare animals.
            Therefore, there are rare animals.

Inference rules similar to JC and LC are needed for particular propositions $I(NP', NP)$, as in the classical syllogistic case (with semantic analysis shown on the right):

$$\frac{A(NP) \; I(NP', NP)}{I(NP')} \qquad \frac{[NP] \subseteq [VP] \quad [NP'] \cap [NP] \neq 0}{[NP'] \cap [VP] \neq 0}.$$

I shall not develop the analogues of JC and LC here for the above instance. The methodology is apparent from what has preceded. Further rules are also needed for $T(NP)$ replacing $I(NP', NP)$, as in

$$\frac{A(NP) \quad T(NP)}{I(NP)} \qquad \frac{[NP] \subseteq [VP] \quad [NP] \neq 0}{[NP] \cap [VP] \neq 0}.$$

Furthermore, the two classical rules of conversion are needed

$$E \quad \frac{E(NP, NP')}{E(NP', NP)} \qquad I \quad \frac{I(NP, NP')}{I(NP', NP)}.$$

I also take as an axiom schema

$$A \quad A(NP, NP).$$

Thus, we have as a logical truth *All men are men*, but not *Some men are men*, in agreement with the conventions of modern rather than Aristotelian logic.

A rule for reductio ad absurdum proofs is needed as well. To state this rule, the concept of a contradictory $K(S)$ of any proposition S is needed. It is also stipulated that if $K(S)$ is the contradictory of S, then S is the contradictory of $K(S)$, that is, the relation is symmetric.

$$\begin{aligned}
K(A(NP)) &= O(NP) \\
K(E(NP)) &= I(NP) \\
K(T(NP)) &= N(NP),
\end{aligned}$$

where we use $O(NP)$ for $EQ + NP + NegVP$. The rule of reductio ad absurdum may now be stated in simple form using the turnstile notation $\vdash$ for derivability.

$$RAA \quad \text{If } \mathcal{S}, S \vdash S' \text{ and } \mathcal{S}, S \vdash K(S'), \text{ then } \mathcal{S} \vdash K(S),$$

where $\mathcal{S}$ is a set of sentences.

A formal definition of derivations is easily given in a standard way and will be omitted. A typical derivation, with the rule of inference used to obtain the given line shown on the left, is illustrated by the following familiar example due to de Morgan. (As usual, P is used for premise; I use WP for a working premise used in RAA.)

Example

P	(1)	All horses are animals.
WP	(2)	Some heads of horses are not heads of animals.
$LC1,2$	(3)	Some heads of animals are not heads of animals.
A	(4)	All heads of animals are heads of animals.
$RAA2,3,4$	(5)	All heads of horses are heads of animals.

What has been set forth in this section is obviously an incomplete beginning to logical rules of inference in English. Completeness is less important at this stage than is idiomatic faithfulness and assessment of weaknesses of the approach. It seems to me that a version of what might be called *logic-classroom* English can be modeled rather accurately. Representing correctly more general usage is another matter. The questions of prosody touched upon several times are only a part of the problem. Some other problems of extension are raised in the next section.

EXTENSIONS

The rules of inference considered in the previous section governed *of*, but it might be questioned whether *of* is a logical particle. Whatever the answer, the classification of the high-frequency prepositions *to, in, for, with, on, at,* and *by* really seems unclear, as does the classification of *as*, serving as either an adverb or a conjunction. For example, should this sentence be classified as a logical truth? *John is as much like John as Mary is like Mary.* But the issue of whether these words are logical particles is not the crucial one. The real problem is to understand their semantics in ordinary usage and the corresponding rules of inference that reflect uncontroversial intuitive practice.

I restrict myself to the important example of the preposition *in*, which presents many difficulties. Sentences like *Some people are in the house* might suggest a simple inclusion relation for the denotation of *in* corresponding to a spatial geometry in which figures are identified as certain sets of points. In this case, as before, we begin with the production rule and associated semantic function

$$S \rightarrow EQ + NP + VP$$
$$[S] = [\mathcal{F}[NP] \cap [VP] \neq 0],$$

and then add a restriction to VP, for example, by the rules (where $PrepPh$ intuitively stands for prepositional phrase)

$$VP \rightarrow VP' + PrepPh$$
$$[VP] = [VP'] \cap [PrepPh]$$
$$PrepPh \rightarrow \underbrace{Prep + NP}$$
$$[PrepPh] = [Prep]\,{}^{\text{“}}[NP].$$

In this analysis, *in* would denote a certain binary relation $[in]$, and it would seem natural to treat it on the same level as other substantive words or phrases that denote objects in $\mathcal{E}(D)$. But the analysis is wrong.

Consider *John is pouring water in the pitcher.* The analysis given above would imply that John is in the pitcher, which is clearly not a valid consequence, and would in all but absurd cases be false. The point is that the prepositional phrase locates the action denoted by the main verb phrase and does not spatially locate the subject of the sentence. Moreover, there is apparently no satisfactory solution at the level of complexity of $\mathcal{E}(D)$.

In a preliminary way, the most intuitive approach would seem to be a semantic version of something like a case grammar. The models used must be made much richer in structure than arbitrary relational structures or the extended relation algebras introduced at the beginning of this article. Unfortunately the geometry of ordinary experience, as reflected in the use of spatial prepositions like *in, to, on,* and *at,* has not as yet received much attention, but no doubt three-dimensional Euclidean space could be used as a first approximation. Inferences using the common spatial prepositions would assume this constant spatial background, but I must leave to another occasion any attempt to formulate explicit rules of inference governing these matters.

PART IV
ROBOTS

16

NATURAL-LANGUAGE INTERFACE FOR AN INSTRUCTABLE ROBOT

This article is concerned with the problems of understanding the grammar and semantics of English as it would be used to instruct a robot. We describe a working prototype system, programmed in Standard LISP, which translates English sentences into an operator language and then executes them. Imperatives become actions that are performed while declaratives become assertions that are checked for truth. We describe the context-free grammar and parser that are the first stage of translation, the postparser that uses context-sensitive information to eliminate the many bad parses permitted by context-free grammar, and the table-driven final stage of translation. We also describe the semantics of the operators and arguments, including the context-referent we invented to construct loops rather than the artificial means (such as labels and goto, or begin-end pairs) usually employed in programming languages. Finally, we discuss the general question of designing systems which build new procedures out of already-known procedures in ways that are similar to how a human being is taught new procedures in terms of old procedures.

The overall purpose of this article is to approach the problems of un-

*Reprinted from *International Journal of Man-Machine Studies* 1985, **22**, 215-240. Written with Robert Elton Maas.

derstanding the grammar and semantics of English by asking what is required to implement a program of instruction for robots. The use of robots rather than children, for example, is to keep important problems from being hidden by the verbal and perceptual facility of children. Children understand too much that we cannot make an explicit part of theory. Robots, at least the kind we consider as prototypes, are rather stupid and do not offer a helping hand to weak theories in the way that children do. We have also put the emphasis on executing procedures rather than the handling of declarative sentences in order to focus on bringing the analysis and understanding of language to the point of execution. We recognize, of course, that one can test the understanding of declarative sentences by asking for judgments of their truth value, but we are more concerned with procedures, partly because the kinds of responses required are more complex.

We are especially interested in the problem of instruction. A robot, like a child at any given stage, must have available a certain set of primitive procedures. A central problem of instruction is to teach the robot new complex procedures by formulating in English new procedures in terms of given ones. To certain readers this may sound like automatic programming. Later we shall discuss the ways in which it is different. In fact, the ideas for the instructable robot came out of the extended experience of one of the authors with the teaching of elementary mathematics.

Our work relates in different ways to various earlier efforts to develop language-understanding systems, to provide a procedural semantics for perceptual words and phrases, or to write programs that learn from various forms of instruction. We say something about the first two topics here and delay further remarks about programs that learn until the fourth section.

Winograd's SHRDLU program (1972) is one of the best known natural-language understanding systems. Its aim is to be able to converse with a person about manipulating objects in a simple world of toy blocks. The system answers questions and accepts commands that are to be executed (in simulation). It is designed to take account of current context, both in the sense of recent past discourse and in the sense of the perceptual scene. Our system improves on SHRDLU most importantly in the interactive facilities for teaching our "robot" new complex procedures. In other respects our system is more restricted than SHRDLU because of our almost exclusive emphasis on interactive instruction.

The same general comparative remarks apply to such recent efforts as the Hearsay-II speech-understanding system (Earman, Hayes-Roth, Lesser & Reddy, 1980). This system has as a goal, the understanding of spoken language and thus embodies important features that we have not even considered. Apart from the handling of spoken language, the problem-solving capacities of Hearsay-II much exceed ours. Our efforts are somewhat closer to the HARPY system (Lowerre & Reddy, 1980) for understanding speech, in that both systems are more sharply focused than Hearsay-II. But even here the comparison is not a close one because HARPY has compiled knowledge as a central feature. The only significant virtue of our system in comparison with these two more powerful ones is the one already emphasized, i.e. the capability of interactive instruction to build new procedures.

The highly interactive features of our system are closer to central features of interactive theorem provers than to any of the three systems just discussed. Several detailed articles on such theorem provers are to be found in Suppes (1981). Our interactive instruction, like interactive construction of a proof, can be viewed as a dialogue or conversation between program (or robot) and person, but unlike the three systems mentioned, general problems of knowledge representation are avoided. Complex proofs can be given or complex procedures can be constructed, but the framework for either is sharply delineated. What is critical is not knowledge representation but powerful methods of construction. Of course, neither the interactive theorem provers mentioned nor our system described in this article are nearly as powerful as we would like, but we do think that their current implemented interactive features compare favourably with the other systems discussed.

Another line of work pertinent to our efforts, even though it does not consist of developing a speech-understanding system, is the extensive work on procedural semantics of perception words, best exemplified in Miller & Johnson-Laird (1976). Their summary of control instructions of cognitive importance in human perception overlaps with our list of primitive atoms, although the earlier list in Suppes (1973c) for our very restricted perceptual world is the actual initial source of our list. Miller & Johnson-Laird (1976) provide a great deal of invaluable analysis and comment pertinent to any language-understanding system that aims to handle any significant part of the perceptual language of English. Compared to the many issues they focus on, we have been able to consider only a small number.

This article naturally divides into four main parts. The first section deals with the grammar and parser. As we shall discuss later, the parser itself actually consists of a preparser, a main parser, and a postparser. The second section is concerned with semantics and translation. We translate parsed English into LISP operator language and then provide a semantic interpretation for the new primitive atoms we add to LISP. New primitive atoms are given a particular semantics relevant to the particular procedures being dealt with. The third section focuses on the execution of

procedures and the interpreter. From the standpoint expressed above, we
are not content with an abstract or even a partially abstract procedural
semantics but consider it important to give a full analysis of the execution
of procedures. Finally, the fourth section deals with instruction from the
standpoint of learning new procedures.

The procedures we deal with in this article are all ones that arise in
teaching a child elementary arithmetic; we emphasize that we include a
perceptual component. Before saying more, it will be useful to give a
very simple example of the parsed English, the operator language translation, and the execution of the operator language translation of one of
our simplest English commands.

English:
Look at the top number.
Parsed English:
(IMPERATIVE VP+Advs look (PrepPh at (NP+ Adjs num-
ber the top)))
Operator language translation:
(SEQUENCE (LOOK TOP) (CHECK NUMBER))
Execution:
Sequence...
(LOOK TOP)
1 see "3" at row 1 (from the top) and column 1 (from the
right).
(CHECK NUMBER)
Ok.
... end of sequence.

The overall dataflow for an interactive session with the robot is shown
in Figure 1. Prior to an interactive session, the whole training corpus
can be compiled, which means applying the parser and translator to each
different sentence in the corpus, to produce lookup tables relating input
and output of parser and translator, and formatting the original corpus
and the lookup tables for fast access later during the interactive session.
(This compilation and formatting process is referred to as "batch mode"
in the dataflow chart.) During the interactive session, sentences from the
corpus can be input from the database just mentioned, or new sentences
can be typed interactively at the terminal or can be read from various
program-debug rigs, as shown at the top of the chart. Each sentence is
then parsed and translated, to yield the operator-language expression.
The robot then recursively executes that expression in the environment
of the example being worked out, asking the user for help in resolving
ambiguities the robot could not resolve itself. Finally, the compiled and

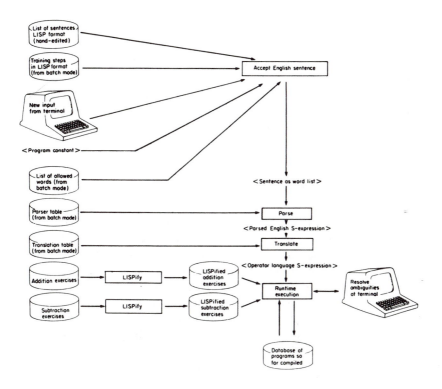

Figure 1. DATAFLOW-INTERACTIVE MODE

disambiguated program is given a name, written into a database of known algorithms, and may later be loaded back in to be applied to a different example without having to be compiled and disambiguated again.

The perceptual component of the procedures we consider is admittedly highly schematized. The perceptual plane is taken to be a coordinate grid of unit squares, and the recognition of a finite alphabet of symbols is assumed, with at most one symbol occurring in a given unit square at any one instant. On the other hand, the simplified perceptual scheme has enough elements of realism, especially in movement around the grid in terms of current points of attention or gaze, that it has been used for the detailed study of eye movements in doing arithmetic exercises (Suppes, Cohen, Laddaga, Anliker & Floyd, 1982; Suppes, Cohen, Laddaga, Anliker & Floyd, 1983).

A training sequence of steps leading to the standard school algorithms for addition and subtraction formed the test bed of initial instruction for our robot program. The instructions were all in English and derive from those given in Suppes (1980). To illustrate ideas, let us restrict ourselves to the case of one-column addition. In principle, two registers suffice in our scheme of analysis. There is a stimulus-supported register that holds an encoded representation of a printed symbol to which the student—child or robot—is perceptually attending. In the present case the alphabet of symbols consists of the 10 digits and the underline symbol. As a new symbol is attended to by a change in the point of visual focus, a previously perceived symbol is lost from memory unless transferred to a second register which is non-stimulus-supported. A typical instruction for this transfer is "Remember this number". In our formulation the student is assumed already able to add a one-digit number to a given number, but this capacity could itself be built up from more elementary operations such as that of counting.

GRAMMAR AND PARSERS

This section is divided into four parts, first the grammar, then the preparser, next the main parser, and finally the postparser.

The grammar. There is nothing very notable about the grammar we have written. We had available on the Institute's computer system a program written by Robert Smith some years ago, which will accept any context-free grammar and parse utterances appropriately prepared in terms of the given context-free grammar. The grammar we have written is strictly a parsing grammar. It would not be adequate for output of English, because we have not in the present formulation provided explicit indication of subject and verb agreement, verb tenses, and other central features. We do not pretend for a moment that this grammar is adequate to further developments but we have constructed it to have something in a framework that was already easily available to us. It needs to be refined considerably for future extensions but it is good enough to exhibit the main features of concern in this first article on our approach to procedural semantics. A typical top-level rule would be one for conjunction of sentences.

S1 ← S0, Conj S1
S2 ← S1, Conj S2

Another rule that generates a complex sentence from parts is the rule for *then*:

S ← S, then S.

We also have the following rules to distinguish between declaratives and imperatives. The rules for each of these are as follows:

S0 ← D
S0 ← I
I ← continue S, until D
I ← VP
D ← NP VP
D ← Dadv NP.

Notice that the first two rules for imperatives introduce at the top level familiar, but rather special, English constructions of importance in our context. An example we used is "Continue doing everything from those steps up through the most recent step, until you see a space".

Our fragment of grammar is rather standard, but we have also introduced a number of specific details to handle the kinds of procedures we have encountered in dealing with our particular subject matter.

Preparser. Robert Smith's parser, called "CREATE", requires that input be in a special form. To permit sentences to be typed in ordinary form, we wrote a program, which we refer to as the preparser, to convert sentences to the special form.

Main parser. The main parser program was written by Robert Smith, using SAIL (Reiser, 1976), a version of Algol 60. Various modified versions of it exist, CREATE being the one we use for the robot. It has no detailed documentation, but a general description is given in Smith, Rawson & Smith (1974). It uses a reasonably efficient algorithm, the Cocke-Younger one (Younger, 1967) for compiling a context-free grammar into a set of tables that permit rapid determination of all parses of a given sentence, avoiding the laborious backtracking that would be needed by a brute-force algorithm that used the grammar directly without compiling it.

When the program is started, it first loads the grammar in from a file (the syntax of this grammar file is given later) and compiles it, checking for loops. A loop is where some symbol (token) is defined to be exactly itself directly or indirectly. For example, "S1 ← S1 P" is legal because each time that production is used an extra P must occur, but "S1 ← S1" is not legal. Similarly, "S1 ← S2" and "S2 ← P S1" is a legal combination, but "S1 ← S2" and "S2 ← S1" is not a legal combination.

The grammar file consists of one production per line, each production being in three parts: (1) the symbol being decomposed, (2) the decomposition, i.e. syntax, (3) the resultant output, i.e. semantics. The general form of a production is ⟨symbol⟩ ← ⟨syntax⟩⟨tab⟩ "⟨semantics⟩".

Here is a sample line from our current grammar:

VP ← VP Conj VP "(;2;;1;;3;)".

This defines one form of a Verb Phrase to be a smaller Verb Phrase followed by a Conjunction followed by another smaller Verb Phrase. For example, if "look" is one Verb Phrase, "see" is another, and "and" is a conjunction, then "look and see" is parsed as a larger Verb Phrase. Output consists of a three-element list consisting of first item #2 (the Conj) then item #1 (the first VP) and finally item #3 (the final VP). Note that the three items in the list are the results of recursively applying the semantics. For example, if the semantical representation of "look" is "LOOK", that of "and" is "SEQUENCE", and that of "see" is "SEE", then that of "look and see" is "(SEQUENCE LOOK SEE)".

It is possible to give the program a command that will enable a trace of the syntax tree for each parse found, as is familiar in context-free grammars. Unfortunately the program has no similar feature for showing the semantics (output).

Postparser. The output from CREATE is not suitable for our purposes. First of all, CREATE often generates multiple parses, due to deficiencies in our grammar. These are placed one after another, and only look-ahead can detect when we have reached the end of the multiple parses and started to read the next sentence in the file. Also, the output is not prettyprinted, so it is hard for us to see from the output it makes which parses (if any) are good when debugging the grammar. Finally, there are usually many obviously bad parses in addition to the one correct parse and a few almost-correct parses. With our present context-free parser and our present grammar that does not know about case, mode, and many other things, we needed to flush the obviously bad parses before further processing the parsed sentences. We thus decided to write a post-parser, which collects all multiple parses into a data structure, rates them according to acceptability of the parse, removes those parses which are inferior to others, generates a warning when no parse achieves a desired acceptability level, and prettyprints the single accepted parse or the list of parses not inferior to any other parse.

The general mechanism of rejecting inferior parses is by weighted demerits. Each proposed parse is recursively examined, looking for any pattern that indicates an obviously bad parse, and checking the type (case or mode) of an overall expression against the types of its parts. Each bad pattern or each type mismatch causes a demerit to be assigned to the parse as a whole. Each type of demerit has a number associated with it, and these numbers for demerits are added to decide how inferior the parse is to a "perfect" parse. That is, a weighted sum of demerits is used to rate the badness of each parse. Among the various parses competing for the title of "best" parse for a given sentence, any parse inferior to another is eliminated, leaving one or more parses, all with the least weighted demerit.

At present, all demerits have a weight of one (except for one class that has zero weight), and every sentence in our original corpus parses with a demerit score of zero. When new sentences are added to implement new robot algorithms, sometimes there is no parse at all that has zero total demerits. In that case, a parse with the smallest weight of demerits is chosen. Definitions and examples of each class of a demerit are given later.

After eliminating all inferior parses for a given sentence, there is usually exactly one parse remaining, which is then flattened and prettyprinted to the output file. This flattening involves bringing obviously parallel structure to the same level of expression (parenthesis), such as all adjectives modifying a noun, all adverbs modifying a verb or other word, and subject-verb-object of a transitive sentence. These structures were not already flattened when they left the main parser because the grammar was written to minimize the number of rules by decomposing structure one step at a time instead of all at once. For example, we did not parse "now look two spots down" by a special rule that allowed exactly one adverb phrase preceding a verb and two adverb phrases following it ("two spots" is a single adverb phrase here, and "down" is the other adverb), and "look two spots down" by a completely different rule that allowed zero adverb phrases preceding and two adverb phrases following a verb, and "look down" by yet a third unrelated rule. Instead we built all parses of this type by two rules, one that allowed a single adverb phrase preceding a verb and gave back a verb, and one that allowed a single adverb phrase following a verb and gave back a verb. These two rules suffice for an arbitrary number of adverb phrases preceding or following a verb, but instead of getting a flattened parse like "(V+Advs look now (two spots) down)" we get a tree-like structure such as "(VP+Adv (VP+Adv (VP+Adv look now) (two spots)) down)". If the main parser had a way to make dotted pairs—technically the basic elements in a list in LISP—which could be strung together to make a list of variable length, it would not be necessary for the main parser to produce such inscrutable output. But dotted pairs are not supported in the main parser. The only way to get rid of the mess of nested 3-element lists and produce a single list of variable length is by some additional processing after the main parser. The postparser does this.

Here is an example of a parse before and after flattening by the postparser. We have manually reformatted (prettyprinted) the S-expressions for maximum legibility. (A fully-parenthesized LISP expression is called an S-expression.)

Original English text: Continue looking at the next spot down adding and remembering until a bar appears.

Output of the correct parse from the parser (ignoring about fifteen other parses that also appear before demeriting). Note that "A, B and C" parses as "(SEQUENCE A (and B C))" instead of the more reasonable but not possible in the main parser "(SEQUENCE A B C)":

> (IMPERATIVE (CONTINUE-UNTIL
> (SEQUENCE(IMPERATIVE
> (VPR + Adv (VPR+ Loc looking
> (PrepPh at (NP+ Adjs spot the next))) down))
> (and (IMPERATIVE (Shortform adding))
> (IMPERATIVE (Shortform remembering))))
> (Subj + Verb (NP+ Adjs bar a) appears))).

Correct parse after flattening, which includes changing the idiom "A B and C" to have the desired parse, and bringing sub-expressions up to the same level as single-argument parent expressions, as well as flattening multiple adverbs:

> (IMPERATIVE CONTINUE-UNTIL
> (SEQUENCE (IMPERATIVE VP+ Advs looking
> (PrepPh at (NP+ Adjs spot the next)) down)
> (IMPERATIVE Shortform adding)
> (IMPERATIVE Shortform remembering))

(Subj + Verb (NP+ Adjs bar a) appears)).

Here are the two classes of demerits most frequently used by the post-parser, with an example of each. The number after each class name is the count of times this demerit is applied in our whole corpus of training steps. These are in descending order, so the most important (troublesome) cases are first.

MIXED-MODE (292)
(IMPERATIVE CONTINUE-UNTIL
(SEQUENCE (IMPERATIVE VP+ Advs looking down)
(or (IMPERATIVE VP + Advs looking (PrepPh for (NP+ Adjs
number a)))
(DECLARE Subj + Verb
(NP+Adjs bar a)
(and (Shortform adding)
(Shortform remembering)))))
(Subject+Verb you (TV+ NP see (NP+Adjs bar a))))).

In the above example, an "or" joins an imperative and a declarative. This is clearly wrong because conjunctions are supposed to join phrases that are parallel in structure, such as two imperatives, or two declaratives. There are other obvious errors in the above parse, such as a declarative sentence (inside the "or" part) whose verb consists of present participles instead of present-tense forms, and the use of "or" instead of "and" to terminate a sequence, but our postparser does not presently detect these errors.

CONTINUE-IN-DOUNTIL (77)
(DO-UNTIL
(TV+ S continue
(SEQUENCE
(IMPERATIVE VP+ Advs looking (PrepPh at (NP+ Adjs spot the
next)) down)
(IMPERATIVE Shortform adding)
(IMPERATIVE Shortform remembering)))
(DECLARE Subj + Verb (NP+ Adjs bar a) appears)).

The problem here is that the grammar is redundant. Any sentence that parses as (DO-UNTIL (TV+ S continue...)...) will also parse another better way in which "continue" and "until" are treated as a single idiom. The robot is set up to understand this idiom rather than to attempt to handle "continue" inside an "until" structure. The grammar-production for "until" by itself is set up to handle sentences that do not contain the word "continue" such as "Look down until you see a number", but a context-free grammar can not easily exclude the use of one production inside another.

For practical work it is almost certain that certain exception lists will need to be added, because it is not possible to make a "perfect" postparser that eliminates 100% of the bad parses for correct reasons. We have done just that, creating a file of bad parses that our program cannot presently eliminate by any normal means. In some cases the bad parse is obviously wrong, sometimes in rather subtle ways, but there is no simple mechanical rule for eliminating them. In a few other cases there is a simple rule but modifying the daisy-chained postparser code to try to include these cases was deemed too difficult to be worthwhile doing at this time, considering that we plan to rewrite the postparser to be table-driven anyway. These latter will be included in a proper way when the postparser is rewritten to be table-driven. Both these non-rule cases and these rule-but-not-programmed cases are included in an explicit exception list. When the parsed English exactly matches any of these exception-list parses, it is assigned the demerit KNOWN-REJECT-PAR. We present here one example for illustration.

English: "Write out the answer in the next spot open."

The bad parse is:

(IMPERATIVE TV + NP
(TV-IDIOM write out)
(NP+Adjs answer the
(PrepPh in (NP+ Adjs spot the next open)))).

This parse implies that something is to be written out, but without a location where to write it, and that the existing thing is the answer in the next open spot, i.e. the answer is already in the next spot open before writing it out to location unknown. The correct parse for this sentence is:

(IMPERATIVE VP + Advs
(TV+ NP (TV-IDIOM write out) (NP+Adjs answer the))
(PrepPh in (NP+ Adjs spot the next open))).

This good parse provides a place for the answer to be written, and the object to be written out is merely the answer, which does not have to be already in the next spot open.

SEMANTICS AND TRANSLATION

To get to semantics we translate from parsed English to operator language. The semantics is then easily specified in terms of the standard syntax of LISP—we used Utah Standard LISP (Hearn, 1969; Frick, 1978). We first say something about semantics and then turn to translation.

Semantics of atoms. In our applied version of LISP, three kinds of primitive atoms occur. First, there are operators. Examples would be LOOK-AT and ADD. Second, there are *actors.* In this case, an example is DEFAULT-NUMBER. Third, there are *data.* An example would be BOTTOM. Use is made of the standard atom NIL but this never appears in any printout and is in one sense not a proper part of our operator language.

The semantics of operators follows one of three patterns. One pattern is a standard recursive evaluation of EXPRs in LISP, whereby each of the arguments to a function is recursively evaluated before calling the function, for example, the standard LISP function LESSP for numerical *less than.* The second is treating the arguments of the operator as data and passing them to special coercion routines before performing the main operation. An example is the operator SUBTRACT in our robot operator language, which must have its arguments coerced to numbers by calling COERCE-TO-NUMBER on each. Another example is the operator LOOK-DIRDIS which passes its first argument to COERCE-DIRECTION-TO-DEL-COLROW and its second argument to COERCE-DISTANCE-TO-NUMBER. The third pattern is a case analysis on the operator's arguments and in this instance nothing else is called to analyze the semantics. For example, the operator LOOK-AT checks the form of argument beforehand and then passes on a sub-expression to another function.

The semantics of actors mainly consists of search and return of a datum. For example, the actor DEFAULT-SUM searches the memory stack as a database and returns the datum found as is.

Model theory. From a model-theoretic standpoint the semantics is based upon the grid world of our arithmetic examples, which contains a perceptual component based upon a small fragment of mental functions as, for example, the operator *remember* and a very elementary fragment of arithmetic used in teaching the algorithms of addition and subtraction, for example, add 2 to 7. In addition, there is a recursive evaluation similar to that of arithmetic of Boolean expressions which constitutes the logical component of the model. Finally, there is a control aspect. Do something whether a given expression is true or false. The truth or falsity of the expression changes the execution behaviour.

In this discussion we have distinguished perceptual, mental, arithmetical, and logical terms, but in the semantics of the operator language no explicit distinction occurs.

Translation. The translation table consists of a set of token names, and for each token name a sequential list of rules. Each rule consists of a template (also called the "syntax") and a result (also called the "semantics"). One of the token names is TOP which corresponds to the top-level parsed sentence that comes out of the parser. Other token names correspond to sub-expressions, a matter discussed below.

The list of rules associated with TOP is applied at the top level of the parsed sentence that is fed into the translator. Sometimes the TOP rules may also be used for some sub-expression that is really a sub-sentence embedded in the overall sentence, for example, if the top-level sentence is a conditional (if...then...) or a loop (do...until...). Other token names correspond to sub-expressions that need different rules, for example, prepositional phrases and nouns.

To translate a sentence, the overall expression is matched against the list of rules associated with TOP, except only the templates are used, not the semantics. The templates of the rules are searched sequentially until one is found that matches. Typically some idiomatic form of English sentence structure is matched *en masse*, sort of a gestalt recognizer for idioms. The first template that matches determines the rule to be used. All later rules in the list, even if their templates also match, are ignored.

Each template has constant-atomic parts, constant-structure parts, and variable parts. The constant parts are the places where an exact match must occur to accept the template match. In the case of an atom, exactly that atom must appear. In the case of a dotted pair (the basic unit for building lists), a dotted pair must appear, and then the two branches of the template are matched against the corresponding branches of the actual expression. All constant parts must match exactly for the template to be accepted. That is, if at any point in the matching process a constant-atom in the template corresponds to a dotted pair or to the wrong atom in the expression, or if a dotted pair in the template corresponds to an atom in the expression, the match of the expression against that template is immediately deemed a failure, and the matching attempt moves on to the template of the next rule in the list. The only place where the corresponding sub-expressions in the template and the expression may differ is where a variable occurs in the template. Here anything may appear in the expression, atomic or dotted-pair.

Note that backtracking is implicit in the template-matching process. However, once a template has been selected, no further backtracking at that level occurs.

Once the correct template is selected, the variable parts are used. Each variable part of the template has a different name that corresponds to one of the token names in the overall translation table. The same name also performs as a pseudo-variable, which is now bound to the sub-expression at the corresponding place in the overall expression of parsed-English. (In LISP this is called "destructuring", as in the DESETQ and LET macros.) Here is an example:

Parsed English: (IMPERATIVE VP+ Advs look (PrepPh at (NP+ Adjs number the top)))
Template: (IMPERATIVE VP+ Advs look (PrepPh at [NOUN]))
Successful match—resultant binding: [NOUN] = (NP+ Adjs number the top)

The constant parts of the template are "IMPERATIVE", "VP+ Advs" *et al.,* in addition to the dotted pairs that are used in the internal representation. The one variable part is [NOUN]. The template matches the parsed English because "IMPERATIVE" *et al.* all match the corresponding places in the parsed English. The spot marked by [NOUN] is ignored during matching. Then, after getting the successful match, the pseudo-variable "[NOUN]" corresponds to the parsed-English subexpression "(NP+ Adjs number the top)", so that binding is made.

After the top level of template-matching and pseudo-variable-binding is done, the translator is called recursively on each of the bindings. Instead of "TOP", the name of the variable is used, for example, "NOUN" in the above example. The same process is repeated as many levels deep as there are further pseudo-variable bindings. The results (described below) are passed up, and the pseudo-variable is rebound to the final result from translating "(NP + Adjs number the top)" according to the rules associated with "NOUN". In this example, the result will be:

New binding: [NOUN] = (INTERSECT-CUES (OBJECT NUMBER) (LOCATION TOP))

Now the original rule is consulted again, except instead of the template, the result (semantics) part is used. With the above example, in our current translation grammar, the semantics happens to be:

Semantics = (LOOK-AT [NOUN])

The "new binding" of [NOUN] given just above is now substituted into the semantics, replacing the occurrence of [NOUN] given in the semantics. The result is:

(LOOK-AT (INTERSECT-CUES (OBJECT NUMBER) (LOCATION TOP)))

When a template has no pseudo-variable spots, then no binding occurs, no recursive call to the translator occurs, and no substitution in the semantics occurs. Instead, the semantics is returned as is, as the result of the parse. This is how the recursion "bottoms out", avoiding infinite recursion depth. In the above example, the [NOUN] happened to invoke such a variable-less rule, thus the recursion depth was two, one level for the TOP-level matching, and one level for the NOUN-level matching.

When a template has more than one pseudo-variable spot, each of them is in turn recursively translated, each with the set of rules associated with the name of the pseudo-variable. When all are done, each of the results is substituted for the correspondingly-named pseudo-variable in the semantics, and that result is returned.

It is possible to enable a trace feature whereby all of this recursive translation is printed on the terminal, with each level of recursion causing a level of indentation. (To make the trace easier to read, the details of each recursion are indented a half-level. Currently a level of indentation is four spaces and a half-level is two spaces.) First, the token name (TOP at the outermost level of recursion) and the expression are printed. Then the matching syntax is found and printed. Then variables are bound and the binding list is printed as an ASSOC list, i.e., each element is one binding, with the CDR of that element being the variable name and the CDR being the sub-expression to which it is bound. Then the recursion occurs on each binding, shown at deeper level(s) of indentation. Then the new bindings which came back from the recursion are printed as "Results" in the same way the initial bindings are printed as "bindings". Then the result (semantics) part of the rule is shown, and finally the result of substituting the "Results" into the "Semantics" is shown preceded by "= =". Figure 2 shows one of these traces, for the simple example shown above.

```
TOP = (IMPERATIVE VP+Advs look (PrepPh at (NP+Adjs number
    the top)))
Syntax = (IMPERATIVE VP+Advs look (PrepPh at [NOUN]))
Bindings = ((NOUN NP+Adjs number the top))
NOUN = (NP+Adjs number the top)
Syntax = (NP+Adjs number the top)
Semantics = (INTERSECT-CUES (OBJECT NUMBER) (LOCATION TOP))
== (INTERSECT-CUES (OBJECT NUMBER) (LOCATION TOP))
Results = ((NOUN INTERSECT-CUES (OBJECT NUMBER) (LOCATION
    TOP)))
Semantics = (LOOK-AT [NOUN])
== (LOOK-AT (INTERSECT-CUES (OBJECT NUMBER) (LOCATION TOP)))
```

Figure 2. Simple example of translation.

Figure 3 shows a more complicated example where more than one pseudo-variable appears at one level of recursion. (Note that some lines are too long to be printed in one piece. They are broken at the right margin and continue on the next line, slightly indented.)

There is one special case in the semantics. If an exclamation mark appears where an atom (word) would ordinarily appear, the rest of that sub-expression is treated specially: call some function to perform additional processing before returning the translation. The next element in the list, at the same level as the exclamation mark, is the name of the function to be called. Ordinarily this is T2-REC which invokes yet another recursive call to the translator besides the normal recursive binding and substitution. The remaining elements are arguments to that function, which first get all variables substituted just like the ordinary semantics part of the rule. Thus, any such extra call occurs after the normal recursion which gives sub-results that are the new bindings for the variables, and just after the argument sub-expression result has been formed by substituting the sub-results for the variables in the argument sub-expression. But this extra call occurs before passing this sub-expression up to the next level of building the overall expression to return.

```
English.
Add this number to the number you remembered.
Parsed-English.
(IMPERATIVE VP+Advs   (TV+NP add (NP+Adjs number this))
(PrepPh to (N+rclause (NP+Adjs number the)
(that you remembered THAT&SLOT))))
Translator running with trace on:
TOP = (IMPERATIVE VP+Advs (TV+NP add (NP+Adjs number this))
  (PrepPh to (N+rclause (NP+Adjs number the) (that you
  remembered  THAT&SLOT))))
Syntax = (IMPERATIVE VP+Advs (TV+NP add [NOUN1]) (PrepPh to
  [NOUN2]))
Bindings = ((NOUN1 NP+Adjs number this)
  (NOUN2 N+rclause (NP+Adjs number the) (that you
  remembered  THAT&SLOT)))
NOUN1 = (NP+Adjs number this)
Syntax = [NOUN]
Bindings = ((NOUN NP+Adjs number this))
NOUN = (NP+Adjs number this)
  Syntax = (NP+Adjs number this)
  Semantics = DEFAULT-NUMBER
  == DEFAULT-NUMBER
```

```
Results = ((NOUN . DEFAULT-NUMBER))
 Semantics = [NOUN]
 ==  DEFAULT-NUMBER
 NOUN2 = (N+rclause (NP+Adjs number the) (that you
  remembered THAT&SLOT))
 Syntax = [NOUN]
 Bindings = ((NOUN N+rclause (NP+Adjs number the)
 (that you remembered THAT&SLOT)))
NOUN = (N+rclause (NP+Adjs number the) (that you
 remembered THAT&SLOT))
 Syntax = (N+rclause [NOUN] (that [MOVER] [VERB]
 THAT&SLOT))
 Bindings = ((NOUN NP+Adjs number the)
 (MOVER . you)    (VERB . remembered))
NOUN = (NP+Adjs number the)
 Syntax = (NP+Adjs number the)
 Semantics = DEFAULT-NUMBER
   == DEFAULT-NUMBER
MOVER = you
 Syntax = you
 Semantics = ROBOT
  == ROBOT
VERB = remembered
 Syntax = remembered
 Semantics = REMEMBER
  == REMEMBER
 Results = ((NOUN . DEFAULT-NUMBER)
    (MOVER . ROBOT) (VERB .  REMEMBER))
 [Semantics omitted because it uses a feature not
  yet explained.]
 ==(SOMETHING-ACTED-UPON ROBOT REMEMBER ANY-NUMBER)
 Results = ((NOUN SOMETHING-ACTED-UPON ROBOT
  REMEMBER ANY-NUMBER))
 Semantics = [NOUN]
  == (SOMETHING-ACTED-UPON ROBOT REMEMBER ANY-NUMBER)
 Results = ((NOUN1 . DEFAULT-NUMBER)
  (NOUN2 SOMETHING-ACTED-UPON ROBOT REMEMBER ANY-NUMBER))
 Semantics = (ADD [NOUN1] [NOUN2])
  == (ADD DEFAULT-NUMBER (SOMETHING-ACTED-UPON ROBOT
      REMEMBER ANY-NUMBER))
```

Figure 3. Complicated example of translation.

When T2-REC is the function being called, there are exactly two arguments, the first being the token name associated with the desired rules to use, and the second being the form to be retranslated in that way (according to those rules). In the above example, at the spot where we omitted the semantics because they used a mechanism that had not yet been explained, that is what happened. Here is that portion of the above trace now:

Results = ((NOUN. DEFAULT-NUMBER)
(MOVER. ROBOT)
(VERB.·REMEMBER))
Semantics = ((SOMETHING-ACTED-UPON [MOVER] [VERB]
(! T2-REC ANYIFY [NOUN]))
ANYIFY = DEFAULT-NUMBER
Syntax = DEFAULT-NUMBER
Semantics = ANY-NUMBER
==ANY-NUMBER
==SOMETHING-ACTED-UPON ROBOT REMEMBER
ANY-NUMBER)

As shown by the above trace, the results from recursion were:

NOUN=DEFAULT-NUMBER
MOVER=ROBOT
VERB=REMEMBER

The semantics called for building the trivial expressions ANYIFY which is a constant and [NOUN] which becomes DEFAULT-NUMBER, then passing these two arguments to T2-REC. The call then occurs, which has the effect of translating DEFAULT- NUMBER according to the ANY-IFY rules. The result is ANY-NUMBER. This expression is then passed up to the main expression being built. This is a list of four elements, the first being the constant SOMETHING-ACTED-UPON, the second and third values of MOVER (i.e. ROBOT) and VERB (i.e. REMEMBER), and the fourth this expression passed up (i.e. ANY-NUMBER).

Here is another example:

Semantics = ((! T2-REC NOUN-TO-PREDICATE [NOUN])
DEFAULT-OBJECT)

Suppose that "NOUN" was originally bound to some parsed-English sub-expression that returned "BAR". When running the semantics, first T2-REC is called with "NOUN-TO-PREDICATE" as first argument and "BAR" as second argument. The effect is as if the pseudo-variable "NOUN-TO-PREDICATE" existed and was bound to the sub-expression "BAR", except that here "BAR" comes not from the parsed-English but from the translation of something according to the "NOUN" rules. Anyway, the translator is called recursively, using the rules for "NOUN-TO-PREDI-CATE", with "BAR" as input, and suppose the result is "BARP". Now "BARP" is substituted into the expression in place of the (! T2-REC NOUN-TO-PREDICATE [NOUN])" and the result is:

Result: (BARP DEFAULT-OBJECT)

This result is then returned up to the next level.

INTERPRETATION AND EXECUTION

Because the operator language is standard LISP with the exception of the primitive atoms, interpretation has strict LISP sense in our system. The CAR of an expression says what to do. On the other hand, evaluation is not standard LISP. In LISP terminology everything we do is assumed to be an FEXPR (an F expression). Evaluation does not take place without looking at the CAR of an expression. The CAR of an expression is ordinarily a function, and this function decides when and how to interpret the arguments and thus when and how to do evaluation. For example, in standard LISP consider the expression

(PLUS X 3).

The standard LISP method is to recursively evaluate the arguments first. For example, suppose the variable "X" had been assigned earlier the value 8. Then the function would be evaluated to give the sum 11. In contrast, when PLUS is treated as an FEXPR the trace of a computation would look the same but the function PLUS would be called first.

It is also true that, in general, execution is that of standard LISP but this does not mean too much because each primitive FEXPR has its own execution. Of course, this is irrelevant for actors and operators which have no arguments. It is also true that statistically most operators with arguments act like EXPRs which have the standard LISP recursive evaluation of arguments.

Coercing data. Sometimes the argument given to a function does not meet the needs of that function. For example, an arithmetic function, needing numbers as arguments, might be given characters or variables as arguments. In a strongly-typed language such as PASCAL it is hard to get around this problem, but in an object-oriented language such as LISP where every object carries its type around with it at runtime and where functions exist for checking the type of an object at runtime, it is not too hard to coerce data of the wrong type into data of the right type at runtime.

When the robot is requested to do an arithmetic function such as addition, COERCE-TO-NUMBER is called on its arguments to convert them to numbers if they are not already. COERCE-TO-NUMBER calls the function MAY-COERCE-NUMBER to do most of its work. MAY-COERCE-NUMBER either converts the object to a number or returns a failure indication. If it fails, COERCE-TO-NUMBER then generates an error message, sets a flag indicating a number was needed (to be used by an error-recovery procedure not yet written), and aborts the current step.

If the object is already a number, then of course it is kept as is and the coercion succeeds. The most common case where the object needs coercion to a number is when it is a character of text from the input data matrix. For example, the character-object !5 must be converted into the number 5. The only other case currently handled is when the text of the command contains a number-word such as "two" or "ten". This is converted into the appropriate LISP numerical representation.

The opposite sort of coercion happens when the command is to output something, for example, writing a character in the arithmetic-example matrix. In this case only characters can be written, so whatever the argument is must be converted to a character. The way it does this is to do an EXPLODEC and check to see if the length is 1. If not, that object needs more than one character to print, and cannot be coerced into a single character. If the length is indeed 1, then that single element, the single character in the print-name, is returned as the result of COERCE-TO-CHARACTER. If the datum was already a character, taking the only element of the EXPLODEC gets back to that character again.

When we want to move the point of attention somewhere, via the LOOK command, or when we want to perform an input or output at some location relative to our current location, various words having to do with direction must at some point be converted into actual coordinates. That is the job of COERCE-LOCAT-TO-COORDS. First it converts keywords into coordinate offsets. According to the semantics of our operator language, HERE is (0 0), LEFTWARD is (1 0), DOWNWARD is (0 1), UPWARD is (0 − 1), etc. Then it adds these offsets to the current coordinates to get the new coordinates. These are later used as the actual arguments to the operator function such as LOOK.

Locating references to past steps. A major facility of our English-understanding robotics approach is the ability to create program loops without the artificial methods of standard programming languages. For example, BASIC has every line numbered for editing, and GOTOs can specify one of these line numbers. FORTRAN has lines numbered only when they will be referenced, and they do not have to be in numerical order. ALGOL and LISP have alphanumerical labels, again only when needed. But all of these methods are artificial compared to the way students in school are taught algorithms for arithmetic. Even explicit loop primitives used in structured languages such as PASCAL are unnatural. Imagine the very first time you are guided through column addition you are told "O.K., now here's a loop that will be executed over and over until an exit condition is satisfied, and here are the steps in the loop..." before any of the individual steps has been performed even once.

We adopted the following approach, which is the closest we have come to the natural method. First we take the "student" through the individual steps in the loop one at a time, with no reference to any of the steps being "in a loop" and no mention of specially marking any of the steps with a "label". We require only that the student keep a list of the steps in sequence, possibly translated from the description we give to his own internal notation. Then at the point when we have guided the student through all the steps of the loop once and we are ready to collect them into a "loop", we refer to the first step in the loop, not by numerical order but by context. We can either tell the student all in one command where the loop starts and ends (it always ends with the most recent step before the loop-making command) and what the exit condition is, or we can separate the label-making (context-matching) part from the loop-making part, as we found necessary due to deficiencies in the parser. But in both cases we need a way to specify some past step based on context (syntactic) information. This is the job of NEWMAT, the new pattern-matcher for past steps. (Previous versions did not work in difficult cases, so the routine had to be completely rewritten using a different approach.)

Before discussing the internal workings of NEWMAT, let us discuss its external interface and how it is used. NEWMAT take as argument a list of cues into past steps. These may be complete repeats of the steps, paraphrases, or very truncated skeletons of them. For example, if the original step was "look down at the next number" the cue given to NEWMAT may be "look down at the next number" or "looking down at the next number" or "looking for the next number" or "looking down", etc. In all cases NEWMAT will find (or at least is supposed to find) the correct step being referred to. Given a list of cues into past steps, it returns a list of numbers of those steps as currently listed in the memory of the robot-student's memory. Note that because earlier some steps may have been collapsed into single steps, these numbers do not necessarily correspond to the sequence of commands originally given to the robot, and later, if further collapsing is done, these numbers will become invalid. They must be used very soon, typically in the current command or the next, to be valid.

When everything is combined in a single command, it is in the form "Continue...until..." which invokes the function O-CONTINUE-UNTIL. NEWMAT is called, and the numbers that come back from it are immediately used to fetch the corresponding steps from the memory. These steps are formed into a loop which is executed in single-step mode with exit check at the start and end and between steps as described below. Upon completion of the loop, any just-preceding steps which match final steps in the loop (after the exit condition) are rolled into the loop, causing those steps to disappear from the top level of memory and to appear at the start instead of end of the loop.

When the reference and the loop are separated, the reference is invoked by "Refer back to when you..." while the loop itself is invoked by "Continue doing everything from that step up to the most recent step, until...". The "Refer back..." calls NEWMAT which returns a list of step numbers as above. But here all the numbers except the oldest are thrown away, and the oldest is set as the value of a global variable, which represents the label that would be present in an ALGOL program. The "Refer back..." step is not saved in memory for later reference because it is not something that might later be repeated. This is the one exception (currently) to the rule that the student (robot) remembers all past steps executed. Then the "Continue doing everything..." resolves the argument "that step" by fetching that saved number (the index, i.e. the label, of the referred-to step), and resolves the argument "the most recent step" by fetching the number of the most recent step. It then creates a list of all numbers between those two bounds, i.e. a list of indexes of all steps to be included in the loop. Finally it does the same thing as O-CONTINUE-UNTIL, fetching all steps whose indexes are in the list, making a loop, stepping thru it, and rolling preceding steps into it where possible.

Thus NEWMAT converts cues into the indices of the actual steps to be brought into the loop, and those indices are used to fetch the past steps to make the loop. Either just the steps mentioned or all steps, from the oldest mentioned to the most recent executed, are included, depending on whether the "continue... until..." or the separate "refer back..." and "continue doing everything..." syntax was used.

Now we will describe the internal workings of the current versions of NEWMAT. It is given two items of information, its argument consisting of cues to past steps, and the global variable listing past steps in reverse chronological order. The first thing it does logically is to convert each list into a list of lists of keywords. That is, each cue and each past step is converted into a list of keywords, so that each list of cues or list of steps is converted into a list of lists of keywords. In the case of the list of cues this is done *en masse*, via MAPCAR, but in the case of the past steps this is done in a lazy way, using a "lazy evaluator" to do only as much of MAPCAR as is needed in actual processing. We shall not go into the details of the lazy MAPCAR, except to say that it creates a partial list of results with a blip at the end indicating the rest has not yet been computed and pointing at the place in the original list where not-yet-processed data reside. When CDR is attempted at the point where the blip stands, one more element is fetched from the original list, processed into keywords, and patched into the result list, then the blip is advanced past that new processed data and the pointer to the original data is advanced past the data which have now been processed. The reason for this lazy MAPCAR instead of simply calling MAPCAR to convert all past steps *en masse* is that often a loop refers only to two or three past steps, and if there are thirty steps in all it is a gross waste of computing to process all thirty steps if the pattern-matching algorithm is not even going to look at more than two or three steps.

After the list of past steps (via lazy MAPCAR) and the list of cues (via normal MAPCAR) have been converted to lists of keywords, the cues are reversed so they are in reverse chronological order (like the past steps). Then these lists of lists of keywords are collated to find the most recent place in reverse past steps where something like the cues occurs. The first (latest) cue is matched against the first (latest) past step. If the match succeeds, then the next (earlier) cue is matched against both the same and the next (earlier) past step. If either succeeds, recursion continues until a mismatch occurs or the list of cues is exhausted. If failure occurs at any level, a re-try of any alternative pending at a higher level is tried. If a failure at the top level occurs (either directly or by all lower-level alternatives failing somehow), the pointer into the past steps is advanced and the whole process is retried. The effect of all this is that if a success occurs, it corresponds to the MOST RECENT sequence that matches, and because it immediately returns at the top level, all older sequences that might also match are suppressed. Thus NEWMAT finds the most recent CONTIGUOUS sequence of past steps that matches the cues given.

For example, suppose after conversion to keyword-lists, the past steps (in reverse chronological order) are:

    –1 (SPACE WRITE ZERO)
    –2 (LOOK LEFT)
    –3 (LOOK DOWN)
    –4 (WRITE NUMBER)
    –5 (LOOK RIGHT)
    –6 (LOOK RIGHT)

    −7 (REMEMBER NUMBER)
    −8 (SPACE WRITE ZERO)
    −9 (LOOK LEFT)
    −10 (WRITE NUMBER)
    −11 (LOOKRIGHT)
    ... (steps farther back irrelevant here)

Suppose the English command that specified a reference point in these past steps was something like "Refer back to when you looked to the right, wrote out a number, looked to the left, looked for a space, and wrote a zero", which converted to keywords and reversed becomes:

((WRITE ZERO) (LOOK SPACE) (LOOK LEFT) (WRITE NUMBER (LOOKRIGHT))

The most recent place where (WRITE ZERO) matches is at −1. NEW-MAT tries to find (LOOK SPACE) at the same or preceding step, i.e. at −1 or −2, and finds it at −1 only (it is not an exact match, but let us assume it is above the threshold). It then tries to find (LOOK LEFT) at −1 or −2, and finds it only at −2. It then tries to find (WRITE NUMBER) at −2 or −3, but can not find it at either, causing this whole attempt to fail. The next most recent place where (WRITE ZERO) matches is at −4 (again an inexact match). But (LOOK SPACE) does not match at −4 or −5 so this aborts quickly. Next farther back (WRITE ZERO) matches at −8, (LOOK SPACE) matches at −8 or −9. In the former case, (LOOK LEFT) matches at −9, (WRITE NUMBER) at −10, and (LOOK RIGHT) at −11, completing the desired match. Possible matches starting with (LOOK SPACE) at −9 are never tried now. The result returned is the list of indices (−8 −8 −9 −10 −11), of which only the −11 is used in the case of "Refer back to..." as here.

Only one detail of NEWMAT remains to be defined: in the above recursive algorithm, when considering whether the keyword list from a particular cue matches the keyword list from a particular past step, what is the criterion for a successful match? First of all, keywords are coerced into a standard form of paraphrasing. Thus "looking", "looked", and "look" all come out the same. This makes it possible to find a match when the original step was "Look at the next spot down", while the cue came from "Refer back to when you looked at the next spot down" or "Continue looking down, adding and remembering". All versions of the pattern matcher do this coercion the same. The original pattern matcher scored a success whenever any keyword in the cue, after this coercion, matched any keyword in the step, after the same coercion. This worked fine for the main loop of addition and also for the little loops in both addition and subtraction, but was too lenient (willing to find a match) for the main loop of subtraction, finding a false match consisting of only the most recent six steps when actually the past 30 steps were supposed to be included. We fixed it by requiring a particular percentage of keywords in the cue to match any keywords in the past step. Note that we could not do the converse, requiring a particular percentage of keywords in the past step to match keywords anywhere in the cue, because of the possibility that the past step is a loop composed of several small steps and that the cue is referring to one of those small steps. We needed a successful match even in cases when one of the steps referred to in the cue was merely one very small part of the large loop that was a past step.

We tried various thresholds, various required percentages of keywords to match, to see which values of the threshold got a false match that masked the deeper correct match, which values skipped over the false matches to reach the correct match, and which values skipped past even the correct match to find no match at all. We found that the false match for subtraction matched half the keywords, thus we needed a threshold greater than 0.5 to get past it. The correct match matched all the keywords; thus, any threshold greater than 0.5 and less than 1.0 would be satisfactory. But then we went back and checked the threshold for the other loops, and found that the correct match for a small loop found only half the keywords in one of the cues, thus requiring a threshold less than 0.5. This put us in a dilemma. The threshold had to be less than 0.5 for one match to work and greater than 0.5 for another match to work. In both cases the English was quite reasonable, so we decided not to force the English to be modified to make the pattern matching come out consistently. Our only easy alternative was to "tune" the program, having a different threshold in the two cases. This can be a dangerous thing to do, because the program is so carefully tuned on the test data it has been developed with that it cannot handle other test data that are identical as far as human judgment is concerned but for which the tuning is not right. We have tried as much as possible to make our mechanisms general, to match parts of sentences in reasonable ways rather than simply to hardwire our program to understand exactly the complete sentences we used as our training data.

Our solution was interaction with the user. The program has a default threshold that works in most cases, although not, for example, in the main loop of the subtraction algorithm. It uses that threshold to find the match, and tells the user both the complete step that it found and the number of steps from that step to the most recent step. This gives the user enough information to decide whether that is the right step or not. If not, the user must supply a new threshold to try. Again the program gives feedback and the user considers the result. When the threshold results in finding the correct step and the user confirms it, the program proceeds with the rest of the processing as before. This method is not totally satisfactory since it requires the user to understand the concept of threshold, an internal aspect of the robot's program, in addition to understanding the problem domain. Perhaps we should change this so the user merely says whether the step found is correct, too far back or too recent. The robot would then use that information to pick a new threshold silently instead of asking the user (teacher) to give it a new threshold.

Finally, we describe the workings of the single-step mode for loops mentioned above. Initially, the exit condition is tentatively located at all possible points in the program, at the start and end and also between each two adjacent steps. Then when executing the loop, if one of these copies of the exit condition is satisfied, the user is asked if it is the correct one. If it is not, that copy is deleted so that the user will not be bothered with the exact same query during a later pass through the loop. If it is the correct one, all others are deleted, leaving just that one exit condition at the correct location in the loop. If there is only one remaining copy of the exit condition when the user answers "no" to the query, the remaining loop contains no exit condition at all and thus can never terminate. The single-step mode detects this error and aborts immediately, flagging the whole loop as invalid. When copies of the exit condition are not satisfied, however, they are left as is, since they may be satisfied during later passes through the loop.

LEARNING AND INSTRUCTION

A notable feature of current work in computer science and artificial intelligence is the relative neglect of a sustained effort to develop concepts and techniques of learning, an exception being Michalski, Carbonell & Mitchell (1983). A liberal definition of "learning" includes any change in behaviour. Under this definition a computer "learns" when it is given a new program to execute. In fact our work instructing a robot is very similar to programming in that we give the robot a sequence of commands which the robot compiles into a more machine-oriented language and then executes or stores for future execution. Our use of a reduced set of English is not even unique. Recall that COBOL was designed to be like English, and several companies now advertise programming languages that are claimed to be fragments of English. But there are important differences between our efforts to create an "English language programming language" and these others. Whereas prior attempts have tried to make the English precise in the same way that programming languages make their source language precise, we allow ambiguities to exist in our English source language. During debugging, rather than requiring the user to go back and modify the English source to resolve ambiguities, we resolve ambiguities during a test run. Most of the resolution is obtained not by direct interactions with the user but by interactions with the test data. Thus if the program has more than one interpretation, but only one interpretation makes sense in conjunction with the test data, the robot can resolve the ambiguity without needing any help from the user-instructor. Even where not all but one interpretation can be eliminated, the number of possible interpretations can be greatly reduced, giving the user a small list of interpretations to choose from. Furthermore, the possible interpretations are presented to the user as practical questions such as "is this the right time and place to exit the loop" in the course of working through the test data, instead of as *in vacuo* questions about the structure of the program. (An example is discussed later.)   Thus the user is relieved of the burden of mentally simulating the program to figure out where the exit condition needs to be, the robot does the test run for him and asks for help at exactly the point in the test run when it is easy for the user to see what needs doing and answer the query correctly. Also the robot is relieved of the burden of anticipating all possible problems before starting execution. Instead the robot can plod ahead as if the program were unambiguous, and ask for help only when it is already bumping into possible trouble.   We believe this is analogous to a teacher giving instruction to young children, where a child is incapable of anticipating all the trouble he will have in learning a new algorithm, and the teacher is incapable of knowing ahead of time all the possible ambiguities in the student's mind and giving unambiguous instruction from the start. Ambiguity of instruction is perhaps the most important feature differentiating teaching children from programming computers. The child resolves residual ambiguity by asking questions, and so should the robot.

It is not our objective in this article to give an overall view of types of learning or a classification of possible tasks. Without attempting to give a less liberal definition of learning than the one mentioned above, we restrict ourselves to the learning that is closely associated with instruction. We have in mind tasks of the kind that correspond to much instruction that is given in school, especially to young children; for example, algorithms of elementary arithmetic and approaches to beginning reading. Many other perceptual and motor-skill tasks fall under this category of being explicitly instructable. We emphasize, of course, that much learning does not fall under this concept of instruction. It does represent, in our judgment, an area of great importance and we are concerned here only with it. The central feature of such learning from instruction is, we believe, the synthesis of complex procedures from simpler ones in accordance with the instructions given, in English or some other natural language.

We now give a couple of concrete examples of new procedures that we synthesized from primitive procedures available. (We emphasize that a limitation of the present system is that new procedures must be built up directly from primitive procedures rather than calling other complex procedures that have been previously built up. The main reason is that we do not yet have a mechanism for the procedures we build to take arguments. They are effectively inline-code macros rather than parameterized subroutines.) From a formal standpoint these examples are trivial. They are meant to illustrate three things: the use of English for formulating the new procedures, the problems we encountered, and a comparison of the English formulation of the new procedure to the LISP S-expression generated as the final product of the compilation of the English. Note the compilation involves three parts, (1) the translation of the English into operator language which initially contains some ambiguities, (2) the interaction of that translation with the problem domain, which resolves some of the ambiguities, and (3) interaction with the user (playing the rôle of the teacher) which resolves the remaining ambiguities. This is different from traditional programming of computers where the source language must have no ambiguities.

The first example takes any addition problem in standard column format and simply places in the answer the first row of digits—for simplicity we assume that the first row has as many digits as any other row in the exercise. The English that successfully constructed the algorithm was the following:

> Look at the top number.
> Remember this number.
> Look one space down until you see a bar.
> Look one space down.
> Write the number you remembered.
> Look at the top of the next column to the left.
> Refer back to when you remembered the number and looked down.
> Continue doing everything from that step up thru the most recent step, until you see a space.

The S-expression which is the final product of compilation is as follows:

```
((LOOK-AT (INTERSECT-CUES (OBJECT NUMBER) (LO-
    CATION TOP)))
```

```
(LOOP (REMEMBER DEFAULT-NUMBER)
(LOOP (LOOK-DIRDIS DOWNWARD (DISTANCE 1))
(IF (BARP DEFAULT-OBJECT) (DONE)))
(LOOK-DIRDIS DOWNWARD (DISTANCE 1))
(WRITE-OUT (SOMETHING-ACTED-UPON ROBOT RE-
    MEMBER
ANY-NUMBER))
(LOOK (INTERSECT-LOCATION-CUES TOP LEFTWARD))
(IF (SPACEP DEFAULT-OBJECT) (DONE)))))
```

It is easy to establish the correspondence between the lines of the S-expression and the English. The most important general feature is the use of the "continue" idiom to establish the loop.

The English is not as precise as the S-expression but it is more readable and much easier for the user to understand. The directions given to the robot here are more explicit than one would use with a child but not enormously so. It would be easy to devise an experiment to give something very similar to six- or seven-year-old children.

Because of the length of the record of the interaction by which we constructed this simple algorithm successfully, we have not presented it. However, there are one or two useful comments about the kinds of difficulties we encountered with the current version of our program in constructing the algorithm given above. First, we had some difficulty with the program's accepting the English we first used for the third line above. Our first try was "Look downward until we get a bar". Unfortunately the three words "downward", "we", and "get" were not in the grammar. The next attempt was "Look down one space until you see a bar". We got several parses of this instruction but no operator-language translation. The difficulty was that the grammar treated "down" occurring "before one space" as a preposition. In the parse of the sentence that was translated into the proper operator language and given above, "down" occurs after "one space" and is classified as an adverb.

Permuting columns. This example is more complicated but still quite simple. Given an addition exercise in standard format with two columns but with not all numbers required to be two-digit numbers, the algorithm permutes the columns. It is understood that a zero is first to be placed in the tens column of a one-digit number.

The 23 English commands that led to successful construction of this algorithm are the following:

Look at the top number.
Look one space to the left.

Look one space to the left.
Look one space to the right.
If you see a space write out a zero.
Look here again.
Remember this number.
Look one space to the left.
Write out the number you remembered.
Look one space to the right.
Look one space to the right.
Remember this number.
Look one space to the left.
Write out the number you remembered.
Look one space to the left.
Remember this number.
Write out a space.
Look one space to the right.
Look one space to the right.
Write out the number that you remembered.
Look one space down.
Look one space to the left.
Refer back to when you wrote a zero.
Continue doing everything from that step up thru the most
recent step, until you see a bar.

We feel that the readability of the procedure described in English is
very much better than that of the generated S-expression:

```
((LOOK-AT (INTERSECT-CUES (OBJECT NUMBER)
(LOCATION TOP)))
(LOOK-DIRDIS LEFTWARD (DISTANCE 1))
(LOOK-DIRDIS LEFTWARD (DISTANCE 1))
(LOOK-DIRDIS RIGHTWARD (DISTANCE 1))
(LOOP (IF (SPACEP DEFAULT-OBJECT)(WRITE-OUT 0))
(LOOK DEFAULT-LOCATION)(REMEMBER DEFAULT
-NUMBER)
(LOOK-DIRDIS LEFTWARD (DISTANCE 1))
(WRITE-OUT (SOMETHING-ACTED-UPON ROBOT
REMEMBER ANY-NUMBER))
(LOOK-DIRDIS RIGHTWARD (DISTANCE 1))
(LOOK-DIRDIS RIGHTWARD (DISTANCE 1))
(REMEMBER DEFAULT-NUMBER)
(LOOK-DIRDIS LEFTWARD (DISTANCE 1))
(WRITE-OUT (SOMETHING-ACTED-UPON ROBOT
```

```
REMEMBER ANY-NUMBER))
(LOOK-DIRDIS LEFTWARD (DISTANCE 1))
(REMEMBER DEFAULT-NUMBER)
(WRITE-OUT SPACE)(LOOK-DIRDIS RIGHTWARD (DIS-
    TANCE 1))
(LOOK-DIRDIS RIGHTWARD (DISTANCE 1))
(WRITE-OUT (SOMETHING-ACTED-UPON ROBOT
REMEMBER ANY-NUMBER))
(LOOK-DIRDIS DOWNWARD (DISTANCE 1))
(LOOK-DIRDIS LEFTWARD (DISTANCE 1))
(IF (BARP DEFAULT-OBJECT)(DONE))))
```

It is evident from this example that there are many obvious improvements to be made in our system to provide a flexible environment for interactive instruction. Some are at the level of language. For example, it is desirable to extend looking to any finite number of spaces, so that lines (2) and (3) could be replaced with the single command "Look two spaces to the left". A second feature concerns access to memory. Our "robot" can access only the top of the stack and the topmost stack item satisfying some property such as being a number or a sum or a difference, etc. Also the stack cannot be purged of items that are no longer needed. This was no problem in handling the algorithms of addition and subtraction, but is already a problem in the present example. There are various grammatical devices in ordinary English for making multiple references to memory–anaphoric reference being among the most prominent. We see no problem in principle of matching the internal workings of our robot program to these various devices, as long as the relevant grammatical theory has been developed.

We promised earlier to give an example of using test data to disambiguate loop control, and we now do so using the above program as an example. That program contains a major loop with 18 steps plus one exit test which happens at the end. But the English description of the algorithm does not tell that it is bottom-tested. Indeed top-tested loops are more commonly useful, and tests in the middle are useful too in some cases. In fact, there are 19 possible places to put the exit condition, and the English does not give any information as to which of them is correct. With full mathematical analysis it is possible to eliminate seven of them, leaving 12, but this is very difficult analysis which requires full knowledge of the semantics, in particular that having written a number at one spot and moving two units to the right and two to the left we are back at the same spot which is still a number and thus cannot be a bar now. Such mathematical analysis is pushing the state of the art of program verification. Also, mathematical analysis does not give us any idea which of the 12 is more likely to be the desired exit location. Our program, by comparison, requires no mathematical analysis, yet still reduces the search space to 12, and in this example gives the correct answer as the second choice. When processing these particular test data (or any similar example with bars only at the bottom), the first time a bar is seen is just after the next to last step, and the second time is after the final step of the same iteration. Therefore the user has very little trouble picking the correct location to insert the exit test in the final algorithm.

As we indicated already in the introduction it is not our present intention to extend our system so as to make it capable of general knowledge representation. But as in the case of interactive theorem provers, at this stage of development our aim is to handle efficiently and easily the rather specialized facts and procedures of a given restricted domain. Every major component of the system reported on in this article can obviously be improved, and we hope to do so in the future.

17

TYPES OF VERBAL
INTERACTION WITH
INSTRUCTABLE ROBOTS

An instructable robot is one that accepts instruction in some natural language such as English and uses that instruction to extend its basic repertoire of actions. Such robots are quite different in conception from autonomously intelligent robots, which provide the impetus for much of the research on inference and planning in artificial intelligence. This paper examines the significant problem areas we see in the design of robots that learn from verbal instruction. Examples are drawn primarily from our earlier work on instructable robots (Suppes & Crangle, 1988; Maas & Suppes, 1984, 1985) and recent work on a Robotic Aid for the physically disabled (Michalowski, Crangle, & Liang, 1987).

We start our enquiry in the first section with a discussion of natural-language understanding by machines. In the next section, we examine the possibilities and limits of verbal instruction. We also discuss the core problem of verbal instruction, namely, how to achieve specific concrete action in the robot in response to commands that express general intentions. The final section of the paper, examines two major challenges to

*Reprinted from G. Rodriguez (Ed.), *Proceedings of the Workshop on Space Teler-obotics*, Vol. II (JPL Publication 87-13, Vol. II). Pasadena, CA: NASA Jet Propulsion Laboratory, California Institute of Technology, July 1, 1987. Written jointly with C. Crangle and S. Michalowski.

instructability: achieving appropriate real-time behavior in the robot, and
extending the robot's language capabilities.

Our work on the interpretation of natural-language commands rests on
the assumption that many English commands can be precisely interpreted
only in the actual situation in which they are issued (Suppes & Crangle,
)1988). Some examples are straightforward, *Go to the chair*, for instance.
When there is more than one chair in the surroundings, which chair is
being referred to? If only one chair is within the robot's field of vision,
however, that chair may in many circumstances be taken as the correct
referent of *the chair*. Another straightforward example, this time at both
the syntactic and the lexical level, is the command *Move the cup to the
right of the spoon*. This command is ambiguous in that *to the right of
the spoon* may indicate which cup is to be moved or where some cup is
to be moved to. Furthermore, *right of* may be interpreted relative to
the speaker, the robot, or the spoon itself (taking it to face away from
its handle). The topic of the previous discourse can help disambiguate
the command, as can the actual arrangement of cups and spoons. If
earlier commands have clearly established the robot's point of view as
pre-eminent, that can suggest an interpretation for *right of*.

A third example, discussed in more detail, reveals the ways in which a
robot must exploit the context in which a command is given to interpret
that command. Of particular importance is the perceptual situation, by
which we mean those aspects of the physical environment accessible to
the robot through its sensory apparatus. Our example shows how the
perceptual situation contributes to the precise interpretation of the word
next.

The intuitive idea behind the semantics of *next* can best be understood
if we talk about *the next x*, where *x* may, for example, be *chair*, *table*, or
wooden chair. When we say *the next x*, we are referring to the first *x*, by
some ordering relation, relative to some present reference entity. Three
things have to be fixed by the context for the interpretation of this word:
the ordering relation, the class of *x*-type entities from which one will be
selected, and some encompassing class of entities which are ordered by
the relation. This encompassing class must be specified because it makes
perfect sense to talk about the next *x* even when the present reference
entity is not itself an *x*. A clear example is given by the robot emulator of
Maas and Suppes which accepts instruction in elementary mathematics
(1984, 1985). In the usual contexts of use for *next*, the robot has been, and

is expected to continue, scanning down a column. Thus for most uses of *next* in the arithmetic instruction context, the ordering relation required by *next* is given by the relation **vertically below**, a strict partial ordering on the perceptual objects (the digits and blank spaces of an arithmetic exercise) such that each perceptual object that has a successor has a unique immediate-successor by this relation and similarly for predecessor. Suppose the robot is focused on the blank space at the top of the tens column of an arithmetic exercise. That blank space plays the role of the reference entity for the interpretation of *next* in the phrase *the next number*. For that blank space to function as the reference entity for *next number*, both the digits (numbers) and the blank spaces must stand in the relation **vertically below**.

The perceptual situation will not always have to yield the semantically important information for *next*. These may be set explicitly by the verbal command. Consider, for instance, the command *Choose the next person in order of height* where the ordering relation is given by the phrase *in order of height*. In the absence of such explicit directions, however, the perceptual situation imposes its own choice of ordering relation. For instance, suppose the robot is in a room containing ten chairs arranged in a row. That very arrangement of objects will tend to establish an ordering relation for sentences in which the adjective *next* qualifies the noun *chair*. If the robot were positioned alongside the second chair, facing down the row towards the third chair, and if there had been no prior discourse, the command *Go to the next chair* would probably be interpreted as a command to move to the third chair. It is clear that the appropriate ordering relation must not only be available perceptually (or by some other means such as memory), it must also be established as a focus of attention. If the robot has no ability to adduce an ordering relation from the perceptual situation, the first time the adjective *next* is used to refer to objects of a certain type, the robot must query the user for help in fixing an ordering that is known to it, which should subsequently be used as the default unless explicit instruction changes it.

Sometimes two of the three contextual factors required by *next* are set explicitly by the command. Consider the room containing only the row of chairs again, with the agent at the second chair in the row. Suppose the agent were being instructed to clean the wooden chairs by applying a furniture polish, and the row included two cane chairs, one of which was in the third position and the other in the eighth. The command *Clean the next wooden chair* would then direct the agent to the fourth chair in the row, the first wooden chair relative to the present chair. In this case, the adjective *wooden* specifies the class of wooden objects, of which one must be selected, and the noun *chair* specifies the encompassing class of chairs, both wooden and cane.

There are many different ways a command may specify the contextual factors required by *next*. Consider the command *Go to the next chair to the left*. Here *to the left* specifies the ordering relation, a relation, call it **L**, which could be defined informally as follows: for all **a** and **b**, **aLb** if and only if **a** is positioned to the left of **b** and within the compass of an arc of 30 degrees radiating horizontally from **b**. Consider, however, the command *Go left to the next chair*. Here *left* does not make a contribution to the interpretation of *next*; it serves rather as an adverb directly qualifying the verb, acting as an extra constraint on where to go. There are many other examples like this. In the command *Search for the next file in alphabetic order*, the ordering relation behind the use of *next* is given explicitly by the phrase *in alphabetic order*. In the command *Search from A to Z for the next file*, on the other hand, that same ordering relation defines a direction in which to search, but leaves open the question of what ordering lies behind the use of *next*.

Contextual information is also required to fix the interpretation of intensive adjectives, such as *large*, and comparatives and superlatives, such as *larger* and *largest*. The adjective *large*, for instance, may be thought of as a procedure that uses an underlying ordering relation of size to determine if an object, the one said to be large, stands in the appropriate size relation to some criterion object. This criterion object is also given by the context. What counts as a large book in the context of a shelf of dictionaries is not the same as in the context of a shelf of poetry volumes. Perhaps the most striking example of the role of the criterion object is given by the phrases *large elephant* and *large ant*. While the ordering relations for *large elephant* and *large ant* will both use some measure such as mass or girth, the criterion objects will be quite different.

Our emphasis on the role of context leads inevitably to another emphasis, namely the essential role that interaction must play in the interpretation of natural-language commands—interaction between the robot and the user and between the robot and the perceptual situation. The next section examines verbal instruction in more detail, at the same time identifying its place within a spectrum of interactions between robots and humans.

A PLACE FOR VERBAL INSTRUCTION

Two types of verbal interaction with robots may be identified, one in which learning occurs as a result of the interaction and the other without learning. When there is no learning, the robot responds to each verbal command or enquiry as it is given, never using its experience to extend its basic repertoire of actions. In our work we refer to such a robot as a commandable robot. The mobile base of the Robotic Aid is commandable in that it obeys a range of motion commands expressed in English, commands such as *Whenever you are within three feet of the ramp, stop.* A commandable robot may be given detailed step-by-step instructions to open the door of a microwave oven, insert a plate of food, close the door, set the timer, and switch the oven on. Yet the next time the user wants the robot to prepare a meal, the same or a similar set of detailed instructions has to be issued. There are obvious advantages if the user could give that behavior a name, such as *Prepare the meal*, and use that name later to invoke the behavior. In this way, the robot would have learned from its verbal interaction with the user.

This prescription—issuing a sequence of commands, baptizing the sequence, and invoking it later by name—describes just one of many possible forms of instruction. There is also non-verbal instruction, as presently provided by the head-tracking mechanism of the Robotic Aid, for instance, which allows the user to describe a trajectory for the robot to follow. Verbal correctives, such as *Slow down!*, given while the robot is in motion are also important in communication. And non-verbal means of correction also have their place. Nonverbal methods are extensively used in the training of animals, by direct procedures of reward and punishment, and they have also been used in simple experiments with very elementary robots learning mazes. More sophisticated examples arise when the robot or system in question has a criterion for evaluating correctness of its responses, as for example in speech recognition systems where parameters must be adjusted to individual speakers. The operator does not know how to do this; the robot or system learns to adjust parameters by the correctness of its responses. It learns about the correctness of its responses by comparing its guess with the given correct answer. It does not learn how to make corrections by being given verbal instruction on the parameter adjustments that are needed. Clearly, verbal instruction is but one of several ways of producing corrective and adaptive behavior in robots.

Some important general points about verbal commands must be discussed before we examine instructability in any detail. Take the command *Pick up the cup and put it on the saucer.* This command expresses the result we would like to see. It says nothing about the process of achieving that result. Typically, ordinary language, like ordinary conscious thinking, is oriented toward results not processes. The detailed movements that are part of some action—either one we intend to take ourselves or one we want the robot to take—are not easily accessible to our conscious thinking and in fact for some actions quite beyond the descriptive powers of ordinary language. Two examples: we cannot verbally describe a specific trajectory to be followed in crossing a room nor can we describe the exact motion of the roll of a die from the instant of its being thrown until it comes to rest. Many actions we would want the robot to perform are for us a matter of automatic, that is, unreflective response—flicking a switch, picking up a cup, using a screwdriver—and are in fact actions that are seldom acquired by us through explicit verbal instruction. Other activities we would require of a robot are more amenable to verbal description— manipulating a toggle switch, navigating with reference to objects in the environment, for example. Many tasks are ideally suited to explicit verbal instruction. The elementary mathematics emulator mentioned earlier is especially designed for primarily verbal instruction, but other kinds of robots dealing with physical equipment also engage in tasks suited to explicit verbal instruction. A good example is the activity of assembling and disassembling a piece of equipment. Not every motion involved in the assembly or disassembly is described but what is described explicitly in words is the sequence in which disassembly and assembly should take place. Also well suited to verbal instruction is the transfer of information about objects. Here the user helps the robot learn to recognize objects by directing its sensors to specific parts of the object, naming those parts, and letting the robot use autonomous procedures to determine their shape and location. The user can also provide information that is not accessible to the robot's sensors, such as what the object is used for.

There is a further complexity to actions and their verbal descriptions that we must face. In requesting action, from a robot or a human, in terms of a result description such as *Bring me the book on the table*, we seldom have in mind a detailed algorithm for executing the command. The particular path taken by the agent satisfying the command is not part of the meaning of the expressed intention. On the other hand, if the agent knocks over a chair in fetching the book, in ordinary circumstances we regard the movement of the agent as satisfying only partially or rather poorly the request made. Similarly, if when asked to pick up a cup the agent spills its contents, we do not consider the request to have been fully satisfied. Expressed intentions carry with them a bundle of ceteris paribus conditions that impose a variety of constraints on the specific procedures actually executed. These ceteris paribus conditions are not given concretely or in advance but depend on the particular context in which an action is carried out.

The semantics of a command such as *Pick up the cup* thus apparently has conflicting demands to meet. In the first place, this intention, expressed in terms of a result, must for its satisfaction be interpreted to produce a specific action-process. That is, a specific procedure must be executed. (We do not of course necessarily mean a simple sequential procedure; a highly parallel complex collection of processes may be involved. The point is that out of the many distinct actions that could take place to pick up the cup, one specific one is taken in a given situation.) We cannot specify in advance a particular set of motions for the specific action-process. Such specifications are not part of the meaning of the command and they would too narrowly delimit the contexts in which the command could be given. At the same time, however, there are the many ceteris paribus conditions we expect to be met in the satisfaction of the command.

As with the interpretation of individual words, the key lies in the context. We want specific action to be produced in response to a command but we cannot explicitly build the details of that response into the semantics. These details are to be taken from the actual situation in which the command is given. In this way they will not have been inappropriately specified in advance and they will include those ceteris paribus conditions accessible from the context. Take the example of *Pick up the cup*. The particular motions of the joints and the gripper that will pick up a given cup in a given situation cannot be specified in advance. What can be specified are generic procedures for moving the arm which are selected and combined as required by the fact that a cup not a book is to be picked up, by the present position of the cup, by its dimensions, and by the nature of its handle if present—in other words, by the context. That is the challenge we face: devising generic procedures which can be combined to accomplish a wide range of navigation and manipulation tasks as demanded by the specific context in which a command is issued. Just as important as the procedures themselves is the control environment in which the procedures execute, for it is this environment which determines the temporal and logical connections allowed between procedures. And there is the parallel challenge of devising the rules of semantic interpretation that connect the surface structure of a command, that is, the English words in their given order, with the executing procedures.

Our design of the commandable base of the Robotic Aid and of the natural-language interpreter for it bore these considerations in mind. A range of motion commands can now be successfully interpreted and obeyed in the context of a room containing fixed items of furniture. An important next step in this work will be to interpret commands that better exploit the perceptual functioning of the robot (which is still under development) for it is through perceptual functioning that many details of the context are made known to the robot, especially in a changing environment.

There is one tempting approach to the problem of achieving specific action in response to requests that entail few specifics in their expression as natural-language commands. The approach is a familiar one in programming practice, namely specifying defaults that operate in the absence of explicit information and that are overridden by the presence of explicit information. So, for instance, a picking-up procedure would be designed, one that as a default looked for and used the handle of the object and that moved the object at a default speed, one that for most liquids and most cups would prevent spilling. While we accept that some default specifics will inevitably be built into the procedures of an instructable robot (our motion procedures for the mobile base of the Robotic Aid individually move the robot at a default speed), we have two reasons for rejecting this as a general solution to the problem of achieving specific and appropriate behavior in response to natural-language commands.

First, such an approach will make robot instruction too much like programming: everything of importance must be anticipated. Secondly, the problem of overriding defaults in real-time is non-trivial. The "solution" offered through defaults does not reduce the technical difficulty of achieving appropriate behavior in a robot. What we propose rather, and therefore acknowledge as an important part of the research effort in instructable robots, is that the robot's initial understanding of explicit verbal commands must be adjusted over time through learning. Here we have in mind forms of learning studied extensively in psychology, learning that advances by making successive discriminations and by generalizing from past experience. In learning to make discriminations or generalizations along any dimension that has a continuum of values it is essential that smoothing distributions of some sort be added to the experience gained from specific learning trials. Detailed mathematical analyses of such smoothing procedures and their application to learning data are to be found in Suppes (1964). Other forms of machine learning have been explored in artificial intelligence research and they too are relevant. We mention just a few key studies here, all to be found in Michalski, Carbonell, and Mitchell (1983): learning by experimentation (Mitchell, Utgoff and Banerji), learning from examples—a comparative review (Dietterich and Michalski), and learning from heuristic-guided observation (Lenat).

To return now to instruction, we can see how the same set of concerns outlined for the semantics of a command such as *Pick up the cup* surround verbal instruction. Ordinary language, as we pointed out earlier, is oriented towards results not processes. Giving explicit verbal instruction that details a step-by-step process will not be easy for many actions. For some, it will in fact be inappropriate and should be forgone in favor of other forms of learning. But even for those tasks for which verbal instruction seems suitable, our instruction, to be concrete and testable, will often be aimed at the execution of a specific action whereas what we really want in the end is for the robot to take whatever specific action is appropriate in the context. To take a simple example, we may instruct the robot to pick up a cup by finding and grasping the handle and then raising the cup without disturbing its vertical orientation. But when there is no handle we want it to grasp across the rim and if the cup is empty we want the robot to tilt the cup as necessary to get it through a constricted space. The final section of this paper therefore addresses the following problem. In giving explicit concrete instruction how are we to ensure that the robot will later exploit the context in which it is operating to successfully perform the action?

THE CHALLENGE OF INSTRUCTABILITY

To examine the problem posed at the end of the last section, we take for discussion a simple example. Suppose we want to teach a mobile base equipped with sensors to circumvent an obstacle it has encountered. Specifically, we want the robot to "bounce" its way around the obstacle by retreating from it, moving to one side, and then advancing in the original direction of travel. We represent two such cases in Figure 1, indicating the mobile base by a triangle with the front of the robot shaded in. This recoil action is to be repeated each time the sensors detect the obstacle, until the robot has moved beyond it. Suppose we, as the operator, start by teaching the robot the following basic recoil behavior. We assume that when the robot encounters the obstacle, it is facing in the direction of its travel and that when the robot moves left in response to a command to go left, it retains its forward-looking orientation. We issue the following set of commands:

> *Stop moving!*
> *Go back twelve inches!*
> *Go left twelve inches!*
> *Carry on as before!*

These commands are assembled off-line and given the label *Recoil* after which the action described by them is tested for appropriate real-time behavior. That is, the commands are interactively interpreted and obeyed in a particular situation. Only through interaction will the intended meaning of *back* and *left* be established. That interaction must establish whether *back* is relative to the direction of travel (a possible interpretation only if the robot possessed path-following behavior, not now present in the

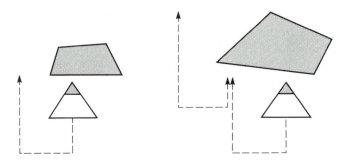

Figure 1.

Robotic Aid) or whether it is relative to the direction the robot is facing. If the robot were moving backwards as it approached and hit the obstacle (contrary to our stated assumption that the robot is facing in the direction of its travel), this second interpretation should not be considered. But to eliminate it would require a highly sophisticated understanding of the intention of the instruction—that it was to avoid the object not push it, for instance. In the absence of such understanding by the robot, a short dialogue with the user must establish one of the two interpretations. Interaction is also required for *left*: is it left relative to the operator or the robot? Again, a brief dialogue with the user establishes the desired interpretation.

For the two cases depicted in Figure 1, the recoil routine would produce satisfactory results with one call to recoil for the obstacle on the left, two for the obstacle on the right. If in such early test situations the recoil sequence proves satisfactory, the operator can embed the *recoil* command in the more general command *Whenever the bumpers are hit, recoil*. At this point, the operator would have made certain assumptions about the physical environment in which the robot will be obeying these commands—for instance, that the obstacle is not shaped as in Figure 2. In such a case, the robot would hit the object again during its leftwards motion and when another call to the recoil routine were issued, the robot would be unable to go back except by scraping along the edge of the object, prompting repeated calls to recoil that, as they were successively executed, would steer the robot far to its left, significantly off course.

The operator has also assumed that the robot is not acting under the constraints of other general commands. Suppose, for instance, the

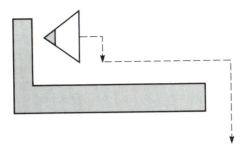

Figure 2.

following command had been issued earlier: *Whenever you are within one foot of the chair go right one foot.* And suppose the chair is immediately to the left of the obstacle in such a way that as the robot took its leftwards step during the recoil action it came within one foot of the chair. The robot would never complete the leftwards motion and so never finish the recoil action and resume its original motion. Under such circumstances the operator should be able to interrogate the robot about its behavior. In answer to the operator's enquiry, the robot should indicate (verbally or graphically) that it is reacting to the earlier command. Note that such interaction between robot and operator requires a degree of "self-understanding" by the robot.

At this point we can see that the successful execution of the learned recoil routine depends on two factors. First, there must be a congruence between the robot's and the operator's perception of the physical environment. Although the perceptual situation does not have to be perfectly comprehended by either the operator or the robot—it is not necessary to know exactly how many obstacles are present and where they are nor their precise dimensions—the operator's judgement about the absence of irregular shapes does have to be consistent with the robot's perception of the objects through its sensors. Secondly, the operator must have an accurate understanding of the robot's functioning. The operator must know, for instance, that the robot "remembers" what it is doing when told to stop moving and recalls that action when told to resume.

It is easy to produce other examples where both these factors are critical to instruction. For example, suppose the user issues the following sequence of commands for changing the arrangement of furniture in a

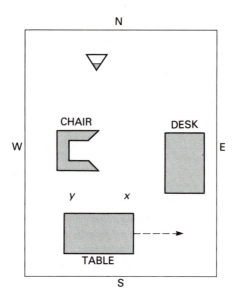

Figure 3.

room, giving the sequence the name *Rearrange the furniture* (as seen in Figure 3).

> *Move towards the table while avoiding the chair!*
> *Go to the other side of the table!*
> *Go west two feet and north six inches then face the table and*
> *   move it east two feet !*
> *Now go to the back of the chair, without hitting the chair!*
> *Face the chair and move it forward until it is within one foot*
> *   of the desk*

The purpose of these commands is to move the table, as shown by the arrow, towards the center of the room and to shift the chair up to the desk. But if the robot's position were slightly more west than depicted, and if the robot were the Robotic Aid, it would approach the table via the west side of the chair, not the east as the commands presuppose. Consequently, the robot's position before obeying *Go to the other side of the table* would be somewhere around *y*, not *x* as required for the successful execution of the rest of the sequence of commands. The problem may seem to lie in the non-determinism of the robot's behavior. If when we said *Go to the table* we knew exactly where the robot would stop, we would have no trouble choosing the right commands. Or so the argument would go. But, as we have discussed, natural-language instruction demands flexibility in the interpretation of commands, as shown by our normal and customary use of English. We freely use any of the following commands and each time impose no restrictions, other than those explicitly given, on how they should be obeyed: *Go to the table; Go to the table, avoiding the chair; Go to the table by skirting around the back of the chair; Go to the table, performing pirouettes along the way.* The interpretation of a natural-language command should ideally introduce no restrictions that are not explicitly given.

These two examples, as simple as they are, suggest that an operator will seldom put together the right set of commands the first time around. The operator can try to anticipate the execution environment by including appropriate conditional commands in the instruction, commands such as *Recoil whenever your bumpers are hit* or *Go forward until you see the line*, commands that exploit the robot's sensory capabilities. That will not be enough, however. What is needed is for the robot to accept real-time adjustments to its behavior as it obeys commands. If, for instance, the robot encounters an irregularly shaped obstacle during the execution of the recoil routine, one that prevents it from completing the recoil action, the operator should be able to adjust the robot's motion by giving a corrective command such as *Move right a little!*. Furthermore, in the end, we will want more than real-time response to corrections. We will want the robot to incorporate adjustments into its learned routines. Such a capability is beyond our present endeavors but we acknowledge its importance and inevitability in our program. It would be intolerable if the operator were to be responsible for the repeated correction of an action. For instance, if initial instruction to the robot caused it to push too hard on a button so that on its first test run the user intervened by saying *Pull back!*, the user would not want to monitor each pressing of a button to give the same corrective command.

The discussion in the first section of this paper anticipated several of the remarks in this section about the real-time testing of verbal command sequences. We saw how many ordinary English words can be precisely interpreted only in the actual situation in which they are used and only in interaction with the person using the word. In light of that semantic fact and of the remarks above, it is clear that the off-line assembly of command sequences is less useful than the more complex form of instruction we call real-time trial-run instruction. In this form of instruction the robot immediately obeys each command as it is given, interpreting the command in context and in interaction with the operator who, in monitoring the robot's performance, is adjusting it as necessary by interjecting other commands to achieve the desired result. During this time, the robot assembles the interpreted commands, together with the real-time adjustments made by the operator, to produce a new routine that it adds to its repertoire of actions.

One important point about these newly learned routines should be mentioned. To allow the robot to fully exploit information in its environment, routines acquired by the robot through instruction should be more than simple "in-line macros"; they should be parameterized subroutines. Such routines will rely on learning through discrimination and generalization to set the right parameter values. For each parameter, a smoothing distribution of a given form with a given variance will be assumed, that is, built in to the robot. For mathematical simplicity, parameter changes may be restricted to adaptation of the mean of the distribution (for examples, see Suppes, 1964). In many cases, however, we expect that it will be essential during learning to modify the variance as well as the mean of the distribution to enable the robot to adapt fully to the environment.

We introduce one more example at this point to emphasize the role of interaction in instructable robots. Interaction between the robot and its environment was essential to the robot emulator that was taught elementary mathematics. Here is a brief description of one interactive encounter to illustrate the kind of solution offered by interaction. Consider the following commands which appear in sequence as part of the instruction on how to add multi-digit figures.

> *Look at the next spot down until you see a number or a bar!*
> *If it is a number then add it to the total so far and remember the sum!*
> *Continue looking down, looking for a number or a bar, adding and remembering until you see a bar!*

The third command makes reference to the preceding two steps, forming a loop. It is not clear whether this loop, when compiled as a program, should be top-tested or bottom-tested or tested in the middle. That is, it is not clear where the test for the presence of a bar should be placed. In fact, for well-formed arithmetic problems, a bar can never appear during execution of the top or bottom of the loop; it can appear only during the execution of the middle of the loop. The operator lets the robot emulator discover this fact by running the program on test data, that is, on a particular addition exercise. Tentatively, the emulator places the exit condition after each step of the loop. The loop is then run in trial mode, showing the operator what takes place. If an exit condition, when encountered, is not satisfied, control is simply passed to the next step of the loop. If, however, the exit condition is satisfied, the operator is asked if this is the right time and place to stop repeating the sequence of steps gathered into the loop. If the operator answers *Yes*, the exit condition is installed at that location and all remaining trial locations are eliminated. If the operator answers *No* (it is not the time and place to stop repeating), the exit condition is removed from that location since it cannot be consistently satisfied and chosen as the right exit point on a later pass. If all possible exit places are rejected in this way (unlikely since in most loops the exit condition will not be satisfied at all places), a fatal error is signalled. A successful interactive session will locate the exit condition in the right place. The robot's ability to be instructed thus lies in its capacity to resolve ambiguities (such as exactly when to stop repeating a set of steps) through attempting to follow a given instruction and interacting with the operator and with test data in its execution environment.

To summarize briefly, we have identified several forms of interaction that contribute to the operation of verbally instructable robots. First the robot must interact with its perceptual environment in interpreting individual words, individual commands, and sequences of commands to resolve the inevitable ambiguities that characterize ordinary language. Secondly, the robot must interact with the operator to resolve those ambiguities when its perceptual abilites are limited or when the operator's intent must be determined. Thirdly, the robot must interact with its perceptual environment to meet those ceteris paribus conditions that accompany natural-language commands. Fourthly, there must be interaction between the robot and the operator to ensure that they share a common understanding of the perceptual environment and of the robot's behavior. Lastly, the robot must accept and acknowledge real-time adjustments to its behavior.

We end this paper with one further major challenge in the design of instructable robots. The problem lies in naming new routines. The suggestion made above, without comment, was to name a routine such as the one for moving furniture *Rearrange the furniture*. That raises the problem, however, of how to integrate this new use of language into the robot's lexicon and grammar. The robot can easily be made to respond to the phrase *Rearrange the furniture* as an unanalyzed semantic whole. But if the robot is to respond naturally to the following commands where *rearrange the furniture* appears embedded in a compound command and the verb *rearrange* occurs in the past tense and in the declarative mood, the robot's lexicon will have to have appropriate entries for *rearrange* and *furniture*.

>*Rearrange the furniture without bumping the cat!*
>*Switch off the lights after you have rearranged the furniture!*

The extent of the problem can be seen when we ask what is an appropriate entry for *rearrange*? First, the category of the verb has to be correctly assigned so that the verb's occurrence in a range of sentences can be recognized. In addition, various grammatical features have to be identified and correctly assigned. Consider the verbs *turn* and *face*, for instance, which at first glance seem to require parallel syntactic treatment that could be achieved simply by assigning the words to the same category:

> *Turn towards the wall!*   *Turn away from the wall!*
> *Face towards the wall!*   *Face away from the wall!*

But, of course, *turn* may be used in ways for which there is no natural parallel for *face*, and similarly for *face*, as suggested by the examples *Turn to the wall* and *Turn clockwise until you are facing the wall.*

The most challenging problem lies with the semantic entry for a new verb. This problem affects the very choice of instruction tasks, particularly what tasks should be taught first. For instance, we could choose for initial instruction those activities that correspond to single verbs and label the learned routines by those verbs. The problem of embedding this new word in the robot's lexicon and grammar does not become any easier however. Tense and mood remain semantically significant. Furthermore, one verb may be used to express many different intentions, which will give rise to many different interpretations. Consider the following three commands.

> *Move towards the table!*
> *Move three feet forward!*
> *Continue going towards the door until you have moved forward*
> *   six feet!*

Each of these commands expresses a distinct intention and consequently, despite the fact that the verb *move* occurs in each command, distinct procedural interpretations are produced by the mobile base of the Robotic Aid. The first command uses the **RegionSeeking** procedure, the second the **Piloting** procedure, and the third the test procedure **Distance-Covered?**. The partially specified interpretations of these commands are as follows. Full details of the interpretation process can be found in Michalowski, Crangle, and Liang (1987).

> *Move towards the table!*
> (Sequence(RegionSeeking ⟨the region around the table⟩ To-
>   wards))
> *Move three feet forward!*
> (Do (Piloting Shift Forward)(DistanceCovered ⟨three feet⟩ For-
>   ward))

Continue going towards the door until you have moved forward
*   six feet!*
(Do ⟨going towards the door⟩ (DistanceCovered? ⟨six feet⟩
    Forward))

No one semantic entry for *move* suffices for these three uses of *move*. If this were the new word being taught to the robot, that semantic complexity would also have to be acquired.

While we have not yet attempted any verb acquisition in our work on instructable robots, we once again recognize the role that interaction will play in it and report here on related work by Haas and Hendrix (also to be found in Michalski, Carbonell, and Mitchell, 1983). The goal of their work was to create a computer system that could hold a conversation with a user in English about a subject of interest to the user and subsequently retrieve and display the information conveyed in the conversation. Whenever a new word was presented to the system, a special procedure was called that temporarily assumed control of the dialogue and prompted the user for relevant information. The system would try to find out if a verb was transitive or if it took an indirect object, for instance, by introducing sample sentences and asking the user to complete them if they displayed acceptable uses of the verb. The system would also ask directly for the -ed and -en forms of the verb, showing the user the example of *went* and *gone* for *go*. Interaction with the user was thus exploited to obtain important syntactic and semantic information about a new word.

CONCLUSION

Through our initial efforts with two robot systems—one in simulation, the other implemented in hardware—we have identified several ways in which interaction (between the robot and its perceptual environment and between the robot and the operator) is essential to instructable robots. Such robots need interaction to interpret ordinary English commands in context, to determine the intentions of the operator when a command or sequence of commands is ambiguous, and to ensure that the robot and the operator share a common view of the environment and of the robot's functioning. At the same time, our work has shown that explicit verbal instruction must be accompanied by other forms of communication and learning if the robot is to function successfully in its environment.

18

CONTEXT-FIXING SEMANTICS
FOR THE LANGUAGE OF
ACTION

In this paper we develop the view that the specific interpretation of many ordinary English words can be fixed only within their context of use and not before. It describes an approach to the interpretation of natural-language commands in which the context of utterance is brought to bear on the interpretation of words used in the command. We also argue for a view of procedural semantics that is grounded in intentions. From this standpoint we outline the concept of a natural model for the interpretation of commands. Next we deal with those aspects of context we stress: the perceptual situation in which a command is given, the cognitive and perceptual functioning of the agent being addressed, and the immediate linguistic surround. The final section shows how our context-dependent view of the lexicon is integrated with the syntactic analysis of a sentence. Here we come into conflict with much conventional linguistic wisdom about the construction of grammars.

An important general point about much of the analysis in this paper is that it is done from the perspective of our work on instructable robots.

*Reprinted from J. Dancy, J.M.E. Moravcsik, & C.C.W. Taylor (Eds.), *Human Agency: Language, Duty, and Value* (pp. 47-76, 288-290). Stanford, CA: Stanford University Press, 1988. Written with Colleen Crangle.

The reasons for this emphasis are made explicit at the end of the next section.

Before turning to details we want to make some general remarks about context. The fundamental assumption of our work on the lexicon is that the precise interpretation of many words can be fixed only after the context in which the word is used has been taken into account. Contextual information, we claim, is an integral part of what a word means. Words do not in general have determinate meaning; their semantic significance is fixed by the actual occasions of their use (Crangle, 1984; Crangle and Suppes, 1986). Our purpose in this paper is to present evidence of the context dependency of ordinary words and to discuss the mechanisms by which the context fixes the precise interpretation of those words. We pay particular attention to the language of action—exemplified in imperatives—which places special demands on model-theoretic semantics. We argue that the language of action calls for a procedural semantics, and we discuss something of the potential of procedural semantics and the new problems it poses.

The fact that context must play a role in the interpretation of utterances has long been acknowledged. This is a familiar and obvious fact in the theory of demonstratives. A detailed logical treatment of their dependence on context is given by David Kaplan (1978). A more general analysis of context is given by Jon Barwise and John Perry (1983), who distinguish three aspects of context: the discourse situation (the time and place of utterance); speaker connections (a speaker's experiences, past and present, providing connections to objects, places, etc.); and resource situations (the use of one state of affairs to convey information about another). Our emphasis on the semantics of the lexicon leads in a direction that is orthogonal to the works of Kaplan and Barwise and Perry. A complete theory of context would need to include both kinds of analysis. Indeed, there is no general agreement on just what the complete role of context is. One prevailing view in both linguistics and philosophy is that an analysis of context is to be superimposed on the study of morphology, syntax, and semantics, all of which may be specified independently of the context of actual utterances. Our view is that context intrudes strongly at the lexical level and makes itself felt in ways that greatly affect traditional approaches to syntax. Suppes (1973b) has examined some of these consequences for syntactic structure; we examine them again in the final section of this paper, showing the expanded force of those arguments for the language of action.

INTENTIONS

There is a fundamental point about the nature of intentions that is central to our analysis. When an intention is expressed, as in "Go to the other side of the room," the meaning of the expression does not include a detailed algorithm for executing the command. The particular path taken by the agent satisfying the command is not part of the meaning of the expressed intention. If it were, the meaning specificity of intentions and the commands expressing them would be computationally intolerable.

A vast array of scientific evidence is available to show that the central and peripheral nervous systems of humans (and other higher animals) are organized hierarchically, but also in a decentralized, pluralistic way (Whiting, 1984). Instructions for detailed movements that are part of some intended action are not transmitted from the central to the peripheral nervous system—again, the computational load of doing so would be intolerable. This decentralization of responsibility for the execution of details is well reflected in our intuitive ideas about the satisfaction of a command. In no sense do we compute a specific trajectory that must be followed in crossing a room or in carrying out any other sort of movement. Even in cases of instruction, we simply cannot verbally describe a specific trajectory. Most actions in fact execute a kinematic path in the four-dimensional space-time of classical physics, the details of which are quite beyond the descriptive powers of ordinary language .

Context enters these considerations in several different ways. Part of the decentralization of action execution is that the expressed intention satisfied by the execution ignores details of context that must be taken into account at a lower level of the agent's system in order for an action to be successfully carried out; for example, an action that required a path through several traffic lights would not ordinarily have been guided by any mention of the traffic signals in the verbal expression of the intention. But the traffic lights would automatically—in ordinary cases—be taken care of at a lower level. Notice that this sketchy character of the expressed intention with respect to any actual path taken is characteristic both of intentions expressed about one's own future behavior and of commands given to another agent.

However, if an agent—person or robot—is asked to fetch a book from a table on the other side of the room, and if the agent knocks over a chair in doing so, in ordinary circumstances we regard the movement of the agent as satisfying only partially or rather poorly the request made. Expressed intentions carry with them a bundle of ceteris paribus conditions that impose a variety of constraints on the specific procedures actually executed. These ceteris paribus conditions are not given concretely or in advance but depend on the particular context in which an action is carried out. From a psychological standpoint, these conditions become embodied in habits. Learning in all its forms is needed for the unspoken consonance between intentions and habits to develop. If someone is driving a car while thinking intently about some problem, the person will, as we say, *automatically* stop for red lights. Other cases of habit are even more ordinarily a matter of automatic, that is, unreflective, response. If I am walking somewhere on an errand, the motor control and perceptual feedback required for normal walking operate quite outside of consciousness. These habits are efficient but unconscious ones. Moreover, even if we try to reflect consciously on how we are walking, our cognitive insight into the details is poor unless we are specialists in the psychology and neurophysiology of such matters. And even specialists can be directly aware of only very limited aspects of their own procedures of movement.

The kinds of considerations just set forth support the view that habits take care of many contextual details of action execution—the *expected* details, we might want to add. Before we circle back to semantics, we will introduce a useful distinction about actions. The distinction we have in mind is familiar in the theory of events as ordinarily developed in probability theory. Suppose we roll two dice and bet on the *event* of a sum of eight coming up. Several different *outcomes* will realize this event, namely the pairs (6, 2), (5, 3), (4, 4), (3, 5), and (2, 6). In the elementary probability cases, the description of the outcomes is nearly as simple as the description of the event, but in more complicated, less regimented cases this is not so. If, for example, a meteorologist forecasts moderate rain tomorrow afternoon, he does not begin to describe the many different configurations of the atmosphere, that is, outcomes, that could produce this event. Notice that the elementary probability cases strip away by obvious convention most of the details of the outcomes. Essentially, the process of getting to an outcome is not recorded at all. Only the end result matters, provided—and this is an important provision—the process satisfies a set of mostly unstated ceteris paribus conditions. The analysis of these conditions is no part of elementary probability theory, but is a necessary part of professional practice for those who love to shoot craps. The most obvious standard condition is that the dice must be thrown against the vertical side of the crap table opposite the shooter before coming to rest on the horizontal surface of the table. It has been known since the time of Poincaré that the detailed analysis of the motion of dice from the instant of their being thrown until they come to rest, that is, the analysis of the process of reaching the outcome, is a matter of great mathematical difficulty. The listing of the possible outcome *results* for the pair of dice is trivial, but the full listing or description of the possible outcome *processes* is in fact impossible.

In the case of actions, the initial distinction we have in mind is between an *event* and an action outcome or *specific action*. It will also be useful occasionally to distinguish between *process* and *result*. We therefore introduce the following technical terms: "event result," "event process," "specific-action result," and "specific-action process."

We can now turn back to semantics. The semantics of commands have, from a process standpoint, an appalling lack of concreteness. When Susan says to an agent "Bring me the book on the table," we naturally tend to think that the command's satisfaction is evaluated just in terms of the result—what we have termed the event result. Here we are close to the situation in elementary probability theory. In the pretty little model of elementary probability theory, the command to the crapshooter "Roll an eight!" has a simple result-semantics. The command is satisfied by any of the pairs listed above, and not satisfied by any of the other possible pairs. No context to worry about. No ambiguity. The same is true of the command "Bring me the book" if only the result-semantics consisting of the pair (brought the book, did not bring the book) is considered. But lurking in the background are those nebulous and troublesome ceteris paribus conditions. An ideal process-semantics of the book command should, at the specific-action process level, consist of all possible acceptable paths of movement to the table and back, together with a probabilistic measure of their likelihood of occurrence. But this is hard enough to do for the simple, idealized models of classical statistical mechanics. It is out of the question in a situation like the present one, in which the component forces determining the motion are so diverse and subtle. Something less detailed is essential; this is reflected in the inevitable vagueness of ordinary descriptions of such processes. Ordinary language, like ordinary conscious thinking" is oriented toward results, not processes.

Even this last claim is too general. There are many devices in ordinary language for distinguishing between process and result. The many distinctions of aspect and tense that are available in English and other languages reflect important semantic features that are essential for accurate and subtle communication. It is just that we do not usually think in terms of any very elaborate schemes for expressing at the appropriate level of detail the semantics of process referred to in ordinary talk.

Although the usual discussions of aspect in English center on the indicative mood, it is easy to generate imperative examples. Contrast the perfective (1) to the imperfective (2):

(1) Stop at the table.
(2) Keep going until you reach the table.

With respect to the process-result distinctions introduced above, we immediately think of (1) in terms of results. The case of (2) is less clear. The imperfective aspect suggests process, but all the same the primary semantic evaluation would probably be result oriented, unless the agent stopped on the way to the table. We are not really certain about this, but when possible a result is probably looked for.

In many cases, however, the only semantic possibility is to make some crude appraisal of process satisfaction. Consider these imperfective imperatives expressing a demand for habitual action:

(3) Take walks every day.
(4) Keep working regularly.

We would ordinarily accept very sketchy behavior reports to judge (3) or (4) satisfied—nothing like process specificity would be asked for. To use our earlier distinctions, we would accept event-process reports at quite a high level of generality.

Given the difficulties of these semantic problems, we have adopted a standard strategy. We have retreated to a simpler framework than that of human response to a verbal command or request for action. The simpler framework is that of instructable robots, which are vastly more simple and simpleminded than people—at least at present. Such robots accept commands in a natural language such as English and use those commands to extend their basic repertoire of actions. The kind of detailed semantic analysis required for instructable robots forces us to confront problems that may remain hidden in more abstract philosophical inquiries. Even here the semantic difficulties are daunting. Although our work in this area has been going on for some time, we are far from having anything definitive to show. Nevertheless, because we can lay out the underlying procedures in an explicit and systematic manner, our robot world, in spite of its severe limitations, provides an opportunity for a kind of detailed analysis that is not possible for human execution of commands. Many of our examples will reinforce this point, particularly those in the penultimate section, which discusses intentions and procedures for the robot that has been the focus of our recent work.

NATURAL MODELS FOR THE INTERPRETATION OF COMMANDS

In a recent phase of our work on instructable robots, we have used a robotic aid that was designed to assist the physically disabled. Earlier work made use of a robot that was taught elementary mathematics (Maas and Suppes, 1984, 1985). All instruction to these robots is interpreted relative to a set of models that define the agent to whom instruction is being given and the perceptual situation in which the instruction takes place. The command "Find the empty space" to the arithmetic robot of R. E. Maas and Suppes, for instance, is interpreted relative to the rows and columns of an arithmetic problem. That same command given to the mobile base of the robotic aid is interpreted relative to the configuration of objects and their parts in the room in which the instruction is taking place.

One natural semantical outcome of the viewpoint of experimental robotics is that one is not interested in the set of logically possible models satisfying a given utterance or piece of discourse. In all cases of the kind of work we are considering—and we would claim for almost all natural discourse—it is appropriate to take a subset of the set of possible models by holding rigid, at the very least, ordinary mathematics and physics, but in fact a larger body of knowledge about the real world. What this larger body of knowledge is and how it restricts the set of models may be expressed as a question about how one deals with the concept of something's being possible. We are not at all talking about the kind of possibility usually thought of in terms of logical possibility but about the ordinary notion of the possible that lies behind ordinary discourse. This notion of possibility assumes as given the kinds of fixed structures familiar in ordinary talk. Moreover, we really want to say something more radical. For the completely detailed and implemented semantic analysis needed in robotics work, we restrict even more severely the fixed set of models to ones that just encompass a particular environment, for example, the room and its physical contents in the case of the robotic aid for the physically disabled. In this set of models the frozen metaphors of abstract language so common in much ordinary talk would be ruled out. Only quite literal physical language would be understood, which means that the set of models is severely restricted to models of physical phenomena.

It is necessary, however, to include in the set of models a framework for the cognitive, perceptual, and motor functioning of the agent—person or robot—to whom the commands are addressed. This means that if we are talking about the robotic aid we are not simply restricting ourselves to the physical objects in the room but must have a way of integrating the models with the cognitive and perceptual states of the robot. The language of communication will, as we envisage it, be almost entirely physical in character. In a command like "Go to the table and pour me a glass of water," all of the terms have a direct physical interpretation. But satisfaction of the command in a set of models requires some apparatus to express as part of the model the cognitive state and perceptual and motor activity of the robot. This point has special plausibility when one considers the verbs "remember" and "look at" in commands such as "Remember where you placed the cup" or "Look at the chair to your left."

Reducing the possible set of models to a relatively small set helps to fix the context of an utterance. The semantic content of the lexical items is given in terms of these models, and the rules of semantic composition are expressed in terms of these models. But—and this is crucial—for many words, residual contextual factors remain and the precise interpretation of a word gets fixed only on the actual occasion of its use, and gets fixed normally, to use our earlier distinction, in terms of results, not processes. It is the residual contextual factors that are of special interest in this paper and are the subject of the next section.

Our use of a set of models to define the context of an utterance has something in common with the "commonsense metaphysics" approach to the lexicon in which core theories are constructed about physical objects— and about time, space, material, and so on—and in which the lexical items are characterized in terms of those theories (Hobbs, Croft, Davies, Edwards, Laws, 1986). Our work is different, however, in that we focus rather more closely on specific contexts of use, and we make provision in the lexical items for those contexts, at the time of utterance, to make their contribution.

In our work on the lexicon for the language of action, our search has been for semantic content that is specific and psychologically plausible in the context in which the language is being used. Consider the word "avoid," for instance, which in many of its ordinary uses carries the sense of evading or shunning or keeping out of the way of something. It is possible to give a general characterization of what this word means, a characterization that charts the interesting relationship between avoiding, evading, shunning, and keeping out of the way. However, such a characterization of the word is neither necessary nor sufficient in the language of action. It is not enough to enable an agent to understand in a detailed way a command such as "Avoid the chair." And the agent can understand and obey that command without ever understanding the words "shun," "evade," and "keep away from." Procedural or operational denotations are most appropriate for the language of action. Verbs such as "avoid," "look at," "put," and "remember" function semantically as operations on the natural physical models and are expressed in terms of the models that define the agent's cognitive, perceptual, and motor functioning.

The idea that a natural-language utterance may be represented semantically as a procedure performed by the language user is an old one, championed at one time by T. Winograd (1972) and supported in various ways in the work of S.D. Isard (1974), G. A. Miller and P. N. Johnson-

Laird (1976), Suppes (1980), and J. van Benthem (1985). But as yet little has been done to offer a theoretically grounded view of procedural semantics for natural languages comparable to the effort for programming languages that began many years ago with J. McCarthy (1963) and R. Floyd (1967). In principle, we would like to be able to answer the following question of adequacy: Why these procedures and not others?

We propose the following approach to procedural semantics as a way of answering that question. In broad outline this is what we do. We describe, intuitively and informally, a class of intentions. These are intentions we want to communicate to the agent—human or robot—through the natural-language commands whose semantics we are concerned with. We then propose a set of procedures whose satisfactory execution should demonstrate that the intentions were successfully communicated. Next, we state satisfaction conditions for these procedures, that is, conditions under which the procedures can be said to have been executed satisfactorily. Finally, we construct proofs that these satisfaction conditions can be met, proofs expressed in terms of the set of models that define the robot's cognitive, perceptual, and motor functioning in the given instructional context.

In terms of the distinction stated above in the section on intentions, we intuitively tend to define satisfaction in terms of event results, the most general of the four categories we introduced. But as we said earlier, satisfaction of a command at this level assumes a variety of unspoken ceteris paribus conditions. When we are interested in a fine-tuning of behavior, as in many instructional contexts, we want to move all the way down to analyzing satisfaction in terms of specific-action processes. Take, for instance, the two commands "Go to the table" and "Go left to the table." The first command simply expresses the result we would like to see. The second command interposes a process condition—that the table be reached by moving to the left. Yet other commands are less clear about the result to be achieved. "Go left toward the table," for instance, may be satisfied even if the table is not reached. And other commands are specific about process "Keep moving slowly to your left until you are at the table."

It is evident that the construction of proofs of adequacy will vary considerably according to the level at which satisfaction is characterized. Here is a pair of contrasting examples to make the point. Perhaps the most familiar construction of "turtle geometry" as represented in the programming language LOGO is the drawing of a circle, for which an instruction could be "Draw a circle by repeatedly going forward one unit then left one unit." In this case it is easy to prove, for a given unit of measurement relative to the display used, how nicely the generated polygon approximates a circle. However, for the command to the robotic aid "Go to the chair," which expresses the result we would like to see, what is of interest is not the particular path taken but whether the robot reaches the chair or not. We ordinarily judge the satisfaction of the command "Go to the chair," addressed to a person or a robot, in terms of results, not in terms of process—unless something alerts us to do otherwise. If, for instance, a bystander picks up the chair and carries it over to the person, we would be obliged to consider the process whereby the person came to be by the chair.

To what extent can these questions of adequacy be posed at the lexical level? Individual lexical items are themselves often thought to denote procedures, with rules of composition stipulating how these lexical procedures are combined to form a more complex procedure for the whole command. Can we ask of each lexical procedure, Why this procedure and not some other? Consider, for example, the following procedural denotation of the verb "avoid" taken in the context of our work on instructable robots. This procedure uses information about the robot's position and the position of the object to be avoided to generate a velocity vector away from the object. The magnitude of this vector is greatest when the robot is close to the object; it declines in proportion to the robot's distance from the object. At a distance greater than D standard units of measure from the object, the velocity vector is zero. When this procedure is being executed, the robot is never allowed to get within d units of the object. But equally plausible, in the absence of further argument, is another procedure that generates a velocity vector away from the object only when the robot comes within d units of the object, thereby bouncing the robot around the perimeter of the region that surrounds the object.

If, as we propose, intentions are semantically primitive, the procedures that are of primary interest are those "at the level of" the intentions. What is required of the lexical procedures is whatever allows these higher-level procedures to be executed satisfactorily and is in accordance with the class of natural models. But is that the only semantic condition that lexical entries are subject to? Certainly not, and our concern in this paper is to present an important source of semantic constraints on the lexicon, namely, the context at the time of utterance. We emphasize that context plays a central role even at the most general level of satisfaction, that of event results.

To return to the original question of adequacy it should be clear that the approach outlined allows the following restricted question to be answered: Why these procedures? It also implicitly shows why many other procedures would not be adequate: it would not be possible to give satisfaction conditions for them, conditions, that is, that could be proved to be met in terms of the class of models. The approach we advocate therefore allows a criterion of sufficiency, but not of necessity, to be met. This is as it should be. At the level of computational detail at which we are working—which is not the level of particular hardware and software or a particular neurophysiology but is the level of particular algorithms—we should expect to find more than one procedural account that is adequate.

What remains, of course, for procedural semantics as we conceive it is to show how the procedures associated with the intentions tie up with the English commands that express those intentions. This is where semantic grammars play their role. In a semantic grammar, rules of semantic composition are attached to the phrase-structure rules of the grammar to stipulate how the denotations of individual words are combined to produce a denotation for the whole expression. We return to this step in the final section of this paper.

EXAMPLES OF CONTEXT FIXING

Context-dependent words are not hard to find. The examples of indexical and anaphoric pronouns and adverbs of place and time are familiar. Our claim is that these are the obvious examples of a pervasive semantic phenomenon, especially in the language of action. A first, straightforward example illustrates the role of the perceptual situation in fixing the interpretation of words. This example will come as no surprise; the words of interest in it—"left" and "right"—are generally understood to have context-dependent meaning (Cresswell, 1978). The example is given here, however, in preparation for the examples that follow, in which the perceptual situation is required for the interpretation of words that are not as widely recognized to be context dependent.

Consider then the commands "Turn left" and "Move to the right of the chair." There are clearly several ways to interpret a command to turn left: is it to your left (the speaker's) or to my left (the one being instructed), or am I to turn left relative to some path I have been following, as one turns left along a footpath or road? Clearly, information about the orientation of the speaker, or the listener, or any path being followed, will be required for the precise interpretation of "left" in this command. For the command "Move to the right of the chair," since many chairs are thought to have their own left and right (identified by the position of the backrest), "right" could be interpreted relative to the chair and its orientation. But if the chair has no perceptually obvious front and back, "right" must be interpreted relative to the position and orientation of the speaker or relative to the position and orientation of the agent being instructed.

Contextual information is also required to fix the interpretation of intensive adjectives such as "big" and comparatives and superlatives. Our treatment of an adjective such as "large" in the instructable robot project closely follows the analysis of Suppes and E. Macken (1978) in recognizing the existence of an underlying ordering relation on the objects referred to by the noun the adjective qualifies. The denotation of the intensive adjective "large" is thought of as a procedure that uses the underlying ordering relation of size to determine if an object, the one said to be large, stands in the appropriate size relation to some criterion object. While this ordering relation is often given by the perceptual situation, particularly for adjectives such as "red" and "large" that refer to physical attributes, there are contexts of use, even for a word such as "large," in which the ordering relation is not immediately accessible by perception—take the phrase "largest donation," for instance, as in "Our company gave the largest donation to the United Way." Our emphasis, however, has been on those uses of language for which the ordering relation is given by the perceptual context.

The criterion object for an intensive adjective is also given by the context. A simple example is provided by the adjective "large" in "large book." The criterion object will typically be different when the context is a shelf of dictionaries and when it is a shelf of poetry volumes. Perhaps the most striking example of the role of the criterion object is given by the phrases "large elephant" and "large ant." While the ordering relations for "large elephant" and "large ant" will both use some measure such as mass or girth the criterion objects will be quite different. Here we see that the criterion object will sometimes be set not only by extralinguistic factors such as the perceptual situation but also by the immediate linguistic surround of the word: the words "elephant" and "ant" serve to limit the range of entities that may be used as the criterion object.

Many of the words we have encountered in the instructable robot project rely on the perceptual situation for their precise interpretation. We will discuss in some detail as our next example the word "next." This word is similar to the intensive adjectives in that it relies on an underlying ordering relation. There are several other words like this: the ordinals ("first," "second," "last," and so on), the adjectives "top" and "bottom," and the adjective "previous." The intuitive idea behind the semantics of "next" can best be understood if we talk about "the next x," where x may, for example, be "chair," "table," or "wooden chair." When we say "the next x," we are referring to the first x, by some ordering relation, relative to some present reference entity. Three things have to be fixed by the context for the interpretation of "next": the ordering relation; the class of x-type entities from which one will be selected, and some encompassing class of entities that are ordered by the relation. This encompassing class must be specified because it makes perfect sense to talk about the next x even when the present reference entity is not itself an x. A clear example is given by the arithmetic robot of Maas and Suppes(1985). For most uses of "next" in the arithmetic instruction context, the ordering relation required by "next" is given by the relation *vertically below*, a strict partial ordering on the perceptual objects such that each perceptual object that has a successor has a unique immediate successor by this relation, and similarly for a predecessor. That is, in the usual contexts of use for "next," the robot has been, and is expected to continue, scanning down a column.˙ Suppose the robot is focused on the blank space at the top of the tens column of an arithmetic exercise. That blank space plays the role of the reference entity for the interpretation of "next" in "the next number." Thus, for the blank space the robot is focused on to function as the reference entity for "next number," the blank spaces and the digits (numbers) in an arithmetic exercise must all stand in the relation *vertically below*.

A command may explicitly fix the ordering relation required for the interpretation of "next." Consider, for instance, the command "Choose the next person in order of height," in which the ordering relation is given by the phrase "in order of height." In the absence of such explicit directions, the perceptual situation imposes its own choice of ordering relation in many cases. For instance, suppose the agent being instructed is in a room containing ten chairs arranged in a row. That very arrangement of objects will tend to establish an ordering relation for sentences in which the adjective "next" qualifies the noun "chair." If the agent were positioned alongside the second chair, facing down the row toward the third chair, and if there had been no prior discourse, the command "Go to the next chair" would probably be interpreted as a command to move to the third chair. It is clear that the appropriate ordering relation must not only be available perceptually (or by some other means such as memory), it must also be established as a focus of attention. (The robotic aid at present has no ability to adduce an ordering relation from the perceptual situation. The first time the adjective "next" is used to refer to objects of a certain type, the person instructing the robot is queried for help in fixing an ordering known to the robot. That ordering is subsequently used as the default unless explicit instruction changes it.)

Sometimes two of the three contextual factors required by "next" are set explicitly by the command. Consider again the room containing only the row of chairs, with the agent at the second chair in the row. Suppose the agent were being instructed to clean the wooden chairs by applying a furniture polish, and the row included two cane chairs, one of which was in the third position and the other in the eighth. The command "Clean the next wooden chair" would then direct the agent to the fourth chair in the row, the first wooden chair relative to the present chair. In this case, the adjective "wooden" specifies the class of wooden objects, of which one must be selected, and the noun "chair" specifies the encompassing class of chairs, both wooden and cane. Because there are no objects other than chairs in the room, the class of wooden objects is a subclass of the class of chairs. The restricting class given by the adjective will not in general be a proper subset of the encompassing class, given usually by the noun. In general, the intersection of the two classes must be found before the next x can be selected.

There are many different ways a command may specify the contextual factors required by "next." Consider the command "Go to the next chair to the left." Here "to the left" specifies the ordering relation, a relation, call it L, which could be defined informally as follows: for all a and b, aLb if and only if a is positioned to the left of b and within the compass of an arc of 30 degrees radiating horizontally from b. Consider, however, the command "Go left to the next chair." Here "left" does not make a contribution to the interpretation of "next"; it serves rather as an adverb directly qualifying the verb, acting as an extra constraint on where to go. There are many other examples like this. On one hand, in the command "Search for the next file in alphabetic order," the ordering relation behind the use of "next" is given explicitly by the phrase "in alphabetic order." In the command "Search from A to Z for the next file," on the other hand, that same ordering relation defines a direction in which to search, but leaves open the question of what ordering lies behind the use of "next."

There are also occasions on which the perceptual situation does not play a role in fixing the interpretation of the word "next," as in the phrase "Susan's next book." Here the underlying ordering relation is on publication date, something that is seldom available in the immediate perceptual situation.

Our last extended example in this section draws directly on the functioning of the robotic aid that is the focus of our current work in instructable robots. Here we will examine how the agent's cognitive functioning comes into play in the interpretation of the word "avoid," as used in commands such as "Go to the door, avoiding the cat on the rug" or "While avoiding the table, move three feet left."

As part of the robotic aid's basic repertoire of perceptual and motor functions, there is a procedure that provides the core interpretation for "avoid." This procedure was described earlier. It generates a velocity vector away from the object when the robot is close to the object and prevents the robot from ever getting within d units of the object. At a distance greater than D units from the object, the velocity vector is zero. As described earlier, the procedure has three parameters: the first specifies the object to be avoided and the second and third the distances d and D. The value of the first parameter is given by the interpretation of the object noun phrase in the "avoid" command. The values of d and D may also be fixed explicitly by the command. "Avoid the heating element by at least one foot" sets d to be one foot, for instance. In the absence of such explicit instruction, however, the context of utterance must provide values for these parameters of avoidance. While perceptual feedback may tell the robot when it is within d or D units of the object, it is the robot's cognitive functioning—specifically, the robot's knowledge of the object that is to be avoided—that will set these values appropriately. In general, different objects demand different parameters of avoidance: a fire and a delicate table lamp, for instance, require distinct d and D values. There are further complexities arising from objects that are part of other objects. If the object is physically part of a larger object (it is the back or the leg of a chair, for instance) and if the robot does not have the motor functioning to allow it to avoid the subpart independently of the larger object (the robot cannot, for instance, maneuver around the base or around and between the legs of the chair), the whole object must be used for the setting of the d and D parameters.

The significant point of this extended discussion of several examples is that for many ordinary words, there must be mechanisms for fixing the precise interpretation outside the language itself. In the final section we discuss how these mechanisms are brought into play in coordination with the grammatical analysis of a sentence. The next section examines in some detail, as required for the discussion in the final section, the procedural semantics developed for the robotic aid.

INTENTIONS AND PROCEDURES

We turn now to the specifics of the mobile robotic aid operating in a room containing ordinary items of household furniture. The robotic aid consists of a six-jointed arm mounted on the front of an omnidirectional mobile base. The base is fitted with sensorequipped bumpers. The intentions we want to communicate to this robot concerning its movement across the floor are:

> that the robot go to a given region of the room
> that the robot move in a given direction
> that the robot avoid a given region

that the robot stay within a given region

that the robot stop doing whatever it is doing at that time

that the robot perform any specific motion at a faster than normal speed

that the robot perform any specific motion at a slower than normal speed

that the robot speed up

that the robot slow down

that the robot pursue two goals simultaneously (the goals are not necessarily achieved simultaneously)

that the robot pursue one goal after another has been achieved

that the robot pursue a goal until a given condition is met (the pursuit of the goal will be interrupted)

that the robot repeatedly pursue a goal until a given condition is met

that the robot pursue a goal if a certain condition is met

that the robot pursue a goal when a certain condition is met

that the robot pursue a goal whenever a certain condition is met.

The conditions we want the robot to detect are:

that a given distance has been traversed

that a given time has elapsed

that the robot's bumpers are hit

that the robot is in a certain region.

In this discussion we are interested only in the movement of the robot across the floor. We therefore restrict our attention to the omnidirectional base of the robot. This mobile base can best be described as a collection of simultaneously executing motor, perceptual, and cognitive processes that communicate with each other under the control of a scheduler. This scheduler has seven modes of operation, corresponding to the following seven procedures (presented here in the notation that places the procedure name followed by its arguments in parentheses):

(*Sequence* $A_1 A_2 \ldots A_n$)	Execute A_1 then A_2, and so on in sequence to A_n
(*Parallel* $A_1 A_2 \ldots A_n$)	Start A_1, A_2, $\ldots A_n$ executing simultaneously
(*If* $X A$)	Execute X, and if X returns True, execute A
(*When* X A)	Repeatedly execute X until X returns True, then execute A

(*Whenever X A*)   Repeatedly execute X until X returns True, then start A's execution and begin repeatedly executing X as before

(*Do A X*)   Start the execution of A and repeatedly execute X until it returns True, then interrupt A's operation

(*Repeat A X*)   Repeatedly execute A and then X, until X returns True.

Each of these seven procedures (also known as *control structures*) specifies a temporal order for the execution of its argument procedures, along with any logical connections that hold between the procedures. Each A can itself specify a control structure, or one of the robot's primitive procedures (described below). Each X specifies a test procedure that returns the value True or False. One test procedure available to the robotic aid is *DistanceCovered*, a procedure that takes two arguments. The first argument specifies a distance in inches; the second gives the direction along which distance is measured. The procedure returns True if the distance covered since the procedure began to be executed is greater than or equal to the distance specified, False otherwise. Another test procedure is *RobotInRegion*, a procedure of one argument that returns True if the robot is in the region specified by the argument, False otherwise.

The overall motion of the robot base results from the simple linear sum of motions contributed by the individual procedures operating at any time. A simple motion is expressed as a two-dimensional linear velocity plus a third component for rotation. Motions are relative to one of two coordinate systems: the first is embedded within the robot and the second is given by the room in which the robot is being instructed. The linear motion may be left or right, forward or backward in the robot coordinate system, and north or south, east or west in the room coordinate system. The rotation about the vertical axis may be clockwise or counter-clockwise.

Three of the primitive procedures that contribute to the movement of the robot base are of interest to our discussion. The first, a procedure of three arguments, produces movement away from an object as described in our earlier remarks on the verb "avoid." We will return to this procedure in the next section. The two other primitive motion-procedures are *Piloting* and *RegionSeeking*. The *Piloting* procedure takes three arguments: the first specifies whether the movement is linear or rotational; the second specifies the direction of movement (north, for instance); and the third specifies whether the default speed of the mobile base is to be increased, decreased, or not changed at all. The call (*Piloting Shift Left* +), for instance, starts a process that shifts the robot to the left at a speed one unit greater than the default speed. Calls to the *Piloting* procedure such as this one are usually embedded in a *Do* structure, with the result that the robot stops moving to the left only when the condition specified by the *Do* structure becomes true. The *RegionSeeking* procedure takes three arguments: the first specifies a region whose nearest point the robot moves toward or away from; the second argument indicates whether that movement is toward or away; and the third argument specifies speed as for the *Piloting* procedure. The procedure stops executing as soon as the robot reaches the region.

While we will not offer satisfaction conditions for these procedures or proofs that the conditions can be met, we want to communicate a sense of such proofs by showing the extent to which the commands, the intentions, and the procedures fit together. Consider the following three commands.

> Move toward the table.
> Move three feet forward.
> Continue going toward the door until you have moved forward six feet.

Each of these commands expresses a distinct intention, and consequently in our analysis, despite the fact that the verb "move" occurs in each command, distinct procedural interpretations are produced. The first command uses the RegionSeeking procedure for "move," the second the *Piloting* procedure, and the third the procedure *DistanceCovered*. The partially specified interpretation of these commands are as follows. (We use square braces for the denotations; the denotation of "forward," for instance, is shown as [forward]. The speed arguments of *Piloting* and *RegionSeeking* are omitted for simplicity.)

> Move toward the table.
> (*Sequence(RegionSeeking*[the table] *Toward*))

> Move three feet forward.
> (*Do (Piloting Shift* [forward]) (*DistanceCovered* [three feet] [forward]))

> Continue going toward the door until you have moved forward six feet.
> (*Do* [going toward the door] (*DistanceCovered* [six feet] [forward]))

Consider also the command "Move three feet north west." (It is convenient semantically to treat "northwest" as two separate words.) The robot's Piloting procedure knows only about the four compass directions of north, south, east, and west given by the room coordinate system. The only way to accomplish movement in the northwest direction in response to this command is to simultaneously execute (*Piloting Shift* [north]) and (*Piloting Shift*[west]). A *Parallel* structure is thus embedded within a *Do* structure with the test procedure (*DistanceCovered* [three feet] *Trajectory*). The second argument value, *Trajectory*, specifies that distance is to be measured along a straight line (computed off a map) from the robot's position at the time the command was given to its present position.

> Move three feet north west.
> (*Do* (*Parallel* (*Piloting Shift* [north]) (*Piloting Shift* [west]))
> (*DistanceCovered* [three feet] *Trajectory*))

As a final example, consider the command "Go left toward the table." In response to this command, the robot will simultaneously execute (*Piloting Shift* [left]) and (*RegionSeeking* [the table] *Toward*) embedded within a *Do* structure with the test (*RobotInRegion* [the table]). Note that a simple *Parallel* structure of *Piloting*, and *RegionSeeking* is not adequate. With that interpretation, *RegionSeeking* would end when the robot reached the table, but *Piloting* would not, and the robot would continue moving left. Note too that it makes sense to issue this command only if in moving leftward the robot would indeed reach the table.

> Go left toward the table.
> (*Do*(*Parallel* (*Piloting Shift* [left]) (*RegionSeeking* [the table]
> *Toward*)) (*RobotInRegion* [the table]))

One could argue that the command "Go left toward the table" does not necessarily express the intention that the robot move all the way to the table and then stop but merely that it begin to move leftward in the direction of the table. It could be seen as semantically incomplete from the point of view of the intentions listed at the beginning of this section, since it specifies neither how far to move exactly nor for how long. However, if the robot did not stop moving when it reached the table but sailed on past it or, even worse, bumped into it, we would in ordinary circumstances consider the command to have been poorly understood or inadequately obeyed.

This observation takes us back to our earlier remarks, in the sections on intentions and the interpretations of commands, about the distinction between process and result and about the unstated ceteris paribus conditions that often accompany verbal commands. We have already noted the extent to which process conditions are present in some commands and absent in others. Satisfaction of a command that primarily expresses a desired result is not without process constraints, however, as our examples have shown. The question how these constraints are gleaned from the context is a major challenge in our work and one we have made a small start on by recognizing the role that interaction plays. So the command "Go left toward the table," for instance, will in fact not immediately be interpreted as above, but will initiate a dialogue between the robot and the speaker to determine the speaker's intent.

We end this section with some further remarks on lexical procedures and the context. As suggested by our extended discussion of "next" and other words, the context of use should fix certain details of a lexical procedure's operation. What is in fact required for the denotation of many words is a procedural *schema*. In the next section we show how procedural schemata for "next" and "avoid" are used to produce a procedural interpretation for the command "Avoid the next chair." We close this section with a brief discussion of the verb "pick up" as used in a command such as "Pick up the cup."

If one particular procedure functions as the interpretation of "pick up," a procedure that stipulates exactly how a cup is picked up, the details of that procedure will be inappropriate for many commands, for there are indefinitely many ways to qualify a command and so modify the action associated with it. Consider, for instance, the commands "Pick up the cup without using the handle," "Pick up the cup by its handle," and "Pick up the cup at its rim directly across from the handle." In general, it seems as if any procedure that serves as the interpretation of a verb of action must be open to an indefinite number of modifications in its actual execution. At the same time, however, the interpretation of a command such as "Pick up the cup" is in most circumstances subject to various ceteris paribus constraints—that the vertical orientation of the cup not be disturbed, for instance. The question we must face is whether or not the notion of a procedural schema allows the appropriate degree of procedural variation for verbs of action such as "pick up." One additional way of looking at this problem is to identify a default way of performing each action, recognizing that in certain contexts the default must be overridden. Under this view, the study of context would have to embrace an analysis of "normal" circumstances given by partially unstated ceteris paribus conditions in which the default holds, and other circumstances in which the default is to be overridden.

On the question how defaults are overridden, one approach is to embed procedures in a highly parallel processing environment. The special circumstance that signals the override of a default will then contribute its own procedure and the parallel execution of procedures will produce the appropriately modified action. There are cases in which this approach works and cases in which it does not. Again we draw on the robotic aid for an example. On the one hand, the procedure for "go to," as used in the commands "Go to the table" and "Go to the table without hitting the chair," produces straight-line motion of the robot toward its goal. The procedure invoked by "without hitting the chair," on the other hand, produces motion that avoids the chair. Together, these procedures have the effect of modifying the robot's direct movement toward the table, allowing it to skirt around the edge of the chair. However, not so successful a story can be told for the "pick up" command. If the default action for picking up a cup has the robot grasping the handle of the cup, and if "without using the handle" keeps the robot's gripper away from the handle, the overall effect is that the cup is not grasped at all. Much remains to be done to develop a sense of context that characterizes normal circumstances, default actions, and ways to override default actions.

GRAMMARS AND THE LEXICON

The process governing the synthesis of lexical procedures to form a complex procedure for the whole sentence is as follows. A semantic tree is generated from rules of semantic composition, called semantic functions, that are attached to the phrase-structure rules of the grammar (Suppes, 1973). A simple example illustrates the main ideas. Although the example features a simple context-free grammar, the process is not restricted to such grammars. The grammar currently in use for the robotic aid in fact has its phrase-structure rules augmented with constraint equations, in the spirit of lexical-functional grammars (Kaplan and Bresnan, 1982) and the unification-based formalisms of S. M. Shieber, F. C. N. Pereira, L. Karttunen, and M. Kay (1986).

Consider the parse tree in Figure 1 for the imperative "Avoid the next chair." The non-terminal labels shown are I (for imperative), VP (for verb phrase), NP (for noun phrase), V (for verb), N (for noun), DA (for definite article), and ADJ$_{ord}$ (for ordering adjective).

This parse is produced by a context-free grammar that we extend by assigning at most one semantic function to each production rule of the grammar. The resultant grammar is called a *potentially denoting* grammar, following Suppes (1973b). In the grammar, we use square braces to show denotations. For instance, [NP] stands for the denotation of NP, [chair] for the denotation of "chair." The lexical denotations are, following our general strategy, relative to the set of models that define the agent being instructed and the perceptual situation in which instruction takes place. Without going into the details of the models, let us again use for our example the mobile base of the robotic aid. Suppose it is being instructed in a room containing several chairs arranged in a row. We will

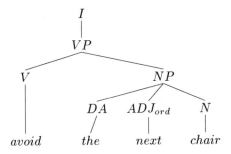

Figure 1.

describe the denotations of "avoid," "next," and "chair." The definite article "the" is treated syncategorematically in this context.

Following our earlier discussion of "avoid," suppose the denotation of "avoid" is a procedural schema with three parameters that must be set to generate a specific procedure. Let us call it Proc1. The first parameter specifies the object to be avoided. The second and third are the perceptual parameters of avoidance discussed earlier: the first one establishes the minimal distance the robot must maintain from the object; the second fixes the region within which the robot's proximity to the object must be monitored. We use the familiar lambda notation for abstraction to represent procedural schemata. The schema for "avoid" is thus shown by the expression $(\lambda xyz)\text{Proc1}(x, y, z)$.

Suppose the denotation of "next" is a procedural schema, Proc2, with three parameters corresponding to the three contextual factors identified above in the section on context fixing. That is, the first specifies the objects—chairs or tables, for instance—of which one is to be selected as the next one relative to a present reference entity. The second specifies the ordering relation that holds for the encompassing class of objects. The third specifies that encompassing class of objects.

Finally, suppose the denotation of "chair" is a simple procedure, Proc3. We will not go into the details of how the robot picks out objects in its environment. We will suppose that Proc3 returns a list of all chairs in the given perceptual environment, each chair being designated by a triple $\langle x, y, \theta \rangle$ that specifies its position and orientation in a coordinate system that is fixed relative to the room.

The semantic functions below stipulate how the denotation at each node of the tree is obtained from the denotations of its daughter nodes. The extended context-free grammar for the sentence "Avoid the next

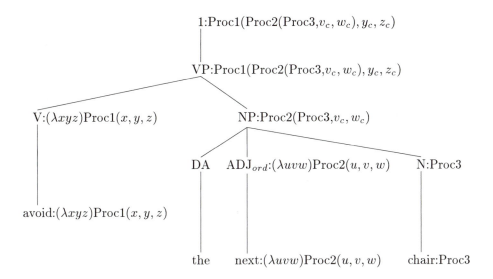

Figure 2.

chair" is as follows. Note that not all contextual parameters are set within the command itself. The notation y, indicates the parameter value y given by the extralinguistic context of utterance.

Production Rule	*Semantic function*
$I \to VP$	$[I] = [VP]$
$VP \to V + NP$	$[VP] = [V]([NP], y_c, z_c)$
$NP \to DA + ADJ_{ord} + N$	$[NP] = [ADJ_{ord}]([N], v_c, w_c)$
$V \to avoid$	$[V] = [avoid] = (\lambda xyz)Proc1(x, y, z)$
$N \to chair$	$[N] = [chair] = Proc3$
$ADJ_{ord} \to next$	$[ADJ_{ord}] = [next] = (\lambda uvw)Proc2(u, v, w)$

The extended grammar yields the semantic tree in Figure 2 for "Avoid the next chair." To the left of the colon at each node is the terminal or non-terminal label. To the right of the colon is the denotation of that label.

At the top of the tree we have a procedure specified for the command "Avoid the next chair," stated in the imperative mood. We call this the semantic interpretation of the sentence. If the sentence were a declarative, such as "The next chair is empty," the semantic tree for it would specify a procedure that determines the truth or falsity of the declarative. Although this example uses only one operation in its semantic functions—namely, function application—in general other operations are also used.

As the semantic functions show, not all parameter values are set within the semantic tree. In examining several examples in the section on context fixing, we saw how the precise interpretation of a word may be fixed by any of several means: the immediate linguistic surround, the perceptual situation, or the cognitive functioning of the agent. We see that same variability in this example. While the VP rule given above, for instance, is required for the sentence "Avoid the next chair," the sentence "Avoid the next chair by six inches" would require a rule such as the following one to produce the result shown on the right. Here the phrase "by six inches" sets the parameter that determines the minimal distance the robot must maintain from the object.

$$VP \rightarrow V + NP + AdvPhDist$$

[Avoid the next chair
by six inches]

$$[VP] = [V]([NP], [AdvPhDist], z_c)$$

$$= [avoid]([the\ next\ chair],$$

$$[six\ inches], z_c)$$

Once the semantic tree has identified the parameter values still to be set, mechanisms must be invoked for obtaining those values from the perceptual situation, from the agent's cognitive functioning, and from interaction with the user. The theory of such mechanisms is as yet not very well developed, and many would regard their consideration as outside the proper domain of semantics. But given the drastic incompleteness of meaning if context-fixing mechanisms are not invoked in most ordinary conversation and communication, we take a contrary view. Moreover, a working understanding of these mechanisms is essential for developing adequate language capabilities in instructable robots. A central point of this paper is to show how essential they are. In other publications already mentioned we have begun a more detailed study of their nature.

Some final remarks have still to be made. The example in this section is but one of many in which the appropriate semantic interpretation of a command requires syntactic rules that are not in accord with many standard approaches to syntax. Several other examples from the instructable robot project can be found in Crangle and Suppes's report (1986); we mention one here briefly.

Consider the command "Go three feet left." Its interpretation by the robotic aid is given by the following procedure: $(Do(PilotingShift[\text{left}])$

(*DistanceCovered*[three feet][left])). Note that "left" makes a contribution to both the *Piloting* procedure and the *DistanceCovered* procedure. In *Piloting* it gives a direction of movement. In *DistanceCovered* it supplies a direction along which distance must be measured. (The path traced by the robot's movement may wind and turn—a point more easily seen with the command "Go three feet left while avoiding the cat"—but the intention is for the robot to move left three feet, and it is distance traversed in the leftward direction that must be measured, not distance along the path.) If "left" is to make its contribution in a straightforward way to both procedures, a relatively flat tree structure is called for in the parse of this sentence, a point we will return to in some detail in the next section. We of course want to claim that our syntactic rules are not merely the result of an inappropriate assignment of semantic content to words. To produce support for our use of what we call *semantically driven grammars*, we close this paper with a final section on grammars and the lexicon.

Perhaps the most unusual feature of the semantically driven grammars we have developed is the flatness of the derivation trees for sentences. We can illustrate our approach by considering a pair of simple sentences. What we prove for this pair is this. If the denotations of the lexical items are just the natural sets they should be—"tables" denotes a set of tables, and so forth—and no sets of the hierarchical kind characteristic of Montague grammars are permitted, then the trees must be flat. (See Partee, 1976 for detailed presentation of Montague's theory of grammar). Both philosophical and scientific intuition support this restricted view of sets. Philosophically there is a natural skepticism about sets of sets of sets, and other sets higher in the hierarchy. We never talk about them in any natural concrete way. Moreover, in the part of mathematics most powerfully adapted to quantitative science, namely, classical analysis, there is only a low-level hierarchy of numbers, vectors, and functions. It seems highly unlikely that the qualitative formulations so characteristic of natural language would have in back of them a more elaborate hierarchy than is required for classical physics. A modern structuralist point is that the mind must reflect the structure of the world—at least that part we most often encounter. Perceptual language and naive physical language seem most naturally analyzed semantically by a low-level hierarchy of sets.

The analysis we give of the following pair of sentences can be extended to more complex cases:

(1) If all tables are empty, stop!

(2) If some tables are empty, stop!

In fact, for complete simplicity, we restrict ourselves just to the antecedents of (1) and (2), that is,

(1') All tables are empty.

(2') Some tables are empty.

First, some concepts need to be explicitly defined, even if they are familiar. A *model structure* of a grammar G with terminal vocabulary V_T is a pair (D, v) in which D is a non-empty set and v is a partial function from V_T to a *hierarchy* $H(D)$ of sets built up from D by closure under the operations of union, intersection, and other set-theoretic operations. A model structure (D, v) of a grammar G is *Boolean* if and only if for any string s of V_T^+ for which v is defined, $v(s)$ is a subset of D. (V_T^+ is the set of all finite sequences of terminal symbols, minus the empty sequence.) A potentially denoting grammar G is Boolean if and only if for any Boolean model structure (D, v) of G, every semantic function of G has as its value a subset of D whenever its arguments are subsets of D.

We also need a Boolean formulation of the Frege function for the top of the tree. Using U for the universal quantifier function and E for the existential quantifier function, we have for any set A:

$$U(A) = \begin{cases} D \text{ if } A = D \\ \cdot\phi \text{ if } A \neq D \end{cases}$$

where ϕ is the empty set, and

$$E(A) = \begin{cases} D \text{ if } A \neq \phi \\ \phi \text{ if } A = \phi \end{cases}$$

To show how a flat Boolean grammar works, we have the following top-level rules and the associated semantic functions:

$$S \rightarrow UQ + NP + VP \quad [S] = U(\neg[NP] \cup [VP])$$
$$S \rightarrow EQ + NP + VP \quad [S] = E([NP] \cap [VP])$$

Note that the non-terminal symbols UQ and EQ for the universal and existential quantifiers have no denotation but operate as control-structure words at the top level. The non-terminal label S is for sentences.

Probably most linguists think of "all tables" and "some tables" as noun phrases, and consequently assign a complex denotation to such phrases, at least when pressed semantically. We do not deny there are good reasons for wanting "all tables" and "some tables" to be noun phrases, just as there are good reasons for wanting the semantics of simple sentences like (1') and (2') to be Boolean. There is a natural clash between grammar and semantics here. Our point is that the clash cannot be avoided.

We sketch the argument behind this claim (for details see Suppes, 1982b). Rather than the rules just given for a flat grammar, let the top-level rules be:

$$S \to NP + VP$$
$$NP \to UQ + N$$
$$NP \to EQ + N$$
$$VP \to Copula + Adj \quad [VP] = [Adj]$$

The semantic functions for the first three rules are our object of study. Suppose there were Boolean semantic functions for these three grammatical rules. Then, without any loss of generality we may assume that UQ and EQ themselves do not denote, so we must have semantic functions h, f, and g such that:

$$[S] = h([VP], [NP]) \quad \text{for } S \to NP + VP$$
$$[NP] = f([N]) \quad \text{for } NP \to UQ + N$$
$$[NP] = g([N]) \quad \text{for } NP \to EQ + N$$

What we can then show is that there are Boolean models of (1′) and (2′) such that the Boolean functional equations in terms of h, f, and g cannot simultaneously have a solution.

The Boolean analysis just given generalizes to relation algebras. In particular, if lexical denotations are held down to sets of physical objects and relations among such objects, then the same argument given above forces the use of flat trees for prepositional phrases, as in "Go to all empty tables" and "Go to some empty tables." The technical details of this semantic analysis of prepositional phrases is rather lengthy, and so it is not given here. But the message for the lexicon is clear: there is an uneliminable tension between syntax and semantics.

19

APPLICATION OF LEARNING MODELS TO SPEECH RECOGNITION OVER A TELEPHONE

In October of 1972, the decision was made at the Institute for Mathematical Studies in the Social Sciences to apply psychological learning models to the problem of computer recognition of human speech. In this investigation of speech recognition we used the standard home telephone as an inexpensive terminal for verbal communication in dealing with a mathematics curriculum. We subsequently describe two mathematical learning models and their properties, their implementation as part of a speech recognition system, and two system experiments with children as subjects.

Speech recognition can be viewed as three separate conditions:

1. the internal representation of each utterance.

2. the actual recognition process.

*Reprinted from Suppes, P. (Ed.). (1981). *University-level computer-assisted instruction at Stanford: 1968-1980*. Stanford, CA: Institute for Mathematical Studies in the Social Sciences, Stanford University, Stanford, CA. Written with Douglas G. Danforth and David R. Rogosa.

3. the change of the internal representation upon the discovery of errors by the recognition process (learning).

In our approach, the representation of each utterance is given by a vector of numbers U. These numbers are the digitized amplitudes and frequencies from three band-pass filters that take as input the analog signal from, say, a telephone. In this study we deal only with recognition of individual phrases, and consequently each utterance may be normalized in time to a fixed length, .5 secs. Our recognition process utilizes what can be called the nearest neighbor approach. A metric (see below) is introduced into the space and a distance is calculated from the unknown utterance U to each of the members of a set of vectors $\{V\}$ representing known phrases; the name of the V closest to U is assigned to U.

The correction process entails updating the representation vectors $\{V\}$ by a linear function of the old representations and new utterances of each word. This approach is not entirely new to the literature. Variants of it have been used for some years in the area of pattern recognition (Abramson & Braverman, 1962; Ford, Batchelor, & Wilkins, 1970). We wish to present two approaches that bear some resemblance to previous work but have special emphasis on psychological learning models and their associated learning curves.

Theta process. We now consider a linear process. The correct vector V is updated using the following learning model. Let $0 < \theta < 1$ be an arbitrary scalar parameter and let V be the old vector representing the word from which U is a sample. The new V representation can be constructed from a weighted average of U and the old V, namely,

$$(1) \qquad\qquad V \leftarrow (1 - \theta)V + \theta U.$$

Note that as θ ranges from 0 to 1 the new representation ranges from V to U. Process (1) is patterned after psychological models developed by Bush and Mosteller (1955) and Estes and Suppes (1959). If we consider U as a random sample from a distribution with mean M and covariance matrix $\sum$ then it can be easily shown that V is an unbiased estimate of this population mean ($EV = M$ where E is the expectation operator). It is well known that the sample mean (a process where θ is replaced by $1/n$) is also an unbiased estimate of the population mean. However, V has the property of giving greater weight to recent utterances than to earlier ones. This responsiveness of V is useful in providing a more accurate representation of the speaker's current pattern of speaking. Abramson and Braverman (1962) have considered this process for tracking wandering patterns.

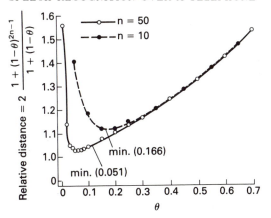

Figure 1. THE ABOVE PLOT DISPLAYS THE EXISTENCE OF VERY PRO-
NOUNCED MINIMA AT $\theta = .166$ FOR $n = 10$. MINIMA SUCH AS THESE
OCCUR FOR EACH TRIAL NUMBER n. WHEN θ ASSUMES ONE OF THESE
MINIMIZING VALUES, IT IS REASONABLE TO BELIEVE THAT THE PROBA-
BILITY OF AN UTTERANCE BEING CORRECTLY CLASSIFIED AS V IS MAX-
IMIZED.

The covariance matrix of V is readily calculated to be a scalar multiple,
c^2, of $\sum$ where

$$(2) \qquad c^2(n, \theta) = \frac{\theta + 2(1-\theta)^{2n-1}}{1+(1-\theta)}, \qquad n = 1, 2, \ldots$$

The expected distance of a sample U to its representation vector V can
be calculated in terms of c^2 if we use a Euclidean metric. Let $d(U, V) =
(U - V)'(U - V)$ be this distance (X' is the transpose of X). Then since
the new U is independent of V and both have the same mean we find that
the expected distance may be written as

$$(3) \qquad Ed(U, V) = (1 + c^2)Ed(U, M)$$

where $Ed(U, M)$ is unknown but independent of θ and trial number. Thus
we have an expression for the expected distance between a member of the
population and its representation vector V. Figure 1 shows explicitly the
form of $Ed(U, V)/Ed(U, M)$ as a function of θ for $n = 10$ and $n = 50$.
The minimum of (3) may be found analytically for arbitrary n.

Delta process. The theta process is essentially an estimate of the first
moment of the population. In the standard problem of statistical classification (Anderson, 1958), estimates of the covariance matrix are necessary
to determine a hyperplane separating two populations. In order to avoid

the inversion of a full covariance matrix, which is necessary with the classical Bayesian procedure, one may use other less precise but computationally more efficient techniques. One of these, which we call the delta process, estimates the variances of the utterance components. Let δ be a parameter that lies in the interval $(0,1)$, then S given by the learning equation

(4) $$S \leftarrow (1 - \delta)S + \delta(U - V)(U - V)', \quad 0 < \delta < 1,$$

is an estimate of the covariance matrix, where U, V are as before. The diagonal elements of S are the estimates of the component variances. Using the two quantities V and S, we may calculate a *distance* between the utterance U and a representation vector V by

(5) $$D(U,V) = (U - V)'W(U - V),$$

where

(6) $$W = \tfrac{A}{\mathrm{Tr} A} \qquad (\mathrm{Tr} = \mathrm{Trace})$$

and

(7) $$A = [\mathrm{diag}(S)]^{-1}, \quad \mathrm{diag}(X) = \text{diagonal matrix}$$

which differs from the Euclidean distance $d(U, V)$ by the replacement of I (the identity matrix) by W. Notice that components with high variability are weighted less than those of low variability. Sebestyen (1962) derived W using the sample variance instead of equation (4) for the minimization of within group distances.

Beta process. Alternatively, we may introduce the concept of a strength associated with each component of V and then increase or decrease its value depending upon whether that component correctly or incorrectly classifies an utterance. Let L be a vector of strengths associated with V. Then L_i can be changed by multiplying by a quantity β_i such that

(8) $$L_i \leftarrow \beta_i L_i.$$

Thus, $\beta_i > 1$ if i is a good component and $\beta_i = 1$ if it is bad (equation 10). The weights subsequently associated with the components of V are related to the strengths through normalization, namely,

(6a) $$W = \tfrac{A}{\mathrm{Tr}\ A}$$

where

(9) $$A = \mathrm{diag}(L).$$

Again the distance between an utterance and a representation vector V is given by

(5a) $$D(U, V) = (U - V)'W(U - V)$$

A good component is defined when an error in classification has occurred. Let V^* be the incorrectly chosen representation vector and V the true vector with which U should be identified. Then component i is good if

(10) $$(U, V)_i W_{ii}(U - V)_i < (U - V^*)_i W_{ii}(U - V^*)_i$$

and bad otherwise. Changing the strengths according to (8) is Luce's beta process, which has been studied extensively in Lamperti and Suppes (1960). We call the combined processes (theta,delta) the delta model and those of (theta,beta) the beta model.

Internal versus external learning models. Our use of the delta and beta models is at variance with what is usually done in the psychological investigation of human learning. A task is presented to subjects and a mean learning curve is obtained by measuring the average number of correct responses as a function of the presentations of the task (trial number). A theoretical model is then proposed as a possible explanation for this correct response curve, and the parameters of the model are estimated from the data. We may consider such models *external models.* In contrast, we specify explicitly the internal response processes. Consequently, the delta and beta models, as used here, may be considered *internal models.* The theoretical link between the internal-external responses of the machine is suggested through the comparison of the minimum expected distance of an utterance to its representation vector and the measured percentage misclassified of Experiment A (see below). Further theoretical investigation of this link is underway. Later we discuss the application of an external model to the learning curves of Experiment A.

IMPLEMENTATION

A call placed from a standard home telephone to an Institute number is automatically coupled with an Institute high-speed line that feeds the analog signal to our hardware filters. These filters are patterned after those used in Vicens (1969, 1970) and consist of three solid-state bandpass filters whose ranges were chosen to approximate the human formant structure—150–900 Hz, 900-2100 Hz, 2100-5000 Hz. Since the telephone frequency response is in the range 300-3000 Hz, the filters adequately span this interval. The output from each of these detectors then is amplitude and frequency sampled at 10 msec intervals and the digitized results are shipped by high-speed line to our PDP-10. This is done in real time.

The raw, digitized utterance data flow into an internal buffer until the hardware stops transmitting, which occurs whenever the input analog signal falls below a hardware-specified threshold for longer than a hardware-specified time. The buffer is dumped when the flow of input data ceases. The dumped data are then reformatted and time and amplitude normalized for input to the recognition programs in a convenient standardized form. The form is a vector of 300 numbers (3 amp + 3 freq)(100 samples/sec)(1/2 sec).

The recognition process simply entails calculating the distance from utterance vector U to each representation vector V of the vocabulary using the weighted sum of squares of component differences as previously described. The word with the minimum distance is deemed the best choice. The recognition rate is such that some 30 words per CPU second can be compared. In experiment B, where a 14-word vocabulary is used, actual recognition times in a time-sharing environment and optimal recognition times are comparable (about 1/2 sec).

Changes of the internal representation of the word spoken are accomplished by the learning algorithms based on the theory previously mentioned. Specifically, this entails modifying each component of the representation vector V and its associated strength vector $(\mathrm{diag}(S)$ or $L)$.

The programming requirements of the two models are quite minimal. The programs are written in SAIL (Stanford Artificial Intelligence Language), which is a superset of ALGOL. The full curriculum of experiment B occupies, when running, only about 35K of core memory including the child's state vector, the recognition algorithms, and the audio output routines.

The production of spoken output is presently accomplished by retrieving digitized representations of the words stored on magnetic disk and by software regeneration of the analog signal. Again this audio process is executed in real time. Consequently, the interchange between student and computer is sufficiently fluent for verbal communication in a curriculum setting.

EXPERIMENT A

Description. In an effort to provide a practical test of the two models under actual operating conditions of telephone transmission and reception, we designed and executed an experiment of two parts (A and B). In A we acquired a data base of 14 children's voices spoken over the local

Palo Alto telephone system. The telephone arrangement entailed calling a local Palo Alto number connected to the Institute from a University extension. The children, 3 girls and 11 boys, ranged in age from 6 to 13 years. A 14-word vocabulary consisting of the digits 0 (a commonly investigated set; see Sebestyen, 1962; Pols, 1971; von Keller, 1971) and command words *yes, no, repeat,* and *stop* were chosen for compatibility with an elementary-mathematics curriculum, Dial-A-Drill (Computer Curriculum Corporation, 1971). In the experiment the vocabulary was presented sequentially on a cathode-ray tube terminal and was repeated by the child into the telephone for a total of 11 repetitions of each word. The time and amplitude normalized form of each utterance was recorded on magnetic disk.

For the analysis the data were sequentially presented to the beta and delta learning models in a machine representation of actual speaking conditions. A parameter grid space was spanned for each model and the percentage of correct classifications were examined to determine the optimal parameter settings.

Learning curves of correct classification. We can represent the results of this experiment by learning curves for both the delta and beta models. To form each learning curve, we combined each of the 14 subjects and their 14 responses per trial to form a curve with ten points, with each point representing 196 subject-items on that particular trial. Since we have 11 repetitions of the vocabulary for each child (one for training), each learning curve has ten data points. The use of learning curves for speech recognition gives the investigator a quantitative measure of not only the asymptotic performance of training but also the rate of learning. Systems that perform well but take a great deal of training do not always satisfy the criterion of expediency. In contrast, systems that are set to learn quickly do not always exhibit their optimal asymptotic performance (Noda, 1971).

In Figure 2, we see that the learning curve for the delta model attained a value of about 95 percent correct responses. Also shown is a curve using the sample mean as the learning model with no component weighting which reaches 89 percent. The deviations, for the delta model curve, of percentage of correct classifications from the average across children are indicated by the ± one standard deviation error bars for each trial number. The shape of the learning curve indicates that at least five repetitions of the vocabulary are necessary for good recognition. The learning curve for the beta model (not shown) reaches 91 percent correct responses, which is lower than the delta model and similar to the sample mean.

We also examined the mean learning curve. A broad class of psy-

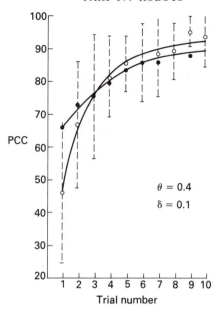

Figure 2. LEARNING CURVE FOR THE DELTA MODEL (OPEN CIRCLES) WITH THE SOLID CURVE OBTAINED FROM THE BEST FIT OF THE REGRESSION ANALYSIS ON THE THEORETICAL LEARNING CURVE. FOR COMPARISON, THE PERFORMANCE OF THE SYSTEM USING THE SAMPLE MEAN AS THE LEARNING MODEL IS GIVEN BY THE CURVE CONNECTING THE SOLID CIRCLES.

chological learning models give rise to a mean learning curve of the form (Atkinson, Bower, & Crothers, 1965)

$$(11) \qquad P(\text{correct on trial } n) = \pi - (\pi - p_0)X^{n-1}$$

where p_0 is a *guessing* parameter, π is the asymptotic recognition probability, and X is a learning parameter between zero and one.

Since our concern was the average learning curve we performed a regression analysis on the data instead of conventional, model-dependent parameter estimation. The regression analysis yielded values for π of .923 and .914 for the delta and beta models, respectively.

Parameter grid spaces. With both the delta and beta models we varied the parameter settings in stepwise fashion, theta and delta ranging from 0 to 1 in steps of .1 and beta ranging from 1 to 5 in steps of .1 to span the parameter space. For the delta model, the parameter space displays a definite and regular structure with the group maximum of 94.1 percent

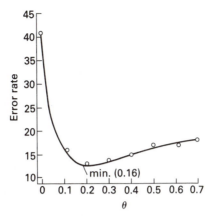

Figure 3. ERROR-RATE CURVE FOR THE THETA PROCESS ALONE. NOTE THE AGREEMENT OF THE MINIMUM WITH THE PREDICTION OF FIGURE 1 FOR THE MINIMUM OF THE EXPECTED DISTANCE OF AN UTTERANCE VECTOR TO ITS REPRESENTATION VECTOR.

at grid point $\theta = .4$, $\delta = .1$. The parameter space for the beta model is noticeably flat even out to $\beta = 5$. The group maximum is 89.8 percent at grid point $\theta = .3$, $\beta = 2.2$.

Using individual maxima, rather than the group maximum, we selected optimal parameters for each student, which raised the percent of correct classification to 95.7.

In terms of either the group or individual maxima, we found no age dependence for the percentage of correct classification with the age range of our subjects—6 to 13 years.

Theta process (experimental). Let us consider the theta process alone. Figure 3 gives the percentage misclassified as a function of theta for $\delta = 0$. We note that to the accuracy of the curve the minimum occurs at the same value of theta that the curve of Figure 1 predicts for the minimum of the expected distance of an utterance vector to its representation vector on the tenth trial. This correspondence between the minima of the percentage misclassified and the minima of the expected distance lends strength to the expectation that minimization of distance minimizes the percentage misclassified. Note that this analysis holds for an experiment consisting of a 14-word vocabulary. That is, nothing has been said concerning the alternative populations surrounding a given population.

EXPERIMENT B

Description. The follow-up experiment was designed to determine whether or not the results of A had valid correspondence to actual working conditions of real-time recognition in a child's learning situation. It entailed investigating percentage of correct classifications for a telephone CAI mathematics curriculum with audio output based on Dial-a-Drill (Computer Curriculum Corporation, 1971), which incorporates the delta model into the learning scheme. The system runs in a fully automatic mode in that a telephone call placed to an Institute number is automatically answered by a coupler that connects the outside phone line to an Institute high-speed data line. The TENEX executive program of the PDP-10 has been modified so that upon sensing the input data over the high-speed line it will log in a job and run a prespecified program.

The mathematics curriculum is extremely simple. It uses only the 14-word vocabulary described in the previous experiment, and randomly generates five types of questions (sum, difference, product, integer division, and ratios). The computer-student dialogue consisting of these arithmetic questions produces audio output that is accessed quickly from magnetic disk and transmitted to the student over the telephone.

Dial-a-Drill curriculum structure. A typical segment of the dialogue could consist of the following:

> COMPUTER: WHAT IS 7 MINUS 3?
> STUDENT: 4
> COMPUTER: 6 OVER 3 IS WHAT?
> STUDENT: 2
> COMPUTER: DID YOU SAY 0?
> STUDENT: no
> COMPUTER: SORRY, MY MISTAKE. PLEASE SAY 2.
> STUDENT: 2
> COMPUTER: THANK YOU!
>
> COMPUTER: 5 TIMES 0 IS WHAT?
> STUDENT: 5
> COMPUTER: DID YOU SAY 5?
> STUDENT: yes
> COMPUTER: TOO BAD, 5 TIMES 0 IS 0.

We used noncontingent learning for the delta model on all correct responses and also updated the representation vector on all requested repetitions.

Seven subjects from Part A each answered 100 mathematics exercises from the curriculum. The recognition mechanism was loaded with a state vector for each subject obtained from the data of Experiment A using the delta model at the optimal parameter settings.

Comparison of Parts A and B. The resulting percentage of correct classifications for the telephone curriculum averaged 13 percent below the best percentage of correct classifications for the subjects in Experiment A. The decrease in percentage of correct classifications in Part B can be accounted for by educational and psychological factors. We did not have an introductory session to acquaint the child with the system. Also, in an effort to approximate natural home conditions we gave no instructions to the child about speaking carefully. When faced with a mathematical question instead of a mere request to repeat a number, the student sometimes stammered or changed his mind in the midst of an utterance (e.g., "ONE—NO—TWO!"), which had obvious degrading effects on the percentage correctly classified. Even under these conditions the percentage of correct classifications were all above 75 percent.

CONCLUSIONS

We have constructed and tested two learning models for the purpose of computer recognition of human speech over the telephone. The delta model was found superior to the beta model in all comparisons. The delta model learning curve reached a correct recognition percentage of 94 for a 14-word vocabulary with 14 subjects ranging in age from 6 to 13 years. All the recognition was done using a standard home telephone.

We are conducting real-time recognition in a time-sharing environment without any linguistic restrictions and with relative computational simplicity. Consequently, the system can be used on any language from English to Swahili. We also tested the recognition system on an elementary mathematics curriculum entirely over the telephone. From our observations we found that the children seemed quite tolerant of nonperfect recognition and, indeed, were amused when the computer made a mistake.

We are approaching speech recognition from the direction of machine learning. We find that learning indeed occurs and is amenable to theoretical analysis for the purpose of predicting the learning performance from the structure of the model.

20

ROBOTS THAT LEARN: A TEST
OF INTELLIGENCE

One of the most notable features of current work in computer science
and artificial intelligence is the absence of a sustained effort to develop
concepts and techniques of learning. At the present time there are very
few programs in the world that exhibit any remarkable features of learning
at all. The inattention to learning is also characteristic of foundational
discussions of artificial intelligence and of cognitive science in philosophy.
The overly emphasized focus on intentionality has dominated much of
the debate between philosophers and computer scientists interested in
artificial intelligence, with that debate centering upon whether computers
can exhibit genuine intentionality or not.

Without denigrating the central importance of intentionality, for not
only human and machine behavior, but also for almost all animal behavior, learning ability is in many ways a stronger test of intelligence than
intentionality. Fortunately, in the last decade there has been a considerable interest in machine learning, and a broad range of developments in
neural networks. The hope that new computers can be built that work on
principles of the human brain has brought learning to the fore of research
in computer science.

Yet it is still true that in the discussions of the foundation of in-

*Reprinted from *Revue Internationale de Philosophie*, **44**, 1990, pp. 5-23. Written
with Colleen Crangle.

telligence, learning has not received the attention we believe it is due. What is paradoxical and fascinating about this neglect is that in American psychology up to about 1960 or 1965, the various theories of learning dominated the theoretical concerns of experimental psychologists. The development of stochastic theories of learning in the 1950s was driven by the view that it might well be possible to emulate the development of theory in physics by concentrating on relatively narrowly defined experiments, the results of which could be appropriately generalized. Unfortunately, what was not realized as much as it is today is that generalizations that lead to accurate predictions of a wide range of phenomena are also not possible for many physical theories. The recent recognition of chaos in the behavior of simple mechanical systems has shown that what seemed to be the simplest sorts of systems, e.g., three bodies interacting by gravitation, cannot be theoretically understood in any complete and deep way, if depth of understanding is meant to imply predictability of behavior. In psychology, the move was not the same as in physics. The drift was off to a new range of experiments and a set of theoretical ideas that were much less developed and had a broader cognitive sweep. The moral of the story in psychology in the last two decades is that in learning theory, as in other subjects, it is not possible to have a high degree of theoretical predictability and a broad sweep of conceptual coverage.

Luckily, as in the frequent move from physics to engineering, the possibilities of building devices that learn, as opposed to understanding the subtle way in which learning takes place in biological organisms, holds separate promise of its own. Furthermore, apart from the possibilities for constructive quantitative theory of such devices of design, there are foundational issues that cut across the consideration of artificial or biological organisms.

It is not our purpose in this short article to preach a foundational sermon about learning. What we have done rather is to try to lay out the many different kinds of learning that are required for robots that can do a variety of tasks. This classification and analysis of types of learning are meant to show how complicated the issues of theory really are and how much there is to be done. What our analysis is meant to do is to put constraints on philosophical views about artificial intelligence, as one species of intelligence. In particular we look with skepticism on claims that there are fundamental differences in principle between the learning capability of artificial devices and biological organisms. At a given level of technological development actual differences certainly exist. Everyone agrees that current robots are pretty stupid in most respects, but that widely accepted conclusion is not a proper basis for an impossibility argument. In mathematics, to give such an argument based on the current status of an open problem would be like saying that because a certain proposition has not been proved in spite of the effort of many persons, it is unprovable. The difficulty of finding a proof is good ground for conjecturing unprovability, but nothing like a proof. Those philosophers most devoted to the uniqueness of the intellectual powers of their own species are, however, unlikely to produce such fundamental impossibility arguments of a valid kind. (This conclusion of ours is an inductive one, from sampling over many years the discussions of intentionality in this same context.)

In this connection we want to compare the philosophical analysis of intentionality to the philosophical foundations of mathematics. In the case of mathematics, any philosophical foundations must reproduce an enormous amount of details regarding the foundations of arithmetic and analysis at the very least. In fact a proposal that does not provide a foundation or a serious technical reworking of classical mathematical analysis is not regarded as really worthy of discussion. Unfortunately, the philosophical analysis of intentionality is not faced with similar detailed constraints, because the technical theory of intentionality is not comparable to the development of mathematics itself. In our judgement, the detailed analysis of learning which has been made by many scientists from many different viewpoints in the last half century provides the framework for stiffening the requirements on an adequate philosophical analysis of artificial intelligence, or of intelligence in general. Ability to learn is recognized in a general way as a central criterion of intelligence by almost everyone. What is not agreed upon is any single measure of this capability to use in comparing the capabilities of different animals or, more pertinent to the rest of this discussion, in comparing human and artificial intelligence. Many aspects of the discussion are rather like the discussions of the relative power of different computer systems. Neither natural or artificial intelligence is uniformly better. Certainly everyone has to agree that when it comes to arithmetic, computers are very much better than humans, and there is something of importance about intelligence in the doing of arithmetic quickly and accurately. It has been a criterion for judging humans for centuries. On the other hand, everyone would also agree that such a criterion is by no means enough and is certainly not as important as, for example, the ability to form new concepts to solve nontrivial problems.

Philosophical debates comparing natural and artificial intelligence have played a useful role in clarifying various issues, but it is not really our own point of central concern. What we think is useful at the present stage is to understand, for example in the case of robots, what kind of tasks are important to be mastered and what types of learning can be built into robots to address these tasks. On a foundational level it is then important and useful to compare what can be expected of robots with what we do expect from humans. It is not a question of competition between robots and humans, but rather a way of gaining perspective on the potential and limitations of robots as a major kind of system using artificial intelligence.

The explicit analysis of various tasks and types of learning can also lead to positive results of a variety of kinds about what is possible and what is not possible along a given line of attack. What such positive and negative results can do is establish definite constraints on design approaches to learning by artificial devices such as robots, and at the same time rule out such theories as viable theories of human learning, when the negative results especially are violated in a clear way by actual cases of human learning.

Without attempting anything like a survey of such results, it may be useful to give an excellent example of a pair of theorems, one positive and one negative due to Gold (1967). The negative theorem is the following:

THEOREM 1 (Gold). *Regular or context-free classes of grammars are not text-learnable.* By *text-learnable* is meant that just by presenting instances of text, including auditory text, the grammar as such cannot be learned, that is, asymptotically identified. What is important about this theorem is that it shows that just comparing positive instances as such is not going to work, even when an infinite number of trials is available.

On the other hand, when an informant can be queried as to whether a given expression is grammatical or not the asymptotic results are positive.

THEOREM 2 (Gold). *Regular or context-free classes of grammars are informant-learnable.*

We want to be clear that we are not suggesting theorems like those of Gold are of real constructive help in designing artificial devices like robots. The negative results, however, can be useful in eliminating certain fantasies that are sometimes held about approaches that are thought to be possible if only more effort is applied to working them out.

Again we want to stress that we will anticipate no single theorem which establishes a decisive result giving a single unitary criterion for relative measures of intelligence. Just as we give below a classification of tasks and types of learning, we would expect a variety of theorems, not necessarily according to our classification of tasks and types of learning, but positively correlated with what we have proposed.

The second point we want to emphasize from a foundational standpoint about learning is that by moving up to a middle level of abstraction, good comparisons can be made between artificial and human intelligence, between different artificial systems or between different species of animals. This middle level of abstraction is one that moves away from the particular hardware of biological organisms, robots, or whatever other devices are contemplated, to the abstract problem of learning particular tasks without commitment to the hardware that supports the learning software. On the other hand we are not interested in the concept of abstraction that is only about "learning in general." We have in mind a level of abstraction that is in terms of hardware, but is addressed to a variety of specific learning tasks, some of which we mention in the next section.

In concluding these introductive remarks, we want to emphasize our own belief that the real outcome of success in creating robots that learn would be an interplay between human and artificial intelligence. Progress in one area should help progress in another. Above all, relatively deep positive results will almost certainly have major impact on our general theories of learning as applied to humans. Moreover, the ability to have a grasp on the fundamental processes in the case of artificial learning in a way that may not be possible for a very long time in learning of biological organisms will provide a range of new insights, but in no sense is this meant to suggest that these insights will be a substitution for new experimental and scientific findings about the learning of biological organisms.

Finally, it is very likely the case that for some considerable time progress in robotic learning will depend upon our good intuitive even if unsystematic understanding of how to instruct another person. In fact, we also hold the stronger belief that even if such models are somewhat inefficient from a learning standpoint, they will be widely used because of the importance of the simple and easy interaction between human and robot. We give in the last section a simple but already somewhat complex example of instructing a robot directly by modifying and correcting its performance with natural-language commands very similar to what would be used in dealing with another person. The complexity of even the very simple issues we deal with shows how much will need to be accomplished in the future. Moreover, we have not dealt in this example in any serious way with the details of the mechanisms of perception that are implied by the example we consider. We are assuming in our analysis of learning, however, that perceptual mechanisms will be an essential part of any sophisticated robot.

Progress in solving perceptual problems for robots and other artificial devices has already had a major impact on the theories of perception for biological organisms, especially theories of vision. It is not unreasonable to predict similar results for progress on artificial learning.

CLASSIFICATION OF TASKS AND TYPES OF LEARNING

The kinds of tasks that robots need to learn seem naturally to fall into four categories.

Programmable tasks. These are the simplest kinds of tasks, ones in which the robots would not do any genuine learning but a new program would be introduced from the outside. The new program would change the behavior of the robot but there would not be any intrinsic learning by the robot.

Explicitly instructable tasks. Tasks of this kind correspond to much instruction that is given in school, especially to young children. For example, algorithms of elementary arithmetic are taught to children in an explicit way. Many other perceptual tasks and motor skill tasks that robots must be able to perform fall under this category of explicitly instructable.

Perhaps the most important intellectual attack on learning of this kind is the synthesis of complex procedures from simpler ones by explicit instructions, preferably in English, to make such a synthesis.

Implicitly instructable tasks. A typical task of this kind is one where one would expect a robot, like a child, to learn from examples but the detailed synthesis of a new complex procedure from simpler ones already available would not be laid out. There is, of course, in the literature on learning in children, especially learning in school subjects like mathematics and science, a considerable controversy on where to put the emphasis—whether it should be on explicit or implicit instruction. That controversy in educational psychology is sometimes described as the controversy between learning by example and learning by rule. It seems important that a properly sophisticated robot should have the capacity to do both. Certainly the evidence is overwhelming that human learning uses both approaches.

The philosophical literature on rule following does not seem to have pursued the many details of the distinctions that can be made here. For example, is ordinary walking rule-following? Perhaps more pertinently, is a particular individual's style of walking, of smiling, or of talking rule-following? On the one hand, we may tend to think so, even if we cannot formulate the rule and perhaps go so far as to claim that explicit formulation is not possible. On the other hand, rules controlling a formal game like chess or tennis can be completely learned either by example or by rule.

The important point is that most perceptual and motor tasks cannot be fully described by rules, and so many essential tasks can only be implicitly instructable. Think of describing in complete physical detail the kinematics and dynamics of taking the lid off a bottle of milk and pouring out half of it.

Autonomous tasks. This category of task consists of those in which the robot must be able to adapt to a new environment, for example, without any instructional guidance from the outside. It is easy to conceptualize the kind of environmental adaptation required. Many surveillance tasks and control tasks require such capacity on the part of robots that are to have proper task flexibility.

The importance to biological organisms of autonomous learning is recognized on all sides. In the case of the extensive classical studies of animal learning by experimental psychologists the goal has often been to study learning in very controlled environments with precise regimes of reinforcement, in order to discover the general laws that should govern unsupervised learning in nature. The intended parallel to the role of experiments in physics is apparent. As we have learned in the last several decades in the study of chaotic phenomena, predictable results from restricted experiments do not necessarily generalize even in physics.

At one time learning was thought to be characterized by a rather unitary set of closely related laws but the recent literature, as well as the older literature in educational psychology in the learning of school subjects, has shown that learning really has many different aspects that are at the present stage of theoretical development not easily put in a tightly unified framework. We have identified eight kinds of learning that are important for robots. A substantial scientific literature exists on human learning of these various kinds, but it would expand this article beyond an appropriate length to provide detailed documentation. Articles in *Annual Review of Psychology* for the past two decades provide an excellent lead into the literature.

Pattern recognition. At an elementary level this is one of the areas best developed for computers at the present time. It already has many practical applications. Study of human methods of pattern recognition is very far from complete.

Parameter setting. In the literature on control mechanisms and operations research, adaptive setting of parameters is also an area that has been widely studied and in a number of practical cases implemented. The basic scientific approach to learning in this area is easily set out in terms of relatively simple mathematical models of learning. Good examples would be fine tuning of speech recognition systems for different speakers.

Procedure synthesis. The synthesis of new complex procedures from simpler procedures already available has already been remarked on. We regard this as one of the most important aspects of learning for robots. The general idea of such learning is easy to see, but what is known from the current literature on automatic program generation is that the technical problems of doing things easily and well are formidable. Of special interest are synthesis procedures based on English instructions. We believe that serious headway can be made on this problem but we do not underestimate the technical difficulties of a robust and powerful implementation.

Formalization and consolidation. Almost without exception, current computer programs have none of that marvelous flexibility of human beings to improve performance with practice. It is easy enough in a general theoretical way to conceptualize how one thinks that might be done. From a practical standpoint it is an important feature of robots that must execute well intricate tasks with serious time constraints. We believe that this is an area in which progress can be made and in which we can learn a good deal from what is known about human learning in this respect.

Acquiring facts. In theoretical discussions of learning in psychology it is often the case that little attention is paid to the simple acquisition of facts, but the acquisition of facts is an important part of human behavior. It is obviously a practical and important part of robot behavior. The conceptually difficult problem is how to integrate new facts into the body of knowledge already under the control of the robot.

There is a large pertinent literature on these problems, especially the literature on probabilistic inference and nonmonotonic logics and memory. There is less as yet done in terms of specific implementation.

In fact, to say that little attention has been paid in the psychological literature to the acquisition of facts is misleading. It is true of the learning literature, but not of the large literature on human and animal memories. Moreover, some of the most conceptually interesting recent theoretical work on memory has come from computer science (Kanerva, 1988).

Hypothesis formation. This is a classical part of learning in psychology. The advances that have been made on hypothesis learning in the last twenty years of research in cognitive psychology need to be brought into focus in order to determine to what extent there are ideas there that can be implemented in a robot. It is understood, of course, by everyone that much fundamental research is still needed.

Acquiring representations. The need for internal representations of the world outside is one of the most striking conclusions of the past decade of research in cognitive psychology. Robots like humans almost certainly need the power of acquiring such representations. A specific study needs to be made of what one can hope to implement within the framework of theoretical ideas now available and the extent to which theoretical developments have to be made to provide a sufficiently mathematically definite framework for implementation. The work on mental images seems especially important for robots moving about in the physical world.

Transfer, discrimination, and generalization. This is the classical triad of behavior learning theory. It remains important and any properly constructed robot with learning powers needs to have these classical capacities. Again there is a problem of the extent to which the classical literature on these three aspects of learning provides sufficiently definite mathematical models or computer models for implementation in a robot prototype.

Shephard (1987) has argued that any intelligent being, natural or artificial, terrestrial or not, must obey a universal law of generalization. Analysis of this kind has only begun, but in so far as the program is successful it will provide a universal theory of learning, comparable in intent to a universal theory of language.

AN EXAMPLE: LEARNING THROUGH INSTRUCTION

In this section we discuss instruction dialogues between a human user and a robot system. The purpose of each dialogue is to teach the robot a new skill or to improve the performance of a skill it already has. Our particular interest is in natural-language dialogues but the techniques we illustrate can be applied to any high-level language. Our primary purpose is to show how verbal instruction can be integrated with the robot's autonomous learning of a skill.

The learning techniques we apply are based on a set of concepts developed within mathematical learning theory and thoroughly tested in human learning (Suppes, 1959, 1964, 1989; Suppes & Crangle, 1988; Suppes & Zinnes, 1966). These techniques relate directly to skill-performance tasks in which the subject (human or robot) learns to make responses along a continuum of values. A great many tasks we would want a robot to perform fall into this category. Whenever the robot is required to position its end-effector, for instance, some specific point on a line, or on a surface, or in 3-dimensional space, must be selected.

Although the task skills and learning techniques we discuss here would form just a small part of the entire repertoire of an intelligent robot, they relate to the classification given in the previous section in several places. First, the instruction is explicit, but some autonomous generalization is also required of the robot. Furthermore, the robot improves its performance over time through practice and corrective feedback. Finally, the robot acquires a geometric representation of some aspect of the task being taught. With the addition of perceptual capabilities, more extensive representations of the tasks will be possible.

Each instruction dialogue is seen as a sequence of trials or steps. On each trial, the robot responds to a natural-language command from the operator by taking the action described in the command. This response is followed by feedback from the operator indicating whether the response was acceptable or not. The feedback is itself a natural-language command, either a congratulatory command such as *That's fine!* or *OK!* which indicates that the response was acceptable, or a corrective command such as *Further to the left!* or *That's way out!* which indicates that the response was unacceptable. When the response is acceptable we refer to it as a "hit," when unacceptable a "miss." After a hit, the operator typically repeats the original command to check that the robot has learned to respond appropriately to it.

Skills or tasks to be taught in this manner are categorized by the number of response variables involved. For many robot tasks, each response variable will have the dimension of space or the dimension of time and we therefore talk of tasks being one-dimensional or two-dimensional, and so on. A typical one-dimensional task is that of learning to select an interval on a line. This learning problem would arise, for instance, with a request to put one object on another much larger object — a box on a table, for instance — if the robot did not know the desired position for the box along the length of the table. The task becomes two-dimensional if the setback of the box from the front of the table were also to be learned. A two-dimensional learning task arises whenever the robot is directed to go somewhere (or move its arm someplace) in order to perform a specific action. For instance, if the robot is to go to a refrigerator unit or a storage cabinet to fetch something, it must stop in front of the refrigerator or cabinet at a point where it will not impede the door's opening. The set of points that are near enough to the refrigerator or cabinet but not in the way constitutes the region the robot must learn. Another two-dimensional task is the seemingly straightforward one of setting the table for dinner. This activity entails a large number of learned skills: what the orientation of each knife, fork, and spoon should be relative to the plate, how far right of the plate the dinner knife should go, how far from the edge of the table the dinner plate and side plate should be placed, and so on. A wide range of three-dimensional task skills are required in any assembly or disassembly process — placing one part in, under, or next to another part, for example. When the dimension of time is introduced, motions and sequences of motions can also be learned. We concentrate on one-dimensional tasks in the discussion that follows and we conclude with a sample instruction session.

The corrective feedback given during instruction is nondeterminate in that it does not let the robot know exactly what its response should have been. It merely indicates what the robot can do to improve its response on subsequent trials. Typically, there is no one correct response on a trial anyway but a range of acceptable responses within the target interval or region, or a range of motion paths. In addition, the operator will often not be able to provide determinate feedback. He or she will have a target interval, region, or motion in mind but will be unable to specify the endpoints of the interval or the exact coordinates of the region or the precise trajectory of the motion path. Instead the operator will use his or her judgement to determine whether the observed response appears acceptable or not. Although an essential guide to the robot's learning, that judgement is not infallible.

There are three categories of feedback: congratulatory feedback given after a hit (*Good!*, *That will do!*, *OK!*, *Fine!*, etc.), positional feedback given after a miss (*To the right!*, *Much further to the right!*, *A little bit to the right!*, *Too far right!*, *Much too far right!*, *Not that far!*, *More!*, *Again!*, *Further still!*, *A bit more!*, etc.), and accuracy feedback given after a miss (*Be more careful!*, *No need to be so cautious!*, *Slower!*, *Faster!*, *Slower next time!*, etc.). Figure 1 gives an example of an instruction dialogue. Note that there is no immediate motor response to congratulatory feedback or accuracy feedback. In either case, the robot waits for the original command to be repeated or for positional feedback. It is assumed that on each trial the state of the robot with respect to the skill being taught is represented by a probability distribution. This distribution enters into the interpretation of the original command (the one that describes the skill being learned) and it comes into play in the interpretation of all feedback from the operator. In addition, the distribution changes in response to the operator's feedback, which in turn alters the interpretation of all subsequent commands.

The distribution plays another important role. It represents the target interval, region or motion associated with the skill being learned. For one-dimensional tasks, therefore, we have a single distribution of one variable. We use the notation $k_{m,v}(x)$ where m is the mean of the distribution, v the variance, and x a value of the response variable. If on trial, n, $m = m_n$ and $v = v_n$ and the robot responds to the original command, then the probability that the response on this trial will lie between a and b is given by $\int_a^b k_{m_n,v_n}(x)dx$. After the robot has made response x_n on trial n in

		Robot's response
Original command:	*Put the wrench on the shelf!*	x_0
Positional feedback:	*Not that far left!*	x_1
Congratulatory feedback:	*That's fine!*	–
Original command:	*Put the wrench on the shelf!*	x_2
Positional feedback:	*A little further to the right!*	x_3
Positional feedback:	*More!*	x_4
Accuracy feedback:	*Be more careful!*	–
Positional feedback:	*A little to the left now!*	x_5
Congratulatory feedback:	*Good!*	–

Figure 1. EXAMPLE OF AN INSTRUCTION DIALOGUE

response to a natural-language command, i.e., after it has selected a point on the response continuum as seen by its moving to that point in response to the command, one of the two kinds of events described earlier occurs: the robot is either told that it was unsuccessful, i.e., it missed the target interval, or that it was successful, i.e., it landed within or hit the target interval. Known as a *smearing* or *smoothing* function, $k_{m,v}(x)$ has the effect of spreading the effect of feedback at a point m around m on the continuum of responses.

The question we face in designing the robot so that it learns from its interaction with the operator is as follows: What effect should a hit or miss have on the function $k_{m,v}(x)$? For one-dimensional tasks the probability distribution we use is the beta distribution. It has two parameters α and β and is defined as follows for $0 < x < 1$ (Γ designates the gamma distribution):

$$\beta(x) = \frac{\Gamma(\alpha+\beta)}{\Gamma(\alpha)\Gamma(\beta)} x^{\alpha-1}(1-x)^{\beta-1}, \qquad\qquad \alpha > 0, \quad \beta > 0.$$

The mean, m, and variance, v, of the distribution are calculated as follows:

$$m = \frac{\alpha}{\alpha+\beta}, \qquad\qquad\qquad v = \frac{\alpha\beta}{(\alpha+\beta)^2(\alpha+\beta+1)}.$$

The beta distribution has several properties that make it suitable for our purposes. First, its usefulness in models of learning has already been demonstrated in studies of human learning (Suppes, 1964; Suppes & Zinnes, 1966). In addition, with appropriate values of α and β the distribution quite effectively represents target intervals we wish the robot to learn. For instance, with $\alpha = \beta = 1$ the distribution is the uniform distribution on $(0, 1)$ and represents the intervals described by phrases such as *anywhere on the shelf* or *anywhere in front of the desk.* (The $(0,1)$ interval must, of course, be mapped onto the actual interval of interest for the task — that corresponding to the length of the shelf or the width of the desk, for instance.) The uniform distribution is also generally used to represent the state of the robot before all instruction starts. Figure 2 shows various curves for different choices of α and β along with the natural-language expressions describing the intervals associated with the curves. The response variable is plotted along the x-axis, the probability distribution along the y-axis.

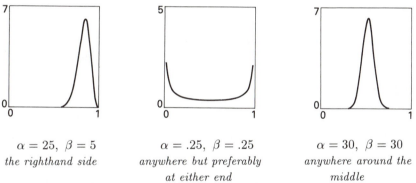

$\alpha = 25, \ \beta = 5$	$\alpha = .25, \ \beta = .25$	$\alpha = 30, \ \beta = 30$
the righthand side	*anywhere but preferably at either end*	*anywhere around the middle*

Figure 2. THE REPRESENTATION AND DESCRIPTION OF TARGET INTERVALS

We will not discuss the process by which commands are interpreted by the robot nor the control mechanisms that enable the robot to move in response to a command. Our earlier publications describe this work in some detail as implemented for the robotic aid, a device being developed for people with severe physical disabilities by the Rehabilitation and Research Center of the Veterans Administration in Palo Alto (Crangle, Liang, Suppes & Barlow, 1988; Michalowski, Crangle & Liang, 1987). A description of the link between natural-language interpretation by the robot and its probability distribution can be found in Crangle and Suppes (1989b). More general discussions of our work on natural-language understanding for robots can also be found in other publications (Crangle, 1989; Crangle & Suppes, 1987, 1989a, 1989b; Crangle, Suppes & Michalowski, 1987; Maas & Suppes, 1984, 1985; and Suppes & Crangle, 1988).

Our discussion here will focus on the effect of feedback on the probability distribution in our current model of instruction. For positional feedback, the robot must move left or right as indicated by the natural language command. The extent of this move is proportional to the variance of the current distribution. If the variance, v, is small, a move leftward or rightward will be correspondingly small. If the variance is large, the move will be correspondingly large. In addition, a correction such as *Much further left!* will generate a larger move than a correction such as *Left just a little!* Clearly, the adverbial, and sometimes the adjectival, component of the language must be allowed to make its contribution. Currently, all positional corrections fall into three equivalence classes: those that generate a relatively small move, those that generate a relatively large move, and those that generate a move of intermediate extent. Three range constraints are therefore needed, c_L, c_M, and c_S for "large," "medium," and "small" moves respectively. These constants are set for the robot and the task (in our current instruction model, $c_L = 2$, $c_M = 1$, and $c_S = .5$). The total displacement for a move is given by the product of the appropriate range constant and the square root of the variance. A request for a "large" move therefore generates a displacement of $c_L \sqrt{v}$. The robot must never move outside the $(0, 1)$ interval; extreme leftmost and rightmost points (*min x* and *max x* respectively) are therefore designated. They too are set for the robot and the task. Once the robot has moved, the mean of the distribution shifts to the robot's response and the variance is squared, which is just a simple rule in this context for reducing it.

For accuracy feedback such as *Be more careful!* which asks for greater accuracy in the robot's responses, we decrease the variance of the current distribution. For feedback such as *No need to be so cautious!* which encourages the robot to make larger adjustments, we increase the variance. We determine the appropriate amount of increase or decrease from the slope of the tangent to the variance, $f_\beta(\alpha) = (\alpha\beta)/((\alpha + \beta)^2(\alpha + \beta + 1))$, at α. Specifically, if we are at step $n + 1$ of the instruction dialogue ($v = v_n, \alpha = \alpha_n, \beta = \beta_n$), we increase or decrease v_n by the square root of the absolute value of the derivative of the variance (with respect to α) evaluated at α_n. The mean of the distribution is unaltered.

For congratulatory feedback, the mean of the distribution shifts to the robot's previous response, the response judged to be successful. The variance is squared, as it was for positional feedback, to reduce it.

In each case, whether for positional feedback, accuracy feedback, or congratulatory feedback, a new probability distribution is produced by solving for α and β given the new mean and/or the new variance. Each kind of physical robot has its own performance limits, both accuracy limits and, for a manipulator, limits of reach. We discussed above how range constants are used to determine the extent of a move to the left or right. Other performance constraints will be reflected in maximum and minimum values for α and β. In the instruction model described here, the maximum value α or β can take is 100 and the minimum is .063.

In our current instruction model, the interpretation of a command giving accuracy feedback during instruction does not generate any motor response from the robot. Nor does the interpretation of a command giving congratulatory feedback. Both forms of feedback change the probability distribution, however. Note that we are assuming congratulatory feedback to be thoroughly effective in that the mean and variance of the distribution always change in response to the feedback. It is common practice to introduce a learning parameter θ into the model and to assume that with probability θ feedback is effective on any trial (the distribution changes), and with probability $(1 - \theta)$ it is not effective (the distribution stays the same). We have in effect set θ to 1 in our instruction model. We made this choice in part because of the explicitness of verbal instructions — congratulatory feedback, in particular, is hard to misconstrue — but also because we are assuming that the robot's total cognitive resources are dedicated to learning from instruction. This assumption would change if the robot were simultaneously attending to some other task. For example, in many applications the robot might be monitoring the status of a process for an emergency condition to which it had to respond.

Whenever the original command is given during instruction, the robot's response is generated by sampling the (0,1) interval using the current probability distribution. If $k_{m_n,v_n}(x)$ is the current probability distribution (step n of the instruction dialogue has just been completed), a response to the original command at step $n + 1$ is generated by the following sampling procedure: Take the cumulative probability distribution $K_n(x) = \int_0^x k_{m_n,v_n}(x)dx$, generate a random number y between 0 and 1, and find x such that $K_n(x) = y$. This x gives the robot's response at step $n + 1$.

We now show a sample instruction session. The one-dimensional skill being taught to the robot is where to stop in front of double swing doors so that the robot can enter through the righthand door when it opens. The doors swing out; the robot is on the outside. Taking the combined width of the two doors as the interval of interest, we want to teach the robot to select any point somewhat to the left of the midpoint. The robot begins with the beta distribution initialized to $\alpha = \beta = 1$. In Figure 3 we show at each step what the distribution looks like before the step, what the instruction is at this step, what the robot's motor response x is (if there is indeed a response), and what the resulting distribution looks like.

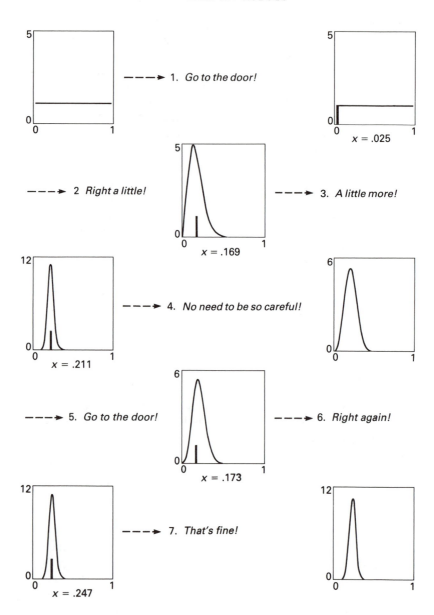

Figure 3. A SAMPLE INSTRUCTION SESSION

The robot's response is indicated by a vertical bar. The response variable is plotted along the x-axis, the probability distribution along the y-axis. The y-axis on each graph goes from 0 to 5 or the least integer greater than the maximum distribution value plotted. The data and the setup are very similar to those in the human experiment reported in Suppes and Zinnes (1966).

In Crangle and Suppes (1989b) we have discussed a different one-dimensional learning model, one that is computationally more efficient but which gives less immediate response to the instruction. Our current concerns are to extend the models to two-dimensional and higher tasks and to extend the range of natural-language expressions used in instruction. An important overall change we plan is to allow feedback to be given, and to take effect, while the robot is still responding to the previous command. So, for instance, if the robot is moving forward in response to a command from the operator, the operator should be able to say *That's far enough!* and have the robot stop where it is. Not only is this form of feedback entirely natural, it should provide faster learning.

This example illustrates another point that is fundamental in our thinking about the learning capabilities of artificial devices. For our own convenience in instructing them they need more than universal principles of learning implemented. They need to understand English or another human language, and to react to instruction in ways we feel comfortable with. We therefore obviously start thinking about instructing robots in a style that is modeled after the way we instruct children in school or apprentices on the job. As robots become much cleverer, i.e., much more intelligent, our approach to instructing them will in all likelihood evolve into something more like a dialogue with a colleague, but that time still seems quite distant.

21

ROBOTIC MACHINE LEARNING OF NATURAL LANGUAGE

We first describe, even if intuitively and somewhat too briefly, our probabilistic theory of natural-language learning. More than most other current approaches, we have taken a very explicit route that uses principles of association and generalization derived from classical psychological principles, but as will be evident enough, the theory we develop is in no sense something that falls within the domain of classical behavior theory — if for no other reason than the extensive internal memory structure we introduce.

A second point we want to emphasize is that our theory has been developed to simultaneously learn English, German, and Chinese. For quickness of reference, what we have to say here will almost entirely be in terms of English, but it is important to stress that the ideas set forth have been tested as well on the learning of German or Chinese. The third general point is that we have also carried out an implementation on Robotworld, a robotic system now extensively used in experimental work in robotics in the United States.

There are two other general points about our work to be stressed. Our viewpoint toward language learning is in most respects semantical, rather than syntactical. The formation of grammatical forms, a key aspect of

Reprinted from L. Lam and V. Naroditsky (Eds.), *Modeling Complex Phenomena.* New York, NY: Springer-Verlag, 1991. Written with Michael Böttner and Lin Liang.

our theory, is driven by a uniform set of semantic categories, rather than grammatical categories, which may vary from one language to another. The final general point that is an important limitation on the theory as currently developed is that it is solely concerned with language comprehension. Nothing that we have to say in this paper will deal in a serious way with problems of language production.

The rest of this section is focused on an intuitive description of the learning theory we develop. Section 2 states in systematic fashion our learning axioms, and Section 3 outlines the structure of the internal representations we use. Section 4 develops the theory of mean learning curves, with emphasis on their complexity. Section 5 describes briefly our grammar generation process. In Section 6, the final one, we sketch the relation between our work and some similar projects.

Background cognitive and perceptual assumptions.

Before formulating the learning principles we use, we need to state informally certain assumptions about the cognitive and perceptual capacities of the class of robots we work with.

Internal language. We assume the robot has a fully developed internal language which it does not learn. It is technically important, but not conceptually fundamental that in the present case this language is LISP. (For more details, see Section 3.) What must be emphasized is that when we speak here of the *internal language* we refer only to the language of the internal representation, which is itself a language of a higher level of abstraction, relative to the concrete movements and perceptions of the robot. There are several other internal language modules that were either developed by us or that come in the software package with Robotworld. It has been important to us that most of the machine learning of a given natural language can take place through simulation of the robot's behavior just at the level of the language of the internal representation.

Objects, relations and properties. We furthermore assume the robot begins its natural language learning with all the basic cognitive and perceptual concepts it will have. This means that our first language learning experiments are pure language learning. For example, we have assumed that the spatial relations frequently referred to in all the languages we consider in detail are already known to the robot. This is of course contrary to human language learning. There is good evidence, for example, that most children do not understand the relations of left and right, even at the age of thirty-six months when their command of language is already extremely good.

Actions. What was just said about objects and relations applies also to actions. There are in the internal language symbols for a fixed set of possible actions. The problem is only to learn their particular linguistic representation in a given language. What has been said about objects, relations, properties and actions constitutes a permanent part of memory of the robot. This memory does not change and is therefore not involved in the learning theory we formulate. (It is obvious that in a more general theory we will want to include learning of new concepts, etc.)

Intuitive description of the process of learning.

What we want to describe now is the process of learning in terms of the various events that happen on a given trial. First, the robot begins a trial in a given state of memory. There are three parts of this memory that are changed due to learning. The first is the association relation between words of a given language and internal symbols that represent denotations of members of categories in the internal representation language. For example, the action of putting will be represented internally, let us say, by the symbol $p and will have three different linguistic representations in English, German and Chinese. The problem will be to learn in each language what word is properly associated with the internal representation $p. The same process of association must be learned for objects, properties and spatial relations. But knowing such associations is not enough, contrary to some naive theories of associationism.

It is also important to have grammatical forms. We will not try to lay out everything about grammatical forms that we have in our fully stated theory, but it will be useful to give some examples. Consider the verbal command *Get the screw!* This would be an instance of the grammatical form *A the O!*, where *A* is the category of actions and *O* is the category of objects. As might be expected we do not actually have just a single category of actions, but several subcategories, depending upon the number of arguments required, etc. The central point here, however, is the nature of a grammatical form. The grammatical forms are derived only from actual instances of verbal commands given to the robot. Secondly, associated with each grammatical form are the first associations of words with their internal interpretations. So for example, if *Get the screw!* had been the first occurrence on which the grammatical form just stated was generated, then also stored with that grammatical form would be the associations *get* $\sim$ $g, *screw* $\sim$ $s—we use $g for the internal symbol corresponding correctly to *get*, and sometimes we just use *g* for *get*, as in the trees shown later. Similar conventions apply to other denoting words. The third part of memory that varies is the short-term memory that holds a given verbal command for the period of the trial on which it is effective. This memory content decays and is not available for access after the trial on which a particular command is given. So at the

beginning of the trial this short term buffer is empty, but is filled by the
second step in learning. A verbal command is given to the robot and it
is held in memory in the short-term buffer.

The third step is for the learning program to look up the associations
of the words in the verbal command that has been given. If associations
exist for any of the words, the categories of the associations, which are
the categories of the internal interpretation, are also retrieved. The categories are substituted for the associated words and an effort is then made
to generate recursively the resulting grammatical form. For example, if
mistakenly the word *get* had been associated to $s, the internal symbol
for *screw,* and *screw* had been associated with $g, the internal symbol
for *get,* then the grammatical form that would have been generated and
now found upon a second occurrence of the verbal command would be
O the A! Now if there were no such grammatical form generated, once
the associations were formed such a grammatical form would be created
by the process of generalization which is used to generate grammatical
forms.

When a grammatical form is stored in memory, also associated with
this grammatical form in memory is its internal representation. This is an
important part of the memory that changes with learning as well. If the
grammatical form is generated, the internal representation is then used
to execute the verbal command that has been given. If the command is
executed correctly then the robot is ready for a new learning trial.

The important case of learning is when no grammatical form can be
generated recursively from the grammatical forms in memory to match
the form of the given verbal command. In this case the robot is unable
to make a response. The correct response must be coerced. On the basis
of this coercion, a new internal representation is formed. At this point
the critical step comes of a probabilistic association between words of
the verbal utterance and the internal denoting symbols of the new internal representation. This probabilistic association is assumed to be on a
uniform probability basis. For example, if within the new internal representation there are two internal denoting symbols and there are no words
in the verbal command associated to either of these internal symbols, and
there are four words in the verbal command, then any pair of the four
will be as likely to be associated with the pair of internal symbols as any
other pair. After this association is made, a new grammatical form is
generated, and possibly because of the new associations at least one of
the old grammatical forms is deleted, for one of the axioms states that
a word or internal denoting symbol can have exactly one association, so
when a new association is formed for a word any old associations must
be deleted. (This strong all-or-none uniqueness assumption is undoubt-

edly too restrictive for actual language learning by children, but there is some evidence that it holds in the early stages of language learning. It works very well for the kind of systematic language and grammar we are concerned to use in robot discourse, at least at these early stages of development.) With the new associations formed and old ones possibly deleted, the robot is ready for the next trial in a new state of memory.

LEARNING PRINCIPLES

To facilitate the statement of principles governing the learning process just described, certain notational conventions are useful. First, generally we use Latin letters to refer to verbal commands or their parts, whatever the natural language, and we use Greek letters to refer to internal representations or their parts. The letters a, a_i a'_i, etc. refer to words in a verbal command, and the Greek letters $\alpha, \alpha_j, \alpha'_j$, etc. to internal denotations. The Roman letter t, as well as t_i, t'_i refer to terms of a verbal command, and correspondingly τ, τ_i, τ'_i to terms of an internal representation, i.e., in the present setup, LISP expressions. The symbols s, s' and $s(t)$, showing that t is a term of s, refer to entire verbal commands, and correspondingly $\sigma, \sigma', \sigma(\tau)$ for entire internal representations. Grammatical forms — either sentential or term forms — are denoted by g or also $g(X)$ to show a category argument of a form; correspondingly the internal representations of a grammatical form are denoted by γ or $\gamma(X)$. We violate our Greek-Latin letter convention in the case of semantic categories or category variables X, X', Y, etc. We use the same category symbols in both grammatical forms and their internal representations. We now turn to the statement of the axioms of learning in intuitive form. We will give a more formal and explicit statement in a longer version. We have delayed until Section 5 statement of the most technical axioms, the one on term association and the one on term form substitution, which are used to generate recursive grammatical forms.

Axioms of learning.

1. (*Association by contiguity*). If verbal command s is contiguous with a coerced action that has internal representation σ, then s is associated with σ, i.e., in symbols $s \sim \sigma$.

2. (*Probabilistic association*). If $s \sim \sigma, s$ has a set $\{a_i\}$ of denoting words not associated with any internal denotations of σ, and σ has a set $\{\alpha_j\}$ of internal symbols not associated with any words of s, then an element of $\{a_i\}$ is uniformly sampled without replacement from $\{a_i\}$, at the same time an element of $\{\alpha_j\}$ is correspondingly

sampled, and the sampled pair are associated, i.e., $a_i \sim \alpha_j$. Sampling continues until there is no remaining a_i or α_j.

3. (*Prior associations*). When a word in a verbal command or an internal symbol is given a new association (Axiom 2), any prior associations of that word or symbol are deleted from memory.

4. (*Forgetting associations of commands*). An association $s \sim \sigma$ of a verbal command s is held only temporarily in memory until the action represented internally by σ is executed or until all word associations are complete (Axiom 2).

5. (*Correction procedure*). If a verbal command s cannot be executed or is executed incorrectly with $s \sim \sigma$, and if a correct response with internal representation σ' is coerced, then s is associated with σ' for application of Axiom 2.

6. (*Category generalization*). If $t \sim \tau$ and $\tau \in X$ then $t \in X$.

7. (*Grammatical form generalization*). If $g(t) \sim \gamma(\tau)$, $t \sim \tau$ and $t \in X$, then $g(X) \sim \gamma(X)$.

8. (*Term specification*). If $g(X) \sim \gamma(X)$, $t \sim \tau$ and $t \in X$, then $g(t) \sim \gamma(\tau)$.

9. (*Memory trace for a grammatical form*). The first time a grammatical generalization (X) (Axiom 7) is formed, the word associations on which the generalization is based are stored with it.

10. (*Elimination of a grammatical form*). If a memory-trace association $a \sim \alpha$ for g is eliminated (Axiom 3), then g is eliminated from memory.

INTERNAL REPRESENTATION

In this section we sketch the language of internal representation we use. As already mentioned, for purposes of our robotic application we use LISP as the language of representation. Internal representations will therefore be LISP-expressions. A LISP-expression is any string $(E_1...E_n)$ where $E_1, ..., E_n$ are either atoms or LISP-expressions.

The fragments of natural language are meant to instruct a robot to perform elementary actions in a simple environment. Due to the capabilities of the robot the tasks are moving around in a 3D space and opening (and closing) the gripper. The environment is a collection of objects like screws, nuts, washers, plates, sleeves of a limited number of colors, sizes, and shapes. Commands that typically arise in this context are: *Open the gripper! Move forward! Turn to the left! Put a nut on the screw! Go to the right! Go to a screw! Lift the black screw which is left of the plate! Drop the washer! Get a nut! Put the nut near the screw! Turn the screw to the right!* and *Stop!*

So we will have in our internal language symbols for each content word of a command. The English command

Get the screw!

will have the following internal representation

$$(fa1 \; \$g \; (io \; (fo \; \$s \; *)))$$

where $\$g$ and $\$s$ occur in the internal language as counterparts of the content words *get* and *screw* of English. The internal representation has three more symbols: *fo, io,* and *fa1.* These symbols are abbreviations of the semantic operations *focus on object, identify object,* and *form action.* The purpose of these operations is to provide what we think is the procedural structure of the natural language command mentioned above. Before it can perform the action denoted by $\$g$, the robot has to determine the object of this action. The object that is intended to become the object of the action is returned by the operation *io.* This operation identifies one out of a set of objects. The input for *io* is a set of objects. This set of objects is the output of the operation *fo*: it takes a property and the set of objects in the robot's environment and returns a set of objects. The environment is represented by the symbol $*$ in our internal language. In our example, the property the environment is checked for is the presence of screws. The procedure *io* then takes this set of all screws of the environment as input and returns a unique screw from this set. This particular screw together with the action $\$g$ is the input of the operation *fa1.*

According to the semantic category of the object that it denotes, each expression of our language of internal representation belongs to a certain category. In the above example, e.g., the expression *screw* belongs to the category property, more specifically: object property, and the expression *get* belongs to the category action. The list of categories is as follows: Property (P), Spatial Relation, (R), Action (A), and Object (O).

Semantic categories can be further divided into subcategories. The category R of spatial relations is split up into subcategories R_1 and R_2

depending on whether its elements are binary or ternary relations. Associated with the category R is the semantic operation *form property*,
abbreviated as fp, which takes a relation and object as input and returns
a property — examples are to be found in Section 5. The category A
of actions has six subcategories depending on the valency of the action
expression. So we have a subcategory for actions that do not require any
complement like *stop*, another subcategory for actions that require an object like *get*, a subcategory for actions that require a region as complement
like *go* as in, e.g. *Go near a plate!* a subcategory for actions that require
both an object and a region like *put*, as in e.g. *Put a screw near a plate!* a
subcategory for actions that require a direction as their complement like
turn, as in e.g. *Turn left!*, and a subcategory for actions that require both
an object and a direction as in e.g. *Move the screw forward!* Unlike the
subcategories of relations the subcategories of actions are not disjoint, i.e.
an action like, e.g. *turn*, occurs in more than one category.

MEAN LEARNING CURVES

Mean learning curves represent the average of all possible individual learning curves. Such mean curves have several important features. First, by
abstracting from the details of individual curves they give a sense of the
rate of learning to be expected. In the case of machine learning this can
be important in evaluating the practicality of the theory proposed. If
the expected number of trials to reach a satisfactory learning criterion is
2^{1000}, for example, then the theory is not of practical interest. Second,
mean learning curves typically exhibit a theoretical robustness that is not
characteristic of individual learning curves, i.e., in probabilistic terms, individual sample paths. Many minor theoretical details and, on occasion,
major ones as well, can be modified without changing the theoretically
predicted mean learning curve. A familiar example is the mean learning curve that is identical for one-parameter linear incremental models
of simple learning and one-parameter all-or-none Markov models of the
same phenomena. The predicted individual sample paths are completely
different for the two kinds of models, but the mean learning curves are
identical.

Simple examples.
     Because in simple cases we can theoretically compute the mean learn-
ing curve from the axioms of Section 2, we will first consider some very
simple cases that give an insight into how things work. These cases are
so simple that no actual simulation is needed. In the analyses we shall
consider, let

m = number of distinct commands,

d = number of distinct denoting words,

k = average number of denoting words per command.

In the case of parameter k, in the simple cases we consider k is not simply an average but a constant.

Case 1. $m = 3$, $d = 3$, $k = 1$. An example of this case would be simply three commands: *Forward!*, *Left!* and *Right!* Because we have three commands and three denoting words with one occurring in each sentence, it is quite easy to derive the mean probability of a correct response on trial n. It is apparent at once under the condition that we present a block of the three commands randomly sampling without replacement. Such a block is then repeated under the same conditions, that is, random sampling without replacement. In the present case, it is clear that on first appearance each command is not understood by the robot and consequently there will be no response, so the probability of a correct response is zero. Secondly, once each command is given it will be learned with probability 1. In this framework it is easy to see that

$$p_1 = p_2 = p_3 = 0 \text{ and } p_n = 1,$$

for $n \geq 4$. In this case it is also obvious that the mean curves and the individual learning curves are identical because of the simplicity of the situation.

Case 2. $m = 2$, $d = 2$, $k = 2$. An example of this case would be the two commands: *Left, right!* and *Right, left!* It is easy to write down the tree structure from which we may derive the mean learning curve. Let ℓ stand for *left* and r for *right*. We use a superscript $*$ to show the probabilistic association is correct. Thus $\ell^* r^*$ means the command *Left, right!* has the correct associations for both denoting words, whereas $\underline{\ell}\,\underline{r}$ means both words have wrong associations. The command given at the beginning of a trial is shown in parentheses. So $(\ell\, r)$ at a vertex means the trial in question begins with the command *Left, right!* In the tree (see Figure 1) we start trial 1 this way, followed by the two branches of possible associations, each branch having probability $\frac{1}{2}$, in accordance with Axiom 2. But in this special case, no further branching after the first trial need occur for the responses are always correct. So $p_1 = 0$ and $p_n = 1$ for $n \geq 2$. It will clarify the way the grammatical forms work to explain this result. For this purpose we examine only the right branch of the tree. On this branch on trial 1 the associations are the incorrect ones.

$$\ell \sim \$r \ ,$$

$$r \sim \$\ell \ .$$

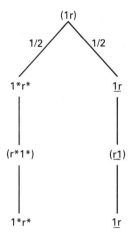

Figure 1. Partial Tree for Case 2. $m = d = k = 2$.

The grammatical form generated and its associated internal form are then:

$$A'\ A\ \sim\ I(A, A')$$

Note that on the left branch this reversal of order of A and A' between the grammatical form and the associated internal form does not take place:

$$A\ A'\ \sim\ I(A, A') \qquad (\textit{left branch})$$

But in this restricted, simple-minded but instructive, example, either grammatical form works for its branch.

The next two cases are perhaps the simplest which have a nontrivial mean learning curve, i.e., the curve is not just a $(0,1)$ step function.

Case 3. $m = 2, d = 3, k = 2$, *but with a special sampling procedure.* The special sampling procedure is that rather than randomizing separately each block of two commands, the two commands are simply alternated on each trial. An example of this case would be: *Get nut!* and *Get screw!*, which, following our earlier notation, we abbreviate as $g\,n$ and $g\,s$ respectively. The association tree in the first few trials has the form shown in Figure 2 (where the choice of which command to begin with clearly does not matter). So, as is easily shown on trial n

$$P_n\ (\text{Correct response})\ = 1 - \frac{1}{2^{n-2}},$$

for $n \geq 2$, and thus $p_1 = 0$, $p_2 = 0$, $p_3 = \frac{1}{2}$, $p_4 = \frac{3}{4}$, etc.

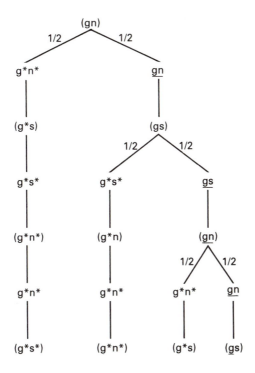

Figure 2. Partial Tree for Case 3. $m = k = 2$, $d = 3$.

In this simple case the curve has a degenerate S-shape, the first point of inflection being at the end of trial 2.

Case 4. $m = 2$, $d = 3$, $k = 2$, but with our standard sampling assumption. The same language example as was used for Case 3 will work here. The only change from Case 3 is in the sampling procedure. We now sample independently to begin each block of 2 trials. Thus every odd-numbered trial has probability $\frac{1}{2}$ of being either of the two commands, and the even-numbered trials must be different from the preceding trial, i.e., must sample the other command with probability 1. The tree, from which we can derive the mean learning curve, for four trials is shown in Figure 3. What is unusual and conceptually important about this case is the *decrease* in the mean probability of a correct response on trial 4. It is a consequence of the wrong association in trial 2 of $g\,s$ not producing an incorrect response on trial 3 when the command *Get screw!* is repeated,

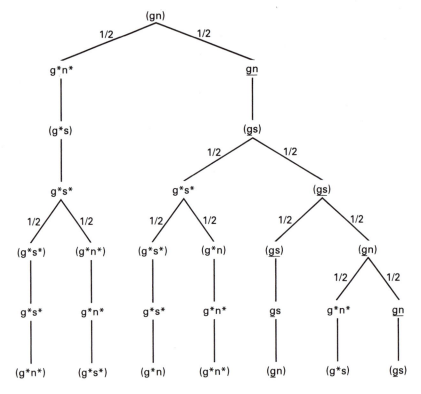

Figure 3. PARTIAL TREE FOR CASE 4. $m = k = 2$, $d = 3$.

but leading to an incorrect response on trial 4 when the command *Get nut!* is given. This pattern of decrease, though of smaller magnitude, occurs on every even-numbered trial. In simple homogeneous stimulus conditions such decreases in the mean learning curve never occur, but they are natural and to be expected in language learning. See Figure 4 for the mean learning curve of Case 4. Numerically, the theoretical results are $p_1 = p_2 = 0$, $p_3 = .75$, $p_4 = .625$, $p_5 = .891$, $p_6 = .859$, $p_7 = .953$, $p_8 = .941$.

Case 5. $m = 4$, $d = 2$, $k = 1$. From the parameters of this case it sounds simpler, but in fact it has, as well as two denoting words, two non-denoting words, namely *please* and *now*. Thus the four sentences of Case 5 are *Please forward!*, *Now stop!*, *Now forward!* and *Please stop!* What makes the learning more complicated in this case and is an important concept for language learning is that the number of denoting symbols in

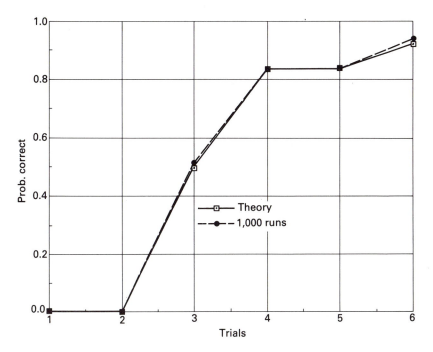

Figure 4. MEAN LEARNING CURVE FOR CASE 4. $m = k = 2$, $d = 3$.

the internal representation is in every case, that is, in each of the four sentences less than the number of the words in the sentence. So there is a special opportunity for wrong associations to be formed. As might be expected the learning is slower and more complicated. The results of the first four trials are shown partially in Figure 5. Only part of the tree is drawn because it is too large to put on the page, but enough is given to show the nature of the results. In the tree the word that has no association to a denoting symbol at a given stage is printed at the corresponding node. Thus at the top of the figure, just below (pf), we print *please*, because *forward* has the only association. A star next to an input command like (nf) indicates a correct response with probability one. The mean learning curve is the following: $p_1 = p_2 = 0$, $p_3 = .083$, $p_4 = .3125$, $p_5 = .727$, $p_6 = .686$, $p_7 = .718$, $p_8 = .794$. This case also exemplifies the nonmonotonic mean learning curve found already in Case 4. In Section 4.3 we examine more carefully with a number of further examples the learning curves when nondenoting words are present. The examples considered there are too difficult to compute theoretically.

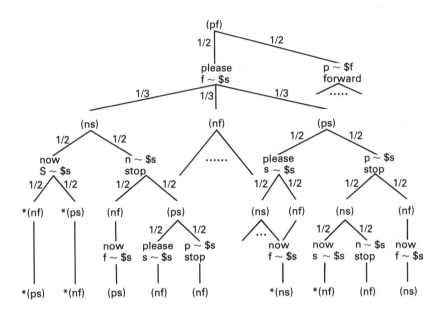

Figure 5. PARTIAL TREE FOR CASE 5. $m = 4$, $d = 2$, $k = 1$.

Computational complexity of mean learning curves.

The concept of mean learning curves has been central to the study of learning in experimental psychology over many decades. In almost all experimental situations in which mean learning curves were computed theoretically, as well as presented empirically, it was quite easy in stochastic models of learning familiar from the 1950s and 1960s to compute explicitly the functional form of the mean learning curve for computation of mean learning curves in some zero-sum, two-person situations see (Suppes and Atkinson, 1960), and for the case of a continuum of responses (Suppes, 1959). Even though the conceptual framework in the two-person situations analyzed in detail in Suppes and Atkinson and the situation with a continuum of responses seem complicated, the methods developed for simpler cases generalize nicely to these more complex ones. The situation unfortunately is quite different in the case of our theory of language learning. The mean learning curves have the same conceptual meaning and force but they are computationally intractable. It is easy to see why in the examples considered in the previous section. The number of verbal commands is extremely small and from a linguistic standpoint uninteresting. On the other hand, even small samples of language lead to computationally unmanageable mean learning curves. For example, in our first robot demonstration which has Robotworld assembling a small shelf structure with nuts and bolts we trained the robot on a sample of 360 sentences in each of three languages, English, German, and Chinese, with each language being treated independently. Without introducing any further special assumptions, several cycles of random sampling without replacement of the entire block of 360 trials is needed for learning with a low error rate. But as is easy to see, just from the assumptions about random sampling of the verbal commands, the number of branches of the tree structure is $m!^n$, where m is the number of distinct verbal commands and n is the number of blocks of trials, each block consisting of 360 trials. Even for our restricted experiment this is an intractable computation. We can state this result more generally in the form of a theorem.

THEOREM. *With random sampling of sentences, the computation of mean learning curves is not feasible.*

The proof of this theorem is immediate from the considerations just introduced above. Notice that the computations are far from polynomial as a function of m.

Conjecture: polynomial bound on mean learning rate.

Although we are not able to theoretically compute the mean learning curves, extensive simulation studies lead us to the conjecture that in almost all cases the learning rate for a sample of m verbal commands is a polynomial function of m. We have in mind here that a rather strict criterion of learning is used, for example, at least 95 per cent correct responses.

Here are the series of examples which led us to the conjecture that in most cases the learning rate is quite fast even though the simplest theoretical concept, the mean learning curve, cannot be theoretically computed. In these examples, adding to our earlier notation of m, d *and* k, we now add $\bar{d} =$ the number of distinct nondenoting words and $\bar{k} =$ average number of nondenoting words per command. As in the previous cases, in the examples we consider, k *and* $\bar{k}$ are not simply averages but constants. We also emphasize that the concept of denoting here is a very restrictive one. It refers just to denotations within the semantic categories of actions, objects, properties and spatial relations. It is important that we have not had to introduce this concept in our learning axioms, but the presence of a large number of nondenoting words certainly has an impact on the rate of learning. This is why we have constructed examples with as many nondenoting as denoting words. We number the cases consecutively with those of Section 4.1.

Case 6. $m = 4$, $d = 4$, $\bar{d} = 4$, $k = 2$, and $\bar{k} = 2$. An example of this case are the following four verbal commands:

Please turn the screw!
Please get a nut!
Now turn the nut!
Now get a screw!

The mean learning curve for this case, computed numerically from the average of 100 individual sample paths, 1000 and 10,000 is shown in Figure 6. All three curves reach the criterion of 95 per cent correct in about 24 trials. Because the learning rate took more than 2^m trials to learn the four sentences we were hopeful that larger examples would confirm this rate, but the next cases show that this was mistaken.

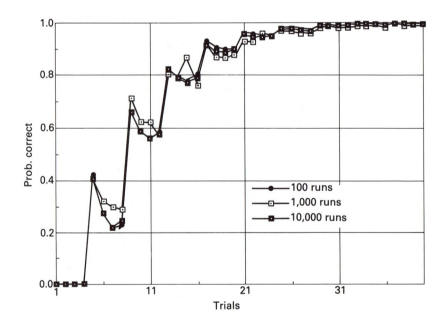

Figure 6. Mean Learning Curve for Case 6. $m = d = \bar{d} = 4$, $k = \bar{k} = 2$.

Case 7. $d = \bar{d} = m = 6$, $k = \bar{k} = 3$, $r = 2$. Here we have also introduced a new parameter r to indicate the number of times each word is repeated in the sentences being learned. We held r to 2 in the expectation that this would slow the rate of learning. In this example and in the others that follow, we artificially constructed the language to test the rate of learning, although of course it would be possible to substitute real natural language commands for the structures we have studied. But the point here is really just to study the rate of learning for given types of structures. So we lay the language out artificially using the capital letters at the beginning of the alphabet for denoting words and the capital letters at the end of the alphabet for nondenoting words. Here are the two sets of words:

$$d \;=\; |A\ B\ C\ D\ E\ F\,|$$
$$\bar{d} \;=\; |U\ V\ W\ X\ Y\ Z|$$
$$U\ C\ Y\ F!$$
$$X\ A\ V\ E!$$
$$W\ B\ V\ F!$$
$$W\ C\ Z\ E!$$
$$X\ B\ Y\ D!$$
$$U\ A\ Z\ D!$$

The learning rate for this case with 1000 individual runs as the basis for the numerical computation for the mean learning curve is shown in Figure 7. As can be seen from the figure, approximately, the 95 per cent criterion of learning was reached on average in about 42 sentences which is far below 2^6.

Case 8. $d = \bar{d} = m = 8$, $k = \bar{k} = 4$, $r = 2$. The artificial sentences were constructed in the same fashion as Case 7. The mean learning curve constructed from 1000 individual sample paths is shown in Figure 8 where the criterion of 95 per cent correct is reached at about trial 61.

Case 9. $d = \bar{d} = m = 6$, $k = \bar{k} = 3$, $r = 3$. In this case we increase the number of words in each sentence to 6 with each word therefore occurring in three sentences. In two of the sentences each denoting word cooccurred with the same nondenoting symbol, but not in the third occurrence. We conjectured that this positive correlation, which was of course not 1, would lead to a slowing of the learning, but it did not have a large effect as can be seen from Figure 9. The 95 per cent criterion of learning is reached at about 50.

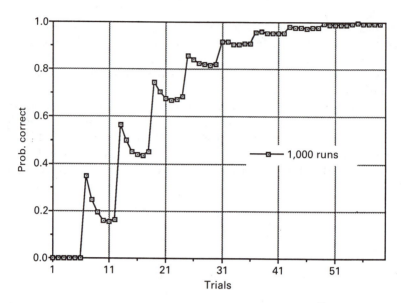

Figure 7. MEAN LEARNING CURVE FOR CASE 7. $d = \bar{d} = m = 6$, $k = \bar{k} = 3$, $r = 2$.

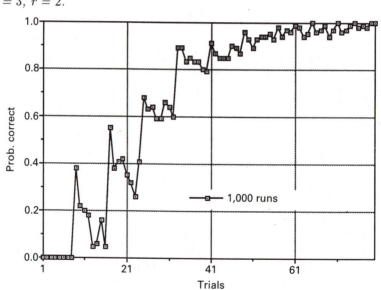

Figure 8. MEAN LEARNING CURVE FOR CASE 8. $d = \bar{d} = m = 8$, $k = \bar{k} = 4$, $r = 2$.

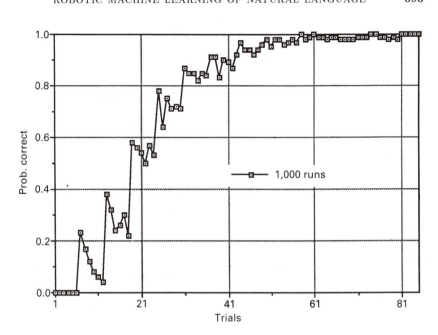

Figure 9. MEAN LEARNING CURVE FOR CASE 9. $d = \bar{d} = m = 6$,
$k = \bar{k} = 3$, $r = 3$.

Case 10. Finally, we describe briefly, the results for the learning of 360 Chinese verbal commands as preparatory training for executing the demo construction by Robotworld. The learning results were essentially the same for English and German. In this case the learning was accelerated by labeling the nondenoting words, which were then excluded from the probabilistic association. With this labeling, as can be seen from Figure 10, the 95 per cent learning criterion was reached in less than one cycle of the 360 verbal commands, in fact, in about 100 trials.

GRAMMARS CONSTRUCTED FROM LEARNING

We have just begun the investigation of the complexity of the grammars that can be learned from a finite sample of sentences. In a sense, it is better to say grammars *constructed* from learning a fragment of a language, because the robot does not learn an explicitly formulated grammar fixed in advance, but constructs one on the basis of learning some initial fragment of a language. In any case, we present here only our first preliminary results. We stress that the context-free grammars are generated

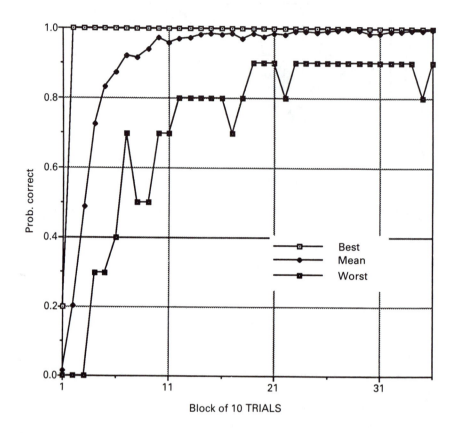

Figure 10. Mean Learning Curve for Case 10. 360 Chinese Commands.

from scratch from the grammatical forms learned by the robot. They are not constructed as an extension or transformation of a grammar given *a priori*, i.e., prior to, and separate from, the learning process.

To generate the grammars we consider here, two more axioms are needed, the recursive axiom for term association mentioned earlier but not stated, and the axiom of term form substitution.

To make the statement explicit we need to extend the earlier discussion of association of words with internal symbols to include terms, both of the given natural language and of the internal language. Formally, such associations of terms, $t \sim \tau$, were already used in the statement of Axioms 6, 7 and 8, but explicit explanation was given only for the special case of t being a single word, all that is essential for developments up to this point.

First, if σ is an internal representation of a verbal command s, the denoting *atoms* of σ are just the LISP atoms that are the internal symbols associated with words of the given natural language. By a *minimal* LISP *expression* of σ containing given occurrences of denoting atoms $\alpha_1..., \alpha_n$ in σ we mean the smallest LISP expression, as defined at the beginning of Section 3, containing the atoms $\alpha_1...\alpha_n$. For example, if $s = Get$ *the red screw!*, and $s \sim \sigma = $ *(fa*1 *\$g (io (fo \$r (fo \$s *))))*, then there are three occurrences of denoting atoms in σ, one of *\$g*, one of *\$r* and one of *\$s*. The minimal LISP expression containing the one occurrence of *\$s* in σ is *(fo \$s *)*.

We postulate a separate association relation for terms — separate from the association relation $\sim$, although we use the same symbol. Thus stored in memory we have

$$screw \sim (fo\ \$s\ *)$$

for the above example, as well as *screw* $\sim$ *\$s* stored under word associations. Also a string w of s is *purely nondenoting (relative to $s \sim \sigma$)* iff no word of w corresponds to each occurrence of a denoting atom in σ.

Second, given a verbal command $s \sim \sigma$ and t a nonempty substring of s, the string t is a *pure complete denoting term (relative to s and σ)* iff (i) every word of t has a corresponding association to each occurrence of a denoting atom in σ, where *corresponding* means in accordance with the association relation $s \sim \sigma$, (ii) the minimal LISP expression τ containing the corresponding occurrences of all the denoting atoms of σ associated with words of t contains no other occurrences of denoting atoms. We now use the concepts introduced to state the recursive axiom needed.

Axiom 11. (*Term Association*). First, if $a \sim \alpha$ and $\alpha \ \epsilon \ P$ then $a \sim$ *(fo α *)*. Second, if (i) *awt* is a substring of a verbal command s, with $s \sim \sigma$ and $a \sim \alpha$, (ii) t is a pure complete denoting term of s with $t \sim \tau$, (iii) w is the substring, possibly empty, of purely nondenoting words between a and t, (iv) $\tau'(\alpha, \tau)$ is the minimal LISP expression of σ containing the occurrences of α and denoting atoms in τ corresponding to occurrences of denoting words in t and $\tau'(\alpha, \tau)$ contains no other occurrences of denoting atoms, then $awt \sim \tau'(\alpha, \tau)$. Moreover, the axiom applies to *twa* with w following t.

In the first part of the Axiom it follows from the category structure of the internal language that *(fo α ∗) ε O*. Notice that as the axiom is formulated in terms of pure complete denoting terms, in the intended correct associations, the atomic term *red* in the command *Get the red screw!* discussed above, is not a pure complete denoting term because the minimal LISP expression containing this occurrence of $r also contains $s.

Axiom 11 is the most complicated single association axiom we state and one that in a further development of the theory might be simplified. We did not find easy ways to do so in the present setup. On the other hand, the role of Axiom 11 is central to recursively generating from a fixed finite sample of sentences a grammar that can comprehend an infinite set of sentences.

We also need a new axiom on substituting term forms, so, for example, in the sentential form A_1 *the O!* we can substitute the form *PO* for *O*, since $PO \subseteq O$, to derive the new sentential form A_1 *the P O!*

Axiom 12. (*Term form Substitution*). If $g(X) \sim \gamma(X)$, $g'(Y_1,...,Y_n) \sim \gamma'(Y_1,...,Y_n)$ and $g'(Y_1,...,Y_n) \subseteq X$, then $g(g'(Y_1,...,Y_n)) \sim \gamma(\gamma'(Y_1,...,Y_n))$.

We can illustrate the nature of the recursion by the following example, where we show the LISP internal representations, as well as use both Axioms 11 and 12.

Assume that, on the basis of previous experience, memory holds the following associations:

$$O \quad \sim \quad (fo\ P\ *) \tag{1}$$
$$A_1\ the\ O! \quad \sim \quad (fa1\ A_1\ (io\ O)) \tag{2}$$
$$get \quad \sim \quad \$g \tag{3}$$
$$screw \quad \sim \quad \$s \tag{4}$$
$$plate \quad \sim \quad \$p \tag{5}$$
$$black \quad \sim \quad \$b \tag{6}$$
$$large \quad \sim \quad \$l \tag{7}$$
$$right \quad \sim \quad \$r \tag{8}$$

Coerce:

$$Get\ the\ black\ nut! \quad \sim \quad (fa1\ \$g\ (io\ (fo\ \$b\ (fo\ \$n\ *)))) \tag{9}$$
$$Get\ the\ nut\ which\ is\ large! \quad \sim \quad (fa1\ \$g\ (io\ (fo\ \$l\ (fo\ \$n\ *)))) \tag{10}$$
$$Move\ right\ of\ the\ nut! \quad \sim \quad (fa1\ \$m\ (fp\ \$r\ (io\ (fo\ \$n\ *)))) \tag{11}$$

Term association applied to (9) - (11) yields:

$$nut \quad \sim \quad (fo \; \$n \; *) \tag{12}$$

$$black \; nut \quad \sim \quad (fo \; \$b \; (fo \; \$n \; *)) \tag{13}$$

$$nut \; which \; is \; large \quad \sim \quad (fo \; \$l \; (fo \; \$n \; *)) \tag{14}$$

$$right \; of \; the \; nut \quad \sim \quad (fp \; \$r \; (io \; (fo \; \$n \; *))) \tag{15}$$

G.F.generalization applied to (13) - (15) yields:

$$P \; O \quad \sim \quad (fo \; P \; O) \tag{16}$$

$$O \; which \; is \; P \quad \sim \quad (fo \; P \; O) \tag{17}$$

$$R \; of \; the \; O \quad \sim \quad (fp \; R \; (io \; O)) \tag{18}$$

Category generalization applied to (12) - (15) yields for purposes of computation, but not permanent storage in memory:

$$nut \quad \in \quad O \tag{19}$$

$$black \; nut \quad \in \quad O \tag{20}$$

$$nut \; which \; is \; large \quad \in \quad O \tag{21}$$

$$right \; of \; the \; nut \quad \in \quad P \tag{22}$$

From (19) - (22) we get

$$P \subseteq O \tag{23}$$

$$P \; O \subseteq O \tag{24}$$

$$O \; which \; is \; P \subseteq O \tag{25}$$

$$R \; of \; the \; O \subseteq P \tag{26}$$

The robot can use (1) - (26) to comprehend the more complex sentence

$$Get \; the \; black \; screw \; which \; is \; right \; of \; the \; large \; plate! \tag{27}$$

The parsing and comprehension of (27) will use the small context-free grammar $\mathcal{G}$ generated by association and coercion as expressed by (1), (2), (16) - (18) and (23) - (26), which written in conventional style, but without rewrite rules for terminal words, has the following form:

$$A \quad \rightarrow \quad A_1 \; the \; O!$$
$$O \quad \rightarrow \quad P$$
$$O \quad \rightarrow \quad P \; O$$
$$O \quad \rightarrow \quad O \; which \; is \; P$$
$$P \quad \rightarrow \quad R \; of \; the \; O$$

The first step is to identify the words of (27) that are associated with internal denoting symbols. The second step is to look up the categories of the denoting words of (27) to generate the grammatical form

$$A_1 \ the \ P_1 \ P_2 \ which \ is \ R \ of \ the \ P_3 \ P_4! \qquad (28)$$

Using a standard parser for the context-free grammar $\mathcal{G}$ we are able to parse (28). We then use (1), (2) and (16) - (18) to generate the internal representation form associated with (28):

$$(fa1 \ A_1 \ (io \ (fo \ P_1 \ (fo \ (fp \ R \ (io \ (fo \ P_3 \ (fo \ P_4 \ *))))(fo \ P_2*))))) \quad (29)$$

Term specification then yields at once the internal representation of (27), which the robot can then execute:

$$(fa1 \ \$g \ (io \ (fo \ \$b \ (fo \ (fp \ \$r \ (io \ (fo \ \$l \ (fo \ \$p \ *))))(fo \ \$s \ *))))) \quad (30)$$

COMMENTS ON RELATED WORK

We have found most relevant to our research the work of Jerome Feldman and his colleagues at the International Institute for Computer Science in Berkeley and the work of Jeffrey Siskind at M.I.T.

With the approach of the Feldman group (Feldman, Lakoff, Stolcke, Hollback Weber, 1990; Hollbach Weber and Stolcke, 1990; Regier, 1990; Stolcke, 1990) we share the focus on spatial-relation talk. But whereas the Feldman group's work is restricted to the study of static spatial relations in a 2D environment we, in addition, consider dynamic spatial relations in a 3D environment. As a consequence, the Feldman group has no action expressions.

While the Feldman group deals with the acquisition of spatial relations, we are focussed exclusively on the learning of the words for spatial relations and assume that the notion has already been acquired by the learner.

Feldman's group emphasizes the point that their learning proceeds without negative evidence (in line with standard views on the child's learning of syntax but not actions); in contrast we use coercion to correct mistaken actions on the part of the learner. Correspondingly they use a declarative language; we use an imperative language.

The Feldman group does not presuppose any linguistic knowledge on the part of the learner and grammatical knowledge is acquired by a connectionist framework. In our approach, some linguistic knowledge is presupposed by endowing the learner with an internal language.

Siskind (1990) develops an operational system MAIMRA (extended to DAVRA in Siskind (1991a,b)) that serves the purpose of language understanding, language generation, and language acquisition at the same time. Since our system so far does not handle generation, we only focus our comparison on the acquisition and comprehension aspects of Siskind's systems.

MAIMRA constrains the possible mappings between natural language structures and scenarios (sequences of events) by three components: a parser, a linker, and an inference component.

Unsurprisingly, there are certain features shared by Siskind's systems and our system:

1. Both systems use verbal and non-verbal stimuli as input (visual scenario and description of it in MAIMRA's case, verbal stimulus and coerced action in our case).

2. Since language learning requires presence of what the talk is about there is a common focus on visually perceptible scenes and spatial relations in particular.

3. The systems have both been exposed not only to English but also to structurally more remote languages such as Japanese or Chinese and Russian (our system).

4. Both approaches make essential use of an internal language.

5. Both systems require that each word has only one meaning (Siskind's "monosemy constraint" matches our "non-ambiguity requirement").

On the other hand, the systems are different in at least the following respects:

1. Siskind's systems acquire language on the basis of assertions, our system on the basis of commands.

2. Siskind's approach appears to require a distinction between denoting words and non-denoting words such as determiners. Initially, our system had a similar condition but we succeeded in removing it.

3. In addition to monosemy but unlike Siskind we also require that a denotation can be expressed by only one word (our "non-synonymity constraint" of Axiom 3).

4. The output of Siskind's system is a lexicon (list of words with syntactic category and meaning) in the case of MAIMRA and a lexicon together with $\bar{X}$-parameters of the language to be learnt in DAVRA, whereas our output is a grammar of the language to be learned.

5. As the language of conceptual representation Siskind uses a language of predicate logic without quantifiers but with variables (to handle argument relationships and arities) whereas our internal language is a variable-free procedural language.

6. Whereas our system assumes a one-one-mapping between denoting words of the verbal command and the denotations in the semantic representation (verbal input is semantically exhaustive), Siskind here can afford a more relaxed position: the verbal input can be less informative than the non-verbal input.

7. We start from a high-level internal representation whereas Siskind works his way up from simple state-descriptions to event-descriptions by his inference component. Siskind's takes the bootstrapping objective more seriously.

8. Siskind uses the lexical categories noun, verb, and preposition. We have carefully avoided the use of syntactic categories and have used semantic categories of action, object, property, and spatial relation instead. Of course there is a close correspondence between semantic categories and syntactic categories but there are also many examples where relations occur as adjectives as in, e.g. *the left hole*, adverbs as in, e.g. *Turn left!*, or nouns as in, e.g. *Go to the left!* and not as prepositions. We also believe that the syntactic categories are more varied from language to language than semantic categories.

We are not suggesting that the work we have just reviewed encompasses everything relevant to our own efforts, for there are many research activities worldwide on the learning of natural language. Undoubtedly we and others working on machine learning of natural language will continue to benefit in many ways from the continuing research of linguists on the structure of language and of psychologists on the acquisition of language.

REFERENCES

Abramson, N., & Braverman, D. (1962). Learning to recognize patterns in a random environment. *Trans. IRE Information Theory*, **IT-8**, 58-63.

Almog, J. (1984). Would you believe that? *Synthese*, **58**, 1-37.

Anderson, T.W. (1958). *An introduction to multivariate statistical analysis*. New York: Wiley.

Atkinson, R.C., Bower, G., & Crothers, E. (1965). *An introduction to mathematical learning theory*. New York: Wiley.

Barwise, J., & Perry, J. (1983). *Situations and attitudes*. Cambridge, Mass: MIT Press.

Biro, J. (1979). Intentionalism in the theory of meaning. *The Monist*, **62**, 238-58.

Bolinger, D. (1967). Adjectives in English: Attribution and predication. *Lingua*, **18**, 1-34.

Brown, R. (1970). *Psycholinguistics: Selected papers*. New York, NY: Free Press.

Brown, R. (1973). *A first language*. Cambridge, MA: Harvard University Press.

Bush, R.R., & Mosteller, F. (1955). *Stochastic models for learning*. New York: Wiley.

Carnap, R. (1947). *Meaning and necessity*. Chicago: University of Chicago Press.

Chomsky, N. (1956). Three models for the description of language. IRE *Transactions on Information Theory*, **IT-2(3)**, 113-24.

Chomsky, N. (1957). *Syntactic structures.* The Hague: Mouton.

Chomsky, N. (1959). On certain formal properties of grammars. *Information and Control,* **2**, 137-67.

Chomsky, N. (1969). Quine's empirical assumptions. In D. Davidson & K.J. Hintikka (Eds.), *Words and objections, essays on the work of W.V. Quine.* Dordrecht.

Chomsky, N. (1975). *Reflections on language.* New York: Pantheon Books.

Chomsky, N., & Halle, M. (1968). *Sound pattern of English.* New York: Harper and Row.

Church, A. (1950). On Carnap's analysis of statements of assertion and belief. *Analysis,* **10**, 97-9.

Church. A. (1954). Intensional isomorphism and identity of belief. *Philosophical Studies,* **5**, 65-78.

Computer Curriculum Corporation (1971). *Dial-a-Drill.* Mountain View, CA: Computer Curriculum Corporation.

Crangle, C. (1984). *A computational approach to lexical meaning.* Doctoral dissertation, Stanford University, Stanford, CA.

Crangle, C. (1989). On saying *Stop* to a robot. *Language and Communication,* **9**, 23-33.

Crangle, C., Liang, L., Suppes, P., & Barlow, M. (1988). Using English to instruct a robotic aid: An experiment in an office-like setting. In *Proceedings of the International Conference for the Advancement of Rehabilitation Technology, 25-30 June, 1988* (pp. 466-7). Montreal: Resna.

Crangle, C., & Suppes, P. (1986). *Studies in natural semantics for instructable robots: Part 1.* (Tech. Rep. 308). Stanford: Institute for Mathematical Studies in the Social Sciences, Stanford University, Stanford, CA.

Crangle, C., & Suppes, P. (1987). Context-fixing semantics for instructable robots. *International Journal of Man-Machine Studies,* **27**, 371-400.

Crangle, C., & Suppes, P. (1989a). Geometrical semantics for spatial prepositions. In P. French, T. Uehling, & H. Wettstein (Eds.), *Midwest Studies in Philosophy Vol. 13, Contemporary Perspectives in the Philosophy of Language II* (pp. 399-422). Notre Dame, IN: University of Notre Dame Press.

Crangle, C., & Suppes, P. (1989b). Instruction dialogues: Teaching new skills to a robot. In G. Rodriguez & H. Seraji (Eds.), *Proceedings of the NASA Conference on Space Telerobotics, Vol. 5* (JPL Publication 89-7) (pp. 91-101). Pasadena, CA: Jet Propulsion Laboratory, Calif. Instit. of Technology.

Crangle, C., Suppes, P., & Michalowski, S. (1987). Types of verbal interaction with instructable robots. In G. Rodriguez (Ed.), *Proceedings of the Workshop on Space Telerobotics*, (JPL Publication 87-13, Vol. II) (pp. 393-402). Pasadena, California: NASA Jet Propulsion Laboratory, Calif. Instit. of Technology. [Chapter 17, this volume]

Cresswell, M.J. (1978). Prepositions and points of view. *Linguistics and Philosophy*, **2**, 1-41.

Curry, H.B., Hindley, J.R., & Seldin, J.P. (1972). *Combinatory logic*, Vol. 2. Amsterdam: North-Holland.

Earman, L.D., Hayes-Roth, F., Lesser, V. R., & Reddy, D. R. (1980). The Hearsay-II speech-understanding system: Integrating knowledge to resolve uncertainty. *ACM Computing Surveys*, **12**, 213-253.

Eifermann, R. (1961). Negation: A linguistic variable. *Acta Psychologia*, **18**, 258-73.

Estes, W.K., & Suppes, P. (1959). Foundations of linear models. In R.R. Bush & W.K. Estes (Eds.), *Studies in mathematical learning theory.* Stanford, CA: Stanford University Press.

Feldman, J. A., Lakoff, G., Stolcke, A. & Hollbach Weber, S. (1990). *Miniature language acquisition: A touchstone for cognitive science.* International Computer Science Institute, Berkeley, CA.

Feldman, S.S. (1972) Children's understanding of negation as a logical operation. *Genetic Psychology Monograph*, **85**, 3-49.

Floyd, R. (1967). Assigning meanings to programs. In *Mathematical aspects of computer science* (pp. 19-32). Proceedings of the 19th Symposium in Applied Mathematics, American Mathematical Society, Providence, Rhode Island.

Ford, N.L., Batchelor, B.G., & Wilkins, B.R. (1970). A learning scheme for the nearest neighbor classifier. *Information Science*, **2**, 139-57.

Frege, G. (1960). *Translations from the philosophical writings of Gottlob Frege* (P. Geach and M. Black, Eds.) Oxford: Blackwell.

Frege, G. (1879). *Begriffschrift: Eine der arithmetischen nachgebildete Formelsprache des reinen Denkens.* Halle, Germany: L. Nebert.

Frick, I.B. (1978). Manual for Standard LISP on the DECsystems 10 and 20. Utah Symbolic Computation Group, Memo TR-2.

Furth, H.G., & Youniss, J. (1965). The influence of language and experience on discovery and use of logical symbols. *British Journal of Psychology*, **56**, 381-90.

Gammon, E.M. (1973). A syntactical analysis of some first-grade readers. In K.J.J. Hintikka, J.M.E. Moravcsik, and P. Suppes (Eds.), *Approaches to natural language*. Dordrecht: Reidel.

Geach, P.T. (1968). *Reference and generality* (amended edition). Ithaca: Cornell University Press.

Ginsburg, S., & Partee, B. (1969). A mathematical model of transformational grammars. *Information and Control*, **15**, 297-334.

Gleitman, L.R., & Gleitman, H. (1970). *Phrase and paraphrase: Some innovative uses of language*. New York: Norton.

Gold, E.M. (1967). Language identification in the limit. *Information and Control*, **10**, 447-74.

Grice, H. P. (1957). Meaning. *The Philosophical Review*, **66**, 377-88.

Grice, H.P. (1968). Utterer's meaning, sentence-meaning, and word-meaning. *Foundations of Language*, **4**, 225-42.

Grice, H.P. (1969). Utterer's meaning and intentions. *The Philosophical Review*, **78**, 147-77.

Grice, H.P. (1982). Meaning revisited. In N.V. Smith (Ed.), *Mutual Knowledge*. London: Academic Press.

Hearn, A. C. (1969). *Standard LISP*. Stanford Artificial Intelligence Project Memo, AI-90. Stanford, CA: Stanford University Press.

Hilbert, D., & Ackermann, W. (1950). *Principles of mathematical logic*. New York: Chelsea.

Hill, S.A. (1961). *A study of the logical abilities of children*. Unpublished doctoral dissertation, Stanford University, Stanford, CA.

Hintikka, J. (1973). Grammar and logic: Some borderline problems. In K.J.J. Hintikka, J.M.E. Moravcsik, & P. Suppes (Eds.), *Approaches to natural language*. Dordrecht, Holland: Reidel.

Hobbs, J.R., Croft, W., Davies, T., Edwards, D., & Laws, K. (1986). Commonsense metaphysics and lexical semantics. In *Proceedings of the 24th Annual Meeting of the Association for Computational Linguistics, New York, June 10-13, 1986* (pp. 231-40). Morristown, NJ.

Hollbach Weber, S. & Stolcke, A. (1990). *L₀: A testbed for miniature language acquisition.* (Tech. Rep. No. TR-90-010). International Computer Science Institute, Berkeley CA.

Hopcroft, J.E., & Ullman, J.D. (1969). *Formal languages and their relation to automata.* New York: Addison-Wesley.

Inhelder, B., & Matalon, B. (1960). The study of problem solving and thinking. In P. Mussen (Ed.), *Handbook of research methods in child development* (pp. 421-55). New York: Wiley.

Inhelder, B., & Piaget, J. (1964). *The early growth of logic in the child: Classification and seriation.* New York: Harper and Row.

Irons, E.T. (1961). A syntax directed compiler for ALGOL 60. *Communications of the Association of Computing Machinery, 4,* 51-5.

Isard, S.D. (1974). What would you have done if . . . ? *Theoretical Linguistics, 1,* 233-55.

Jespersen, O. (1940). *A modern English grammar: On historical principles. V. Syntax* (Vol. 4). London: Allen and Unwin.

Kanerva, P. (1988). *Sparse distributed memory.* Cambridge, MA: MIT Press.

Kaplan, D. (1978). On the logic of demonstratives. *Journal of Philosophical Logic, 8,* 81-98.

Kaplan, R., & Bresnan, J. (1982). Lexical-functional grammar: A formal system for grammatical representation. In J. Bresnan (Ed.), *The mental representation of grammatical relations* (pp. 173-281). Cambridge, MA.

Klein, F. (1893). Vergleichende Betrachtungen über neuere geometrische Forschungen. *Mathematische Annalen, 43,* 63-100.

Knuth, D.E. (1968). Semantics of context-free languages. *Mathematical Systems Theory, 2,* 127-45.

Krantz, D. H., Luce, R. D., Tversky, A., & Suppes, P. (1971). *Foundations of measurement* (Vol. 1). New York: Academic Press.

Lamperti, J., & Suppes, P. (1960). Some asymptotic properties of Luce's Beta learning model. *Psychometrika, 25,* 233-41.

Lewis, D. (1970). General semantics. *Synthese, 22,* 18-67.

Lindenbaum, A., & Tarski, A. (1934-5). Über die Beschränktheit der Ausdrucksmittel deduktiver Theorien. In *Ergebnisse eine mathematischen Kolloquiums,* fascicule 7, 15-22.

Lowerre, B.T., & Reddy, R. (1980). The HARPY speech understanding system. In W.A. Lea (Ed.), *Trends in Speech Recognition*. Englewood Cliffs, NJ: Prentice-Hall.

Luce, R.D. (1956). Semi-orders and a theory of utility discrimination. *Econometrica*, **24**, 178-191.

Luce, R. D., & Suppes P. (1965). Preference, utility and subjective probability. In R.D. Luce, R.R. Bush, & E. H. Galanter (Eds.), *Handbook of Mathematical Psychology*, (Vol. 3) (pp. 249-410). New York: Wiley.

Maas, R.E., & Suppes, P. (1984). A note on discourse with an instructable robot. *Theoretical Linguistics*, **11**, 5-20.

Maas, R.E., & Suppes, P. (1985). Natural-language interface for an instructable robot. *International Journal of Man-Machine Studies*, **22**, 215-240. [Chapter 16, this volume]

McCarthy, J. (1963). A basis for a mathematical theory of computation. In P. Braffort & D. Hirschberg (Eds.), *Computer programming and formal systems* (pp. 33-70). Amsterdam.

McLaughlin, G.H. (1963). Psychologic: A possible alternative to Piaget's formulation. *British Journal of Educational Psychology*, **33**, 61-67.

Michalowski, S., Crangle, C., & Liang, L. (1987). A natural-language interface to a mobile robot. In G. Rodriguez (Ed.), *Proceedings of the Workshop on Space Telerobotics*, (JPL Publication 87-13, Vol. II) (pp. 381-392). Pasadena, California: NASA Jet Propulsion Laboratory, Calif. Instit. of Technology.

Michalski, R.S., Carbonell, J.G., & Mitchell, T.M. (1983). *Machine learning: An artificial intelligence approach*. Palo Alto, CA: Tioga Publishing Company.

Miller, G.A., & Johnson-Laird, P.N. (1976). *Language and perception*. Cambridge, MA: Harvard University Press.

Montague, R. (1970). English as a formal language. In B. Visentini et al. (Eds.), *Linguaggi nella società e nella tecnica*. Milan.

Montague, R. (1973). The proper treatment of quantification in ordinary English. In K.J.J. Hintikka, J.M.E. Moravcsik, & P. Suppes (Eds.), *Approaches to natural language*. Dordrecht: Reidel.

Noda, A. (1971). An inconsistency between the rate and the accuracy of the learning method. In K.S. Fu (Ed.), *Pattern recognition and machine learning*. New York: Plenum Press.

Parsons, T. (1970). Some problems concerning the logic of grammatical modifiers. *Synthese*, **21**, 320-34.

Partee, B. (Ed.). (1976). *Montague grammar*. New York: Academic Press.

Piaget, J. (1957). *Logic and psychology*. New York: Basic Books.

Pols, L. (1971). Real-time recognition of spoken words. *IEEE Transactions on Computers*, **C-20**, 972-78.

Poncelet, J.V. (1822). *Traité des propriétés projectives des figures*. Paris: Bachelier.

Quine, W. V. O. (1960). *Word and object*. Cambridge: Massachusetts Institute of Technology Press.

Quine, W. V. O. (1970). Methodological reflections on current linguistic theory. *Synthese*, **21**, 386-398.

Quine, W. V. O. (1974). Truth and disquotation. In L. Henkin et al. (Eds.), *Proceedings of the Tarski Symposium (Proceedings of Symposia in Pure Mathematics*, 25). Providence, RI: American Mathematical Society.

Rawson, F.L. (1973). *Set-theoretical semantics for elementary mathematical language* (Tech. Rep. 220). Stanford: Institute for Mathematical Studies in the Social Sciences, Stanford University, Stanford, CA.

Regier, T. (1990). *Learning spatial terms without explicit negative evidence.* (Tech. Rep. No. TR-90-057). International Computer Science Institute, Berkeley CA.

Reiser, J.F. (Ed.). (1976). *Sail.* Stanford Artificial Intelligence Laboratory Memo, AIM-289. Stanford, CA: Stanford University.

Russell, B. (1905). On denoting. *Mind*, **14**(NS), 479-93.

Saarinen, E. (1982). Propositional attitudes are not attitudes towards propositions. *Intensional logic: theory and applications* (Moscow, 1979), 130-62, *Acta Philosophica Fennica*, **35**, Soc. Philos. Fenn., Helsinki.

Salomaa, A. (1971). The generative capacity of transformational grammars of Ginsburg and Partee. *Information and Control*, **18**, 227-32.

Schiffer, S. R. (1972). *Meaning*. London: Oxford University Press.

Scott, D., & Suppes, P. (1958). Foundational aspects of theories of measurement. *Journal of Symbolic Logic*, **23**, 113-28.

Searle, J. R. (1980). The background of meaning. In J. R. Searle, F. Kiefer, & M. Bierwisch (Eds.), *Speech act theory and pragmatics* (pp. 221-32). Dordrecht: Reidel.

Sebestyen, G.S. (1962). *Decision-making processes in pattern recognition.* New York: Macmillan.

Shephard, R. (1987). Towards a universal law of generalization for psychological science. *Science,* **237**, 1317-23.

Shieber, S.M., Pereira, F.C.N., Karttunen, L., & Kay, M. (1986). *A compilation of papers on unification-based grammar formalisms: Parts I and II* (Report No. CSLI-86-48). Center for the Study of Language and Information, Stanford University, Stanford, Calif.

Siegel, M. (1976). *Capturing the adjective.* Unpublished doctoral dissertation, University of Massachusetts.

Siskind, J. M. (1990). *Acquiring core meanings of words, represented as Jackendoff-style conceptual structures, from correlated streams of linguistic and non-linguistic input.* (Proceedings of the 28th Annual Meeting of the Association of Computational Linguistics).

Siskind, J. M. (1991a). *Dispelling myths about language bootstrapping.* (AAAI Spring Symposium Workshop on Machine Learning of Natural Language and Ontology), Stanford University, Stanford, CA.

Siskind, J. M. (1991b). *Naive physics, event perception, lexical semantics and language acquisition.* (AAAI Spring Symposium Workshop on Machine Learning of Natural Language and Ontology), Stanford University, Stanford, CA.

Smith, N. (1974). A question-answering system for elementary mathematics. (Tech. Rep. No. 227), Institute for Mathematical Studies in the Social Sciences, Stanford University, Stanford, CA.

Smith, R.L., Jr. (1972). *The syntax and semantics of ERICA.* (Tech. Rep. No. 185). Stanford: Institute for Mathematical Studies in the Social Sciences, Stanford University, Stanford, CA.

Smith, R. L. , Jr., & Rawson, F.L. (1976). *A multi-processing model of natural language understanding.* In *Proceedings of the 1976 COLING Conference at Ottawa, Canada, June 1976.*

Smith, R.L., Jr., Rawson, F.L., & Smith, N.W. (1974). CONSTRUCT: In search of a theory of meaning. *Proceedings of the 1974 Conference of the Association for Computational Linguistics.* Amherst, Mass.

Statman, R. (1974). *Structural complexity of proofs.* Ph.D. dissertation, Stanford University, Stanford, California.

Stolcke, A. (1990). *Learning feature-based semantics with simple recurrent networks.* (Tech. Rep. No. TR-90-015). International Computer Science Institute, Berkeley, CA.

Suppes, P. (1957). *Introduction to Logic.* New York: Van Nostrand Reinhold.

Suppes, P. (1959). A linear model for a continuum of responses. Reprinted in R.R. Bush & W.K. Estes (Eds.), *Studies in Mathematical Learning Theory* (pp. 400-14). Stanford: Stanford University Press.

Suppes P., (1960). *Axiomatic Set Theory*, New York: Van Nostrand. (Paperback edition. New York: Dover, 1972).

Suppes, P. (1964). Some current developments in models of learning for a continuum of responses. (Discrete Adaptive Processes Symposium, American Institute of Electrical Engineers, June 1962.) *The Institute of Electrical and Electronics Engineers Transactions on Applications and Industry,* **83**, 297-305.

Suppes, P. (1965). On the behavioral foundations of mathematical concepts. *Monographs of the Society for Research in Child Development,* **30**, 60-96.

Suppes, P. (1966). Probabilistic inference and the concept of total evidence. In J. Hintikka & P. Suppes (Eds.), *Aspects of inductive logic* (pp. 49-65). Amsterdam: North-Holland.

Suppes, P. (1969). Stimulus-response theory of finite automata. *Journal of Mathematical Psychology,* **6**, 327-55.

Suppes, P. (1970). Probabilistic grammars for natural languages. *Synthese,* **22**, 95-116.

Suppes, P. (1973a). Congruence of meaning. *Proceedings and Addresses of the American Philosophical Association,* **46**, 21-38. [Chapter 1, this volume]

Suppes, P. (1973b). Semantics of context-free fragments of natural languages. In K.J.J. Hintikka, J.M.E. Moravcsik, & P. Suppes (Eds.), *Approaches to natural language* (pp. 370-94). Dordrecht: Reidel.

Suppes, P. (1973c). Facts and fantasies of education. In M.C. Wittrock (Ed.), *Changing education: Alternatives from educational research* (pp. 6-45). Englewood Cliffs, NJ: Prentice-Hall.

Suppes, P. (1974a). On the grammar and model-theoretic semantics of children's noun phrases. *Problèmes Actuels en Psycholinguistique,* **206** 49-60. [Chapter 7, this volume]

Suppes, P. (1974b). The semantics of children's language. *American Psychologist,* **29**, 103-14. [Chapter 6, this volume]

Suppes P. (1976). Elimination of quantifiers in the semantics of natural language by use of extended relation algebras. *Revue International de Philosophie*, **117-118**, 243-59. [Chapter 11, this volume]

Suppes, P. (1979). Variable-free semantics for negations with prosodic variation. In E. Saarinen, R. Hilpinen, I. Niiniluoto & M.P. Hintikka (Eds.), *Essays in Honour of Jaakko Hintikka* (pp. 49-59). Dordrecht: Reidel. [Chapter 12, this volume]

Suppes, P. (1980). Procedural semantics. In R. Haller & W. Grassl (Eds.), *Proceedings of the Fourth International Wittgenstein Symposium, August 28 - September 2, 1979, Kirchberg, Austria* (pp. 27-35). Vienna: Hölder-Pichler-Tempsky. [Chapter 13, this volume]

Suppes, P. (Ed.). (1981). *University-level computer-assisted instruction at Stanford: 1968-1980.* Stanford, CA: Institute for Mathematical Studies in the Social Sciences, Stanford University, Stanford, CA.

Suppes, P. (1982a). The plurality of science. In P. Asquith & I. Hacking (Eds.), *PSA 1978* (Vol. 2). East Lansing, MI: Philosophy of Science Association.

Suppes, P. (1982b). Variable-free semantics with remarks on procedural extensions. In T.W. Simon & R.J. Scholes (Eds.), *Language, Mind, and Brain.* Hillsdale, NJ: Lawrence Erlbaum. [Chapter 14, this volume]

Suppes, P. (1984). A puzzle about responses and congruence of meaning. *Synthese*, **58**, 39-45. [Chapter 2, this volume]

Suppes, P. (1986). The primacy of utterer's meaning. In R. E. Grandy & R. Warner (Eds.), *Philosophical grounds of rationality: Intentions, categories, and ends* (pp. 109-29). Oxford: Clarendon Press. [Chapter 4, this volume]

Suppes, P. (1989). Current directions in mathematical learning theory. In E. Degreef & E.E. Roskam (Eds.), *Mathematical Psychology in Progress* (pp. 3-28). Berlin: Springer-Verlag.

Suppes, P. & Atkinson, R.C. (1960). *Markov learning models for multi-person interactions.* Stanford, CA: Stanford University Press.

Suppes, P., Cohen, M., Laddaga, R., Anliker, J., & Floyd, R. (1982). Research on eye movements in arithmetic performance. In R. Groner & P. Fraisse (Eds.), *Cognition and eye movements.* Amsterdam: North-Holland.

Suppes, P., Cohen, M., Laddaga, R., Anliker, J., & Floyd, R. (1983). A procedural theory of eye movements in doing arithmetic. *Journal of Mathematical Psychology*, **27**, 341-69.

Suppes, P., & Crangle, C. (1988). Context-fixing semantics for the language of action. In J. Dancy, J.M.E. Moravcsik, & C.C.W. Taylor (Eds.), *Human agency: Language, duty, and value* (pp. 47-76, 288-90). Stanford, CA: Stanford University Press. [Chapter 18, this volume]

Suppes, P., & Gammon, E.M. (1973). *Grammar and semantics of some six-year-old black children's noun phrases.* (Tech. Rep. No. 226). Stanford: Institute for Mathematical Studies in the Social Sciences, Stanford University, Stanford, CA.

Suppes, P., Hyman, L., & Jerman, M. (1967). Linear structural models for response and latency performance in arithmetic on computer-controlled terminals. In J.P. Hill (Ed.), *Minnesota Symposia on Child Psychology* (pp. 160-200). Minneapolis: University of Minn. Press.

Suppes, P., Léveillé, M., & Smith, R.L. (1974). *Developmental models of a child's French syntax.* (Tech. Rep. No. 243). Institute for Mathematical Studies in the Social Sciences, Stanford University, Stanford, CA.

Suppes, P., & Macken, E. (1978). Steps toward a variable-free semantics of attributive adjectives, possessives, and intensifying adverbs. In K. Nelson (Ed.), *Children's language* (Vol. 1). New York: Gardner Press. [Chapter 9, this volume]

Suppes, P., & Morningstar, M. (1972). *Computer-assisted instruction at Stanford, 1966-68: Data, models, and evaluation of the arithmetic programs.* New York.

Suppes, P., Smith, R.L., & Léveillé, M. (1972). *The French syntax and semantics of PHILIPPE, Part 1: Noun phrases.* (Tech. Rep. No. 195). Institute for Mathematical Studies in the Social Sciences, Stanford University, Stanford, CA.

Suppes, P., Smith, R.L., & Léveillé, M. (1973). The French syntax of a child's noun phrases. *Archives de Psychologie, **42**, 207-69.

Suppes, P., & Zinnes, J.L. (1963). Basic measurement theory. In R.D. Luce, R.R. Bush & E.H. Galanter (Eds.), *Handbook of mathematical psychology*, Vol. 1. New York: Wiley.

Suppes, P., & Zinnes, J.L. (1966). A continuous-response task with non-determinate, contingent reinforcement. *Journal of Mathematical Psychology, **3**, 197-216.

Sussex, R. (1974). The deep structure of adjectives in noun phrases. *Journal of Linguistics, **10**, 111-31.

Tarski, A. (1935). Der Wahrheitsbegriff in den formalisierten Sprachen. *Studia Philosophica, **1**, 261-405. (Translation: The concept of truth in formalized languages. In A. Tarski (Ed.), (1956), *Logic, semantics, metamathematics* (152-278), J.H. Woodger, Trans, Oxford, England: Oxford University Press.)

Tarski, A. (1941). On the calculus of relations. *Journal of Symbolic Logic*, **6**, 73-89.

Tarski, A. (1953). *Undecidable theories.* Amsterdam, The Netherlands: North-Holland Publishing Co.

Thomason, R.H., & Stalnaker, R.C. (1973). A semantic theory of adverbs. *Linguistic Inquiry*, **4**(2), 195-220.

Truman, H. S. (1956). *Memoirs by Harry S. Truman* (Vol. 2), *Years of Trial and Hope.* Garden City, NY: Doubleday.

van Benthem, J. (1985). *Semantic automata* (Report No. CSLI-85-27). Center for the Study of Language and Information, Stanford University, Stanford, Calif.

Vicens, P. (1969). *Aspects of speech recognition by computer.* Unpublished doctoral dissertation, Stanford University.

Vicens, P. (1970). *Preprocessing for speech analysis* (Project Memo No. AI-71). Stanford, CA: Stanford University, Stanford Artificial Intelligence Laboratory.

von Keller, T.G. (1971). An on-line recognition system for spoken digits. *Journal of the Acoustical Society of America*, **49**(4,Pt.2), 1288-96.

Wason, P.C. (1959). The processing of positive and negative information. *Quarterly Journal of Experimental Psychology*, **11**, 92-107.

Wason, P.C. (1961). Response to affirmative and negative binary statements. *British Journal of Psychology*, **52**, 133-42.

Wason, P.C., & Jones, S. (1963). Negatives: Denotation and connotation. *British Journal of Psychology*, **54**, 299-307.

Wheeler, S.C., III. (1972). Attributives and their modifiers. *Noûs*, **6**, 310-34.

Whiting, H.T.A. (Ed.). (1984). *Human motor actions: Bernstein reassessed.* Amsterdam.

Winograd, T. (1972). *Understanding natural language.* New York: Academic Press.

Younger, D.H. (1967). Recognition and parsing of context-free languages in time n^3. *Information and Control*, **10**(2), 189-208.

Youniss, J., & Furth, H.G. (1964). Attainment and transfer of logical connectives in children. *Journal of Educational Psychology*, **55**, 357-61.

Youniss, J., & Furth, H.G. (1967). Learning of logical connectives by adolescents with single and multiple instances. *Journal of Educational Psychology*, **58**, 222-30.

Yu, P. (1979). On the Gricean program about meaning. *Linguistics and Philosophy*, **3**, 273-88.

AUTHOR INDEX

This book was typeset with TeX on Turing, CSLI's principal computer at Stanford University, by Laura Tickle and Emma Pease, in Computer Modern Roman type, designed by Donald Knuth with his digital-font designing program, METAFONT. TeX, which was also created by Knuth, is a trademark of the American Mathematical Society.